# LANGUAGE CITY

## Also by Ross Perlin

*Intern Nation: How to Earn Nothing and Learn Little in the Brave New Economy*

# LANGUAGE CITY

## The Fight to Preserve Endangered Mother Tongues in New York

ROSS PERLIN

Atlantic Monthly Press
*New York*

FIRST EDITION

*Published simultaneously in Canada*
*Printed in the United States of America*

This book was designed by Norman E. Tuttle of Alpha Design & Composition.
This was set in 11.5-pt. Times New Roman by Alpha Design & Composition of Pittsfield, NH.

First Grove Atlantic hardcover edition: February 2024

Library of Congress Cataloging-in-Publication data is available for this title.

ISBN 978-0-8021-6246-5
eISBN 978-0-8021-6247-2

Atlantic Monthly Press
an imprint of Grove Atlantic
154 West 14th Street
New York, NY 10011

Distributed by Publishers Group West

groveatlantic.com

24 25 26 27 10 9 8 7 6 5 4 3 2 1

For Cecil

# Contents


Preface: The Limits of My Language ix

**I. Thousands of Natural Experiments**

A Room on Eighteenth Street 3

A Home in Queens 12

A Snapshot of Babel 17

A Brief Guide to Radical Linguistics 25

**II. Past**

Minority Port 45

Survivor City 64

Indigenous Metropolis 78

Global Microcosm 93

**III. Present**

Rasmina - सेके, སེ་སྐད་ (Seke) 115

Husniya - X̌ik (Wakhi) 171

Boris - ייִדיש (Yiddish) 200

Ibrahima - ߒߞߏ (N’ko) 233

Irwin - Nahuatl 267

Karen - Lunaape (Lenape) 301

**IV. Future** 339

Acknowledgments 357

A Note on Sources 359

Notes 367

# Preface
## *The Limits of My Language*

Don't ask a linguist how many languages they speak.

Some may blurt out a number just to change the subject ("Fifteen!"), but then people usually want a list, even a quick performance. Rattling off the names of unfamiliar languages tends to end the conversation quickly. Many linguists *are* extraordinary polyglots, like Roman Jakobson, who is said to have been dazed after an accident and started calling for help in the twenty-five he knew. But most linguists study Language, not languages.

Every one of us has a linguistic history, however buried or unexamined. Here, very briefly, is mine. Like most Americans, my family left behind its original languages, moving closer to Dominant American English with every generation.[1] My great-grandma Bessy, who sold corsets in Queens and was known as The General, crossed the ocean by herself at the age of sixteen ("an unaccompanied minor," they would say today). Bessy could get by in Yiddish, Polish, Russian, German, and, starting on the boat, heavily accented English. It was more or less the same with my other seven great-grandparents, all multilingual Jewish immigrants from Eastern Europe with little formal schooling who sailed in steerage into New York Harbor around 1900. Their children, my grandparents, grew up first with Yiddish, seasoned only with bits of the other languages, before shifting wholesale to the New York Jewish English that reigned in Brooklyn and the Bronx in the 1920s and '30s. Despite some telltale tics, my parents tacked hard toward the "accent from nowhere" inculcated at school, piped in by TV, and pushed in a thousand ways, overtly and covertly, in the fast-assimilating neighborhoods and suburbs of the mid-twentieth century city.

I grew up with the privilege of Dominant American English, only a trace of the New York inflection, but I longed for other languages. A city of unprecedented linguistic diversity was rising all around me, although I didn't know it at the time. My chance to become bi- or multilingual—at least to sound like a native speaker, even with a second-grade vocabulary—came and went with the "critical period" before adolescence.[2] "Die Grenzen meiner Sprache bedeuten die Grenzen meiner Welt," wrote Ludwig Wittgenstein. *The limits of my language mean the limits of my world*. So fundamental were my limits that I was hardly aware of them.

Second-language classes started when I was eleven, later than almost anywhere else in the world.[3] Like many monolinguals, I saw them as a graded game confined to school, not a fundamental imperative for living. At the same time, linguistic hierarchies were impossible to miss. Unconsciously I had learned to register most other forms of English as somehow lesser. Now I sensed the same with Spanish, which wasn't offered at school despite being both the city's and the country's second language, crucial for anyone hoping to feel at home in the hemisphere. In theory it was Cervantes and Salamanca, but in practice it was a working-class, immigrant, brown-skinned language at the bottom of the social hierarchy, often spoken at a lower volume when Anglophones were around.

French, on the other hand, was required. Its lingering elite prestige goes back almost a thousand years, when a small group of Norman French speakers conquered a large group of diversely dialected Old English speakers. That's how the resulting hybrid language ended up with different words for animals in the field (Old English–derived *cow*, *pig*, *sheep*, *deer*) versus on the plate (French-derived *beef*, *pork*, *mutton*, *venison*). Century after century, Middle and Modern English were continually forged through French, including not only words like *elite* and *prestige* but *lake*, *mountain*, *flower*, and thousands of others which now seem impeccably English. Like many English speakers, I heard both elegance and arrogance in the roll of French uvular /r/ or a cascade of nasal vowels.[4] I learned to say je ne sais quoi and raison d'être, correctly but not too correctly, not to show I knew French but to show I was a certain kind of English speaker.[5]

Classes in "dead languages" also fed a certain kind of English. Latin and Ancient Greek appeared as codes to crack, *things* to master, lists to memorize and unlock worlds. A smattering of Hebrew at Hebrew school was neither fully dead nor really alive, poised uncertainly between the ancient and modern languages. It felt safer to explore a language if there was no one you could speak it to. If reading is about pressing headlong and half-conscious into a mess of meaning, we didn't even read so much as decipher, where it's the romance of a person alone in a room—Champollion with the hieroglyphs, Ventris the architect tinkering with Linear B after work—incommunicado while cracking ancient communication. Language as form, which is the beginning of linguistics.

In college, I tried inhaling Old Norse, Uighur, Luo, Russian, and Arabic, racing like a bucket-list traveler to stamp the pages of my linguistic passport. Above all I threw myself into Mandarin, keen to go up against its proverbial difficulty.[6] Speakers themselves now know it as 國語 guóyǔ *national language*, 普通話 pǔtónghuà *common speech*, 中文 zhōngwén, or 漢語 hànyǔ *Han/Chinese language*, but Europeans call it Mandarin from an old Indic word for *counsel* (same root as *mantra*) that passed through Portuguese in the seventeenth century and came to mean a type of orange, a senior official, the icy detachment of such officials, and eventually the form of Chinese those officials spoke, 官話 guānhuà. Just one of countless spoken varieties under the heading of "Chinese,"[7] Mandarin is still distinguished in part by its strangely officious flavor, now with a Communist twist: "simultaneously austere and vacuous, intimidating yet elusive, in short stuffy and puffy at the same time," as Perry Link puts it.[8]

A year into classes, I could barely string together a sentence, but my conception of human language was already wonderfully warped beyond recognition. There seemed to be native words for everything, and few clear cognates with or borrowings from other languages. There were complex tones: putting the mantra back in Mandarin, I would play an audio file on loop and mutter the same syllable hundreds of times: mā má mǎ mà . . . There were 成語 chéngyǔ, the elaborate four-syllable phrases derived from Classical Chinese but often used in contemporary speech, distilling poetry and wisdom into the tiniest spaces: 一葉知秋 yīyè zhīqiū. *From one leaf's fall, you know that it's autumn.* From a single sign comes the wider revelation.

As for reading and writing—over fifty thousand characters attested across a three-thousand-year written tradition—you're not sufficiently obsessed until you're constantly tracing them with a wagging finger in the air, each stroke in the proper order. Far from being ideograms that represent meanings directly through images, characters are intricately entangled with the spoken language. Basic literacy is sometimes said to mean memorizing a minimum of three thousand, which is still no guarantee of being able to read a newspaper article.

I moved to Beijing for six months of full-time language study, under a pledge to speak English only on phone calls home. By then I could carry on a conversation, exhausting myself in the process, but it was easier to discuss economic development than to give directions. I still bludgeoned every other sentence, could only dream of nuance, and was haunted by the feeling, in the city's cold smoky beauty, that I was just translating from the nonstop English ticker running through my head. Even when I did (almost) sound like a native speaker, did it make any sense for me to sound that way? For the first but not the last time, I faced the unmistakable connection between language, identity, and appearance. Mandarin may eventually become a global language beyond the global Chinese diaspora, but for now anyone who speaks it without looking Chinese is a curiosity, an anomaly, a question mark. Reactions veer quickly from total incomprehension to overblown praise, while Chinese Americans are unfairly expected to be fluent.

One day in Beijing, I went to a talk by the legendary Chinese linguist 孙宏开 Sŭn Hóngkāi. At first I was just trying to keep up with his Mandarin. Only gradually did I grasp the life's work he was describing: half a century spent documenting as many of China's approximately 300 languages as possible (hardly counting forms of Chinese). That was also the first time I heard the phrase *endangered languages* (瀕危語言 bīnwĕi yŭyán).

A few years later, with a little linguistics, I went to southwest China, as Professor Sun had.[9] Chasing leads from scholars and street vendors, I took buses and shared jeeps from valley to valley across mountainous Yunnan province, home to over a hundred languages. Finally I came to Gongshan, the tiny seat of one of China's poorest counties. In this new frontier town of already rotting buildings, Han Chinese settlers were setting up shop and minority groups from surrounding villages were coming in search of work, education, health care, and consumer goods. Among them were speakers of Trung, whose homeland was a day's journey away by shared jeep on an unpaved road that was life-threatening in summer and impassable in winter. It was literally at the end of the road, on China's remote border with Tibet and a breakaway part of Myanmar, that the Trung world began.[10]

Working first through Mandarin, I gradually learned to speak some of the language, which is only distantly related to Chinese, Tibetan, Burmese, and hundreds of other little-known languages in the Tibeto-Burman family, now also known as Trans-Himalayan.[11] With no formal teachers, dictionaries, grammars, or textbooks, the only way to learn was by living with people, asking endless questions, and developing the materials to teach myself. Grounded in fieldwork and verging on anthropology, language documentation in this vein has been going on for centuries, but is now being dramatically transformed by technology and the urgency of global language loss.

With fewer than seven thousand speakers, Trung had evolved for the way of life in a single valley, but everything was changing. Hunting and swidden ("slash and burn") agriculture, the traditional modes of subsistence, had recently been banned for environmental reasons, upending the group's very basis of livelihood. By fiat the government was replacing all the older log cabins with new houses. Electricity and signal towers were enabling cell phones and TVs, bringing Mandarin directly into hands and homes. Children were leaving the valley for boarding schools, which function completely in Mandarin. The remnants of traditional religious life, shattered by the Cultural Revolution, were being swept away by a local form of evangelical Christianity.

My task was to record, transcribe, and translate all the stories, songs, and conversations I could, analyzing the grammar, probing the dialects of different villages, documenting knowledge of the local environment, and ultimately compiling a dictionary in a newly devised Latin-based writing system, together with three Trung speakers, known in Chinese as Yáng Jiānglíng 杨将领, Lǐ Jīnmíng 李金明, and Lǐ Aìxīn 李爱新.

I spent three years in Yunnan, enough to lay the groundwork for a PhD, but there is enough work involved in documenting any language to last a lifetime. A world was slipping away even faster than the words that referred to it. I barely understood either the world or the words, but I was trying to record them for posterity, or at least as long as the digital files may last. I have never done anything harder.[12]

One night at a village feast, I took out my recorder as the singing started. But this time the singer turned it back toward me: "Menju chuq pvo! *Now sing some of your songs!*"[13]

I couldn't remember a single one.

# I. Thousands of Natural Experiments

# A Room on Eighteenth Street

Up on the sixth floor of an old commercial building along the sunless canyon of Eighteenth Street, there is a room where languages from all over the world converge. Clouds of tangled wires choke overworked recording equipment. Sticky notes whose meaning is lost to time frame the streaky monitors of three beleaguered computers. Tacked up at random are untranslatable posters, yellowing maps of places that few people have ever heard of, and calendars in half a dozen languages and calendrical systems, all turned to the wrong month and usually for the wrong year.

Every surface displays donations proudly shlepped from distant villages, including Garifuna drums in need of repair, a dried-out Mexican corncob, textiles from Timor, and a trilingual shopping bag that teaches Romansh, a minority language of Switzerland. Titles like *Warrabarna Kaurna! Reclaiming an Australian Language*, *The Architect of Modern Catalan*, and *The Sociolinguistics of Borderlands* fill the shelves.[1] Half-busted filing cabinets bulge with linguistic and bureaucratic papers, surrounded by strewn stacks of rare ring-bound studies, hard drives and tapes of every format, and an invaluable "Rolodex," a fragile paper cascade with hundreds of highly unusual business cards.

Speakers of Bishnupriya Manipuri, a minority language of Bangladesh (and now Queens), prepare a song in the corner. A Quechua teacher from Peru (long resident in Brooklyn) gets ready for class at the same table where a Tsou speaker from Taiwan (now living in

California) is correcting the proofs of her children's book. A linguist in over-ear headphones edits recordings in the Gabonese language Ikota, made with the one known speaker in the city, who lives on Roosevelt Island. Just entering is a young Chuvash activist from Russia, recently settled in Harlem, who is here to strategize about the future of his people's language. In the tiny makeshift studio attached, used for an on-and-off Indigenous internet radio station, a Totonac shaman from Mexico (and now New Jersey) declaims into a microphone, calling New York the new Teotihuacán.

This is the Endangered Language Alliance, the only organization anywhere focused on the linguistic diversity of cities, and especially on endangered, Indigenous, and primarily oral languages. ELA (for short) is where an eccentric extended family of linguists, language activists, polyglots, enthusiasts, and ordinary New Yorkers tune in to the deeper frequencies of the surrounding city, and by extension the world.

The languages heard here are generally not recognized by governments, used by businesses, or taught in classrooms, though they are fully capable of expressing anything that any other human language can express. The world's leading libraries have no books about them, let alone *in* them, because there aren't any. Nor, in many cases, are there recordings, dictionaries, grammatical descriptions, or other materials. Google's claim to "organize the world's information" and Facebook's bluster about "bringing the world closer together" ring hollow when those websites operate in just over a hundred languages, and even Wikipedia (at the time of writing) is in only 331.[2]

Of the world's approximately seven thousand languages—not counting all the dialects, sociolects, ethnolects, religiolects, and local varieties—up to half are likely to disappear over the next few centuries. Languages are being lost every year.[3] The least documented are the most threatened. Few nonspeakers have heard of them, and most are used by only the smallest and most marginalized groups: just 4 percent of the world's population now speaks 96 percent of the world's languages.[4] The situation is even more dire for the approximately two hundred sign languages.[5] Hundreds of entire language *families* (groups of historically related languages, typically reaching back thousands of years) are also likely to be lost.

This book is about the most linguistically diverse city in the history of the world: its past, present, and future. Now home to over seven hundred languages, early twenty-first century New York City is especially a last improbable refuge for embattled and endangered languages. Never before have cities like New York been so linguistically various, and they may never be again, but this new hyperdiversity has hardly been mapped, let alone understood or supported. In particular, in just the last few decades, hundreds of thousands of people speaking hundreds of languages have arrived in New York from heavily minority and Indigenous zones of Asia, Africa, and Latin America.[6] At the very moment when languages worldwide are disappearing at an unprecedented rate, many of the last speakers are on the move. Far from being confined to remote islands, towering mountains, or impenetrable jungles, they are now right next door, though to majority groups they remain invisible and their words inaudible. Theirs are the stories that intersect on Eighteenth Street and form the core of this book.

We begin by moving from ELA to the level of a single neighborhood and then to the wider metropolitan area. In outline we describe the linguistic life of cities, the forces threatening linguistic diversity, and how linguists and speakers are fighting back.

Diving into the past, we then explore how a single city, New York, has served as a home for so many languages. In four loosely chronological chapters, we chart how the Lenape archipelago became in turn a polyglot port of minority peoples, a center of refuge for communities of survivors, an Indigenous metropolis, and finally an unprecedented microcosm of global linguistic diversity (albeit a very particular one).

Turning to the present, we follow six speakers of endangered languages from Asia, Europe, Africa, and the Americas, all now living in

New York and striving to find a place in the city and the world for their mother tongues.

In her early twenties, Rasmina feels the burden of being one of the youngest people anywhere who can speak Seke, a language from five villages in Nepal with seven hundred speakers, over a hundred of whom have moved to a vertical village, a single building in Brooklyn, as part of a vast new Himalayan migration of extraordinary linguistic complexity.

Every stage of Husniya's life and education has happened in a different language, with English her ninth (depending on how you count). She feels at home almost anywhere along the new Silk Road that runs through Brooklyn and Queens, but is devoted to developing her native language Wakhi and the other Pamiri languages of Tajikistan, which are spoken by one of the city's smallest and newest communities.

Boris, born after the Holocaust in Soviet Moldova and now living deep in post-Soviet Brooklyn, refuses to be the last Yiddish writer. He believes that a language can linger through literature, as long as a faithful few continue writing and reading. Even as a new spoken Hasidic Yiddish is growing all around him, it's hard for Boris to know who will read his secular creations, including the storied newspaper he spent eighteen years trying to breathe new life into.

Ibrahima, a language activist from Guinea, also counts on the written word and its associated technologies for linguistic survival. He is determined to promote N'ko, a writing system created in 1949 to challenge the dominance of colonial languages and unite over forty million speakers of Manding languages across West Africa, as well as its major new outposts in Harlem and the Bronx.

Irwin is a Queens chef unearthing the roots of Mexican cooking through his native Nahuatl, which is still spoken today by over 1.6 million Indigenous Mexicans and a growing number in New York. Not only Nahuatl, but Mixtec, K'iche', Mam, and dozens of other Indigenous Latin American languages have arrived in the city in the last few decades, though the tens of thousands who speak them—many considered undocumented immigrants in their home hemisphere—struggle for justice at the bottom of the city's social and economic hierarchy.

And Karen, a keeper of Lenape, the land's original language, which she helped bring back to New York for the first time in three centuries. There is only a single elderly native speaker, hundreds of miles away in Canada, but Karen and others both there and across the Lenape diaspora have been courageously reclaiming and reviving the language against all odds.[7]

Six individual voices speaking six languages: this is barely a beginning. Of course it's not possible to mention, let alone discuss in detail, every language community.[8] Among them, the six speakers actually speak over thirty languages. Nor does any of them live entirely or even predominantly in their mother tongue, though mother tongues are the focus here. All need larger regional and national languages to various degrees, as well as some English, and have to move nimbly from one linguistic ecology to another, whether it's home, work, the neighborhood, a WhatsApp group, or anywhere else.

There are special challenges in writing about lesser-known languages, not only around sourcing and translation, but also because most are unwritten and unstandardized. For years I have been working with the six speakers to varying extents on their languages, but I am not a native speaker of any. They are my teachers, but any mistakes are mine alone. I settle for the matrix of English (or translation into what is likely another dominant language) to bring the sound and sense of their languages within earshot and to widen our acoustic range. Their words will not be sequestered in italics; it's the *English* gloss that will.*

We end by approaching the future. Will cities just be last-minute outposts for endangered languages, or can they become sustainable

---

* For languages written in non-Latin scripts, I include key initial words or passages in both the script itself and a Latin-based transliteration, but thereafter stick mostly to transliteration for the sake of simplicity.

sites for linguistic diversity? Can Babel—the real contemporary New York experiment, not the Biblical myth—actually work?

The idea on Eighteenth Street, however crazy, is to make Babel work. Somehow still going after almost fifteen years, ELA has always been a tiny operation, getting by on gumption and grace. It was founded in 2010 by the linguist Daniel Kaufman, who is still codirector, together with the linguist Juliette Blevins and the poet Bob Holman, who are both still on the board. For the last decade I have been codirector with Daniel.

Daniel heard Hebrew at home, but his English is pure New York. Though it clearly shaped him, he claims he was "just a witness" to the East Village underground scene in the nineties, hanging out at the Anarchist Switchboard with the neighborhood's wayward radical punks. He started picking up Tagalog over speed chess in Washington Square Park with a hustler named Junior, "the greatest one-minute chess player in the world." That led to college in the Philippines and an obsession with the Austronesian language family. He's gone village to village in Madagascar, recording undocumented dialects of Malagasy. He listens to the latest rap from Borneo and Guam, digging the beats while scanning for deep prosodic patterns. His laptop and his marriage, to the founder of an Indonesian dance group in New York, run mostly in Indonesian.

Besides word of mouth, ELA has grown partly out of Daniel's uncanny knack for finding speakers of smaller languages wherever he goes in the city. He chats with the cashier at the bodega on the other side of Eighteenth Street, who turns out to speak Ghale, a little-documented language of Nepal. Then he gets to know the speaker of Poqomchi', the Mayan language from Guatemala, behind the deli counter. At an Indonesian wedding in Queens, he hits it off with another guest who turns out to be the city's only speaker of Mamuju, from West Sulawesi. Taking cabs he meets speakers of Chantyal from Nepal and

Chocha-Ngacha from Bhutan behind the wheel. "A rando calls me up by accident thinking I'm his friend," he texts me one morning, "and he happens to be a trilingual speaker of K'iche', Kaqchikel, and Acateco." Neither finished nor unfinished, Daniel's projects are perpetually open, embodying a vision of the city as a greenhouse, not a graveyard, for languages, as well as a crucial site for original linguistic research.[9]

A couple of articles in the *New York Times* and elsewhere also brought a wave of interest in ELA, leading over a hundred New Yorkers of all backgrounds to crowd the old Bowery Poetry Club, form neighborhood teams, and pound the pavement for languages along the Brighton Beach boardwalk, on the streets of Harlem, and in the plazas of Jackson Heights. For years it was all volunteer, though speakers have always been paid for their time, sometimes out of Daniel's pocket. Only later did occasional grants begin to cover a few staff positions, with the work as disparate as analyzing the grammar of a specific Central Asian language and translating public health materials into Indigenous Mexican languages.

Though officially a nonprofit, ELA is more like a loose network of a few hundred people who share a passion for languages, helping however and whenever they can. It's both a physical space and a quasi-official platform where linguists and speakers meet and collaborate on long-term, open-ended projects, as neighbors making common cause. Poets, artists, journalists, filmmakers, researchers, and policymakers are part of the network, bringing new kinds of visibility to languages, sometimes on a global level. Language activists and communities facing similar challenges or speaking related languages share strategies and join forces.

The work at ELA is very different from traditional linguistic fieldwork, which is closer to what I was doing with Trung in China. There can be fundamental problems when even the most dedicated outsider linguist drops into a far-off locale to document a language for the first and perhaps only time, then returns to the ivory tower. Though we have strong ties to universities—I teach at Columbia, and Daniel is at Queens College—ELA remains independent of both the bureaucracy and the narrow scholarly goals that can come with academic affiliation. Few universities anywhere dedicate resources to researching, teaching, or supporting endangered languages, or indeed to any languages beyond the most dominant and lucrative. Instead ELA takes its cue from the surrounding city, answering to language communities that few others know exist. Speakers and activists themselves initiate most of the projects, and through them we connect to communities on the other side of the world.

With its donated office in the heart of Manhattan now spilling into a sizeable new room, ELA itself has become an anarchic switchboard. We are constantly fielding messages from people trying to preserve their languages, record their relatives, get information, or simply find someone else to talk to.[10] When they search online for a language, ELA's website may be the only thing they can find. When they walk in the door, ELA's grungy office at least makes clear, like no other space in the city, that all languages are welcome.

And so it usually starts. Alex, a young speaker of P'urhépecha born in the Michoacán highlands in Mexico, grew up in York, Pennsylvania, where over a hundred P'urhépecha speakers have moved for agricultural work, often on Christmas tree farms. As far as he knows, he's the only speaker in New York, where he moved after college and immediately got in touch with us. Now for the last eight years, whenever time allows, he has been working with ELA to record his family in both Pennsylvania and Mexico, while also digitizing and translating old existing texts. He dreams of teaching the language to anyone who wants to learn it.

A Khasi speaker originally from eastern India, dropping in from Boston, explains how his language's revival could be a model for others. A Pana speaker in the Bronx leaves a voice mail full of longing for the mother tongue he left behind at the age of seven in a village on the Mali–Burkina Faso border. "Has anything been written about my language?" he asks as soon as we meet. "Are there any recordings?"

If there are already extensive, high-quality recordings, which is seldom the case, a dictionary may be needed. If a dictionary has been published, there may not be a grammatical description, or a corpus of transcribed and translated texts. Even if there is robust documentation, it may not be digitized or accessible to the community. Although documenting and archiving can be essential prerequisites, a speaker or a community may be more focused on teaching, maintaining, or revitalizing their language, and this too can take any number of forms.

Language, for all its importance, is nothing without survival and livelihood. During the tumultuous recent years of the COVID-19 pandemic, it became ELA's mission to help speakers of minority languages with timely information and resources, and to document the disproportionate impacts of the pandemic on these overlooked groups.[11] Around the city and the world, there was an unprecedented effort to translate and disseminate COVID-related messages as quickly and accurately as possible. Speakers, linguists, and communities started doing it for hundreds of languages that have no official support and have never had recorded or written public health messages before. Language access saved lives, even as so many essential elders and native speakers of languages the world over, from Ojibwe in Minnesota to Yamalapiti in the Brazilian Amazon, were being lost.

# A Home in Queens

Eighteenth Street is our base, but the real day-to-day linguistic diversity of the city lies elsewhere—in some of its least-known neighborhoods.

We're not talking about Manhattan, which was once a multiethnic labyrinth but is now simply too expensive, though it remains a job center and playground for many better-off international students, tourists, businesspeople, cultural figures, diplomats, and various others, with their hundreds of mother tongues. The United Nations, after all, is both a global political hub and just another city neighborhood.[1] The destruction of the World Trade Center in 2001 was an event of global scale and significance in part because the New Yorkers killed in the towers came from over one hundred countries and almost certainly spoke an even larger number of languages.[2]

But for at least the last half century, it's the city's outer boroughs where hundreds of language groups from around the world have carved out entire communities. This other, more radically cosmopolitan city of low-rise, working-class immigrant neighborhoods both makes Manhattan possible and stands perpetually in its shadows. It encompasses ungentrified Brooklyn south of the terminal moraine, most of the Bronx, and Staten Island north of the expressway. But nowhere on the planet, square mile after square mile, is more linguistically diverse than the borough of Queens.

In terms of what we know about its actual linguistic life, not to mention many of the individual languages spoken, Queens might as well be at the bottom of the ocean. Here speakers of languages like Trung live not eight thousand miles but a block or a subway stop away. For the last decade, since coming home from China, I have been living in one of its quieter corners—a nondescript neighborhood with an extraordinary soundtrack.

Imagine you're on foot. On any given block, passing voices speak varieties of Polish, Ukrainian, Egyptian Arabic, Mexican Spanish, Puerto Rican Spanish, Dominican Spanish, Ecuadorian Spanish, Kichwa, and all the forms of New York City English they give rise to. I can usually pick them out, but only understand a fraction of what people are saying, depending on context, volume, and so many other factors—and you can't learn a language by eavesdropping.

In certain stores, Albanians, Bosnians, Serbs, and Montenegrins all reunite for the immigrant hustle, speaking the languages of the former Yugoslavia as if the country still existed.[3] An old Macedonian selling tchotchkes from a table on the street is a gentle bully in every language. At a grocery stocking goods from Budapest, Baku, and all points between, the owner has a favorite among the dozen sweating blocks of feta: "Romanian" sheep, which is actually made in Bulgaria by a Romanian firm the way the Bulgarians, those masters of feta, used to do it twenty years ago, he says with a faraway look in his eyes.

Some groups in the neighborhood have battled each other to the point of genocide "back home," but here a basic neutrality and balance of power are never questioned. Everyone's homeland is a borderland, and every group is some kind of ethnic or linguistic minority. No nationalism seems simple, no language standard, and all are to different degrees endangered here. People call themselves "Romanian Serbians" when they mean they're from the Banat, "German Hungarians" rather than Danube Swabians, "Slovenian Germans" in case you don't know of the Gottscheers. The "Albanian Montenegrins," to be precise, are from the border town of Ulqin. The "Austrian Italians," to be specific, are from Val di Non, a valley in the Dolomites.

Every group has its clubs, some more private and intimidating than others. At the Val di Non clubhouse, old ladies making doilies hold a halting conversation in Nones, a Romance language which sits somewhere between Ladin, Lombard, and Venetian.[4] Partanna, Castelvetrano, and Santa Margherita di Belice are neighboring towns in western Sicily with neighboring social clubs here going back a century, where the men play cards under blasting TVs, the espresso and Sicilian flowing. At the Banatul Soccer and Folklore Club, people with roots in the Banat, a historical region now divided among Romania, Serbia, and Hungary, gather, presumably, for soccer and folklore.

Gottscheer Hall, still the focal point for an estimated eighteen thousand Gottscheers and their descendants in the New York area, now also hosts quinceañeras and house music parties along with its annual Bauernball (*Farmers' Ball*). While doubling as a neighborhood bar, it's still the headquarters for all things Gottscheer: the Blau Weiss soccer team, the annual Miss Gottscheer contest, the Relief Association, and the multiple choral groups, among other community institutions. This is the last outpost for Gottscheerish, an endangered Germanic language which developed in the isolation of the Gottschee (Kočevje) region in what is now Slovenia. Its speakers packed up seven centuries of history in about as many months, escaping in 1944 and 1945 via displaced persons camps to Germany and Austria, where people largely assimilated, or else here to Queens, where the last speakers live.[5] At the Gottscheer-owned pork store nearby, a placard behind the hanging sausages says "We speak—" in fourteen languages, and they're not counting Gottscheerish.[6]

Danube Swabians, another Germanic group who fled central Europe at the end of the war, gather annually at the local cemetery to commemorate their people's Opfer der Entrechtung, Vernichtung, Verschleppung, Vertreibung, *victims of expulsion, deprivation of rights, extermination, and deportation* (as the memorial stone puts it in German and English). Nearby the community built a very different kind of memorial—one of the oldest soccer fields in the country, where kids born all over the world kick the same ball, as the sun goes down behind a distant skyline.[7]

Two-story vinyl-sided houses with aluminum awnings give little sense of the languages spoken inside. But the Black Madonna of Częstochowa stares out from a living room window, meaning Polish. The twentieth-century saint Padre Pio painted on a passing van is "a point of contact with Eternity" and a sure sign of Sicilian.[8] A store selling off-brand phone chargers and cases is named for a Mauritanian province, a likely indicator of Hassaniya. The scrolling LED sign on a Tibetan momo truck flashes mandalas and hearts that transform into dancing letters, which go from blood red to icy green. The customers know what they're getting, even if the text doesn't fit: "CHICKEN MO. TABLE MOM. ROZEN MO."

Even cars sport signs and symbols of allegiance. A bumper sticker in English: "I am proud to be a Coptic." A license plate holder from the little Puerto Rican town of Toa Baja. The vanity plate BUZAU, for the medium-sized city of Buzău in southeastern Romania. (Unfortunately, the DMV doesn't do diacritics.) A mini swallowtail flag hangs from a rearview mirror: blue and gold with a white crescent moon and an eight-pointed star, for the Székelys of Transylvania.

Peoples from particular places with particular histories now have their places on these particular blocks. Pointedly far from the city's Muslim Egyptians is the Coptic block with its Coptic bodega, Coptic laundromat, Coptic print shop, and Coptic street life all centered on a Coptic church. Tahrir Square refugees pray in Coptic or play backgammon in Egyptian Arabic as their kids play freely on the sidewalk in English, the language often spoken here when parents aren't around. Retired Gurkha soldiers shoot hoops every Sunday morning in the local park, calling for the ball in Nepali, a lingua franca for these native speakers of different dialects of Gurung and Tamang, minority languages of the mountains and the middle hills.

There is something to study here, but nothing to romanticize. Affordability, now vanishing fast, has been key. Many people stick to their own kind, at least the adults, though mostly without walls and without rancor. Historically, not all communities have been welcome. There have been Nazis, and there may be neo-Nazis now.[9] For decades, white ethnic homeowners, whatever their linguistic backgrounds, resisted ethnic succession, using historic preservation and other tools to fight policies like school busing and low-income housing. Broadly speaking, there is a "Latino" side of the neighborhood and a "European" side.

But speakers of Italian "dialects" and different varieties of Spanish communicate through cognates. A retired Puerto Rican cop and a Serbian contractor see eye to eye. Roma and Romanians may meet as fellow Pentecostals. Speakers of Russian, Polish, and Ukrainian somehow communicate along the Eastern Slavic spectrum.[10] People pick up bits of each other's languages, sometimes more. Mixing, code-switching, and other ways of combining languages and dialects are lightning-speed facts of daily life. These blocks sound like nowhere else in the world.

To all these groups, "Americans" in a sense are just another little ethnic group, disproportionately twentysomething and more numerous every year. They were born in the interior, the suburbs of Ohio and Virginia and Florida which some may go back to, but in the meantime they're here making little linkages of their own. To others looking in, the Americans have their foods, stores, and subgroups just like any other group; their tats, T-shirts, and dogs; their particular vowels.

No language group has a majority, or even 15 percent of the neighborhood, and most are at just 5 or 10 percent. No group is in control.[11] Even English is a vital lingua franca, not a linguistic overlord. By and large, linguistic and cultural differences stabilize, even harmonize, the neighborhood. It can be a home for so many groups in part because it's a homeland for none of them, no one's turf. There is breathing room not only for national languages, but even to a degree for Indigenous, minority, and endangered languages.

# A Snapshot of Babel

My neighborhood has its signature sound, but there are several dozen across the outer boroughs that are just as diverse, each in a different way. These are the places where ELA has recorded New Yorkers speaking over a hundred languages which officially are not here, according to the census or any other dataset. Collectively, the communities that speak them comprise hundreds of thousands of individuals. Nor is this massive gap unique to New York or even the US, for no record of any city's languages comes even close to representing everything people actually speak. Majority-language speakers either can't find out the truth, or can't be bothered.

Since 1890, the US Census has generally asked at least one simple question about language, which has varied over time but remained far too limited to reflect the complex and ever-evolving dynamics of migration, diaspora, and cultural change. The way the questions have been asked, and to whom and in which languages, has ensured that Indigenous, minority, and primarily oral languages are systematically undercounted, starting with the question of what even counts as a language.[1] Today the question is asked only on the annual, sample-based American Community Survey, not the main decennial census, with a blank for people to fill in the non-English language they "speak at home." Only one response is used (no room for multilingualism), and the way these are tabulated by the Census Bureau tends to lump smaller languages in with larger ones and for privacy reasons figures aren't even published until a language reaches a certain population threshold.

To fill the gap, we launched a language census of our own at ELA. Of course languages inherently can't be pinned to a map, but move in the mouths of their speakers or the hands of their signers. Whole communities are constantly on the move. This is true even on a daily basis if you consider the subway, the circulatory system that is also fundamentally the city's most democratic public space. Every train on every line, to varying degrees, has at least a superficial tendency to be a kind of Noah's ark, holding in rumbling and often garish suspension a cellular representation of humanity, or at least a single squiggly spaghetti cross section of New York. As the MTA now recognizes, certain languages may be particularly vital on certain lines—Russian on the B/Q, Haitian Creole on the 2/3, etc.—but every line spans two or three boroughs and touches on all kinds of neighborhoods, making any given train a world's fair in motion that fragments and reconstitutes at every stop. The subway might not run throughout the world, but it can contain and display it, at all hours, for anyone who cares to see.

We didn't attempt a subway census, but the map soon became an endless, obsessive work in progress, first in print, now a website at www.languagemap.nyc. At best it's just a snapshot of Babel, created over five years through thousands of interviews and discussions with community leaders, speakers, and other experts. In total we have mapped over 1,200 locations, including restaurants, temples, community centers, and other significant sites across the metropolitan area, where over seven hundred languages are used—seven times the number of languages recorded by the census.[2]

ELA's count makes clear that one out of every ten languages on the planet, including just about all the sizeable ones, has at least one speaker in New York. Hundreds of languages have substantial communities of hundreds if not thousands of speakers, though the reliability of community estimates varies. Nearly 40 percent of the city's languages are from Asia, a quarter from Africa, and just under 20 percent each from Europe and the Americas, with a much smaller number from

Oceania and the Pacific. Linguistically, it's a very different city from what most people imagine.[3]

The language map also shows complex interaction zones, where one group settles next to, near, or after another with which it has linguistic, historical, cultural, religious, national, or other links. Speakers of Geg and Tosk Albanian may not always live side by side, but both are drawn to existing Italian areas because of their linguistic and cultural familiarity. Punjabi speakers buy homes and build businesses near speakers of Guyanese and Trinidadian creoles who may have arrived a few years earlier, united at least loosely by an Indian heritage, and this draws other South Asians in turn. Neighborhoods may be less relevant units than the countless microzones of peoples from particular towns, regions, and language groups clustering in different ways across the city's sixty-six thousand blocks and million-plus residential buildings.

The number of "global immigrant neighborhoods" and "melting-pot census tracts" has exploded in recent decades, but monoethnic enclaves sealed off from other groups are almost nonexistent.[4] In fact, the idea of the "Little [insert foreign country or city]" enclave is just as much a poorly labeled idealization, usually centered around food, as the notion of a monoethnic nation. Even in areas strongly associated with a particular group (from Manhattan's Chinatown to Richmond Hill's Little Guyana), the group in focus is perhaps a plurality but almost never a majority of the population, or is itself made up of speakers of many different languages.

Instead of homogenous enclaves, what ELA's language map reveals are whole regions of the world shrunk down to the size of city neighborhoods, entire linguistic universes recreated in miniature. We will visit them over the course of this book as we meet the six speakers. In both central Queens and central Brooklyn, it will be the languages of South Asia and the Himalaya (Rasmina's world), and then close by the communities from across the Middle East and Central Asia that form the city's new Silk Road (which Husniya calls home). Just beyond, two other worlds collide in southern Brooklyn: the former Soviet Union reconstituted around Brighton Beach, and the fading Jewish diaspora assembled in all of its languages along Ocean Parkway (with Boris at the intersection).[5] Over a hundred West African languages are concentrated in Harlem and the Bronx (where Ibrahima tirelessly promotes N'ko). Across the city there are growing clusters of Indigenous peoples speaking dozens of languages from across the Americas (including Irwin).

The map proves for the first time that hundreds of Indigenous, minority, and primarily oral languages constitute the vast majority of the city's mother tongues.[6] They are not exotic; they are integral. If not always individually, in aggregate they are a force. They have long played an outsized role in the city's on-the-ground history, though their names are largely unknown and almost never mentioned directly. They are an indispensable lens onto the deep dynamics of immigration and diaspora, genocide and displacement, the whole tangled web of inheritances that make the city tick.

Far from straightforwardly representing either America or the world, New York is a constantly evolving collection not just of particular people, but of particular peoples from particular places, often most clearly identified by their languages. With few exceptions, linguistic, religious, ethnic, and other minorities have been *over*represented in diaspora in comparison to their home countries, for they are the ones hit hardest by conflict, catastrophe, and privation and thus impelled to leave.

It's not necessarily the poorest and most desperate who can migrate, but time and again, arrivals in the city have been linked to distant calamities that befall specific ethnolinguistic groups and set in motion particular futures. Whether because it's easier to reach, makes for an essential first stop, is already home to related communities, or promises long-term opportunities of its own, the city has continually served as a new home for survivors and outcasts, opportunists and adventurers, despite being in other ways "the most thrusting, heartless, and demanding environment on earth."[7] Of course it helps that the city is also a magnet pulsing with money and power, drawing all things, including the rarest and most precious, into its vortex.

The archetypal New Yorker is neither an artist nor an actor nor a banker, but a working-class, multilingual immigrant.[8] Close to 40 percent of New Yorkers were born in another country, a figure that is only slightly lower than it was a century ago. Numerically, they form the largest foreign-born population of any metropolitan area in the world.[9] Around half of all New Yorkers speak a language other than English at home, and many of the rest have non-English-speaking parents or grandparents.

Yet paradoxically New York is also one of the capitals of the empire of English—not only the largest English-speaking city in the world, but a preeminent center of English-language media, publishing, and entertainment. Every kind of English is also here, with much more variation than is commonly recognized. Enormous numbers of New Yorkers also speak Spanish, Mandarin, Cantonese, Russian, Arabic, Bengali, and several other major languages. Their importance to the sprawling story of this most multilingual of cities is undeniable but comparatively better documented, and so not in focus here.

Before any of this was here, the whole region spoke Lenape. Among the earliest settlers were Frisian and Flemish speakers, while Fulani and Fujianese speakers are among the most recent. To label these groups only as Dutch, Belgian, Guinean, or Chinese is to miss who they are and where they're coming from, as well what happens when they get here. Nor does language simply reveal more precisely the set-in-stone ethnicity of a speaker or community. Linguistic differences may become more meaningful, not less, through all the interactions of urban life.

Deep linguistic diversity is among the least explored factors in New York's history and makeup. It could be argued that the disproportionate presence of historically oppressed and marginalized groups speaking less common languages quietly informs many of the city's most distinctive political, cultural, and economic arrangements.[10] It is also part of the city's soul, explaining its particular capacity for tolerance and ability to "make room" for others, however fraught and grudging, given long histories of segregation and a thousand local flavors of racism.

All cities, to different degrees, are defined by linguistic diversity. Throughout history, there have been many Babels besides Babylon, but few have left any trace. Imperial Rome must have had speakers, if not whole neighborhoods, of Oscan, Umbrian, Etruscan, and later Visigoth, Ostrogoth, and other languages now unremembered. Tang-dynasty Chang'an (today's Xi'an) must have teemed with speakers of Sogdian, Salar, Tangut, and others from across Eurasia. Chroniclers of Ottoman Istanbul and Mughal Delhi noted the presence of many different peoples, but no one listened to their languages, probably because (much as today) the unwritten held little interest for writers.

Past Babels faded unrecorded, but we should listen to the ones emerging today. They are the most diverse in history, the first with a truly global reach. Many are also outcomes of empire, where the rallying cry "We are here because you were there" rings with particular force.[11] Because of ELA, New York's is now by far the best documented, but every Babel has a dynamic all its own. Colonial history explains why Paris is now home to so many languages of Southeast Asia and West Africa, not to mention Saramaccan from French Guiana, Réunion Creole, and Indigenous Kanak languages of New Caledonia.[12] Today's London is powered by peoples of South Asia, the Caribbean, and Eastern and Southern Africa.[13] Moscow, just beneath the surface, is an unparalleled magnet for speakers of Caucasian, Central Asian, and Siberian languages.

Decolonization, in all its piecemeal chaos, made the metropoles' metropolises themselves into mini empires, reversing the flow of peoples while at the same time doubling down on colonial power dynamics. Migration policies may have left the door ajar, but the once-colonized pushed it open by mastering French, English, and Russian.[14] In time this led other, unrelated layers to develop: Tibetans and Wenzhounese in Paris, Brazilians and Lithuanians in London.

Linguistically diverse Dubai is a revolving door of mercilessly stratified peoples.[15] In Geneva, it's packed into Les Pâquis: Galician and Portuguese social clubs, Ethiopian and Eritrean shops, Lebanese sidewalk cafés, Thai masseuses, Romanian and Bulgarian dentists, African asylum seekers, and Balochi exiles. Hong Kong's Babel really is a single tower.[16] Toronto consists of communities from all over the world, including speakers of endangered languages like Scottish Gaelic, Sri Lankan Malay, Faetar from Italy, and Harari from Ethiopia—perhaps under less pressure to assimilate than elsewhere.[17] Los Angeles holds in its suburban sprawl dozens of Indigenous languages of the Americas, together with a unique linguistic assemblage from the Asia-Pacific.

National capitals like Jakarta, Nairobi, and Port Moresby have their own distinctive linguistic ecologies, differently constructed but no less extraordinary. Especially important, diverse, and challenging because of their proximity to remaining Indigenous lands are regional hubs like Anchorage, Alaska; Darwin, Australia; and São Gabriel da Cachoeira in the Brazilian Amazon.[18] There are also smaller Babels like Manchester and Graz, where careful work by linguists has found much more than at first meets the ear.[19]

Likewise, for one reason or another, many US states, towns, and cities not known for their diversity also serve as vital, substantial diaspora capitals for certain endangered language communities: the Kurds of Nashville, the Hawaiians of Las Vegas, the Tai Dam of central Iowa, the Arbëresh of Sacramento, the Micronesians of Arkansas, the Zomi of Tulsa, the Karen of Utica, and the Somali Bantus of Lewiston, Maine, among many others in an unsung but expanding and very American archipelago of refuge.[20]

Yet, for all these examples, there are no linguistic histories or portraits of any city. In the stories we tell about cities, the total, unconscious focus on the usual dominant languages needs undoing. The story of a city's least-known languages is also the story of its forgotten peoples, told in their own words (in translation where needed). One problem is an overreliance on written sources, which tend to be in the same few languages. We need to read those sources against the grain but more importantly listen to speakers of the other, mostly oral languages. A second challenge is that linguistic minorities, especially in urban centers, often seem to be rapidly subsumed into larger national, panethnic, or racial groupings, hiding the linguistic diversity within those.[21]

Just as confounding are the ways that cities can be crucibles of glorious and intensive contact and mixing, where new linguistic and cultural composites form, or sites of rediscovery, where people learn lost family languages as adults and language movements take wing. Contemporary sign languages in particular have often grown and flourished in cities, where a critical mass of Deaf people can gather at schools and clubs. Some endangered languages may even thrive, under certain circumstances, in the eye of the urban storm.

Today smaller languages will have to survive in urban environments—where a majority of humans, including in many places a majority of Indigenous people, now live[22]—if they are going to survive at all. Yet cities can be like sieves through which languages are continually running.[23] More than ever, cities depend on diversity but swallow it up and spit out a monoculture. Without continuous infusions of new speakers, few immigrant languages typically make it beyond the third generation. Now threats to immigration and immigrant lives, language loss in the homelands, and the gentrification of cities appear to be accelerating the cycle. A city like New York can be a haven but also an endpoint, a "Babel in reverse" metabolizing the languages and cultures of the world until none are left.

# A Brief Guide to Radical Linguistics

The baseless and pernicious myth of Babel in Genesis 11 suggests that linguistic diversity is nothing but confusion, divine punishment for the urban hubris that dared build a tower to reach the heavens. But in Genesis 10, the world was already diverse, with the descendants of Noah listed in a dazzling genealogy seventy names long as the world's original nations, each with its own language—איש ללשני (ish lilshono) or *every one after his tongue*, as the King James Version has it. Even earlier in Genesis 6–9, Noah himself was commanded to safeguard the world's biodiversity in an ark.

In many traditions, linguistic diversity is recognized as primordial and essential. In most of the world, multilingualism has been the historic norm. How we speak is the essence of where we come from, the grounding of self which enables us to connect with other, different selves.[1] More than race or religion, language is a window onto the deepest levels of human diversity. The ubiquitous map of the world's approximately two hundred nation-states is recent and superficial compared to the little-known map of its seven thousand languages. Borrowing, code-switching, mixing, hybridization, creolization, and language shift are all processes which attest to the fluidity of communication, but the core vocabulary of any given language can usually be traced back several millennia.

At the heart of linguistics itself is a radical premise: all languages are cognitively and communicatively equal. Language is a universal and democratic fact cutting across all human societies: no human group is without it, and no language is superior to any other. Some languages may specialize in talking about melancholy, or seaweed, or atomic structure; some grammars may glory in conjugating verbs while others bristle with syntactic invention. Languages represent thousands of natural experiments: ways of seeing, understanding, and living that should rightly form a major part of any meaningful account of what it is to be human.

We are talking about languages, not "just dialects." Linguists use the criterion of mutual intelligibility, meaning that under normal circumstances a distinct language cannot be understood by speakers of any other language.[2] But in popular parlance there is often something irreducibly political at work with these terms, as captured by the famous Yiddish phrase spoken by an unknown Bronx teacher: אַ שפּראַך איז אַ דיאַלעקט מיט אַן אַרמיי און אַ פֿלאָט (A shprakh iz a dialekt mit an armey un a flot): *A language is a dialect with an army and a navy*.[3] Indeed, "dialect" is now such a loaded and unhelpful term that linguists prefer to talk more neutrally about "language varieties," as we will here.[4]

Users of Sanskrit, Latin, Greek, Hebrew, Arabic, Persian, Mandarin, English, and the like have continually proclaimed their languages holier, more perfect, or more adaptive than the unwritten, unstandardized "dialects" they look down on. But from a linguistic point of view, no language as used by a native speaker is in any way inferior, let alone broken. The vast majority have always been oral, with written language a derivative of comparatively recent vintage, confined to tiny elites in a small number of highly centralized societies. Writing is palpably a trained technology of conscious coding, in comparison to the deeply natural and universal human behaviors of speaking and signing.

Perceptions of linguistic superiority or inferiority are not based on anything about the languages themselves, but on the power, class, or status of the speakers. Every language signed or spoken natively is a fully equipped system for handling the core communicative demands of daily life, able to coin or borrow words as needed. "Languages differ essentially in what they must convey and not in what they may convey," said the linguist and polyglot Jakobson.[5] In other words: it's possible to say anything in any language, but each language's grammar *requires* speakers to mark out certain parts of reality and not others, however unconsciously. This is the essence of what makes linguistics fascinating and revealing.

All languages may be communicatively and cognitively equal, but much harder to bridge are the social and historical disparities among their speakers, which have become almost unfathomably large. At present, around half of all languages are spoken by communities of ten thousand or fewer, and hundreds have just ten speakers or fewer. On every continent, the median number of speakers for a language is below one thousand, and in Australia this figure goes as low as eighty-seven.[6]

Today these numbers reflect serious endangerment, and even languages with hundreds of thousands or a few million speakers can be considered vulnerable. In the past, however, small language communities could be quite stable, especially hunter-gatherer groups which typically comprised fewer than a thousand people.[7] Likewise, most older sign languages, now critically endangered, evolved in so-called Deaf villages, where the incidence of hereditary deafness in the population was significantly higher than elsewhere, though still rarely more than 2 or 3 percent.[8] Many hearing people in these villages could also sign, but the core group of signers was typically several hundred at most.

In general, sheer speaker or signer numbers have always mattered less than intergenerational transmission. As long as parents, grandparents, and other caregivers were using it with children, and those children ultimately used it with their children, a small language could apparently remain strong for centuries. Take Gurr-goni, an Aboriginal language from North-Central Arnhem Land in Australia, which has had around seventy speakers as far back as anyone can remember.[9] Far from being an isolated group, Gurr-goni speakers maintained their language in a context of multilingual equilibrium, where each "father tongue" was integrally connected with certain ancestral lands and natural resources. It's this kind of equilibrium that has been vanishing fast as colonial and national languages take over.

But why does linguistic diversity matter in the first place?

For profoundly practical reasons—because children learn best in their mother tongue, and beyond education there are a whole host of positive effects on physical and mental health whenever native languages remain strong.[10]

For all the knowledge, wisdom, and art contained in every single language, which the dominant-language canons almost always overlook and no amount of last-minute translation can salvage.

For our understanding of human expression and communication in general, as the least-known languages are often the ones that prove a certain sound or feature or meaning is even possible.[11] It matters whether Pirahã does or doesn't do recursion (simply put: inserting a phrase inside another of the same kind, potentially ad infinitum), or whether nouns and verbs can be distinguished from each other in Salish.[12]

For the sake of justice—because the powerful, by conquest or commerce or culture or creed, are always actively suppressing, stamping out, and stigmatizing the languages of the powerless. Languages today are not "dying natural deaths" or evolving into new forms the way Latin evolved into Romance. Now more than ever, languages are being hounded out of existence.

Like biodiversity, with which it is clearly linked,[13] linguistic diversity remains strongest today in remote and rugged regions traditionally beyond the reach of empires and nation-states: mountain ranges like the Himalaya and the Caucasus; archipelagoes like Indonesia, Vanuatu, and the Solomons; and zones of refuge like the Amazon, southern Mexico, Papua New Guinea, and parts of West and Central Africa. But these too are under tremendous pressure.

"Que siempre fue la lengua compañera del imperio [*Language has always been the companion of empire*]," wrote Antonio de Nebrija in his 1492 *Gramática Castellana*, which aimed to raise vernacular Castilian Spanish to the level of Latin and other imperial languages, just in time for European conquests across the globe.[14] Though languages have always changed and come and gone, the scope for linguistic imperialism has widened exponentially since Nebrija. A comparatively small number of empires and nation-states, now bristling with twenty-four seven communication and education systems, cover every inch of the earth. Worldwide, centuries of imperialism, capitalism, urbanization, environmental destruction, and nation-building are now coming to a head linguistically. With power behind them, a few hundred languages keep growing and getting all the resources, while the other 95 percent struggle.

Particularly dominant are just a few dozen languages of wider communication, less politely called "killer languages." English, Spanish, and Chinese are on the march, but so are Nepali, Tok Pisin, and Brazilian Portuguese. These languages are spreading through political, economic, and cultural conquest, and the consequences are seeping into everything. When a Nahuatl speaker shifts to Spanish in Brooklyn today, it's the ultimate outcome of the conquest of Tenochtitlán and all the forces and processes it unleashed.[15] At the same time, only under extraordinary circumstances are a few new languages emerging, such as Nicaraguan Sign Language, which was created by Deaf students at new schools, and Light Warlpiri, which developed out of mixing between English and the Aboriginal language Warlpiri in Australia's Northern Territory.[16]

In Anglophone settler societies like the US and Canada, genocide, expulsion, disease, and every form of prejudice and pressure exerted on Native peoples have profoundly altered the linguistic landscape. Around half of the three hundred distinct languages once spoken north of the Rio Grande have already been silenced, and most of those remaining are no longer actively used, with under ten native speakers.[17] Only a few of the largest, including ᏣᎳᎩ (Cherokee), Diné Bizaad (Navajo), and Yup'ik can in any way be considered "safe," though profoundly embattled, for the coming decades.[18] Likewise, most of the hundreds of Aboriginal languages once spoken in Australia are either no longer spoken or else down to small clusters of elderly speakers, with just a few still heroically being transmitted.

Dominant-language speakers opine that everything would be easier and better (and peace on earth!) if everyone would just speak their particular dominant language. But common languages don't unify in and of themselves—look at many of the world's civil wars, or the deep divisions in Anglophone American society today. The imaginative challenge of big differences is quickly replaced with the narcissism of small ones: scrutinizing other people's accents, sociolects, word choice, tone of voice.

That's why even *within* the dominant languages, a dominant standardized variety is usually preached and promulgated to the exclusion of others: Parisian French, Putonghua Mandarin, the "Received Pronunciation" of upper-class southern England. Originally known to a relative few, all were consciously built up: backed by power, turbocharged by technology, consecrated through literature, validated through education, and popularized thanks to media and entertainment.[19] Now that the takeover is complete, few remember what came before. Even closely related varieties like Cajun French, working-class Beijinghua, and Cockney English come to be cast as deviant and defective dialects *of* the new standards, rather than the equal and independent developments they actually are.

The spheres of use for smaller languages and nonstandard varieties are continually shrinking: they often emerge only in private, yielding as soon as a speaker steps outside. Now the shift is happening inside homes as well. Families around the world are hitching their fate to English and other dominant languages—abandoning not just words, but vast traditions of gesture, intonation, facial expression, conversational style, and perhaps even the culture and character behind all these.[20] Only in the face of intense political, economic, religious, or social pressures do people stop passing on their mother tongues to children, but today these pressures are everywhere. The disruption of this basic natural process has come to feel almost normal.

Of course English in particular, supercharged by business, pop culture, and the internet after centuries of colonial expansion, is the real empire of our time—far more fluid and influential than any political entity. Many English speakers go their entire lives without encountering anything significant they can't do or get in their language. Whatever the power dynamics of any given conversation, English is pure linguistic privilege, the reserve currency of communication. The push to learn it is an event of planetary significance, swelling a linguistic community of half a billion native English speakers worldwide, plus another one to two billion who know it as a second language. These numbers are growing every day.

Many people think the world, or at least their corner of it, is growing ever more diverse, but monolinguals are increasingly in charge. The monolingual mindset, bone-deep in almost every Anglophone American, blocks any real urgency about other languages. A multilingual childhood, only now widely recognized as an inestimable cognitive advantage associated with increased empathy and flexibility, can add a whole dimension to one's understanding of the world, with a sense of linguistic and cultural perspective.[21] But to do it right, especially for monolingual parents, can require serious effort or considerable resources.

What should a monolingual do? Every time a person speaks, they embody an inherited chain of choices. It can be profoundly useful to be a native speaker of the dominant dialect of a dominant language. Representing the associated "mainstream" culture with every sound means being able to talk to many and sound good to most, set above the particulars of region, class, or ethnicity, though also lacking those solidarities. Rarely does a dominant-language monolingual need to speak anyone else's language, and it counts as a charming attempt if they do, a mark of open-mindedness and sophistication or an advanced party trick. Since reading and writing usually hew close to the dominant dialect, book learning is that much easier. A person "without an accent" is by default considered to be smarter or better educated as soon as they open their mouth.

Yet people intensely aware of privilege based on gender, race, class, or sexuality seldom consider their linguistic privilege. English (or Spanish or Mandarin or Urdu) may just seem like the air you breathe. "Language" becomes more metaphor than reality—what's *your* love language? The only cure for monolingualism is to learn other actual human languages, but it's at least a start to learn about them, from those who speak them. Maybe there should be a special kind of therapy for monolinguals, where you have to sit listening to a language you can't understand, without translation but with total patience.

For a linguist, this is an occupational hazard. On first meeting, a speaker knows you don't know their language, but there is a useful ambiguity. If not learning languages, what exactly does a linguist do? Sound systems are entire ecosystems for the ear, but even on an initial listen you can try to make out the shapes of syllables, the qualities of vowels, the puff of aspiration, the bent tongue of a retroflex. There may be clues in the intonation patterns: variations in pitch, rhythm, loudness, voice quality, or the length of sounds, which convey not only vibes, but essential information, like how rising pitch in English can signal a yes-no question. Under the rush of unfamiliar sound, flowing at hundreds of syllables per minute, you try to hold back from the scramble for meaning and suss out the structure.

From the glottis to the lips, the whole tract where spoken language happens is just five or six inches long. Across evolutionary eons, a space for eating and breathing gradually took on linguistic uses, not just anywhere but at certain places of articulation: the lips, the teeth, the alveolar ridge, the hard palate and the soft one behind it, the uvula that hangs like a little grape above the throat, the pharynx, and the larynx. The tongue—that great athlete of language, and the near-universal symbol of it—darts and bends to make contact wherever it can. For signers, it happens in the hands. (In what follows, I use terms such as speech and oral for the sake of simplicity, but virtually everything here also applies, mutatis mutandis, to the extraordinarily rich and diverse world of sign languages.) There are also whistled languages, drum languages, and other ways of emulating speech across space, since the unaided human voice rarely carries more than several hundred feet.[22]

The unaided human voice also fails at carrying across time, hanging in the air for just a few seconds at most. How it persists in memory is hard to say, but linguists try to make it last either on the tape or on the page. To document and describe languages while there is still time ought to be the first and most fundamental task for a linguist. Yet a linguist's moment of discovery is also almost always the moment of grasping a disappearance. For any outsider claiming to "discover" any human society or culture or language—that is, announcing the existence of some smaller group to the ruthlessly joined-up juggernaut sometimes known as "us"—is also arriving at, and bound up in, the moment of its destruction. The same forces that bring an outside linguist in are bringing everything else as well.

Individual linguists like the legendary Professor Sun have been out documenting for decades. For even longer, missionaries have been spreading the gospel ever more multilingually in the struggle for souls.[23] But the organized movement to preserve the world's languages is recent. In 1991, the linguist Michael Krauss warned that linguistics would "go down in history as the only science that presided obliviously over the disappearance of 90 percent of the very field to which it is dedicated."[24] This helped light the spark. Inspired by the new push for biodiversity and the growing movement for Indigenous rights, a cohort of linguists and language activists vowed to use new technologies to record and preserve as much as possible of the world's vanishing linguistic heritage.[25] Ideally, speakers record and document their own languages, and this is now increasingly common.

Language documentation may sound like an obvious priority for linguistics, but it flies in the face of what most linguists have been focusing on for the last seventy years: Language, not languages. Following Noam Chomsky, most have been chasing theoretical and computational questions, seeing themselves as Martians trying to document an essentially uniform language called Earthling. Their evidence has come mostly from the largest languages, which happen to be the dominant ones they're familiar with. Few meaningful universals have emerged from all the armchair theorizing and laboratory testing, but new data from thousands of other languages have gradually been trickling in, leading linguists like Joseph Greenberg to posit crosslinguistic tendencies stated with considerably more nuance than the purported universals. Theory has its place, but it's essential that languages be documented on their own terms. The real view from Mars, it turns out, is that linguistic diversity on Earth is far more profound and fundamental than previously imagined.[26]

At the same time, there is an essential toolkit that every language should have: a substantial dictionary, a detailed grammatical description, and a representative corpus of recorded stories, oral histories, and other texts showing the language in action and at least partially transcribed, translated, analyzed, and archived. To the extent speakers are willing, these materials should be maximally accessible and archived for posterity.[27] Not to mention publications, teaching materials, children's books, and other kinds of media. Speakers of larger languages take for granted effectively limitless resources both in and about their languages. Forget Siri, speech recognition, automatic translation, spell-check, and other nifty tools: imagine not having a dictionary, any established way of writing, or any authority on the language at all, aside from an elder you have to find and ask in person.

It's one thing to help build arks, or at least archives, but linguists don't and can't "save" languages. By definition, every language is limitless as long as speakers are still speaking it or signers are signing it. No language ends on the last page of a dictionary. From a finite number of sounds, words, rules, and techniques, speakers form an infinite number of utterances. There is no single way that a community "really speaks," nor any one authoritative type of data to preserve for all time. Language is too fluid to be caught in a net or an audio file, especially by an observer, however dedicated, who is not living and breathing it. Almost everything we say is a unique recombination of familiar elements, tuned to a particular moment, aired, and then gone. You can learn those elements, but you have to live those moments.

Unfortunately, many linguists also dwell on damaging, defeatist abstractions about language "death," "extinction," and "endangerment," while Indigenous scholars state clearly that oppression is the threat, and that reclaiming Indigenous languages is about liberation and recovery from historical trauma.[28] Linguistics, like anthropology, has skeletons in its disciplinary closet.[29] Fighting for endangered languages can only mean fighting on the side of their speakers and signers, and ultimately it's always up to communities whether and how to keep using their languages. Some have been struggling to for centuries; others are less concerned. Of course there are not only pressures, but also always enticements to learn a dominant language, which may grant access, however limited, to the dominant culture's resources.

For some members, the breakdown of a traditional community may feel like emancipation; for others, a disaster. Whether it's a matter of survival or a question of common sense, the logic of abandoning a smaller mother tongue for work, education, migration, marriage, or any number of other reasons can seem unassailable. Once-valued or ingrained connections to ancestors, traditions, territories, and knowledge systems can easily seem irrelevant, obscure, or simply impossible to access under contemporary conditions.[30]

It's a powerful-sounding truism, not quite true, that language and culture are inextricably linked, since group identities in some cases persist after the loss of a language.[31] Nor should anyone feel forced to stay within any particular culture. What matters is that individuals and communities have meaningful options, in an atmosphere of tolerance, respect, and support, for how they relate to their linguistic pasts and construct their linguistic futures. Given the normal and natural human capacity for multilingualism, maintaining a less widely spoken language need not preclude learning a more widely spoken one. The stories of our lives are embedded in the stories of the communities, identities, and traditions we embody and carry on.[32]

Today more than ever, people are trying to recover disappearing ancestral or heritage languages. There are now hundreds of language revitalization movements around the world, most launched in just the past few decades, creating a wealth of experience for others to draw on.[33] It can feel like nearly impossible work, where even a single new speaker of a highly endangered language counts as a serious triumph, requiring years of dedication. At the same time, scattered speakers are now finding each other in virtual spaces, where language learning options are multiplying and reality-augmenting and artificial intelligence possibilities are on the horizon.

Nevertheless, for the revivers of endangered languages, a sense of radical futility may be waiting around the bend of every utterance. Where will I speak this? Who will understand me? Who can even tell me if I'm speaking correctly? Will I ever start thinking in the language? When almost no one else is doing it, matching a string of sounds to a meaning can seem downright arbitrary. And yet it is only after ingesting masses of often arbitrary-seeming words that people can process or produce them at speed, and only then that they can start feeling the indescribable sense of what it is to live in a particular language—just as an actor needs to get her lines down cold before even starting to get into character. To try to communicate with what is no longer a tool of communication—to resurrect a whole worldview which is almost over the horizon—is a wonderful madness.

Linguists try to mark out points along this continuum like semi-speaker, heritage speaker, and rememberer, though such categories may do more harm than good. Familiar-seeming (English) concepts like *native*, *fluent*, and *mother tongue* shouldn't be uncritically assumed. The memory of older capabilities fades quickly: if elders once routinely knew the names of a hundred plants, it can become impressive for anyone to remember any. Ceremonial, symbolic, and "post-vernacular" uses take over: a prayer, a song, a word tattooed on an arm or printed on a T-shirt. Discussions and events start to be *about* the language rather than in it, or else circle around concepts like identity, culture, history, preservation, and endangerment that are almost always borrowed from larger languages. Sometimes what people need most is language affirmation, where the emotional importance of even echoes of heritage languages can be recognized.[34]

If one critical ingredient has been missing from language revitalization movements, it is real financial, political, and technical support from majority populations.[35] Speakers of endangered languages almost never encounter outside interest in or knowledge about their languages, while persecution, mockery, and stigma are still common. To the extent that language policy or discussion is on the agenda at all, it's about framing and flash points in a few dominant languages, not the collapse of linguistic diversity itself.

To tell the story of New York and its languages, we need just one more element: a fast-paced overview of the major areas of linguistics, because documenting languages involves them all.

Linguists study how people *do* speak, not how they *should* speak. Written language serves at best as unruly evidence, if used carefully, for the astonishingly elegant patterns of actual speech. This is why it's so important to document, through fieldwork, how actual linguistic encounters happen. Grammar is not the "prescriptive" set of dos and don'ts often taught in school, like avoiding passive voice or split infinitives, with an eye toward clear communication or sounding "right" in writing. For linguists, grammar is "descriptive," concerned with the nuts and bolts of communication, especially through the study of phonetics and phonology (sounds and sound rules), morphology (principles of word formation), syntax (the ordering of words and phrases), and semantics (the study of meaning). Historical linguists trace how languages emerge and change over time, while sociolinguists ground languages in social variables such as class, gender, race, ethnicity, and sexuality. Let's take each of these in turn, very briefly, leaving aside other fascinating subfields like pragmatics (language in use and context), gesture, and computational linguistics.

Phonetics zooms in on those five or six inches of the human vocal tract and its places of articulation. Here languages get their sonic building blocks, known as phonemes—the basic consonants and vowels which speakers of any given language can differentiate and use to make meaning (while ignoring possible others, like the click sounds used on a regular basis only by languages in southern Africa). There may be tremendous variation in terms of "phonemic inventory": Hawaiian does fine with just thirteen while there were eighty-four in Ubykh, the Caucasian language whose last known speaker passed away in 1992.

Linguists use the International Phonetic Alphabet, or IPA, as a kind of periodic table for phonetics which assigns a unique, often Latin-based but sometimes crazy-looking character like ʟ̝̊ or ʕ to every meaningful sound ever discovered in every human language. With over a hundred unique symbols and hundreds more markers, conventions, and suggestions, it can hurt your eyes if you're not an adept, and to type with any fluency means training your fingers for fearsome keystroke sequences.

Phonology is the study of how all these sounds fit together in action—for instance, the way the English plural, though taught as just **-s**, can be "realized" as /s/, /z/, and /əz/ (using IPA) in *cats*, *dogs*, and *horses*, respectively. It also encompasses a feature like tone, where relative differences in pitch are used systematically to distinguish syllables or words and make meaning. Though best known from the world of Chinese, tone is a common feature of languages in certain regions of the world (East Asia, West Africa, southern Mexico, parts of Papua New Guinea) and can come in many forms—from a simple pitch applied to a whole word to one that mutates over just a single syllable—and serve many functions, including grammatical ones. There are also "pitch accent" systems in languages like Swedish and Japanese that use tone in more limited ways, not to mention intonation, which operates on subtler, less systematic levels, as in the bundle of features we call stress in English, encompassing pitch but also length and loudness.

You might think that *word* at least would be a straightforward concept, but just hitting the space bar or taking a breath doesn't make something a word. Different languages operate on very different principles, raising the question of whether the word is even a universal or linguistically defensible concept. More basic than a word, when it comes to meaning, is the morpheme—linguists love the old Greek suffix **-eme** to mean the most fundamental unit of something—which can just as well be a "free" morpheme like *cat* that stands on its own or a "bound" one that can't, like English plural **-s**.[36] Morphology is the study of word formation, looking at how so-called isolating languages (like Mandarin) may typically use just one morpheme per word, while inflectional languages (like Spanish) use more, and agglutinative languages (like Japanese) can chain up to five or six at a time to form what might be described as an entire sentence. For a linguist, fully analyzing a language involves interlinear glossing, where a transcribed tier of words is broken down morpheme by morpheme in the tiers below it, whether the (abbreviated) gloss is lexical (feline.type for *cat*) or grammatical (PL for -s).

From morphemes and words, however analyzed, come sentences—or better yet utterances, since "sentence" implies a nice full stop with a period at the end, a convention of writing (which texting is calling into question). It's rarely so neat when people are actually talking, though there may be pauses, intonation contours, and other kinds of breaks in the flow of speech. Syntax is the ordering of elements in an utterance, and here too every kind of variation exists across the spectrum of the world's languages. To take a basic example, positing subjects, objects, and verbs as the core constituents of an utterance, these three can be ordered in any logically possible way (SOV, SVO, VSO, VOS, OVS, OSV), though in practice the first two are overwhelmingly dominant and the latter known to be possible only thanks to a handful of Amazonian languages.[37]

None of this explains how we mean what we mean, which is the role of semantics. Every language carves up its semantic space into different fields, where the words relate to and define each other in a variety of ways, whether it's the spectrum of colors or a set of synonyms and antonyms. Or consider how a system of verb tenses is not straightforwardly about what happened exactly when, but a set of relations, which is why the English present can also have habitual, future, and narrative uses. Similar but subtly different from the "parts of speech" taught in school are what linguists call "word classes," of which only nouns and verbs may be universal (depending on Salish), while articles (as in English *a*, *an*, *the*), classifiers (as in Mandarin 個 ge or 本 běn), and even adjectives are apparently not. While a class like the English article is considered "closed" (a small set of items that almost never changes), the classes of nouns and verb are "open" both to neologisms and to loanwords, which are words brought in ("borrowed") from another language.

A language like English lives through loanwords, little though its speakers may realize it, and every other language should be accorded the same privilege without facing questions about purity and authenticity. Though its "own" lexicon is arguably tiny, English carries many spoils in its imperial sweep, always folding in the greatest hits of other languages, just as a universal museum buys, borrows, or loots from all over. Words like alcohol, alchemy, and algorithm bear the Arabic definite article al-, still distantly reflecting a whole world of medieval learning (and there are many more such words, due to the Moorish conquest, in Spanish). Meander was once a river in Turkey; paradise a walled Persian garden; tragedy some kind of goat song in ancient Athens. From Patagonia to Alaska, hundreds of words have entered English from Indigenous languages of the Americas.

Loanwords are an obvious form of language change, but languages are always changing both for natural reasons internal to themselves (which linguistic principles aim to elucidate) and for external, social reasons. Though the ultimate origins of language remain as foggy as so much else in the history of Homo sapiens, historical linguistics reconstructs how the phonology, morphology, syntax, and semantics of languages have changed over the last several thousand years, comparing evidence from present-day languages with any older written materials that may remain. Most of the world's languages can be grouped into families, which include all the descendants of a common, theoretically reconstructible "protolanguage." The languages of the six speakers introduced in this book belong to the Tibeto-Burman, Indo-European (Iranic and Germanic), Mande, Uto-Aztecan, and Algic families—each of which is deeply different from the others, not to mention the massive differences which may exist across all the different subgroups of a single family.

Take the Austronesian family, Daniel's specialty, the product of intrepid sailors who probably started leaving Taiwan around four thousand years ago. Over time, their descendants eventually settled on almost every habitable island in the Indian and Pacific oceans, resulting in one of the world's largest and most widespread language families—some 1,250 languages, according to the latest count. On the other hand, there are also linguistic isolates, like Alex's language P'urhépecha or Basque, Burushaski, and approximately 126 others, which have no established historical connection to any other language on earth. It could be that the rest of the language family vanished without a trace, or that the isolate branched off and evolved beyond recognition, or maybe we just don't know enough yet to say.[38]

Languages may share features by virtue of coming from the same family, by contact due to geographic or other proximity, or in some cases by chance. The influence is rarely completely mutual, as the language with more powerful speakers usually makes its presence felt well beyond loanwords and deep into the grammar. Extreme cases, now becoming the norm, lead to endangerment and loss.

This always happens for fundamentally social and political reasons, because language is a practice shaped by our identities, ideologies, and attitudes. This is the subject of sociolinguistics: how language is lived and embodied in contemporary societies, including how class, gender, race, ethnicity, sexuality, and other factors shape linguistic structure. It also illuminates the linguistic creativity and fluidity of individuals—their ways of managing and mixing languages, for example, or defining themselves by their registers and repertoires—just as we will by listening to the six speakers at the center of this book.

Before we do that, we need to dive into New York's linguistic history. How did all these worlds of words end up in a single city?

# II. Past

# Minority Port

Before the arrival of Europeans, an estimated fifteen thousand people may have been living across Lenapehoking, including all of what is now New Jersey, the southern part of New York, northern Delaware, and sections of eastern Pennsylvania. What is now New York City was just its eastern edge, but running through its heart was the Delaware River, which rises in the Catskills, forms Pennsylvania's eastern border with New York and New Jersey, flows by Philadelphia and Wilmington, and widens into an enormous bay as it approaches the Atlantic. Europeans named it the Delaware for the forgotten grandee Lord de la Warr, governor-for-life of Virginia, and likewise all the Native people who lived near it, especially along its many tributaries.

The name they usually call themselves today is Lenape, covering what was then a constellation of dozens of distinct but related groups, a few hundred members each and all likely considered kin. In New Jersey, these were the Raritans, Haverstraws, Tappans, Hackensacks, and many others; in what is now New York City, the Canarsees, Nayacks, Rockaways, and more. Some of those are place-names now, but they were societies of farmers, hunters, and foragers then, seasonally mobile and adapted to rivers, shores, and bays that remain natural facts, however dramatically altered or forgotten today.[1] Manaháhtaan was *the place where we get bows*. At the southern tip of the island, goes the most plausible theory, there stood a stand of hickory trees, hard enough to make bows from.[2]

All but forgotten until recently, the first non-Native inhabitant of Manhattan was the extraordinary Jan Rodrigues (a.k.a. Juan Rodriguez), who was born to a Portuguese father and an African mother on the island of Hispaniola, then controlled by Spain and today split between Haiti and the Dominican Republic. Rodrigues was working with a Dutch captain who sailed on his own reconnaissance into New York Harbor in 1613, before New Amsterdam even existed. Left there over the winter, Rodrigues is believed to have started a family with a Native woman, learned Lenape, set up a trading post, and then served as an interpreter when the Dutch returned. The first Latino New Yorker, the first Caribbean New Yorker, the first African New Yorker, and the first European New Yorker were thus all the same person.[3] Details are sparse, but Rodrigues apparently spoke at least Spanish, Portuguese, Dutch, and Lenape, if not also an African language or an Atlantic creole. With people like Rodrigues, the new port was diverse in its makeup, with Native Americans, Africans, and Europeans present from the beginning.[4]

In 1624, New Amsterdam was established by the Dutch West India Company where the Hudson meets the Atlantic, as another node in its network of coastal trading posts spanning Brazil, Suriname, Curaçao, Ghana, Benin, and elsewhere. The first permanent settlers to arrive in May of that year were thirty-two Walloon families, originally from Valenciennes and Roubaix in what is today France, close to the Belgian border. Walloon is related to but distinct from French. The Walloon families were members of a religious and linguistic minority who had fled the Catholic takeover of their cities, resettled in the Dutch city of Leiden, and took their chances on a colonial scheme under the influence of their leader Jessé de Forest, who himself never made it to the new settlement.[5] A few years later, it was another Walloon refugee named Pierre Minuit, also employed by the Company, who effected the supposed "purchase" of Manhattan.

Fort Amsterdam rose on the land where hickory trees had grown. Among those who built and maintained it were eleven African men enslaved by the Company. Like the thousands of other enslaved Africans brought in chains to the city over the following two centuries, they must have been highly multilingual.[6] A significant number were likely Kikongo speakers from the Kingdom of Kongo or Kimbundu-speaking Ndongo from what is today Angola—as reflected in names like Paulo d'Angola and Simon Congo. Unfortunately, personal names and group names used by slave traders are the only evidence for African language use in New Amsterdam and early New York. During bilingual court cases involving the enslaved, it's possible that the interpretation was between Dutch and either Kikongo or Kimbundu.[7] It's suggestive too, in terms of language use at home and within families, that the Angolans seem to have married each other rather than other Africans.[8] Regardless, all must have faced intense pressure to give up their African languages, and it is likely that Portuguese or a Portuguese-based creole was important for them at first, followed by a shift to Dutch.

Lenape continued to play a crucial role during the early years of settlement. Several colonists lived among or had close contact with speakers and apparently served as interpreters during legal proceedings.[9] Probably many more Native people learned Dutch, and a substantial number of Dutch loanwords entered Lenape, ironically preserving a piece of colonial history otherwise lost.[10] Drawn by trading opportunities, speakers of other Native American languages including Mohawk, Mohican, and Susquehannock also became increasingly frequent visitors.[11]

Violence was never far from the surface. On the night of February 23, 1643, New Amsterdam's Governor Wilhelm Kieft, avenging the killing of a small number of settlers, ordered a surprise attack that killed over 120 Native people then taking refuge in Lower Manhattan and Jersey City. The following year, now in an all-out war, where the odds were dramatically stacked against the Lenape, the Dutch killed hundreds of others in Westchester and Long Island, effectively eliminating Lenape societies from the area. Some survivors remained while most moved north or west—remarkably, as we will see later, managing to keep their language with them.

Only about half of New Amsterdam's population was actually Dutch, and perhaps considerably less if all Walloon, Frisian, and Flemish speakers are counted separately.[12] The other half included both enslaved and free Africans, a motley mix of mostly northern Europeans, and English-speaking religious refugees from New England like Anne Hutchinson and Lady Deborah Moody, who tended to form their own towns in outlying areas. There were also a number of singular individuals like Pietro Cesare Alberti, "the Italian" from Venice, and Anthony Janszoon van Salee, the Muslim "Turk" whose mother was a Moor from Spain and whose father was a Dutch pirate serving the Barbary Coast city-state of Salé in what is now Morocco.

At a time when Virginia and Massachusetts were fanatically intolerant English-only colonies, commercial opportunity, religious tolerance, and linguistic diversity were all of a piece in New Amsterdam. For these reasons, the Dutch Republic itself in this period was a major hub for refugees and immigrants from across Europe, and New Amsterdam took these qualities even further.

Many of these diverse New Amsterdammers either had some kind of Dutch connection or came from an adjacent area, so Dutch became a handy lingua franca in the early days of the city. Even among the Dutch, however, there was likely considerable dialect diversity, for Dutch was not a standardized national language at the time, and colonists came from Holland, Gelre (Gelderland), Utrecht, and other provinces. Flemish, then part of the same linguistic continuum, was also a mother tongue for many, like the prominent settler Annetje Loockermans, who is sometimes credited as introducing the Santa Claus tradition to America. Also often simply taken as Dutch were the outpost's many Frisian speakers, not only the famous West Frisian Peter Stuyvesant but also many North Frisians from Schleswig-Holstein in what is now Germany.[13] The latter region was still reeling from the Burchardi flood, a storm tide which devastated North Frisia on October 11–12, 1634, overrunning the dikes, killing thousands, and destroying the island of Nordstrand (which still echoes, via the family name, in Brooklyn's Nostrand Avenue). Five years later, Frisians were among those who sailed over with Jonas Bronck, the first settler of the Bronx whose own identity has been variously claimed as Frisian, Swedish, Norwegian, and Faroese and whose library contained books in Danish, Dutch, German, and Latin.[14]

In 1643 the French Jesuit priest Isaac Jogues, who was visiting to perform the first Catholic mass for an Irishman and a Portuguese woman, wrote: "On the island of Manhate, and in its environs, there may well be four or five hundred men of different sects and nations: the Director General told me that there were men of eighteen different languages"—of which a number must have been what are today considered minority languages.[15] It's another indication of the port's extreme diversity that a satirical Dutch pamphlet of 1649 depicts each of eight passengers bound there as being from a different ethnic group.[16] Many just passed through or stayed briefly, like the Lithuanian nobleman and scholar Aleksandras Karolis Kuršius, who founded the city's first Latin school in 1659 before packing up two years later, but the template for the city's ethnic diversity and multilingualism was being set.[17]

At first, the English takeover of 1664 changed little linguistically, with most New Amsterdammers staying on and a diverse mix of new settlers continuing to arrive. Even three decades later, the newly named New York was still "too great a mixture of nations and English the least part," according to one English observer.[18]

An early French-speaking presence, including the Waldensian religious refugees who came to Staten Island in the 1650s, was substantially augmented by a late seventeenth-century wave of Huguenots, a different group of Protestant refugees driven out of France. Likewise, the initial group of Portuguese-speaking Sephardic Jewish refugees were soon outnumbered by Ashkenazi Jews, who also worshipped in Hebrew but spoke Yiddish, German, Polish, and other languages.[19] Besides Dutch, wrote the Reverend Justus Flackner, his Lutheran flock included "High-Germans, also Swedes, Danes, Norwegians, Poles, Lithuanians, Transylvanians, and other nationalities."[20]

In the same period, the acceleration of the slave trade was changing the composition of the city's African community, with the arrival of what were likely Akan speakers (often called Coromantees at the time) from what is today Ghana, as well as speakers of Gbe languages from Benin, then known as Popo. Some also likely knew Malagasy, given the substantial but short-lived trading relationship between the city and various pirates in Madagascar, which included human cargo. Later on, a majority of enslaved New Yorkers came not directly from Africa but via Jamaica or Barbados and may have already learned local English-based creoles. Besides countless unrecorded acts of sabotage and rebellion, there were uprisings of the enslaved in 1712 and 1741,[21] in which it's possible to imagine that linguistic solidarities, whether around African languages or New World creoles, may have played a role.

The elite that brutally suppressed these uprisings itself had distinct Dutch-, English-, and French-speaking segments. Dutch dynasties like the Lefferts, Wyckoffs, and Cortelyous established large agricultural estates in Brooklyn that fed the then-distant city centered on lower Manhattan off enslaved labor. In the city itself, many Dutch men became bilingual, though some Dutch women remained monolingual. Books and pamphlets in Dutch continued to roll off the presses.

It was only in the first decades of the eighteenth century that demographic shift, commercial pressures, and the Anglican church intensified the pressure to switch to English, at least in the city. The British colonial governor Lord Cornbury worked a canny bit of language policy, making licensure difficult for teachers in the Dutch schools as a way of pushing families toward the English ones.[22] Already some were noting how

New York Dutch was both changing under the influence of English and diverging from the Dutch that was evolving in the Netherlands.[23]

Yet Dutch remained vital in the wider region well over a century into English rule and even past the American Revolution, with the Dutch Reformed Church usually seen as the key institution maintaining it. Gertrude Lefferts-Vanderbilt, a product of rural Dutch Brooklyn, wrote that "as late as 1830, and even 1840, when elderly people met together socially, it was quite common for them to drop gradually into the use of the Dutch tongue, even when the conversation had begun in English; a little confidential talk between old ladies was sure to be in Dutch."[24] The language lasted even longer further north in rural areas on both sides of the Hudson and in the Mohawk Valley, with "Jersey Dutch" and "Mohawk-Hudson Dutch" at least partially documented from a few mixed-race speakers, rememberers, and revivers as late as the early twentieth century.[25]

Many enslaved New Yorkers like Sojourner Truth, born in Ulster County in 1797, were also native speakers of the local Dutch; though famous for her oratory in English, she apparently learned it only after the age of eleven. Market days and Pinkster celebrations—which may have played a role in the development of minstrelsy and tap dancing, as well as the spread into English of words like *boss*—brought a Dutch-speaking or -accented Black cultural ambience into the city.[26] Runaway-slave advertisements, which sometimes mentioned the languages spoken by the runaway, testify that many spoke Dutch as well as "a variety of black language styles . . . ranging along a continuum from those who spoke a language close to that of standard English, through creole-speaking blacks to, at the other end, a few speakers of African languages."[27]

If English was ever singularly dominant in New York, as it has been in nearly every other American city, it was probably around the turn of the nineteenth century, as Dutch was receding. The reputation of being home to "a motley collection of all the nations under heaven" remained,[28] and other languages were certainly making it to the city—the large-scale arrival of white and Black Haitians during the 1791–1803 revolution is a case in point—but a majority of immigrants at this particular moment seem to have been English speakers. In fact the consolidation of a distinctive New York City English may date from this period, because it was already being played for laughs in nineteenth-century newspapers and books.[29]

The city's English, of remarkably low prestige for such a powerful and wealthy city,[30] is now in some sense a bundle of "ethnolects," each closely associated with a particular ethnic group and in general with working-class New Yorkers. Take the sound system, with key features like "*r*-lessness" (the lack of /r/ after vowels, as in "bee-ah" for *beer*), "the complex short-a split" (*halve* pronounced differently from *have*), "the raising of the *thought* vowel" (to sound like "thawt"), and "*h*-dropping" ("yuge" instead of "huge") among others. Some of these exist in other East Coast cities that were settled around the same time, but the total package is distinctive, and there is an often untraceable story behind each individual feature. Some linguists point to the impact of immigrants from particular parts of southern England, while others reckon that the colonists imitated and retained fashions in London speech of the period, which Londoners themselves later abandoned. Others see natural processes of sound change at work within the city's English.[31]

English may have dominated for a time, with a new local style fast developing on the streets, but non-English-speaking immigrants would soon again dominate, as has been the case ever since. By the 1850s, there were more New Yorkers who had been born in France than in Massachusetts, for example—and two much bigger immigrant waves from Europe were soon completely transforming the city's linguistic landscape.[32]

Many of the earliest Irish New Yorkers, before the Revolution, were Anglo-Irish (Protestant, English-speaking, sometimes well-to-do), but there were also many Scots Irish (some speaking Scots, which is kin to the Englishes of northern England) and so-called German Irish, transported from the ravaged Palatinate in southwest Germany to County Limerick in 1709.[33] After decades of hardscrabble farming, many of the latter came to New York in the mid-eighteenth century, possibly still speaking their Germanic varieties. It's not clear whether they connected with anyone left from the three thousand mostly Palatine refugees who came to New York in 1710 and were quarantined for a bitter winter on Governors Island—a sudden onset migrant crisis not unlike today's.[34]

At least by the eighteenth century, there were Irish speakers in New York as well, typically Catholics from areas of western Ireland where the centuries-long English effort to stamp out the language had not succeeded. Though still spoken by around half of Ireland's population at the time, Irish was low status and seldom written. Many speakers who reached New York may have been indentured servants, given ads posted for runaway servants that mention knowledge of the language or an accent.[35] Others were exiles from the 1798 rebellion against the English, which culminated in the Battle of Vinegar Hill that gave the Brooklyn neighborhood its name.

The Gorta Mór changed everything, with famine sending an estimated two hundred thousand Irish speakers from the disproportionately affected southern and western parts of the country to North America between 1845 and 1855, and New York the major gateway.[36] By 1860, there may have been seventy-three thousand Irish speakers in Manhattan and Brooklyn, around as many as there are native speakers in the world today.[37] New arrivals often settled with others from the same hometown or county, such that the Fourth Ward (roughly today's Chinatown) informally became known as the Kerry Ward and the Seventh (part of today's Lower East Side) as the Cork Ward, in honor of two counties with significant Irish-speaking populations.[38] Later, the West Side piers and associated industry made Greenwich Village a mini–County Clare, with Chelsea and Hell's Kitchen also heavily Irish. Smaller communities in the city spoke other, quite different Celtic languages, Welsh and Scottish Gaelic, though it's unclear how much these communities interacted during this period.

Protestants proselytized in Irish, at least one Catholic priest preached in Irish, swindlers swindled in Irish, and in 1851 the first Irish poem published in America sang the praises of a pub on Duane Street in three stanzas. Yet the language remained stigmatized and underground until another immigrant wave, along with generational change and the evolving Irish independence struggle, spurred a revival in the 1870s and '80s. Thousands in the city signed up for classes, and the first periodical ever printed anywhere in Irish, An Gaodhal (*The Gael*), was launched in Brooklyn in 1881, full of folklore, original Irish-language poetry, and nationalist appeals.[39]

Rapid shift to English was unstoppable, but immigration continued to bring thousands more Irish speakers to the city, even as the language was continually receding in Ireland itself. If not entire neighborhoods then at least significant clusters used Irish well into the twentieth century, though intergenerational transmission proved difficult. One close look at Chelsea in 1910, for instance, found eight buildings with sixty-one Irish-speaking families, including a single building with thirteen.[40] From the 1930s to the 1950s, the area around St. Teresa's Parish in Crown Heights and Flatbush drew many Irish speakers originally from Donegal, who called their picnicking and football spot in Prospect Park "Donegal Hill." Between a small number of native-speaker immigrants and enthusiastic second-language Gaeilgeoir, New York remains an active Irish language center today.[41]

The other massive mid-nineteenth-century wave of immigrants that challenged English's hold on the city was from the Germanic-speaking lands of central Europe, which were still decades away from political (let alone linguistic) unification. Some eight hundred thousand of these diverse "Germans" passed through the city in the 1850s alone, making New York a Germanic-language metropolis of a scale and diversity rivaled only by Berlin and Vienna. Centered on Avenue B ("German Broadway") and Tompkins Square Park in today's East Village, the hundreds of blocks comprising Kleindeutschland (*Little Germany*) arguably became the US's first sizeable and "institutionally complete" immigrant neighborhood operating predominantly in a language other than English.[42]

In fact, it operated not just in one, but in half a dozen related Germanic languages which people somehow navigated. Among the largest linguistic groups, coming in waves after the uprisings of 1848, were Prussians, (Prussian-avoiding) Bavarians (including Palatines), Swabians, Hessians, Württembergers, Hanoverians, and many others from Austria, Switzerland, the North Sea coast, and elsewhere. Each group was said to be concentrated to a degree in a different East Side ward. By 1850, there were twenty-eight "German"-language newspapers and in 1890, twelve dailies still remained, including ones published in regional languages like the *Plattduetsche Post* (in Low German) and *Schwäbisches Wochenblatt* (in Swabian). There was occupational specialization, with many grocers hailing from Hanover, shoemakers from Baden, and tailors from Prussia.[43] A number of other central and eastern European communities speaking different languages were forming nearby.

Yet there was also intense and increasing contact between the different Germanic groups, from which ultimately emerged a new German American community, especially following German unification in 1871. "German dialects," as they were now seen, gradually faded as most German New Yorkers moved to "second-generation" neighborhoods like Yorkville or Williamsburg. During the world wars, the use of any form of German became stigmatized.

From 1846 to 1940, between fifty-five and fifty-eight million people came from Europe to the Americas in one of the largest migrations in human history, far outnumbering all the settlers from the previous 350 years combined.[44] By far the largest number of these hemispheric transplants were peasants and workers who came to the United States and entered through New York Harbor. Falling mortality rates, land loss, and the vast upheavals of industrialization and urbanization were driving a demographic explosion on the European continent. At the same time, transatlantic travel was becoming easier than ever, with faster and cheaper steamboat routes from Europe to New York increasingly common after 1838. Colonial expansion meant relatively high wages and free land for the new settlers.

By the mid-nineteenth century New York had bypassed rival cities on the Eastern seaboard, taking on the twinned roles of premiere commercial entrepôt and immigrant gateway. If Wall Street increasingly symbolized the former, it was Castle Garden, the country's first-ever "emigrant landing depot," established by city and state officials in 1855 at the foot of Manhattan, that stood for the latter. Over the next thirty-five years, an estimated eight million migrants, mostly from Northern and Western Europe, came through Castle Garden, which became the word keslgarten in American Yiddish, meaning any *chaotic and confusing place*, just as lunapark (from Coney Island's Luna Park) would later become the general Yiddish term for *amusement park*.[45]

In 1892, to bring order to the chaos, the federal government opened the Ellis Island Immigration Station on an artificially extended island in New York Harbor itself, named for its one-time Welsh immigrant owner Samuel Ellis. Nearly ten million migrants, by then overwhelmingly from Southern and Eastern Europe, would pass through before immigrant restrictions took effect in 1924, followed by just two million more before the station's closure in 1954.[46]

No visas were required. First- and second-class passengers could skip the island and its inspections altogether. Despite the urban legend that officials on the island regularly changed immigrants' names—they usually copied them directly from the ship's manifest—Ellis Island was a place of comparative cultural and linguistic sensitivity. Its staff of mostly immigrant New Yorkers could interpret for the twenty most commonly spoken European languages, as well as Arabic and Chinese (given the small but significant communities then forming in the city, as we will see shortly). Even if pragmatically motivated, the island's linguistic accommodations left a deep impression on the new arrivals, as one later wrote (originally in Yiddish):

> *My first contact with my new country was the brief conversation between me and the immigration officials. We were put into short lines as we entered the large buildings at Ellis Island. Each line had to go by a small table next to which officials sat who questioned each immigrant in his language. The new immigrant felt right at home. My line spoke Yiddish. Hence, a big, strange country recognized my language that I had brought here with me from abroad as an official language. In Russia and Germany, I did not receive any such privilege.*[47]

Of the 98 percent of passengers admitted by inspectors, some set out immediately for other parts of the country—railway agencies sold tickets on the island—but many met relatives or were otherwise directed to one of the city's booming ethnic neighborhoods, where they might stay for days, years, or generations. Language skills weighed heavily in such decisions, because sometimes the only part of the country where an immigrant could communicate comfortably was a five-block area of Lower Manhattan or, as the case might be today, a small slice of central Queens. By comparison, those from larger national language groups had more options for a smooth resettlement, and perhaps more hope of replicating agricultural and other livelihoods, only more prosperously than in Europe, somewhere west of the Hudson.

As the city's working class became majority immigrant, the Know Nothings of the 1840s and '50s—a political movement of bitterly anti-Catholic, "native-born Americans" against the new immigrants—gave way to a city fundamentally patterned along ethnolinguistic lines. Politically, this resulted in a particular form of ethnic coalition-building which operates to this day and shapes many of the city's key institutions. Spatially, it meant a city primarily composed of mixed yet specific ethnic neighborhoods—of Cork Wards and Kleindeutschlands—speaking a wide variety of languages, however stratified or stigmatized.

Far from being a dead-end ghetto, an ethnic neighborhood in turn-of-the-century New York typically served the most linguistically vulnerable groups as "a buffer and a way-station," "a mobility launcher," despite the hardships, with an ever-evolving array of personal, political, and economic opportunities. "Assimilation" to Standard German or Irish English often came first. Just as today, there were few mono-ethnic enclaves: a single, unexceptional early twentieth-century block in Manhattan could be home to people born in the US as well as Canadian, English, Scottish, French, German, Irish, Italian, Jewish, Hungarian, Finnish, and Swedish immigrants.[48]

Many immigrants moved rapidly from manual labor into more white-collar work or started small businesses, a sign of upward mobility.[49] Powering it all was blistering economic growth, especially at the city level, as catalyzed locally by five-borough consolidation in 1898, nationally through the dominance of New York's industries, and internationally as the new US imperialism unlocked opportunities for what was becoming the world's busiest port. As a "corporate command post" powered by a multilingual immigrant workforce, the city was positioned on a global level to receive ever-thickening flows of people, ideas, and goods.[50]

Remarkably, that workforce consisted predominantly of the dispossessed and often effectively stateless victims of Europe's ethnic conflicts and internal colonialisms. Emma Lazarus reconceived the Statue of Liberty, fortuitously close to Ellis Island, as the "Mother of Exiles" from whose "beacon-hand / Glows world-wide welcome"—for masses that were not just huddled, tired, and poor, but "homeless, tempest-tost."

Over the course of the twentieth century, virtually every European language and dialect came to be spoken in New York. Nowhere, even in Europe itself, was the continent's linguistic diversity more concentrated, including not only its emerging national standards but dozens of oral, minority, and endangered languages, sometimes from different branches of the Indo-European family, if not other language families altogether. Basque sailors bunked down by the East River piers. Arumanians from Romania claimed a few blocks in the Bronx. Maltese speakers poured into Queens, positioning themselves between Italian, Greek, and Arabic speakers just as they are in the central Mediterranean.[51]

Even those assumed by outsiders to be speakers of national languages have often used something quite different among themselves. Most Spanish New Yorkers—first settling in the "Little Spain" near the Hudson River piers from Christopher Street to Twenty-Third Street and later on the Brooklyn waterfront—were in fact Galicians, whose mother tongue is closer to Portuguese.[52] Besides Galicians and Castilians, Little Spain also drew in Catalans, Basques, and Asturians, as well as Cuban and Puerto Rican political refugees and cigar makers, laying the basis for today's Nueva York, a major melting-pot metropolis for Spanish speakers using every variety of the language.

Many French New Yorkers in the first half of the twentieth century were also from a linguistic minority on their country's Atlantic fringe, speaking the Celtic language Breton. Over three thousand came in the 1900s, mostly from Gourin, to work at Michelin's tire factory in Milltown, New Jersey, and even more after the Second World War to the city's French restaurants, whose owners, maître d's, barmen, dishwashers, and busboys were actually for the most part Breton speakers. By 1967, there were twelve thousand Bretons in the city, if not more, representing over a third of the city's total

French population, with many living in Hell's Kitchen and later Astoria and Woodside in Queens. Living in the Bronx and making a living reproducing Louis XV–style furniture in a factory, the writer Youenn Gwernig wrote Breton-language poetry about the city and published his novel *La grande tribu* (The Large Tribe) in French, describing the trials and tribulations of the city's pan-Celtic "tribe" of Breton, Irish, and Scottish New Yorkers.[53]

Many New Yorkers seen as Russian or Ukrainian have actually considered themselves ethnic Rusyns or Lemkos, native in a continuum of Slavic dialects from the Carpathian Mountains primarily in what is today Slovakia, Poland, and Ukraine.[54] From the 1880s on, they formed the core of the city's eastern European neighborhoods in the East Village, Williamsburg, and later Yonkers and New Jersey, as well as the earliest Byzantine Catholic and Eastern Orthodox congregations. Many headed for Pennsylvania coal country, including the parents of Ondrej Warhola, later known as Andy Warhol.[55] But the city remained an essential site for Lemko activists like bass-playing Brooklyn streetcar motorman Stephen Shkimba, who in 1928 convinced a local label to make dozens of recordings of traditional music featuring him and his fellow immigrants. These remain an early, invaluable archive of a culture already being overrun in Europe—the artistic analog to the 1933 formation to the Organization for the Defense of Lemkivshchyna (as the Lemko homeland is called) on 13th Street in Manhattan. Poland's forced resettlement of its Lemko population in 1947 drove a new wave of refugees to New York.[56]

Living near the Rusyns in Williamsburg and taken to be either "Russians" or "Turks" were the Lipka Tatars, who arrived at the turn of the twentieth century from what is now Poland and Belarus. Some may have still spoken their variety of the Turkic language Tatar, while others likely spoke Polish or Belarusian dialects, which they may have written in the Arabic script. Built in 1931, their side-street mosque was the first in the city and is one of the oldest in North America. Active for decades and still bustling on days like Kurban Bayram (Eid al-Adha), the Powers Street Mosque stands modestly sandwiched between rowhouses today, somehow looking a little Baltic Muslim in its north Brooklyn vinyl siding.

"Italians" are perhaps the most significant example of a collection of particular linguistic groups being taken for speakers of a single national language. The New York metropolitan area has long constituted one of the largest Italian cities in the world, home at one time or another to almost all of the peninsula's substantial linguistic diversity.[57] Yet virtually none of the four million Italian immigrants who arrived in the US between 1880 and 1924, mostly through New York, could speak, read, or write the national language Italian, a literary variety originally based on central Tuscan. In the period following unification, when "Italy" was still a work in progress, only around 2.5 to 10 percent of the new nation's population could. Even fewer could in the desperately poor and marginalized south, where the countryside emptied out as whole communities left for l'America—although many were "birds of passage" who returned or went back and forth.

In fact people from the Italian peninsula came to New York speaking hundreds of related but distinctive village-based dialetti (*dialects*), largely from Sicily, Campania, Calabria, Puglia, Abruzzo and Molise, Basilicata, and Lazio. Campanilismo, which describes the deep local ties binding those born within earshot of the village campanile, or *bell tower*, not only carried over to New York but dictated the terms of the migration. Elizabeth Street in Manhattan's emerging Little Italy became not just a Sicilian street but a series of hometown clusters, with people from Palermo, Marineo, Sciacca, and Santa Margherita di Belice packed into their respective tenements.[58]

This pattern, both reinforced by and in turn reinforcing linguistic difference, continued at least to some extent in East Harlem, Brooklyn, and the Bronx, the next generation of Italian neighborhoods made accessible by the new subway lines that Italian laborers themselves were building. By 1920, there were at least twenty-five neighborhoods across the city with anywhere from two thousand to one hundred thousand Italian residents, and in 1935 East Harlem alone had over a hundred hometown-based società (*mutual benefit societies*), the surest reflection of who was settling where.[59]

Northern Italian communities, of which much less is known, were small but influential early on. In the 1880s, Ligurian speakers from Chiavari near Genoa pioneered the Italian presence in Greenwich Village, and in subsequent years the local entertainment spot Ferrando's Hall held performances in both northern and southern dialects.[60] Likewise, on the Lower East Side's "Lung Block," unfairly stigmatized as a toxic immigrant slum and epicenter of tuberculosis, northerners from Emilia-Romagna, Tuscany, and elsewhere lived alongside a diverse mix of southerners, with the local church named St. Joseph's to be acceptable to all.[61] Near the Hudson piers lived communities of Genoese, Turinese, and Milanese, as well as Neapolitans.[62] A separate "Little Friuli" formed on the East Side roughly from Twenty-Third Street to Thirty-Seventh Street, with a clubhouse on Thirty-Fourth Street which is now an Estonian cultural center.

White-collar prominenti and middleman padroni, many of them earlier immigrants from the north, practiced the time-honored tradition of getting ahead by both helping and exploiting the more recent immigrants.[63] A padrone, contracted by American employers for big jobs, would hire a mass of new arrivals who usually had little English, taking a percentage and sometimes founding a whole new settlement wherever the work was. Prominenti and padroni might even handle the correspondence of illiterate immigrants with their loved ones back in Italy, drafting love letters in "florid prose styles" that likely would have veered away from dialect and toward the national standard.[64]

Further bolstering an "Italianization" beyond the campanilismo of all these diverse groups were a new press and radio in the national language, both in New York and in Mussolini's Italy.[65] Likewise, the city's extensive network of Catholic schools began teaching Italian, at least as a foreign language, as did the New York City public school system with a pioneering bilingual educational program that peaked in 1938, with sixteen thousand students enrolled.[66] Nor were Italians the only group in the city to experience a kind of transnational political "awakening" during this period. Even as many Italian New Yorkers celebrated Mussolini's invasion of Ethiopia, Harlem's African Americans rallied against it.

Yet Standard Italian has remained more the ideal than the reality in homes and neighborhoods. Even after the Second World War, when a new wave of Italians came with more knowledge of the national language, many of the outer-borough neighborhoods they created were dialetti-dominant.[67] Kids in such neighborhoods with immigrant parents became what linguists call sequential bilinguals, because the heritage language they picked up at home was rapidly supplanted by the (New York City) English taught at school and picked up in the streets.

Even today, most of the approximately sixty thousand New Yorkers still listed by the census as speaking "Italian" are actually doing something much more intricate and interesting, communicating along a multilingual continuum that includes "Italianized dialect, pidginized American Italian, and archaic dialects . . . with various degrees of competence, according to generation, time of emigration, and education"—in other words, forging a lingua franca in real time.[68] As for those "archaic dialects," from time to time an Italian New Yorker visiting their ancestral hometown is teased for speaking the way that people there, shifting rapidly toward the national language, haven't done for half a century.[69] Linguistic survival often works best when speakers are not even conscious of what they are doing.

# Survivor City

Beneath the glitter and glamour, New York has long been an archipelago of last resort not only for marginalized minorities but for the remnants of colonized, decimated, and enslaved peoples. Many arrived in the city in the first half of the twentieth century, and their descendants still make up a substantial portion of the population. Their languages, at the brink, may be defended, perpetuated, or indeed consciously abandoned with a special determination. They are speakers of Western Armenian and Pontic Greek, who survived the genocides of the late Ottoman Empire; of Circassian, Kalmyk, Crimean Tatar, and other Caucasian languages, who made it through Soviet deportation; of Yiddish, Judeo-Greek, Ladino, and Romani languages, who came through the Holocaust; and of African American English and Gullah, who fled lynchings and Jim Crow in the American South.[1]

Retrospective platitudes (in English) like *searching for a better life* and *land of opportunity* can be conducive to forgetting, elision, and moving on. But no one knows for certain how deeply or for how long the calamities that befall peoples and cultures remain locked or lingering in the minds or lifeways or even the genes or epigenetic inheritances of the survivors and their descendants. Alleged war criminals from Haiti's Tonton Macoute,[2] Bangladesh's War of Independence,[3] and the Third Reich[4] have lived quietly in the city among, or at least not far from, the survivors they once terrorized.

Survivors rebuild and reinvent in neighborhoods and suburbs. Descendants replace ancestors. At a Manhattan ceremony to commemorate the Pontic Greek genocide, the adults make the speeches, but it's the kids and teens who hold up signs and wear T-shirts to honor the victims and who will speak, dance, and sing at the upcoming Pontic Youth Festival. Hasidic Brooklyn has grown essentially from a small cluster of Holocaust survivors to an estimated one hundred thousand people thanks to women like Yitta Schwartz, who survived Bergen-Belsen and died upstate at the age of ninety-three with some two thousand living descendants—reflecting not just the Biblical imperative ken yirbu (*may they multiply* in Hebrew) but the more recent one to replace the six million murdered, a project which at current rates may succeed by the end of this century.[5]

Compared to the pressing concerns of daily life, survival is an undercurrent, a common strand at an almost subliminal level, an infrastructure of feeling. "You can hear it in people's voices, in the accent, in their body language and facial expressions, and in the kindness and blunt bursts of warmth you'll suddenly get from where you least expect it," writes a contemporary New Yorker, whose family spoke the Greek dialect of southern Albania's Dropoli Valley, of the "sorrow of exile" behind the city's capacity for tolerance, and more concretely its long unshakable pro-immigrant politics:

> *He may not know a word of whatever it was his great-grandparents spoke or seen even a picture of the land they came from, but every New Yorker carries a bit of that sense of loss in him and an innate knowledge of what drove him and his away and brought them here: the destitution of Ireland, the grinding poverty of Sicily, the fear of just being Jewish in Russia, the terror of being Black in Georgia, the violence of Colombia.*[6]

There have also always been connections, recognitions, and echoes across the city's communities of survivors. On Eighth Avenue in Chelsea, survivors of the Armenian genocide performed and recorded alongside Turkish, Greek, Jewish, Balkan, and Middle Eastern musicians who spoke every language of the vanished Ottoman Empire.[7] Starting in the 1920s, dozens of nightclubs like The Egyptian Gardens and Club Istanbul extended for several decades the cosmopolitan world of Istanbul and Izmir that the late Ottoman genocides had forever ruptured. Meanwhile, most Armenian New Yorkers actually lived just across town in the East Twenties and Thirties, which are still home to three Armenian churches of different denominations, as well as the famous international food store Kalustyan's, originally opened as a spice market by an Armenian from Turkey before it evolved into the (now Bangladeshi-owned) anchor of "Curry Hill," the South Asian restaurant row.

As the community of Armenian genocide survivors from Turkey moved uptown to Washington Heights, or to Queens, or the suburbs, they were joined by wave after wave from the wider diaspora: Bulgarian- and Romanian-Armenians escaping communism, Lebanese-Armenians fleeing civil war, and Iranian-Armenians running from the 1979 Revolution (though many of the latter went to Los Angeles). Most spoke endangered forms of Western Armenian, like the Dikranagerdtsi speakers (from Dikranagerd, known in Turkish as Diyarbakır, in today's eastern Turkey) who reunited in Union City, New Jersey.[8] The fall of the Soviet Union brought speakers of Eastern Armenian, now the national language of independent Armenia.

For a variety of reasons, many of the city's Armenian neighborhoods have formed next to Greek ones. By the 1960s, Astoria was becoming the largest and most diverse Greek community outside of Greece and Cyprus, with a tremendous range of cultural, political, religious, and other institutions, including a galaxy of clubs and societies based on islands and towns of origin, from the Amorgos (for an island in the Cyclades) to the Thessalonikian (the largest northern city). There were also thousands of Pontics, speaking a very different and endangered variety of Greek from the eastern shore of the Black Sea all the way from Turkey to Ukraine. Decades after their own genocide at Ottoman hands, many Pontic survivors made their way here via Greece or the Soviet Union to Queens (and Norwalk, Connecticut).[9]

For the multilingual peoples of the North Caucasus, killed or deported first under the Russian Empire and later the Soviet Union, it was a combination of Cold War politics and cross-cultural connections that turned the city and a small corner of northern New Jersey into an unlikely haven.

Leading the way were people like the Circassian leader, businessman, playwright, and historian Kadir Natho, who was born near the Black Sea and escaped the Soviet Union via Europe and Jordan. There at the airport to welcome him when he migrated to New York in 1956 was a representative of the Tolstoy Foundation, founded by the famous novelist's youngest daughter to aid Soviet refugees. A few years later, Natho met his wife, a half-Georgian half-Turkish seamstress on Madison Avenue. Going up against three Ukrainian printers, he opened a print shop in the refugee hub of the East Village, hoping both to make a living and eventually to publish in his mother tongue. Natho also threw himself into building up the Circassian Benevolent Association, which was founded in New York in 1952 but soon moved to Paterson and later Wayne, New Jersey.[10]

At the same time, Natho also started mingling with the leaders of Georgian, Armenian, Azeri, and other organizations at their Manhattan fundraisers, balls, national festivals, and independence celebrations.[11] Many were involved in the National Captive Nations Committee, an anti-communist outfit established by Congress in 1959, which included two dozen "nations" under communist occupation, including Mainland China and Cossackia. Among them, but not explicitly mentioned, were both the Circassians and seven other ethnolinguistic groups of the North Caucasus deported en masse by Stalin in 1943–44 as alleged internal enemies.

Of those seven deported groups, the Crimean Tatars, Meskhetian Turks, Karachays, and Balkars all speak related Turkic languages, but the Mongolic language Kalmyk and the Northeast Caucasian languages Chechen and Ingush are entirely different. As for the Circassians—most of whom had been driven out of Russia and had lived in exile in Jordan, Syria, and Turkey since the nineteenth century—they speak a cluster of languages, including Kabardian, Adyghe, and Shapsug (Natho's mother tongue) from the Northwest Caucasian family. Given what their speakers had been through, all of these languages became endangered in the space of a generation, with massive pressure to shift to Russian, Turkish, or Arabic.

Beyond the varying levels of linguistic, cultural, and religious overlap, what these groups shared most intensely was a recent history of expulsion and suffering, and the Soviet Union as a common enemy. Besides the Circassians who came via the Middle East, all the others arrived in New York after the war, destitute after tortuous journeys across Europe. The factories and neighborhoods of Paterson, New Jersey a substantial and diverse immigrant hub with Russian and Turkish speakers, were an immediate draw. The Tolstoy Foundation, based in nearby Rockland County, also played a major role in resettling many of the North Caucasian groups in the surrounding area.[12]

It was in Howell, New Jersey, not far from a community of Russian Old Believers also aided by Tolstoy, that the Kalmyks planted their diaspora capital. On December 28–31, 1943, over ninety-three thousand Kalmyks, almost the entire population, had been deported to forced labor camps in Siberia. Thousands died, and both a language and a way of life were fundamentally ruptured. Of the small number of Kalmyks who had avoided deportation in Europe, some eight hundred families eventually made it to the US in the early 1950s. In Howell, twenty of those families bought a piece of land they called Olna Gazur, *The People's Gathering Place*, where they managed to build five houses and a khurul, a *Kalmyk Buddhist temple*. Two more were subsequently built, so that all four of the traditional Kalmyk subgroups of the lower Volga River are now represented within a mile of each other in this otherwise unremarkable corner of Monmouth County, New Jersey.[13]

A second group of Kalmyks, a few thousand strong, has come to Brooklyn since the fall of the Soviet Union. Many at first were artists, dancers, or musicians playing instruments like the lute-like dombra and the khuur, or *horsehead fiddle*, but now anyone comes who can because work is so scarce in Kalmykia. The new arrivals are fascinated by how the older ones were able to keep their language and culture alive in Howell, at least for a generation, in ways that the deported families in Siberia were not, though Kalmyks from Xinjiang, of whom only a dozen are now reportedly here, may preserve it most of all.[14] Wider ties are important, too. Because the Kalmyks practice Tibetan Buddhism, the priests in Howell today are usually Tibetans. Because the Kalmyks consider themselves Mongolian, they gather and celebrate holidays with New York–area Mongolians, Buryats, Tuvans, and Hazaras, all of whom claim common descent despite substantial linguistic differences and thousands of miles of separation. Since the days of Genghis and Kublai Khan, there had been centuries of little contact, leading to very different historical experiences, with New York now perhaps the only place where all the Mongolian-identifying groups have the chance to meet in person on a regular basis.

Of the deported Caucasians, it was the Crimean Tatars who established the largest community in the city itself, though some also went to New Jersey. Perhaps it made a difference that a small number of Crimean Jews who spoke the closely related, now lost Turkic language Krymchak had preceded them in Brooklyn, living among Yiddish-speaking Ashkenazim.[15] Never more than a few hundred people, they organized the First Brotherhood of Crimean Jews of America in 1920, with a house on Saratoga Avenue in East New York serving as their synagogue. Of the Krymchak speakers who remained in Crimea, three-quarters were killed by the Nazis, and even some who survived were subject to the Sürgün, the deportations under Stalin which decimated their Muslim Crimean Tatar neighbors.

Survivors among the latter regrouped in Brooklyn in the 1950s and '60s with others who had been sheltering in Turkey. A few had maintained the Crimean Tatar language, but many had started shifting to Istanbul Turkish. Today, members of Brooklyn's Crimean Tatar Ensemble, themselves born in exile in Uzbekistan, keep up the music. A buzzing mosque/community center stands on New Utrecht Avenue in Borough Park, almost completely surrounded by Yiddish-speaking Hasidic Jews, many of them the descendants of Holocaust survivors.

At the corner of Broome and Allen on the Lower East Side stands the only Greek Jewish (Romaniote) synagogue in the Western Hemisphere. It may be the only place where the distinctive Judeo-Greek language is still vanishingly remembered—at least a few words we recorded there from an old member who died a few years later.[16] Formed from the merger of two existing congregations in 1927, the synagogue was named Kehila Kedosha Janina, after the town of Ioannina in western Greece, which then had the largest Romaniote community in the world.[17] Although a majority of the approximately seven-thousand-strong population had moved to New York in the previous several decades, almost everyone who still remained in the town was sent to Auschwitz-Birkenau on March 25, 1944—around 1,860 people in total. There may still be as many as several thousand Romaniote Jews and their descendants in the tristate area, with others in Greece and Israel, but Judeo-Greek is now only a memory.

A few members of Kehila Kedosha Janina do still speak Ladino, the language of the Sephardic Jews who were expelled from Spain in 1492 and settled in the Ottoman Empire, especially what's now Greece and Turkey.[18] Linguists call it Judeo-Spanish (just one of seventy-plus recorded names for the language) because of its well-preserved Old

Spanish core: nuestra casa verde (*our green house* in Spanish) would be muestra caza vedre in Ladino, to take a quick example. In Ottoman lands, this Old Spanish and Hebrew base was topped by layers of Greek, Turkish, and later French; for the smaller number who went to Morocco, the same language (which they came to call language Haketia) was topped off with Moroccan Arabic and later French.[19]

By the early twentieth century, thousands of Ladino speakers from Ottoman cities like Salonika (Thessaloniki), Istanbul, and Izmir were arriving in New York City. Along with the Jews from Ioannina, many settled first on the Lower East Side, though some faced discrimination from the surrounding Yiddish speakers, who found it hard to believe there were Jews who didn't speak Yiddish. Later Ladino-speaking clusters in Harlem, Brooklyn, the Bronx, and Queens usually adjoined, but remained distinct from, Jewish communities where Yiddish, forms of Judeo-Arabic, or other languages were spoken. Besides synagogues, social clubs, and hometown associations, Ladino speakers in New York had their own press and their own literature, written at the time in the Hebrew alphabet, and even their own labor movement.[20]

In New York, for the first time in centuries, many Ladino speakers came into close and frequent contact with Spanish. In Bernardo Vega's memoir, he remembers East Harlem in 1916 as a largely Sephardic "Tower of Babel" where Jewish immigrants who often spoke five or six Mediterranean languages were an important point of contact for newly arriving Puerto Ricans like himself. At the open-air La Marqueta even a few decades later, according to Piri Thomas, "most of the vendors were Jewish, but they spoke Spanish like Puerto Ricans."[21] Their multilingualism meant that in New York many Sephardim "could play the role of Spaniard, Latino, Greek, Turk, Italian, or French person to their benefit in various scenarios."[22]

In Greece itself, nearly the entire Ladino-speaking population was murdered during the Holocaust, and once-substantial Jewish communities like Castoria, Salonika, and Monastir were destroyed. Soon after, almost all the remaining Ladino speakers in the Balkans, Morocco, and elsewhere left for Israel, where the language quickly gave way to Hebrew, with only a tiny group remaining in Turkey.

But in New York as late as the late 1950s, there were not only Ladino-speaking neighborhoods but more or less distinct communities of Castoralis, Saloniklis, Monastirlis, and others along the Grand Concourse close to Yankee Stadium,[23] in Bensonhurst near Ocean Parkway, and in the New Lots section of Brooklyn.[24] Today the kids raised in those places are nonas and papus in Hallandale Beach or Cedarhurst, who may teach their grandkids at least a few words of what their families used to speak. In 2018, at a celebration of Ladino in the basement social room of a synagogue in Forest Hills, I found a growing, globally networked revival, including everyone from high school kids to anusim, the *ones forced* (*to convert*) (in Hebrew) who are rediscovering buried Sephardic roots and trying to learn the language.

While Ladino makes a comeback in a synagogue basement in Queens, the language of the Macedonian Roma is hanging on at a mosque in the Bronx, crowned by a green dome and a crescent-topped spire. Here, nestled among much larger Italian, Albanian, and Mexican communities, is a community of several hundred families whose Romani (at least those not shifting to Macedonian or English) is very different from what other Roma communities in the city speak.[25] Moreover, most other Roma in the city are Christians, increasingly drawn to charismatic churches in Brooklyn, Queens, Staten Island, New Jersey, and beyond.

Little is known about the impact of the Roma Holocaust—the Porrajmos, as it is sometimes called, which means *Devouring* in the Romani language Kalderash Vlax[26]—on New York's diverse, largely invisible Roma communities. What is certain is that the Roma have been a presence in New York since at least the mid-late nineteenth century, when formerly enslaved and chronically persecuted Kalderash and Machvaya began to arrive. They were followed by Ludar, Lovari, Romanichal and probably other Roma groups, each escaping a different part of Europe and speaking a somewhat different dialect.

Some would camp on empty land when they could: tents went up in Williamsburg in 1867 for a season, and a whole village made its home in Maspeth from 1925 to 1939 before the authorities dismantled it. But the largest number settled near other immigrant communities from Southern and Eastern Europe in what's now called the East Village, though they made the West Village famous for its fortune-telling. For some, the city was just a winter base, and summers were for circus work crisscrossing the country. New Roma communities have continually formed in different parts of the city—after the Holocaust, after the Soviet invasion of Hungary, after the fall of the Iron Curtain unleashed new anti-Roma persecutions—but remained largely unknown to outsiders.

Given their history in Europe, many Roma see this as being for the best.

Decades after slavery ended in New York, Manhattan was the epicenter of what can be considered the worst single episode of racial violence in the country's history: the so-called Draft Riots of 1863, prompted by the inequities of Civil War conscription.[27] Across four days of looting and lynching, white New Yorkers, many of them recent Irish immigrants, killed hundreds of Black New Yorkers, prompting five thousand more to flee the island, some for the free settlement of Weeksville in Brooklyn.

Half a century later, it was the ongoing epidemic of anti-Black violence and the Jim Crow system in the South that were driving people *to* New York, just as these other survivor communities from around the world were also arriving in the city. With them they brought the African American English forged in southern slavery and continually developed ever since—numerically and geographically the most remarkable story of linguistic survival in the US.

From twenty-five thousand in 1890, Manhattan's Black population had grown to three hundred twenty-five thousand by 1930, even as the Great Migration was continuing to bring large numbers of African Americans from southeastern states in particular: Georgia, the Carolinas, Virginia, and Florida. Inexpensive shipping and rail lines were crucial conduits. As with immigration from across the seas, "particular southern counties became feeder lines to specific destinations in the North, based on where the earliest migrants went and established themselves."[28]

Within the city, similar though largely unrecorded patterns played out at the neighborhood, block, or even building level, and even today many communities can trace their roots to particular southern counties where some still have relatives, own land, and periodically return, in another echo of transnational immigration patterns. Thus did a significant community of Gullah (also called Geechee) speakers come to Harlem and later Bed-Stuy, once central Brooklyn become the focus of Black settlement after the Second World War. A unique English-based creole with African elements, the Gullah language evolved on the southeast Atlantic coast, especially the Sea Islands of Georgia and South Carolina, until speakers faced large-scale displacement from the late nineteenth century on. A significant minority came north to New York.

Little has been published about Gullah New York, but as of the 1970s anywhere from one thousand to ten thousand speakers may have lived in the city. As with other creoles and with Black speech in general, white society imposed a significant stigma, subsequently internalized by the community, that Gullah was not a proper language. At least one linguist attempted to document the process of "decreolization" by which speakers were shifting en masse toward the more "standard" or dominant forms of English around them. In the process, Gullah speakers in New York and Charleston seemed to be "independently creating

Black-English-like speech forms—thus recapitulating what was probably the earlier course of Black English elsewhere in North America." In other words, by listening to Gullah speakers shift their language in late twentieth-century New York one could understand the evolution, at least a century earlier, of African American (i.e., Black) English more generally.[29]

The continual erosion and loss of creole languages—forged in the context of plantation slavery, and with characteristic linguistic structures as a result—has also been a constant condition of Afro-Caribbean New York. Though ties between New York and the Caribbean go back to the seventeenth century, it was the twentieth century that made the city an unparalleled magnet for people from every single island, speaking every Caribbean creole. Most initially settled in Harlem, where some of their associations remain headquartered to this day: the Nassau Bahamas Association, the Montserrat Progressive Society, the Antigua and Barbuda Progressive Society. There were likewise long-standing mutual-aid associations for those from Bermuda, Barbados, Grenada, Trinidad, and other islands mostly then under British rule.

In this early period, many Caribbean New Yorkers were single young men, and no account of the Harlem Renaissance is complete without figures like Marcus Garvey, who arrived from Jamaica (via London) three years after Claude McKay, whose *Songs of Jamaica* was the first full-length book of poetry in Jamaican Patwa.[30] Hubert Harrison, born in St. Croix in what later became the US Virgin Islands, was a self-avowed "radical internationalist" who married socialist politics with Black liberation. Cyril Briggs, born in Nevis, became one of Harlem's leading journalists and in 1919 founded the African Blood Brotherhood, a short-lived organization of mostly Afro-Caribbean New Yorkers which prefigured later Black nationalist and pan-Africanist movements.

Too little is known of the linguistic dynamics in all this, but the phenomenon of "Harlemese" gives some indication. Stars of the

Harlem Renaissance from the writer Zora Neale Hurston ("Story in Harlem Slang") to the singer/bandleader Cab Calloway (*Hepsters Dictionary: The Language of Jive*) moonlighted as linguists. Whether they deplored or exalted it, everyone seemed to agree that Harlem had a "language all its own," as the writer Wallace Thurman put it, which differed even from forms of African American English elsewhere in the country. Thurman, one of its chroniclers, saw it as a product of Harlem's extraordinary Black diversity: "innumerable colloquial expressions heretofore peculiar to Martinique, the Virgin Islands, Cuba, Trinidad, Jamaica, our own Southland, Liberia, Abyssinia, South Africa, and Senegal are being assimilated into Harlemese, and so corrupted in the process that their origins are lost and only confirmed Harlemites now understand them."[31]

Many expressions entered Harlemese, which was also known as jive or jive talk and often associated with jazz musicians, and diffused widely from there into other forms of English, apparently including the word *hot* as a sexual reference.[32] A contemporary linguist, highlighting usages connected to sexuality, also finds traces from "the language of sex workers (around the world, browned, jelly roll, papa, woofing), language of hobos and tramps (go under the house, wolf), Caribbean English (sissy man), homosexual language in broader US circulation (pansy, queer, dinge queen) . . . and diminutives and other usage drawn from British English and European sources (dandy, daddy)."[33]

More broadly than that, Harlemese gave the city much of its "distinctive lexical culture," which was particularly influential at a national and even international level from the mid-nineteenth to the mid-twentieth century. Indeed New York's traditional "English" lexicon teems with distinctive words about "city streets, nightlife, new forms of transportation and communication, the vertical city of tall buildings, the worlds of poverty, common vices, the array of social types in city streets, and the names of social divisions of class, neighborhood, and of town and country," including many derived from both Harlemese and immigrant languages.[34]

For many, both Harlemese and New Yorkese were just slangy collections of funny, informal, but ultimately improper words and phrases. Then as now, it is hard for white Americans to shake the prejudice that Black forms of English in particular are somehow "broken." But many Black writers of the time were experimenting with and taking "dialect" seriously. James Weldon Johnson, author of *Black Manhattan*, was one of many Black intellectuals who wanted to build up Black English to be more than "the mere mutilation of English spelling and pronunciation," forging "a form that is freer and larger than dialect, but which will still hold the racial flavor."[35]

Though named for a neighborhood, Harlemese was more than a linguistic expression of the Harlem Renaissance. It reflected the birth of a unique Black metropolis, where diverse African American, Afro-Caribbean, Afro-Latin, and ultimately African communities were starting to come into contact after centuries of decimation and enslavement. Their linguistic convergences have also had musical analogues. Continual encounters bringing jazz, mambo, and Afro-Cuban and Puerto Rican musical traditions into dialogue exploded into salsa in the 1970s. Stars, clubs, record labels, and media outlets have made the city a nonstop center for the import, export, and globalization of Afro-Caribbean musical styles, ultimately including hip-hop, born at the intersection of African American music and Jamaican sound system culture in the multicultural Bronx. And this ingathering of Afro-Caribbean musical worlds also has a religious parallel in the ways that Cuban Santería, Puerto Rican Espiritismo, Haitian Vodou, Brazilian Candomblé,[36] and Yoruba religious practices from West Africa itself are combining, changing, and spreading in the city's private temples, circles of devotees, and botanica stores. As in the days of Jan Rodrigues, the city is at the crossroads of Africa, Europe, and the Americas.

# Indigenous Metropolis

Lenape survivors were bought out, forced out, and driven into hiding even at the margins, but even then there were probably always Native Americans, however underground and isolated, coming to and living in the city. By the mid-twentieth century, a new Native New York was coming into being. Today, nowhere else are so many Indigenous languages of the Americas known and used to at least some degree, though all are severely threatened—even more so than immigrant languages arriving from Europe, Asia, and Africa. Of New York's numberless cities, the Native American city is among the hardest for outsiders to see, let alone hear. Its history remains largely unwritten.[1]

Census data, as problematic as it is for language, at least gives a sense of the demographic scale of the Indigenous metropolis.[2] As of 2020, over one hundred eighty thousand New Yorkers identify at least partly as "American Indian or Alaska Native," which is by far the highest total for any city in the country and more than on any reservation.[3] It's also more than double the number from twenty years earlier, and still likely undercounts thousands of recently arrived Indigenous peoples from Mexico, Guatemala, Ecuador, and elsewhere who for numerous reasons are overlooked by the census.

Growing Native pride, the ability to identify on the census as multiracial, and the fact that some Latinos see themselves as Native American are driving this broader surge nationwide. More than half of those identifying as American Indian in New York also list another race, including a mix of Black, white, and other. More than two-thirds say they are also Hispanic/Latino, which is treated as a separate ethnic category. This last factor explains why at least on paper the Native city now substantially overlaps with pan-Latino immigrant neighborhoods, especially those in Queens, where Jackson Heights, Elmhurst-Corona, and Jamaica each registered over seven-thousand-plus Native people.[4]

Native American New York also includes thousands of people who identify with particular North American tribal groupings like Iroquois and Cherokee, whether or not they are enrolled members. Even larger numbers are grouped as “Mexican American Indian” or “South American Indian,” and still more list Dominican or Puerto Rican ancestry. In fact, there are so many Dominican and Puerto Rican New Yorkers that even under 1 percent identifying as American Indian (seemingly a higher percentage than in the Caribbean) has a big impact on the numbers. Differing colonial dynamics mean that substantial percentages of Central and South Americans have at least some Indigenous roots, and New Yorkers of Central and South American ancestry may well use the “American Indian” category more and push the city’s numbers much higher over time.

What about languages? Half of New Yorkers identifying as American Indian speak English and over a third speak Spanish, according to the census, with Native languages, statistically speaking, nowhere to be found. Yet the city is home to at least a few speakers each of many Native North American languages, not to mention the increasing drive to learn and share words, phrases, prayers, and songs. There are now also dozens of Central and South American Indigenous languages, some of them with hundreds if not thousands of active speakers here.

Ernest Naquayouma, from Second Mesa on the Hopi reservation in Arizona, came to New York to escape poverty in the 1930s. By then, others from all over the country, with a wide range of tribal backgrounds, had started converging on the city. Many worked as artists, artisans, and showbiz performers, tapping into the often lurid fascination of white audiences with all things Indian, however offensive and ahistorical the circumstances. ("Indian" almost always meant nineteenth-century Plains Indian as reflected in the mythology of the Wild West, with tipis, traditions, and faces to match.) In extreme cases, explorers and impresarios also brought Indigenous people to the city to be studied or exhibited, as in the tragic case of Minik, an Inuktun speaker from Greenland.[5] Others labored in the port, in factories, or in the homes of the well-off. A small number, like the Cherokee journalist John Milton Oskison from Oklahoma, were formally educated, path-breaking professionals.[6]

Naquayouma was a skilled silversmith, Kachina doll maker, performer, and language bearer. As a native speaker of Hopi, Naquayouma became a key, accessible source for the linguist Benjamin Whorf, then at Yale working on his famous and famously questionable account of how Hopi has "no words, grammatical forms, constructions or expressions that refer directly to what we call 'time.'"[7] Whorf's work on time in Hopi fueled the so-called Sapir-Whorf hypothesis, which controversially posits a fundamental connection between linguistic structure and the perceptions and experiences of native speakers. Whorf and Naquayouma kept up a friendly correspondence for several years, but it's an open question whether the linguist relied too much on data from this single speaker living in Manhattan, far from most of his community.

Yet by no means was Naquayouma entirely on his own. In what was then a working-class area on West Sixty-Seventh Street, later demolished for the development of Lincoln Center, he lived with Morris Mofsie, a fellow Hopi artist from Second Mesa. Mofsie had been touring the country with a dance company from the reservation when he decided to stay and marry Vina Lowry, a Ho-Chunk woman from Nebraska working at the retailer Montgomery Ward. Living nearby was Vina's aunt Red Wing, known as Lillian St. Cyr, one of the first great Native American film stars, who lived in the city until she passed away in the 1970s.[8]

The Mofsies' son Louis, born in Brooklyn in 1936 as part of "the first generation off the reservation," relished moving to and growing up on West Sixty-Seventh Street among German, Italian, Irish, African American, and other Native neighbors. "It gave you even more of an impetus to keep your culture alive, just like these other people," says Mofsie in an interview recorded by the American Indian Community House (AICH).[9] The one thing everyone had in common, he adds, was that they were poor. At times Ho-Chunk, a language now with just a small number of elderly speakers in the Midwest but an active revitalization program, was the language of the Mofsie home, as when an uncle came to stay for a year. Likewise, it was from his father at home in New York, not in Arizona, that Mofsie began learning the Hopi songs and dances.

"Many, many Native people passed through, a lot of them in the [military] service," remembers Mofsie of the forties, "and before they would go overseas they would always stop in New York City." It was the word-of-mouth "moccasin pipeline," he adds, that led many of them to his parents' house, where they were always invited to eat, dance, sing, and stay.

Hopi and Ho-Chunk were by no means the only Native North American languages then spoken in the city, even if only in private homes, judging from all the tribal diversity and the fact that many raised on reservations still would have had their languages at the time. Unfortunately, the extent to which Native languages were actually used is unknown, but from the 1920s onward there were more concerted efforts to create public spaces in the city for Native people to gather and share their cultures, at least somewhat on their own terms.

From 1915 until the 1930s, the Society of American Indians, a key national organization pushing for an official American Indian Day among other things, held annual powwows in Manhattan's last old-growth forest at Inwood Hill Park—prefiguring Drums Along the Hudson, an annual powwow held there since 2002.[10] The same park in that era was home to a traditional-style house built by Emilio Diaz, a Chibcha artist from Colombia, and a cottage where the charismatic Cherokee Princess Naomi was in residence.[11] "All of the Indians in the city, about 600 of them, members of fifty tribes, come to see me," Princess Naomi told a reporter, adding that she served as vice president of the United Indians of America, an organization in Brooklyn.[12]

Another organization, the American Indian Club, was founded in 1926 with a building at 72 Grove Street in Greenwich Village "to unite the many Indians in the city and to welcome Indian visitors," according to the Blackfoot activist Dr. Skiuhushu, also known as Red Fox James.[13] A leading role was played by Mary Newell, also known as Princess Chinquilla, a Cheyenne woman whose vaudeville group toured the US and Europe before she eventually settled down in the city. Club members included white-collar professionals and higher education graduates as well as World War I veterans, film actors, plumbers, and mechanics. Monthly public lectures set out to counter stereotypes and rebut misinformation.

In 1929, over two hundred Native Americans (including Red Wing) rallied in Brooklyn under the banner of the Indian Unity Alliance with an event in Prospect Park, likewise designed to educate the public and advocate for an official day. Among those present, according to the *Brooklyn Eagle*, were Hurons, Abenaki, Mohawk, Seneca, Onondaga, Tuscarora, Chickahominy, Yuma, Aztec, and Kuna.[14]

Like Louis Mofsie, Gloria Miguel was a first-generation Native New Yorker born in the 1930s to parents from very different tribal backgrounds. Her father Antonio was a Kuna sailor from Kuna Yala, the San Blas archipelago off Panama, who came ashore one day at Brooklyn's Erie Basin. He and a fellow Kuna sailor had heard about a house on Degraw Street where a Native family lived—Rappahannocks from

Virginia, it turned out—and where they hoped to find hospitality while in port.

Antonio fell in love with one of the daughters and ended up staying for good. Gloria's grandmother was a midwife in the Rappahannock tradition, and all three girls were born on the floor of that house. Each time the placenta was buried in the backyard, according to Kuna tradition. Antonio became a longshoreman and then got into showbiz, connecting with the Wild West shows, rodeos, circuses, and exhibitions that were always coming to town and befriending the Native people from across the country who worked in them. The neighborhood was Italian, says Gloria, and outside the house the three sisters were on their own: exoticized, objectified, mocked with the hand-over-mouth war cry. "What saved us," she says, "is our tradition."

It mattered, too, that a Native American neighborhood was forming for the first time in the city's history right nearby. This was Little Caughnawaga, a full-fledged Mohawk cluster across several Brooklyn blocks—State, Nevins, Pacific, and others—in what is now the zone of multimillion-dollar brownstones known as Boerum Hill. Beginning in the 1920s, the neighborhood was home to hundreds of Mohawk families from the Kahnawake and Akwesasne reservations on the border between New York State and Canada.[15]

Men drank Montreal ale at bars like the Wigwam and the Spar, and local Italian grocers learned to stock the particular brands of flour and cornmeal that women needed to make corn soup and boiled bread. Families prayed in Mohawk at the Cuyler Church, where the socialist pastor David Cory, a non-Native born in Manhattan, learned the language well enough to preach in it and prepare a hymnal. Mohawk was by all accounts widely used in daily life.

Little Caughnawaga was where it was because of a union hiring hall. Many of the men were ironworkers, famed for fearless work up on high steel that built much of the New York skyline, including the Empire State Building, Rockefeller Center, the United Nations, and the Verrazano Bridge. By the 1960s, however, the ironworkers were retiring: work was drying up, and you needed more formal education to get it. Mohawk kids were staying home, where there were new opportunities. Of those who kept up the ironwork, many became occasional, seasonal, or project-based commuters, as Little Caughnawaga started changing and the new highway north made the four-hundred-mile trip home faster.[16]

In the meantime, however, Mohawk Brooklyn had become a focal point for members of other tribes, including a new generation of New York–born Natives like Gloria Miguel and Louis Mofsie. Having grown up at an exciting crossroads of Native arts and cultures, they wanted to do something different as Native performers and activists. In 1963, they formed Wanbli Cikala (*Little Eagles* in Lakota), devoted to Native dances from all over and still flourishing today as Thunderbird American Indian Dancers. The Mohawks' Cuyler Church was their initial home base, but the dancers came from many different tribal backgrounds, and monthly powwows at the McBurney YMCA on Twenty-Third Street, which drew Natives and non-Natives, became a mainstay.[17]

Like the Thunderbird Dancers, the AICH, conceived by Mifaunwy Shunatona Hines, an Otoe-Pawnee-Wyandot woman living in Queens, and founded in 1969, signaled a new direction. The American Indian movement and the idea of Red power were taking off across the country. Several early AICH leaders were Mohawk, but others were New York born from various tribal backgrounds, and still others were new arrivals from all over the country, many of them artists.[18] Today, close to 80 percent of Native Americans live off of reservations, primarily in urban areas, and the trend toward Indigenous urbanization is a global one.[19]

Though dispersed beyond any single neighborhood, Native American New York has become ever more diverse in recent decades. AICH members are enrolled in seventy-nine different tribes.[20] There are New Yorkers who know Sioux and Cherokee and Apache. For a time, a small cluster of Anishinaabemowin (Ojibwe) speakers were living near each other in Williamsburg. A Lummi woman originally from Washington State works for the Staten Island Ferry and is learning her heritage language with elders over Zoom.

Nor is it only a story of loss when people shift to English, for there is also the new lingua franca which some speakers call "rez talk" and some linguists call Native American English. The common phonological, intonation, and grammatical patterns found in Native American speech across the continent are almost certainly connected to the patterns of dispersion, migration, and mixing which have brought people from so many different tribes together, including in cities like New York.[21]

Nowhere is the diversity of the Indigenous metropolis more in evidence than on the city's flourishing powwow circuit, which besides Drums Along the Hudson includes the Thunderbird Dancers' summer powwow in Queens and a fall powwow in the Bronx, among others. Among those always present are Puerto Rican and Dominican New Yorkers who identify as descendants of the Taíno people murdered, enslaved, or forced to hide their identity by the Spanish colonizers in the sixteenth century.[22]

Once spoken across much of the Caribbean, the Taíno language was suppressed into silence everywhere, though it may have survived longer in isolated areas on certain islands. Documentation is sparse: just a handful of sentences in early Spanish sources, essential loanwords (e.g., potato, maize, cassava, papaya, tobacco, barbecue, hammock, hurricane, canoe), and place-names (e.g., Cuba, Havana, Haiti, Jamaica, etc.). Though most linguists agree that Taíno would have belonged to the widespread Arawakan language family, there are no remaining texts in the language and just one short, fragmentary word list.

This hasn't deterred activists, many of them inspired by and in contact with New York's wider Native American community. According to Rene Çibanakán Marcano, it was being invited to dance at one of the old YMCA powwows that led him to organize the group that became Taíno Nation.[23] After similar encounters, another New York–based Taíno activist started reconstructing the language with material from better-documented Arawakan languages.[24] Numerous Taíno-identifying groups have emerged in recent decades, especially in Puerto Rico and New York, with efforts to revive the language a central goal for several of them. Classes, performances, and other events referencing Taíno words have become regular occurrences in the city, with some activists even teaching themselves to speak and write their different reconstructions in newly devised scripts, though activists may differ significantly in their linguistic approaches.

Even the increasing use of the Taíno word boricua to mean *Puerto Rican*, as opposed to the Spanish term puertorriqueño—like the Dominican use of Quisqueya as a name for their island—is suggestive. The number of people actively involved in Taíno groups or language efforts may not be large, but it seems only to have grown since the naming in 1979 of East Harlem's Taíno Towers, an innovative federally funded housing project, underscored the resonance of the label.

Nor can it be entirely by chance that the Taíno movement coincided with the arrival of one of the most widely spoken living Arawakan languages to the same parts of Harlem and the Bronx, during the same period.[25] For a number of reasons, the Garifuna language today probably looks very different from pre-1492 Taíno, which itself may have varied substantially by island. But Garifuna's survival, transformation, and rerooting in New York, one of its major centers, is nonetheless a remarkable story. Most Garifuna trace their descent from enslaved West Africans who escaped during a shipwreck onto the island of St. Vincent. There they intermarried with Indigenous Caribbean people and adopted cassava cultivation, distinctive singing styles, and the local

Arawakan language, supplemented over time with layers of French, Spanish, and English loanwords.

After an insurrection against the British in 1795 led by their Chief Joseph Chatoyer, the Garifuna were exiled to the Caribbean coast of Honduras and Belize, with smaller numbers going to Nicaragua and Guatemala. (In New York, just twenty-eight years later, Chatoyer's story became the subject of the first known play by a Black playwright in the United States, William Henry Brown's *Drama of King Shotaway*.[26])

In the twentieth century, tens of thousands of Garifuna, if not more, made it to New York, forming what is likely the single largest community in the world and yet another level of diaspora after Africa, St. Vincent, and Central America. What started with sailors and merchant marines became a broad-based migration of entire communities after 1965. In recent years, Garifuna people have again been coming, seeking asylum from gang violence and the Honduran government's violent seizure of their coastal land for tourism development.

The Garifuna may be a comparatively small minority in Honduras and Belize, but they form a significant group within both Honduran and Belizean New York, with distinct communities in different boroughs, even if the complex intersectionality of Garifuna identity renders the community invisible to outsiders. Those speaking English are often taken for African American or Afro-Caribbean. Those speaking Spanish may be seen as darker-skinned Dominicans. Those speaking Garifuna may be lumped in with Africans.

The range of Garifuna organizations in New York reflects both this complexity and the range of possible alliances and connections with larger surrounding groups. There have been not only (sometimes multiple) hometown associations representing every major Garifuna town, but also "pan-Garifuna organizations that unite all Honduran Garifuna; others that unite Garifuna of Honduras, Belize, and Guatemala; pan-Honduran organizations that unite Garifunas and ladinos (similar to mestizos); Hispanic immigrant organizations; and Afro-Hispanic organizations."[27]

Several specifically Garifuna organizations formed after the 1990 arson fire at the Happy Land Social Club on Southern Boulevard in the Bronx, one of the worst disasters in New York City history, in which most of the eighty-seven who died were young Garifuna. Today, despite large-scale shift to Spanish or English, there are Garifuna-language church services, picnics, musical performances, sporting events, and even an annual Miss Garifuna competition where the contestants have to give a speech in Garifuna. ELA's longtime collaborator Milton Guity teaches Garifuna language classes through Casa Yurumein, a community center in the Bronx. Garifuna New Yorker James Lovell, a singer-storyteller who has worked with ELA for over a decade, has even tried to revive the language on Yurumein itself, as the lost homeland of St. Vincent is known in Garifuna.[28]

Only a small number of Indigenous Caribbean languages survived the colonial onslaught, but Latin America has retained substantial zones of Indigenous linguistic diversity, with as many as one thousand living languages from over one hundred deeply different families.[29] Large populations speak a few of them and children still speak many of them, but few can be considered entirely safe from or unaffected by the linguistic imperialism of Spanish and Portuguese. They are concentrated in southern Mexico, Guatemala, the Andes, and the Amazon. In the last four decades, all but the latter have become major sending regions to New York.

While some Puerto Rican New Yorkers were reclaiming a Taíno identity, the city's most famous Puerto Rican politician, then chancellor of the CUNY system, seemed to feel little kinship with the new Indigenous immigrants arriving in the city. "They're Incas and Mayas," said Herman Badillo in 1999. "Little people with straight hair . . . They don't speak Spanish. They speak in Indigenous languages."

Badillo's words were quickly condemned, and he soon faded into political irrelevance, but his dismissive words didn't come from nowhere. Many Puerto Ricans, Dominicans, and Cubans have rallied around a pan-Hispanic, Spanish-speaking identity in New York, and mass migrations, especially from Mexico, Guatemala, Ecuador, and Peru since the 1990s, did bring a dramatic influx of Indigenous peoples, especially into the city's Latino neighborhoods. Some of the new arrivals spoke very different kinds of Spanish as a second language, if at all.

The largest number were Mexican, and the fact that they came disproportionately from the southern states of Puebla and Guerrero has meant that Indigenous languages like Mixtec, Nahuatl, and a dozen others now have a substantial if little-known presence in the city, as we will see later. The Mexican government officially recognizes sixty-eight Indigenous "linguistic groupings," within which linguists have counted as many as 282 Indigenous languages.[30] The 2020 Mexican census found that between seven and eight million Mexicans, representing 6.2 percent of the population, speak an Indigenous language, though that percentage is continually falling. On the other hand, a much larger (and growing) number of Mexicans say they speak only Spanish but nonetheless identify as Indigenous, a situation which is also becoming common in New York.

In Guatemala, on the other hand, Indigenous people constitute fully 40 percent or more of the population, though that has not stopped discrimination and extreme marginalization. During the Guatemalan civil war from 1960 to 1996, US-backed military dictators decimated Mayan communities, leading many to hide their identities. Violence and poverty in the country's highlands are still causing people to flee, including unaccompanied minors, to the point where Mam, K'iche', Q'anjob'al, Q'eqchi', and Kaqchikel are now among the languages most commonly encountered at the US-Mexico border.[31] Of the two hundred fifty thousand Guatemalan migrants apprehended there in 2019 alone, at least half were Mayan.[32]

Of the country's twenty-two Mayan languages, the five above are the most widely spoken, and each has a presence in New York today, though the city is also home to many ladino Guatemalans. Speakers of K'iche' seem to be the largest Mayan group in New York, dispersed throughout the city but with a critical mass along the D train's Brooklyn route through Bensonhurst and Bath Beach and marked out by the sky-blue awnings of half a dozen Guatemalan bodegas under the elevated tracks. Speakers of Mam have tight communities from particular towns in East Harlem, the Bronx, Staten Island, Queens, and Morristown, New Jersey. There are isolated individuals, too, like the speaker of Chuj who lives in the Bronx but hears the language only during the occasional phone interpretation jobs he does, translating between Spanish and Chuj.

Though many Indigenous Guatemalans now work in the city as deliveristas or in construction, others have gravitated to smaller suburban or even rural towns upstate, on Long Island, or in New Jersey, where like other Central Americans they have found agricultural, landscaping, or other outdoor work, sometimes as day laborers.[33] Many Kaqchikels are in New Jersey and on Long Island, where a community from the Guatemalan town of San Raymundo has established itself in Riverhead. There are Poqomchi' speakers in Bergen County, Q'eqchi'-speaking asylum seekers in Kingston, and a community in Westchester where some may know Ch'orti'.

These particular footholds often reflect the initial decision of a single, still-remembered "pioneer" who found a cheap room, a job, a contact, or proximity to some earlier community.[34] Some who arrive later may have no idea why they ended up in a particular place, except that someone knew someone back in the day. Clemente, a speaker of Tz'utujil living in Great Barrington, Massachusetts, near the New York border, says that all fifty or sixty Indigenous Guatemalans around there are from the little town of San Pedro Cutzán.[35] The migration started twenty years ago with his cousin, who happened to go to the local community college for a training program, and it now includes a few old guerrilla fighters, he adds with a smile, who have tales to tell when they drink.

In contrast to these scattered settlements, the city itself is unquestionably the focal point for Ecuadorian immigrants coming to the US, with over three hundred thousand in the metropolitan area constituting around two-thirds of the national total. Though many of the earliest arrivals in the 1950s and '60s were well-to-do mestizos from the city of Guayaquil, the mass migration touched off by the economic crisis of the early nineties has consisted overwhelmingly of undocumented rural migrants from the south-central Andean highlands of Azuay and Cañar provinces—and thus has a major Kichwa-speaking component.[36]

Kichwa, as it is spelled in Ecuador, is part of a larger family that linguists call Quechuan to capture the remarkable scale and diversity of related languages spoken by some ten million people from Colombia to Argentina. Altogether it represents by far the most widely spoken of all Indigenous languages of the Americas, having spread orally through the Inca Empire and subsequently diversified. In addition to those from Ecuador, much smaller numbers of Peruvians and Bolivians scattered in Brooklyn, Queens, and especially New Jersey also speak their own distinctive forms of Quechua.[37]

Those coming to New York from Azuay, Cañar, and other Indigenous areas of Ecuador like Otavalo and Salasaca may fall anywhere on a linguistic spectrum between speaking Kichwa natively and shifting completely to Spanish, depending on their town of origin as well as whether they stayed first in cities like Quito or Cuenca. They may not be easily slotted into "the trinity *indígena* (indigenous), mestizo (mixed blood), and *blanco* (white, considered of pure Spanish descent) so commonly employed in Ecuador," but rather identify as Cañari, Kisapincha, Saraguro, etc., groups that had their own languages before the shift to Kichwa during Inca times.[38]

Today, some eight to ten thousand Ecuadorian New Yorkers may speak Kichwa, estimates Charlie Uruchima, who helps run Kichwa Hatari, a Kichwa-language radio station broadcasting from the Bronx. Most live near larger Ecuadorian and Latino communities in Ridgewood or Corona (Queens), Parkchester (the Bronx), or the suburb of Spring Valley—though there are also distinctly Kichwa-speaking clusters like the hundreds of Kisapincha families around Bushwick and now Canarsie.[39]

Uruchima himself was born in New York and has worked to build up his proficiency in the language, but his family comes from the typical sending community of Déleg, a town of several thousand people in Cañar. Its "pioneer migrant" was Hugo Callaguaso, who left his subsistence farming family for New York in 1976 and worked various restaurant and janitorial jobs before getting amnesty in 1990. Migrating later became much harder, admits Hugo, with many forced to take a dangerous maritime route, smuggled in trawlers or cargo ships to Central America via the Pacific and some drowning or freezing to death on the way.[40]

"To be a man and to have a family you have to immigrate," says Hugo. But what may start as a "shortcut" to achieving concrete goals like building a house in Deleg often becomes a permanent move.[41] Many who migrate want not just a family, but something they call iony—an expression (pronounced "I-OH-knee") which derives from the logo I♡NY and connotes not only New York (which is also known as Yoni), but the whole glamorous package of North American lifestyles and attitudes. Indeed, for all the factors that "push" minority, survivor, and Indigenous peoples to New York, a whole range of "pull" factors have also always been operative, resulting in a city that now looks more and more like the world itself.

# Global Microcosm

A century ago, a writer took a trip around the world without leaving New York City. Others had focused their tours on particular "quarters," the more exotic and picturesque the better,[1] but Konrad Bercovici, himself a polyglot Romanian Jewish immigrant,[2] claimed that "New York, like no other city, offers the best study of the nations of the world, samples of each being centered in different sections within easy reach of one another."[3]

Judging both from his biography and the sheer pleasure he took in his "peregrinations," Bercovici was the kind of New Yorker who doesn't just celebrate the city's diversity but lives it. "Hating one another, loving one another, agreeing and disagreeing in a hundred different languages," he writes, brooking no comparisons. "Not another Rome, not another Alexandria, not another Paris, another London, but an aggregate of which there is no counterpart anywhere."[4]

Bercovici's conceit was to see the entire world inscribed within city limits, and New York has long encouraged the age-old fantasy of the microcosm, with a grit manifestly missing from Disney's Epcot, Shenzhen's Window of the World, or even the 1939 and 1964 world's fairs, which by some psychogeographic legerdemain set the stage for what the surrounding neighborhoods in Queens would become. In recent decades, the idea of the urban microcosm has been rediscovered, reimagined, and updated, though of course its exact contours are always changing.[5]

So badly does Bercovici want to discover the world next door that he presents a European microcosm with fast-growing communities from Asia, the Middle East, and the Caribbean but almost without assimilation or "Americans" (except for the "American quarter" of Greenwich Village). He desperately wants to believe that his world-city will stay assembled, even if the exact locations move, and that people from the same community "not only . . . live in the same neighborhood, but they lead the same lives, sing their own songs, and speak their own tongue, which is jealously guarded by the older ones."[6]

A requisite stop was Manhattan's Chinatown, already well established since the mid-nineteenth century as the ne plus ultra of cultural and linguistic difference in the city. Yet it was also a very particular community, with its Taishanese-speaking nucleus originally from and remaining connected to a very small area in southeast China. Many had landed first in California, seeking their fortune in the gold fields, but headed to New York as anti-Asian hysteria grew on the West Coast. At once feared and exoticized by other New Yorkers, Chinatown maintained itself in the face of immigration restrictions, occupational limitations (forcing many into laundry and restaurant work), and tight control by the Tong organizations.

Likewise prominent was Little Syria, which grew up in the late nineteenth century along Washington Street in a then deeply diverse part of Lower Manhattan.[7] Most were Maronite, Melkite, and Orthodox Christians from the Mount Lebanon region, part of the Ottoman Empire, and spoke Levantine Arabic. Many worked as peddlers, shopkeepers, or in the garment industry, but a small number of the city's Arab intellectuals came to play a global role in forging modern Arabic literature (the Mahjar movement and Khalil Gibran, most famously), journalism (the newspaper *Kawkab America*, among others), and music (Maloof Records, to name one company).[8] The poet Mikhail Naimy wrote that "Merka" was the name given to all the countries the early Arab immigrants went to, while "Nayirk" meant the US specifically.[9]

In 1924, the same year Bercovici published *Around the World in New York*, the world-in-the-city he so ecstatically described was dealt a serious blow. As early as 1882, the Chinese Exclusion Act had marked the first-ever legal limit on immigration to the United States, with profound impacts on the West Coast.[10] Then the so-called Gentlemen's Agreement of 1907 cut off Japanese immigration. During the First World War, the anti-immigrant lobby, deeply entwined with the eugenics movement and under the sway of racist pseudoscience, continued to gain strength, especially in the Republican Party.[11] Some of its chief theoreticians and proponents, like Madison Grant, were patrician New Yorkers horrified by the diversifying city around them. Ellis Island first felt the effects of their efforts in 1917, with Congress's creation of the oddly shaped "Asiatic barred zone" that stretched from Afghanistan to Micronesia and mandating of a literacy test requiring any immigrant over sixteen years old to read thirty to forty words in their own language.[12]

Four years later, Senator William Dillingham, whose congressional commission had studied immigration in forty-one volumes' worth of exhaustive detail, devised a new quota system based on national origin. For the first time, the Emergency Quota Act established a strict monthly limit on all immigrants from outside the Western Hemisphere, as dictated by the same racial considerations behind the Asiatic barred zone. Every country received a quota amounting to 3 percent of the population born in that country and living in the US as of the 1910 census. Technocratic though this sounds, it had a clear intent: to freeze the ethnic balance of the country.

In the summer of 1921, the "midnight races" began. On the last night of each month, steamships full of immigrants would line up in the Lower Bay, just outside the Narrows. There might be a fleet of twenty ships with a total of twenty-five thousand passengers. At the stroke of midnight, their captains would make a desperate dash into the harbor to be the first to get their passengers to Ellis Island. A few minutes could make all the difference, because a single ship might fill a whole month's quota for a country like Italy or Greece, while all the others would have to return to Europe.[13]

The Johnson-Reed Immigration Act of 1924 not only ended the races but slammed shut the "golden door." Further reduced and made permanent, the quotas would now be based on the 1890 census (not that of 1910), as conceived by one John Trevor, who had obsessively mapped New York's ethnic neighborhoods in search of subversives. Northern European countries were thus assured generous quotas, while the number of southern and eastern Europeans admitted shrunk dramatically, by 99 percent in the cases of Italy and Greece.[14]

Immediately after the act became law, Congress established the US Border Patrol to start enforcing and deporting. Before, immigrants had simply set sail with high chances of being admitted, but now you couldn't even leave home without a visa. With the exception of northern and western Europeans, immigration collapsed across the board: there were one-eighth as many arrivals in 1924 as a decade earlier.[15]

Leaving aside the millions who were thus never able to immigrate, the impact on New York in particular was incalculable. A heavily first-generation immigrant city soon became a second- and third-generation one.[16] Cut off from the source, languages and cultures withered in an atmosphere that increasingly promoted assimilation to white American norms, allowing at most for pride in certain countries, provided they were on friendly terms with the United States.

Restrictive, highly racialized immigration laws remained in place even as exceptional provisions after the Second World War fueled the city of survivors, admitting certain groups of displaced persons, including "refugees" (fleeing persecution), "escapees" (fleeing communism), and "expellees" (ethnic Germans leaving Eastern Europe).[17]

It was only the Hart-Celler Immigration Act of 1965 that would ultimately restore and expand Bercovici's dream of the city as a microcosm of the world.[18] A liberal movement against the nativism and racism of the 1924 law had first swept into the White House with John F. Kennedy, a descendant of Irish immigrants and the first Catholic president, who published *A Nation of Immigrants* in 1958. The Cold War, the civil rights movement, and economic prosperity all set the stage. After JFK's assassination, it was Bobby and Teddy Kennedy who did most of the legislative legwork, getting the act through a heavily Democratic Congress. LBJ signed it into law on Ellis Island, which had become all the more symbolic for no longer being in use. Most of the new immigrants would soon be flying into an airport in eastern Queens just recently renamed for JFK.

Just as a new era of global mobility was beginning, the 1965 act opened up the city and the country to the world as never before. Over the following half century, what had been true of European New York—not only the presence of every major group but also, disproportionately, of certain linguistic minorities—would become true of Latin American New York, Asian New York, Caribbean New York, and African New York. By ending the national-origins quotas, the immigration act put every country on a more equal footing (including those in the Western Hemisphere, which lost their exemption) while emphasizing family reunification and occupational skills. Subsequent legislation (the Refugee Act of 1980, the Immigration Reform and Control Act of 1986, the Immigration Act of 1990) dialed back or enhanced aspects of the earlier law, each time with traceable effects on many specific communities, but without fundamentally altering the terms of Hart-Celler.

Apart from an initial influx from certain European countries like Greece and Portugal, where there was pent-up demand, the most immediate impact on the city was in terms of Asian immigration.[19]

Over the next half century, Taishanese- and later Cantonese-dominated Chinatown would give way to a dozen different Chinatowns and counting across the five boroughs, transforming New York into by far the most populous Chinese city outside of Asia. First came immigrants from Hong Kong and Taiwan, with many of the latter being middle-class, Mandarin-speaking professionals who settled directly in Flushing. Cantonese speakers in particular began moving to Brooklyn, following the N train from Sunset Park to Bensonhurst and beyond. A large wave of working-class Fujianese speakers, especially from in and around the city of Fuzhou, started arriving in the 1980s and '90s after China loosened its restrictions on emigration. Likewise came the Wenzhounese from Zhejiang Province, who speak their own highly distinctive Chinese language, are known for entrepreneurship (owning restaurants, grocery stores, clothing factories, and more), and have made New York one of their main global centers, along with Paris and Prato (Italy).

Still others from various Chinese backgrounds have come after generations in Southeast Asia, Latin America, and the Caribbean. Suddenly there were Cuban Chinese, Guyanese Chinese, Peruvian Chinese, and Malaysian Chinese restaurants. Only in New York. Yet the largest influx of all has been from mainland China, including students, artists, billionaires, and every conceivable kind of religious and political dissident.[20] Thus is Mandarin increasingly dominant, although every major Chinese language and dialect now seems to be present in the city. But it remains to be seen whether languages like Hakka, Hainanese, or Hunanese can survive here, let alone the many distinctive varieties of specific Chinese cities and counties.

On a much smaller scale, Korean and Japanese were also growing their New York presence exponentially from a tiny pre-1965 base, although in both cases the homeland is unusually linguistically homogenous.[21] Far more impactful in terms of linguistic diversity was the upsurge in Filipino immigration, with clusters developing in every borough and beyond, but especially near the hospitals where many women found work. Woodside in Queens emerged as the center, and Tagalog as the unifying language, but there are also substantial numbers who speak Cebuano, Ilocano, and a dozen smaller Philippine languages. More recently, the same area of Queens is also fast becoming the city's main Southeast Asian nexus, with fast-growing Thai, Burmese, and Indonesian communities that among them speak several dozen languages.[22]

In the meantime, speakers of Central Asian languages have been gathering in southern Brooklyn. Following those initial refugee and survivor communities of the 1950s, many more Turks, Tatars, Uzbeks, Kazakhs, and later Azeris and Uighurs began converging in and around Sheepshead Bay in the 1980s—creating what the writer Zohra Saed, from an Afghan Uzbek family that came to the neighborhood via Pakistan, calls "a Turkic palimpsest."[23]

Because these Turkic languages diverged from each other in relatively recent times, many of these people now discovered that they could largely understand one another. They found work as supers, framers, and Persian rug store dealers, often working with or for Russians, since so many spoke that language from living in the Soviet Union. More recently, people from the farthest eastern reaches of the Turkic world have also been arriving in Brooklyn: speakers of languages like Chuvash, Tuvan, and Yakut from deep in Siberia. As if every last language from the Turkic family had to be represented somewhere in the city, Turkish Cypriots apparently made a small community of their own, not far from a cluster of Greeks in the east Bronx.

For centuries, Turkic and Iranic languages have played off one another in a complex counterpoint that defined the linguistic world of Central Asia, in a pattern that has carried over to New York. Iranic, a subgroup within Indo-European, stretches all the way from eastern Turkey to western China. So prestigious and powerful was Persian itself (which is only the group's largest language) that it was used for various purposes in much of India well into the twentieth century.

Speakers of Iranic languages have come to New York in different, sometimes overlapping waves. Multiple, largely separate communities speak very closely related forms of Persian, including Farsi from

Iran, Dari and Hazara from Afghanistan, and Tajik from Tajikistan and Uzbekistan. Many of the Hazaras were translators embedded with US forces; others came via Quetta, in Pakistan.

While there are many secular and Muslim Iranians in the city, many of them middle-class professionals who fled after the 1979 revolution, Iranian Jews in Brooklyn, Queens, and Long Island constitute the largest organized community. Some speak not only Persian, but the quite different Iranic languages of Shiraz, Isfashan, Kashan, and other Iranian cities, long preserved mainly by Jews and Christians but now almost entirely forgotten even by them.[24] At the same time the "mountain Jews," a distinct Jewish community from Azerbaijan and Daghestan, speak the very different Iranic language Juhuri and now have a hub in central Brooklyn.[25] And tens of thousands of Bukharian Jews from Uzbekistan, speaking a Jewishly inflected Tajik, have made their world center in Rego Park and Forest Hills.[26] A small Kurdish community, speaking Kurmanji, Zaza, Sorani, and perhaps other languages, is also continually growing.

Of course the politics are intricate and delicate in every direction. A Kurdish Nowruz (New Year) celebration in New Jersey held in the gym of an Armenian day school—given the groups' shared trauma at Turkish hands—commemorates martyrs and hails the PKK's freedom struggle. Run variously by supporters of the AKP (Islamist), HKP (Marxist), and MLKP (Hoxhaist) political parties, the cafés and restaurants of Turkish Brooklyn may employ Kurds while largely catering to Russian customers.[27] Central Asian Muslims, as newer arrivals, often work for Bukharian Jewish employers. The Uzbek world in Brooklyn is split between Samarkandliks living near Ditmas Avenue (more likely to speak Tajik) and Tashkentliks settled near Avenues X, Y, and Z (more likely to speak Uzbek). Russian may serve as the common language, to which many are still shifting, but not everyone is always eager to use it.

Downtown Manhattan's Little Syria, finally obliterated by the construction of the Brooklyn Battery Tunnel in the 1940s, had already half moved to Brooklyn, first Atlantic Avenue and later down to Bay Ridge. But after 1965, the city as a whole gradually became home to nearly every kind of Arabic as used by Muslims, Christians, and Jews from Morocco to Iraq. Whether it's Yemeni and Moroccan New Yorkers living near each other in the Bronx, or Sudanese and Mauritanian New Yorkers encountering each other in Brooklyn, these Arabic "dialects" are often so different from one another that many get by via the Modern Standard known as الفُصْحَى al-fuṣḥā, *the purest*. Some mosques belong to particular linguistic groups, while others are now among the city's most multilingual spaces, with prayers in Arabic but the chatting afterwards in a dozen different languages. Egyptian Arabic, widely known through music, movies, and television, can also be a lingua franca—along Steinway Street in Queens, for example, which is a hub for North Africans, including speakers of a half dozen Amazigh (or Berber) languages.

Still overrepresented in the city, religious minorities of the Middle East may speak Arabic in daily life but often worship in a very different language. Thus Egyptian Christians, who have numerous churches in Brooklyn, Queens, Staten Island, Jersey City, and elsewhere, live in Egyptian Arabic but pray in Coptic, the last descendant of the pharaohs' language. In Flatbush and Gravesend, a few neighborhoods over, the world's largest community of "Syrian" (actually Syrian, Lebanese, and Egyptian) Jews, estimated at forty thousand if not more, retains traces of a distinctively Jewish form of Levantine Arabic. Likewise Moroccan Jews, who have several synagogues in the city, speak a Moroccan Judeo-Arabic (in places like Fez or Marrakesh) that was sometimes called il-'arbiyya dyalna, *our Arabic*, in contrast to il-'arbiyya dil-msilmin, *the Arabic of the Muslims*, used by other Moroccans. Yemeni Jews have established communities around the city speaking their own Judeo-Arabic but praying in a distinctive liturgical Hebrew. Most Iraqi New Yorkers are Jewish, with synagogues in Jamaica Estates and Great Neck, and some still remember endangered Baghdadi Judeo-Arabic, which was simply called ħaki mal yihud, the *speech of the Jews*. Today, every Jewish form of Arabic is almost gone.[28]

Before Arabic spread with Islam, it was Aramaic that dominated the Middle East. Three millennia since its heyday under the Neo-Assyrian and then Persian Empires, the language of Jesus is alive in all sorts of surprising ways in various corners of New York. Observant Jews of all backgrounds still study Jewish Babylonian Aramaic to read key texts, including the Talmud. No book club in the world can rival Daf Yomi, the practice of studying all 2,711 pages at the rate of one per day (around seven and a half years) and culminating in a massive Siyum HaShas, *completion of the Six Orders* (*of the Talmud*). The recent thirteenth event was the largest ever, packing over ninety thousand people into New Jersey's MetLife Stadium.

Syriac, another Aramaic descendant, is prayed and chanted in every day at a dozen churches across the city, not only by Levantine Christians but also by South Indian Christians of the Malankara Orthodox Syrian Church, whose language of daily life, Malayalam, could hardly be more different.[29] Mandeans, a tiny religious community of Iraq and Iran with about three hundred people in Queens and Long Island, still worship in and, vanishingly, speak their Mandaic forms of what is ultimately the same language.[30] Still other very different and highly endangered forms of Neo-Aramaic are spoken by a community of around two hundred families originally from 'Ayn Wardo in present-day Turkey's southeastern Tur Abdin region, who are now settled in and around Haworth, New Jersey; by recent Chaldean refugees from the Plain of Mosul and Iraqi Kurdistan, now in Brooklyn; by Assyrians in Yonkers; and by older Iranian Jews from places like Bijar, Sanandaj, and Urmia, now living in Queens or Great Neck.[31] All forms of Aramaic are scattered and endangered, but in New York several of them share a ghostly, unprecedented proximity.

Until 1965, it was all but impossible for South Asians to immigrate to the US legally, but many still found their way to New York, especially Muslim seamen working on British steamships, who jumped ashore. Speakers of Bengali, Sylheti, Urdu, Punjabi, and probably other languages, they found work in hotels, restaurants, and factories, marrying into African American and Puerto Rican communities in Harlem and the Lower East Side, as chronicled in Vivek Bald's *Bengali Harlem*.

By the 1990s, three decades after restrictions finally eased, Bengali and Urdu had become two of the city's most widely spoken languages, and by far the largest from South Asia. Bangladesh, a nation forged through language activism, gained its independence from Pakistan in 1971.[32] Beginning in the 1980s, many Bangladeshis won spots in the diversity visa lottery and found jobs in construction, in food service, and as cab drivers. Though Bengali is the shared community language, many actually speak the related Sylheti, including in the East Village, where Madina Masjid on Eleventh Street and the small restaurant row on Sixth Street have been hubs for half a century.

So substantial and varied has the community become, with growing neighborhoods in every borough and beyond, that most of Bangladesh's linguistic and religious minorities are now represented in the city as well. In Queens, there are Bangladeshi Hindus who speak Bishnupriya Manipuri and Meitei; a few dozen Garo speakers from close to Tibet; and even one hundred people or so from the country's Chittagong Hill Tracts, mostly Buddhists who have arrived since 2010 and speak at least five different endangered languages.[33] In Kensington (Brooklyn), the Chittagong Association Building, the Greater Noakhali Society, and the Sandwip Society are all within a few blocks of each other, each representing a region and a language variety distinct from but closely related to Bengali.

Just a neighborhood over, along Coney Island Avenue, is the city's largest Pakistani zone, with its auto body shops (for all the cab drivers), its steam-table joints, and Makki Masjid, its spiritual center. Pressure from immigration officers after 9/11 had a devastating impact here after the booming nineties, with many deported and others leaving voluntarily, often for Canada.[34] Others have been moving deeper into Brooklyn, creating new communities in Bath Beach and Coney Island. Urdu and Punjabi are widely spoken, but there are also speakers of Pashto, Sindhi, Saraiki, and Pothwari, as well as of the endangered languages of Pakistan's mountainous north (Balti, Burushaski, Kalasha, Khowar, Shina, Wakhi), who organize under the regional rubric of Gilgit-Baltistan. Central Brooklyn was also an initial focus for Nepalis, Tibetans, and other Himalayans, as we will see, though more have moved over time to Jackson Heights, the city's other major center of South Asian life.

Many places in New York that outsiders perceive as "Indian" are in fact largely Bangladeshi, Pakistani, and Nepali. Yet the Indian community in greater New York is still by far the largest in the Western Hemisphere. Hindi speakers, many of them middle-class professionals, have often moved directly to New Jersey and Long Island suburbs. There are separate, substantial clusters of Punjabi speakers, mostly Sikhs from the Doaba region (in Ozone Park/Richmond Hill); Malayalam speakers, mostly Christians from Kerala (in Bellerose/Floral Park); and Tamil speakers from a tremendous variety of religious, caste, and cultural backgrounds.

Gujarati is still at the heart of Jersey City, while Edison and the surrounding suburbs have a little bit of everything. The number of Telugu speakers is rising fast, especially in New Jersey. These are all relatively widely spoken languages with official status, at least in certain Indian states, but there are also a few speakers each of nine different Naga languages from Nagaland (in India's northeast)—to give just one indication of how deep the linguistic diversity of Indian New York may go.[35] Meanwhile, Staten Island is home to several thousand Sri Lankans, said to be the largest community outside the island nation, including Sinhalese, Tamils, and apparently still even a speaker or two of endangered Sri Lankan Malay.

Indic languages are also partially retained in the city's massive Indo-Caribbean communities, which hail largely from Guyana and Trinidad but have their roots in nineteenth-century indentured labor migration from India. Bhojpuri and Awadhi were the main north Indian languages that the indentured would originally have spoken, evolving over time into the composite Caribbean Hindustani.[36] This in turn gave way to English-based creoles spoken by both the African- and Indian-origin communities, with the shift to English itself, especially for those born and educated in the US, usually not far behind.

The major move to New York happened in the 1980s, ultimately bringing an estimated one hundred forty thousand Guyanese, a group one-fifth the size of Guyana's entire population, and over half as many Trinidadians. Over time, the Indo-Guyanese and Indo-Trinidadians largely made their world in the Richmond Hill and Ozone Park areas of Queens, while most Afro-Guyanese and Afro-Trinidadians went to live with other Afro-Caribbean groups in Brooklyn. There is proximity and connection, but also separation.

Something similar was at work in the genesis of Caribbean Brooklyn itself, beginning in the 1960s and '70s. As new African American communities emerged beyond Harlem in every borough, Afro-Caribbean communities often moved nearby or in parallel, but there was no straightforward merger between the two. Strained relations and "distancing strategies" have been cited, but it's equally clear that Afro-Caribbean New Yorkers were motivated to create and maintain their own culturally and linguistically distinctive communities.[37]

With few exceptions, however, communities from among all of the Caribbean's seventeen English-speaking island nations and territories have overlapped considerably in New York, especially in central Brooklyn along a stretch of neighborhoods from Crown Heights to Canarsie. As a crossroads for Caribbean peoples, the city has no rival even in the Caribbean itself. Immigrants from every single island have brought to the city both their distinctive English-based creoles and their ability to situate themselves linguistically along a "creole continuum" all the way up to dominant British or American varieties.

They also may be converging, especially in New York, on a kind of "superlanguage": a common Caribbean English Creole.[38] Some features of the different creoles were shared to begin with, whether due to a shared historical origin or to parallel developments: intonation patterns (especially related to syllable timing), grammatical particles, and certain words and expressions. But convergence is also what happens when so many people speaking so many related varieties are in close proximity: Bajans, Grenadians, Vincentians, etc., living on the same blocks and interacting in so many different spheres. Such is the scale and pull of Afro-Caribbean New York that it also effectively includes Belizean Garifunas and Afro-Panamanians, both from Central America's Caribbean coast.

Jamaicans, as the single largest Anglophone group in both the Caribbean and New York, have remained the most linguistically distinct. For the most part unintelligible to English speakers when spoken naturally and at speed, Jamaican Patwa is probably known by most of the one-hundred-eighty-thousand-plus New Yorkers born in Jamaica, not to mention their children.[39] It should thus be considered one of the city's major languages, but Patwa has never been officially recognized or supported anywhere. Many Jamaicans, moving up and down their creole continuum with extraordinary creativity and flexibility, have never considered themselves speakers of a separate language. As elsewhere, class is also a significant predictor of who is likely to speak what when where with whom. Given all this, it's intriguing that an estimated eight thousand New Yorkers do call themselves Patwa speakers on the census, especially in the concentrated Jamaican section of the northeast Bronx around White Plains Road—a tiny percentage but a far higher number than for any other English-based creole.

The one Caribbean language which seems to be on its way to full visibility in New York is Haitian Creole, with over one hundred thousand speakers according to the census. This may include speakers of other "French creoles," notably from St. Lucia, but also from Martinique, Guadeloupe, and French Guiana. Linguistically speaking, two centuries of political independence have helped cement a deep divergence from French, though only in the last few decades (and still not completely) have many Haitians shaken off the stigma of speaking a creole. Many Haitians do continue to learn and use French in certain contexts, but in 1987 Kreyòl at least gained official legal status in Haiti. By that time, an enormous diaspora community was forming in the middle of Caribbean Brooklyn, and it was gradually becoming clear that Haitian Creole was a more widely spoken mother tongue in the city than French itself.[40] Poets write in it, singers sing in it, preachers preach in it, and pirate radio stations broadcast in it. It became an official "citywide language" in 2008, which is why you can now see it on key subway lines, on certain park signs, and in other materials.

There may be a long way to go before any of the city's African languages achieves similar visibility, but an extraordinary new migration since the 1970s is making New York the most African city, linguistically speaking, outside of Africa.[41] The vast majority are West Africans, speaking at least a hundred languages from the region, though there are also speakers of dozens of other languages from all corners of the continent. While Harlem was an initial gateway, the Bronx has become the epicenter. The birth of a new kind of African diaspora capital, with

African American, Afro-Caribbean, and African languages in close, constant, and complicated contact, is now being fully realized.[42]

For African New Yorkers who are Muslims from French-colonized West Africa, as will be described later, Arabic and French remain vitally important intergroup languages. African languages themselves, struggling with low status and little support, are often part of cross-border groupings. Take Fulani, also known as Pulaar or Fulfulde, which some linguists see as consisting of nine distinct but related languages, spoken by some forty million or more people everywhere from Africa's Atlantic coast to the Red Sea. Traditionally the Fulani were pastoralists who moved with their cattle, prompting rivalries and resource struggles with farming neighbors, including the Manding-speaking peoples who themselves live spread across West Africa and are one of New York's other largest and fastest-growing African communities. A degree of separation carried over to New York with the formation of Brooklyn's small Fuuta Town, anchored by the Pulaar Speaking Association's office on Fulton between Franklin and Bedford. But there are also large Fulani communities close to Manding ones and other Africans in Harlem and the Bronx, given that most also know French and Arabic since they hail from Senegal and Guinea.

Like so many Caribbean New Yorkers, those from formerly British-controlled West Africa usually arrive with a preexisting relationship to English and a creole continuum of their own. Many know English from school, including higher education, and may be shifting to it completely. Others speak Ghanaian English, Nigerian English, Liberian English, and Krio from Sierra Leone—likewise English-based creoles, with some shared characteristics, that can connect people from very different mother-tongue backgrounds.

The multilingual complexity of those backgrounds can be substantial. Samuel Owusu-Sekyere of the Ghanaian Association of Staten Island has an Ashanti father, an Akuapem mother, and an Mfantse wife, and he speaks Ga because he lived in Accra, plus a little Ewe because his parents were traders. According to him, every Ghanaian language is now spoken in the city, with either the national language Twi or Ghanaian English serving as a lingua franca. He has friends in the Yankasa Association, founded by Muslims from northern Ghana who have their own mosque in the Bronx and speak several local languages among themselves: Frafra, Wale, Guang, Dagaare, and Dagbani.

A first wave of Ghanaians arrived after the coup in 1966, while others came as seamen with the country's Black Star Line (not to be confused with Marcus Garvey's earlier line of the same name, with its ships docked at Harlem's 135th Street pier). By the early twenty-first century, New York had the largest Ghanaian community outside of Ghana, with major chiefs and famous figures living among the tens of thousands in the Bronx from the Grand Concourse up to Tracy Towers, and the more affluent now pushing out to Westchester.[43]

Nigerian New Yorkers, a significant number of whom are middle-class and highly educated, have set a course of their own, settling all over the city, including areas of Brooklyn and Queens that are majority Black but have few other Africans. Yoruba and Igbo speakers appear to constitute the majority, but there is considerable diversity within those broad categories. There are also many Hausa and Edo speakers and at least a critical mass of Afenmai, Anaang, Efik, Esan, Ibibio, Kalabari, Tiv, and Urhobo speakers, each with an association, as well as organizations for people from particular Nigerian states like Edo and Akwa Ibom, which may correspond partially but not entirely to language groups.

More than economic opportunity, flight from violence has driven the growth of Liberian Staten Island, where refugees from the civil war of 1989–2004 and their children form the majority. The area around Park Hill, also home to many African Americans and Nigerians, has more Liberians than anywhere outside Liberia, apparently including speakers of all seventeen languages spoken in the country. Many are now leaving New York for other parts of the country.[44] Likewise, the brutal civil war in neighboring Sierra Leone from 1991 to 2002 brought many seeking asylum to the city, with communities forming in Staten Island, the Bronx, and Queens, and ultimately elsewhere across the country.

By the reverse effect, survivors coming to the city from official refugee resettlement hubs in Iowa and Indiana helped create Brooklyn's Little Darfur, a hustling outpost of at most a few hundred people that happens to be surrounded by Bangladeshis. Working with a Zaghawa speaker there named Nasseruddin, ELA recorded the story of how Tawila, once a prosperous town of forty thousand people known for its whole-leaf tobacco, was attacked by a genocidal militia in 2004 and subsequently abandoned.[45] The mass killing and expulsion is threatening not only Zaghawa but a dozen other languages of Darfur, belonging to the Nilo-Saharan family that stretches from Timbuktu to Nubia. Many survivors have had little choice but to assimilate to an Arabic-speaking society that aimed at their extinction.

Of course not every language is spoken in New York, and not every part of the world or language family is equally represented in the city. It's comforting to imagine every language getting a word in, in what's arguably the world's most powerful and visible city, just as every nation has a mission to the UN—but the realities of mobility are much starker and stranger. The extraordinary linguistic diversity of Australia, Papua New Guinea, the Pacific, the Amazon, and much of southern and eastern Africa is largely absent for a variety of reasons, at least for now. Partly it's the fact that people from those regions have tended to move elsewhere, often closer by, but in some cases small speaker populations and critical levels of language endangerment may also be at issue.

Regardless, the linguistic landscape of a city is much more than just a list of its groups, though it can be challenging and crucial enough just to register everyone's presence. Day-to-day life in the universes of post-Soviet Brooklyn, the West African Bronx, and Asian Queens—entire multilingual ecosystems tucked inside the city—is far more complex, a linguistic ballet every bit as intricate as the "sidewalk ballet" identified by Jane Jacobs. For that, the skyline view alone won't do. We have to go down into the streets and hear the city through the ears of its most multilingual people—six individual speakers sustaining their endangered languages against overwhelming odds.

# III. Present

# Rasmina

## सेके, སེ་སྐད་ (*Seke*)

### 1

This village has elevators. We step into one of them.

"More of our cousins and relatives live on this side," says Rasmina. "One family is in 6F. Some cousins are on 5. An uncle just moved to 3K. Every floor there's one of my aunts living in it, one of my relatives, someone from the village. We'll start on the sixth floor and come down to the fifth. We'll knock and see if anybody's home, just to say hello." She presses a button, and the box lurches upward.

This vertical village in the heart of Brooklyn is home to a significant percentage of the world's approximately seven hundred Seke speakers. All are originally from five villages in the Mustang region of northern Nepal, near Tibet, but over a hundred live or have lived in this one building seven thousand miles from home. Seke speakers call it 380 because of the address, and it's now the sixth Seke-speaking village.

To gather critical mass in a neighborhood is hard; to carve out space in a single building even harder. Forget the "apart" in apartment living. The city's vertical villages, which don't appear on any map, are intensely communal sites of cultural and linguistic survival. They upend urban theory. They develop a spatial and social logic all their own.[1] They are also vulnerable.

In a vertical village like 380, the future of a language is at stake. Like Trung, the language I researched in China, Seke belongs to the

Tibeto-Burman language family, which includes Tibetan, Burmese, and ultimately all forms of Chinese, but also hundreds of smaller languages spoken across the Himalaya. For centuries, Seke speakers were under Tibetan political, economic, religious, and cultural influence, but Nepali (an Indo-European language closer to Hindi and ultimately English) started spreading up from the south around the eighteenth century. Today Seke is squeezed from all sides.

Two of the five Seke-speaking villages are heavily represented here: Tshugsang and Tsangle, "which almost count as one village," says Rasmina, because people tend to marry one another, as her Tshugsang father and Tsangle mother did. Everyone from these two villages is now said to be related through a dense weave of marriages. English kinship terms are vague to the point of uselessness when Seke speakers need to reference their uma, *paternal aunt's husband*, and at the same time utterly cold for not seeing cousins essentially as brothers and sisters. Likewise, ashang *uncle* or incha *aunt* can be used with anyone a generation older, za *son* or zeme *daughter* with anyone a generation younger.

Today, half of Tshugsang and Tsangle seem to be in 380, especially working-age people with children. Except for elders and a handful of others, the original villages stand almost empty while the one in Brooklyn is full.

Seke villages are small settlements of rammed-earth houses jammed together and surrounded by fields and orchards on what little flat land there is. All around are enormous cliffs eroding into columns and facets in ever-changing shades of ochre and beige, pocked by ancient cave dwellings. It's desert at over ten thousand feet, parched and protected by the Himalayan rain shadow cast by snow-capped mountains twice as high at the edge of the frame. Through the middle runs the river that Seke speakers call Omdi Kyu, better known as Kali Gandaki, which forms one of the world's deepest gorges while concealing in its banks beguiling shaligrams: Cretaceous fossil stones, holy to Hindu pilgrims as symbols and incarnations of Lord Vishnu. Some work the land, raise animals, and run guesthouses, but most young people now leave for New York.

380 is a six-story brick building in Flatbush, built in 1960, of the kind found everywhere in the outer boroughs, because buildings up to six stories don't need a water tower under local law. Instead there's just a flat ordinary roof, technically off limits of course, where smokers and teens look out to the Manhattan skyline at an almost tangible distance. Three acres of space packed into six floors means 136 rental apartments, plus a small Pakistani mosque, a dentist's office, and a medical practice on the ground floor. Three, four, or more people may share a five-hundred-square-foot apartment, splitting $1,500 a month in rent.

No one remembers who came here first from Tshugsang or Tsangle, but for the last few decades almost everyone has followed them. Word of any openings spreads quickly on the WeChat and WhatsApp groups that link Seke speakers in New York and beyond, with new arrivals just staying on the same lease, unbeknownst to super or landlord. Besides being relatively affordable and linguistically and culturally navigable, the building is near nanny and nail salon jobs (for women) and restaurant and grocery store jobs (for men). "There is reliability and safety," says Rasmina, "because at the end of the day, if something goes wrong, your people are there." America is the ultimate goal for virtually all Seke speakers, believes Rasmina, and 380 is a foothold in America.

The village makes many forms of social, cultural, and economic cooperation possible. If someone has just made it to Brooklyn from Nepal via Mexico, they are invited to meals and welcomed with gifts to help them get started. People do keep track of contributions, however, and may not take kindly to those who don't ultimately reciprocate. A particularly vital form of organized reciprocity is called dhikuti, which literally means *a box for valuables* in Nepali, but by extension a remarkable informal institution: a voluntary rotating savings and credit association for Seke speakers linked by hometown and kinship, in some ways better than a bank.[2]

Here's the system as it functions in Nepal. Say there were a group of fifty people, with each putting in $1,000 at monthly meetings. So the pot would be $50,000, and the highest bidder would pledge $10,000 of that to win it, which would go into a common fund. This "winner" would then take home $40,000 to put toward a house, start a business, celebrate a wedding, pay for their kid's degree, or get surgery or treatment for a family member. They would pay it off to the group on a certain schedule, usually interest free, over the next few years. Everyone can win once, and winners toward the end of the cycle would mostly just be getting their savings back. Almost everyone plays, if you can call it playing.

The workings are intricate, but the purpose is clear: to allow people who could hardly hope to get loans elsewhere, or else only at predatory rates, save money, get access to credit, and build up their community. No collateral needed, with default, fraud, and embezzlement all but unheard of, because trust is everything. Any money left in the common fund is divided up, and then that particular dhikuti is done, but sooner or later a new dhikuti group, along the same lines with many of the same players, is sure to start up.

Over two hundred names for practices like dhikuti have been recorded across Asia, Africa, Latin America, the Caribbean, and the Pacific. There are Mexican cundinas, Peruvian juntas, South African stokvel, Japanese ko, Tibetan dukhor, Yemeni hacba, Somali hagbad, Haitian sòl, Guyanese "boxes," Philippine paluwagan. In West Africa, there are susu, a possibly Yoruba word that spread as enslaved Africans transferred the practice to Jamaica, Trinidad, and ultimately New York. Senegalese and Guinean New Yorkers call them tontines, using a name that resonates all the way to Wall Street.[3]

Given all these different names across so many far-flung places, rotating credit associations seem to be a quasi-universal institution, invented again and again from scratch in societies all over the world. If anything, many seem to have grown out of rural realities, as a way for farmers to pool risk in the face of harvest uncertainties. The anthropologist Clifford Geertz, who studied the similar arisans of Modjokuto in eastern Java, argued that they emerged naturally as peasants encountered traders and entered the cash economy.[4]

The elevator rattles to a stop and we step into the hallway, walking the green-and-black checkerboard of vinyl flooring past door after door under fluorescent lights. Whole non-Seke societies are also packed into this building: Pakistani, Caribbean, Nepali. One door is covered by a wrathful-looking but probably protective deity; Rasmina thinks the family is Tibetan. On the next door she tries the knob, which opens a few inches with a deafening creak.

After some talk through the doorjamb, a cousin pops out. Rasmina wants to press him for the latest 380 news. Last year her family moved out to a bigger apartment a few blocks away, with her sister pregnant and her sister's husband having just immigrated from Nepal midpandemic and found work at an H Mart.[5] That meant the rent was now being split four ways, there was room for the baby, and Rasmina had a room of her own for the first time in her life.

"I babysat for you here!" she teases her cousin as we walk down the hall. This is another benefit of life in the vertical village, where the older kids are expected to look after the younger ones whenever needed. He was born in Nepal and came to New York when he was three.

"Do you understand Seke?" she needles him, in English.

He giggles nervously: "Depends on the context. If I know what's going on."

"Maybe you're good at guessing, okay!"

"Well, like I remember one time, we went to Korean barbecue. I was super young and there was a fly in my ramen. I still wanted to eat it, and then my mom yelled at me. I went into the bathroom, and my sister was like, Tu kraze, *Oh, he's gonna cry.*"

Rasmina corrects him, laughing: "The kraze!" (The Seke pronunciation is roughly "tay kraZAY.")

His English, like Rasmina's, carries the inflection of New York City public school, channeled through hip-hop and TikTok. His Spanish, from five years of classes, is better than his Seke. He doesn't tell his Pakistani and Bangladeshi friends, but he can understand at least a little of what they're saying thanks to the Bollywood movies he's been watching with his dad during the pandemic.

Rasmina turns another knob, revealing a warm apartment suffused with the smell of spiced meat. We greet a mother and daughter in Seke, and the mother responds in Seke, the daughter in Nepali, until talk inevitably slips into Nepali with a little mixing. We stay near the threshold, just saying hi for a second, not taking our shoes off. Besides shoes, the shoe rack supports two big bags of flour.

The traditionally dressed mother sits watching *Dance Champion Nepal* on a big flat-screen in the living room, which doubles as a Buddhist shrine room with water bowls, butter lamps, flowers, thangka paintings, and everything else needed for the morning and evening rituals. A curtain encloses a narrow bed in the corner, which is almost certainly hers. The daughter pounds fresh garlic and ginger in a mortar in the kitchen.

"I always used to go to her house to ask for onions and tomatoes," she says, nodding at Rasmina. They miss being down the hall from each other. Everyone is so busy with work these days. They've been here twelve years and like everyone they're trying to buy a house—"in Brooklyn, but everything's too expensive, too hard to find, maybe Jamaica."

The mother has health issues, and Rasmina, as the community's de facto nurse, is called over to read and translate the prescription labels.

To the daughter we say what people departing say: Sena laze truo! *Stay doing well!* And to the mother the respectful form: Sena laze denchaago! They respond with what people staying say, the casual and then the respectful form: Sena laze yaro! Sena laze pheno! *Go doing well!* They insist on giving each of us a bottled water for the road.

Down in the lobby, we can't find a single Nepali or Tibetan name on the nameboard or the mailboxes. (Seke personal names may be Nepali, Tibetan, or a combination.) It's true that many landlords can't be bothered to update them, though there are some newer names here taped over old ones. In some buildings you can tell from the nameboards that there must be speakers of thirty or forty languages; in others, the names haven't been changed in thirty or forty years, reflecting communities already gone to the suburbs. On the walls hang old notices, defunct forms, boilerplate posters, all the city-required things in English bureaucratically canceling each other out. In a small concession to the present, certain taped-up notices from the management which must actually be urgent are posted in both English and Nepali.

This building may be a miraculous site for the survival of Seke, but it's also a piece of real estate being squeezed for profit by the family that owns it, who themselves were probably immigrants to this neighborhood fifty years ago. Rasmina says they turn a blind eye when the Pakistani live-in super charges at least the Nepalis an extra month's rent just for moving in. Sometimes he fixes things only after Rasmina calls 311 for people. One of the oldest tenants in the building is a Jamaican woman, here since 1977, who "does all the activist stuff," from circulating petitions about leaks and mold to putting up the Christmas tree. Rasmina used to help her by going door to door or waiting in the lobby to translate and explain for the Nepali speakers.

A few older tenants may be rent stabilized, but none of the Seke speakers are. Already, says Rasmina, people are buying houses and the community is splitting up and scattering to cheaper areas like outer Queens or Jersey suburbs like Harrison, Lyndhurst, and West New York. They would stay together in the Brooklyn village if they could.

## 2

With the push of a door, we're out of the Seke village and into the street. You can get used to the scale and speed of the city, but never all of its contrasts, proximities, and juxtapositions. Barely even visible under quasi-permanent scaffolding, 380 sits unnoticed off a bustling commercial strip, two blocks from a subway stop, in a neighborhood where Brooklyn's biggest ethnic blocs back up onto one another.

Sometime in the late twentieth century, almost by accident, this became one of the most diverse places on the planet. It all looks very ordinary, but this square mile is home to a Ghanaian evangelical church, a Russian banya, a florist/bar for hipsters, a Juhuri-speaking synagogue for the Jews of Azerbaijan and Daghestan, Dominican hair salons, Pakistani auto body shops, Haitian dollar-van stops, an organization of Darfuri refugees, a Cambodian Buddhist wat, an Albanian mosque, a Panamanian bar, and a restaurant where Uzbek Uber drivers swig bottles of Jameson while savoring fine kebabs. Certain worlds here intersect, but most never do and never need to.

We walk south into streets of rambling old Victorian mansions owned mostly by people known here as "Americans," which usually means white and English-speaking.

"I've had my eye on that house since I was a kid," says Rasmina's cousin.

"Me too!" Rasmina almost shouts. "It's so perfect. It's big—"

"The backyard is nice—"

"—for a family—"

"—and it's brick!"

"Most of our people look for brick."

"Because it looks nice—"

"—and also the houses in Nepal are made out of brick." Rasmina gestures to the mostly wooden houses all around us. "These look like paper houses to us. Like it's just gonna blow away."

With gentrification, the American zone (known as Ditmas Park) is expanding, and even the humblest houses here now have price tags way out of reach.

"Our area was not the safest," says Rasmina's cousin, with a touch of pride. "They were throwing garbage cans at old people. Then lots of white people were coming in, right? All the buildings are becoming nicer, the restaurants. That's like the last ten years. The whole area is super nice now."

So far 380 is unchanged, as are the other two vertical villages we're walking toward, likewise known from their addresses as 611 and 1212—or "Bara Bara", the latter a double fit because बाह्र bāhra is *twelve* in Nepali and many who live in the building come from what is usually spelled Baragaon, the *Twelve Villages* region of Lower Mustang, which today actually comprises nineteen villages and has a language of its own, sometimes also known as Baragaon. Nor are Seke and Baragaon speakers the only groups in the city with vertical villages. The six-story red-brick building at 37 Mott Street in Manhattan's Chinatown has seen generations of Taishanese and Cantonese speakers closely linked by family and village.[6] Two brutalist towers in the Bronx are home to hundreds of Ghanaians, who have their own association, celebrations, and events there. Some Brooklyn buildings with Haitian owners or supers have become entirely Haitian, with family, community, and church networks spreading the word about any vacancies, and fellow tenants serving as tailors, dressmakers, drivers, barbers, electricians, and folk healers.[7] There are rumors of many others.

Everywhere they live, Seke speakers are always also inevitably in close contact with other languages. In Mustang, Baragaon is spoken to the south and Loke is used in the north—and both are much more closely related to each other and to Tibetan than to Seke. This may be an indication that Seke has been spoken in situ longer and was later surrounded by speakers of these other languages. In New York, Seke speakers are part of, but also stand apart from, the larger Mustangi migration. Of Mustang's total population of around ten thousand, at least a quarter are now estimated to be in the city, not including the children born here. These may be tiny numbers in the context of New York or even just Nepali New York, but that's not the view from Mustang, whose fate is now closely linked to New York.[8] One person here may be supporting a whole extended family back home.

To Baragaon and Loke speakers, Seke is a small, strange language, if they've heard of it at all. This in turn is how Nepalis and Tibetans see Baragaon and Loke, if they've heard of *those* languages at all. The once-independent kingdom of Mustang, traditionally closer linguistically, culturally, and religiously to the Tibetan world to the north, is gradually being absorbed, politically and otherwise, by Nepal from the south. The complexity of how different people identify inside Mustang is playing itself out in Brooklyn and Queens, where Baragaon speakers from the south may be more likely to settle with other Nepalis, while Loke speakers from the north stay with other Himalayans. I've met Mustangis in their twenties who grew up speaking Nepali in Nepal and actually learned Loke only in New York, such is the size and strength of the diaspora.

"I'm friends with some of them," says Rasmina's cousin of such other non-Seke Mustangis, as we approach Bara Bara.

"We know *of* them, but I wouldn't knock on their door," says Rasmina. Her own small building actually has a makeshift Buddhist temple run by Baragaon speakers in the basement. "Every Sunday I wake up with their prayers!"

Both Bara Bara and 611 look just like 380: basic, midcentury, red-brick buildings packed with relatively cheap apartments. Rasmina sees a woman struggling with a pushcart of groceries on the steps in front of the building and rushes over to help, in Nepali. "With everyone who passes by here, I can tell they're familiar," she says afterwards. Based on the woman's accent in Nepali and her facial structure, Rasmina is sure she's from Mustang. Monolinguals don't see it, but multilingual people are always making these split-second judgments, deciding which language to open up in. Who can calculate all the linguistic labor, both mental and emotional, involved in the constant accommodation of others?

Seke speakers have stuck together by choice and necessity. "People always prefer someone of their own," says Rasmina of village loyalties in Mustang, "and I feel like our people do the same thing. Let's say somebody is getting married from one village into a second village, they'll say something like, 'Oh, the language doesn't even match.'"

Another crucial factor in both Brooklyn and Queens is the presence of much larger working-class Bangladeshi and Pakistani communities, each numbering in the tens of thousands. Speakers of tiny languages from Mustang can draw on a baseline of cultural and linguistic familiarity with their Pakistani, Bangladeshi, and sometimes Indian neighbors, who might also be their supers, landlords, employers, and neighbors.

Rasmina's cousin points out a school where at first he hung out with the Baragaon-speaking kids and then later with the Bengali- and Urdu-speaking ones, who make up the majority there. They would shoot hoops at the playground, where the "mommy gang" of six or eight Baragaon women formed a circle to share food and keep an eye on their kids. At 611, nearby, the kids would play hide and seek in the bushes, or "ding dong ditching," a game of ringing aunties' doorbells, scramming, hiding, and then hoping to glimpse an auntie coming out, peeved and confused.

Just ahead is the Pakistani bakery where the Seke-speaking uncles of Newkirk drink chai in the summer, and there's the Nepali phone store where they gather in the winter, and over there the grocery store that people call Bengali chowk, chowk in South Asia being a *market* or a *meeting place*. We exchange passing greetings with a group of Seke-speaking aunties.

But if there was any place outside of Nepal where you could hear Seke spoken in public, it was Himalayan Grocery, the "All American

& Asian" bodega where Rasmina used to work, a few blocks up on Cortelyou Road. The store, in a Korean-owned building, had a Sherpa-speaking owner, then a Loke-speaking owner, and finally a Seke-speaking owner named Hale, so people would call it Hale Pasal (*Hale's store* in Nepali). Here the Seke-speaking uncles of Cortelyou could gather and catch up over milky, sugary coffees, sitting on milk crates under the awning. If someone younger came by, they would quickly switch to Nepali—or else Baragaon/Loke, Hindi/Urdu, Tibetan, or even a little English, depending on the person.

The bodega itself has been just as flexible as its resident uncles. Now under Yemeni ownership, it glistens with vapes and snacks. Its previous awning with clip-art mountains promised organic produce, sushi, a juice bar, ice cream, ice-cold beer, and more. There were always a few Nepali products, like the boxes of Wai Wai instant noodles, so beloved that their creator became the country's first billionaire. The juice bar didn't pan out, says Rasmina, but the three-seat sushi bar did well for a while. During that period, the awning read Himalayan Sushi Inc., with a blown-up photo of the Dalai Lama and Barack Obama arm in arm in khata, *white ceremonial scarves*.

Himalayan sushi is even kind of a thing, at least in New York, since many Japanese sushi places hire Himalayans, who then become masters of the trade, never mind how far from the ocean they were born or how unseemly it is at first for them, as Tibetan Buddhists, to handle dead fish all day.[9] More than sushi, though, what sold were momos, so together with a Tibetan partner Hale opened Cafe Tibet, a tiny restaurant next door, where Rasmina also worked. Once a week, a group of Mustangi guys roll in after playing soccer and take over the back, but otherwise most business is from the neighborhood inji, *white people*. Hanging cliffwise almost above the open-cut train tracks, the tables shiver and shake as the tapke train rolls by below.

Brooklyn Himalayans call it the tapke train because early on most could neither speak nor read English, including letters and numbers, let alone comprehend the arcane correspondences of the Metropolitan Transportation Authority. To them, the logo for the Q train (capitalized, Helvetica) looked just like a tapke, *saucepan* in Nepali, with the letter's tail an obvious handle. The Q was their train, the one for going to work in Manhattan, often at Indian restaurants where they were laboring all night over scalding tapke. "Take the tapke train" was essential advice for new arrivals.

How do people name and navigate the city in all their languages? Seke speakers say they live in 380 or Bara Bara and call their neighborhoods after the streets, Cortelyou or Newkirk, not Flatbush or Ditmas Park. In Seke, "Coney Island" is usually the bit of Coney Island Avenue that runs nearby, not the famous fairground and neighborhood miles to the south.

"We wouldn't go past Coney Island," says Rasmina's cousin. "It's like a whole other world over there"—a world of Russian, Yiddish, Azeri, Albanian, and Uzbek speakers.

"A lot of Newkirk people don't go past the train station," adds Rasmina, pointing in the other direction, "and Cortelyou people only go to Eighteenth." Which means Seke Brooklyn is about four blocks long and eight blocks wide—although elders have a walking circuit in nearby Prospect Park and know just the spots there for foraging certain wild greens, which they sometimes return home with bags of.

The English name "New York" seems to indicate a certain familiar city, but many other full-blown cities, in other languages, occupy the same three hundred square miles. Official maps present the bird's-eye view, the planner's angle. They sprawl endlessly in English, even if some street names were originally Lenape or Dutch, even if thousands of business names are obviously in Spanish, Chinese, and many other languages.

The total urban fact, if such a thing is possible, would encompass the thousands of non-English place-names that speakers of all the city's languages use to mark out the places that matter to them. Not Chinatown, Little Italy, Little Haiti, Little Guyana, Little Yemen, etc., which stake symbolic claims for homogenous enclaves in English while making room for cultural tourism. Only marginally better are the various Broadways which proudly graft the name of the city's traditionally most glamorous street onto the commercial arteries of immigrant neighborhoods, whether the old German Broadway of Kleindeutschland, Yiddish Broadway (lower Second Avenue), Czech Broadway (First Avenue in the Sixties and Seventies), Swedish Broadway (Atlantic Avenue near downtown Brooklyn), or Bukharian Broadway (108th Street in Queens).

Loisaida, an ingenious Nuyorican play on both the Lower East Side and the city of Loíza Aldea in Puerto Rico, is the rare non-English name that is breaking through, even quasi-officially, beyond the community that coined it. Same with El Barrio for East Harlem, and to a lesser extent Los Sures for the southside of Williamsburg, marking out Puerto Rican space even or especially as gentrification threatens. Likewise, but less well known, are the Dominican nicknames for their world in Washington Heights: Quisqueya (the Indigenous Taíno name for the whole island of Hispaniola), Plátano (*Plantain Land*), and El Platanal (*Plantain Grove*). Or the Dominican part of Corona affectionately called Sabana Iglesia or Sabana Church, because so many migrated from that particular town in the northern Dominican Republic to that particular part of Queens starting in the 1950s.[10] Meanwhile, the Colombian section of Jackson Heights nearby was becoming known as Chapinero, for a middle-class suburb of Bogotá.

If the Real Estate City is full of neighborhoods named SoBro, ProCro, and NoLiTa, the Immigrant City has Ørkenen Sur, Fuuta Town, Cois Fharraige, Registan, Deh Afghanan. There's no money or power to make these names stick, but each is a story wrapped in a pun and sealed with a wink, a message of belonging both to the city and to a distant homeland.

Ørkenen Sur, *Bitter Desert* in Norwegian, was a vast Depression-era shantytown in Red Hook. Fuuta Town, also in Brooklyn, is a new kind of region, or fuuta, for Fulani people at the intersection of Fulton and Nostrand. Cois Fharraige, *By the Sea* in Irish, is both the "Irish riviera" of Brooklyn's Gerritsen Beach and a coastal, Irish-speaking area near Galway in Ireland. Registan blends the attached houses of Rego Park with the architectural splendor of Samarkand's most famous square, where many in Queens(istan) are from. Deh Afghanan, *Village of Afghans* in Dari (and a place-name in Kabul, too), was applied by arriving refugees to their housing projects in Queens.[11] Jai Kishan (Jackson) Heights, Bronzeville (alias Brownsville), Брайтон (Brighton Beach, pronounced the Russian way) show that even originally English names can take on new textures in the non-English city.[12]

This unofficial creative placemaking extends to streets, blocks, buildings, and even more local units, changing as the groups change. Brooklyn's Eighth Avenue was once called Lapskaus Boulevard for a Norwegian version of beef stew, with the R train nearby dubbed the Norwegian-American line, after the shipping company. Now Eighth is 八大道 (baat3 daai6 dou6 in Cantonese—the numbers marking tones—or bā dàdào in Mandarin), which is literally *Eighth Avenue* but stands in for Chinese Sunset Park as a whole with an especially lucky sound, because the number 八 bā, *eight*, like several other numbers in Chinese, sounds like the lucky word 发 fā, *get rich* (to use Mandarin for the example).

Manhattan's Chinatown is home to a whole host of alternate street names used by Taishanese, Cantonese, Mandarin, and Fujianese speakers, often reflecting a very different layer of history from the English name, including maai6 mou6 gaai1 (*hat seller street*, Cantonese for Division Street) and jiu2 gwai2 gaai1 (*Jews' Street*, Taishanese for Orchard Street), and many others.[13] Nearby Yiddish speakers punningly named Essex Street Esik for *vinegar*, while Brooklyn's Livonia Avenue was turned into Levone, meaning *moon*, and the Bronx's Mosholu Parkway (*smooth stones* in Lenape, possibly) became Moyshele's Parkvey, whether for the Biblical Moses or some more local hero.[14]

What the Parks Department calls Rainey Park is known to Garifuna speakers in the Bronx and beyond as Waporu, after the shape of a traditional boat. It's a place where new immigrants find their feet, romances begin, and punta stars are made.[15] They call nearby Crotona Park Trujillano, after the town in Honduras. Some Hindus who worship at the Ganesh Temple on Bowne Street in Flushing call it Bawa Street, conferring saintliness on the sidewalk through Sanskrit.[16]

## 3

For the last five years, Rasmina and I have been meeting regularly to work on Seke, either near 380 or at ELA's office. The work takes many forms: gradually adding words, definitions, and examples to a dictionary-in-progress; homing in on single points of grammar; or carefully transcribing and translating a previously recorded text, as we're doing today.

Namaste ale! Namaste rinza! She calls me *older brother/cousin* and I call her *younger sister/cousin*, because anyone who speaks the language must be a relative, but we use the Nepali (and Hindi) greeting, originally Sanskrit for *bowing to you* and now entering at least the yoga dialect of English.[17] Like most smaller languages, Seke doesn't have or need a formal, all-purpose hello. In traditional face-to-face societies, where you see the same people constantly and seldom meet a complete stranger who speaks your language, real questions with actionable answers like *Where are you going?* or *What are you doing?* usually make more sense as greetings.

We chitchat. It's getting hard to find time now with her twelve-hour night shifts at the hospital. She started working as a nurse right after COVID's first peak—at the bottom of the pecking order, with the worst jobs and little chance of getting any overtime. First it was a nursing home where she was the only nurse on duty and responsible for giving meds to forty patients, which meant no time to eat, have a sip of water, or even go to the bathroom. Then it was a cushy job doing COVID tests for Goldman Sachs, where she fought for better pay along with the other contract nurses, knowing that the hiring agency was keeping three or four times what the nurses were making. Rasmina tells me she's getting serious about money: saving for a house, paying her own taxes, even trying out Robin Hood and Dogecoin. Of course language work is not the most lucrative proposition: we can barely pay half of what Goldman was paying, but maybe that's not bad given the disparity in budgets.

She shows me pictures of Brooklyn—her two-month-old Brooklyn-born nephew Brooklyn Kyalsang—or rather scrolls through the Instagram account his mother, Rasmina's sister, has been curating for her model or mini-influencer in training. A series of photos show him serene and red-beanied in a brown sweatsuit with abstract Santas from Zara, followed by thirty hashtags like #babyboy #zarakids #myfirstchristmas #infantfashion #newyorkcity. Agents appear to be posting comments. Only his grandma calls him Kyalsang and talks to him in Seke, but this is leading Rasmina's sister to use more of the language too. A baby has a way of putting language questions front and center, at least in the beginning.

Brooklyn may supersede her in time, but Rasmina in her early twenties is one of the youngest people anywhere who can speak Seke. Until she was about seven, more or less that "critical age" for language, she was raised in Tshugsang by her grandmother, while her parents worked in Nepal's cities. Indeed a grandparent is often the explanation for an "unusually" young speaker of an endangered language. At the same time, Rasmina's older sister, her cousins, and just about everyone else in her generation were growing up and going to school in Pokhara (the regional urban hub), Kathmandu (the national capital), or New York. In all three, the shift to Nepali is well underway.

At boarding school in Kathmandu after she turned seven, Rasmina, too, was soon pulled away from Seke. The other students came from dozens of language backgrounds across the Himalayan areas of northern Nepal, but most were already dominant in Nepali, which was also the unquestioned lingua franca of both the school and the surrounding city. A few classes were either in English or Tibetan, since it's both the language of Tibetan Buddhism (which Seke speakers and most other Himalayans follow) and the key to a wider diaspora.

One day Rasmina's mom showed up unexpectedly at school: "She came with a lot of snacks, she even gave me money. I was like, 'Wow!' I was just so happy to show my friends. That was her goodbye. She didn't want me to cry because she was leaving. When I got home for the holidays, she wasn't there. When I asked my dad, he was like, 'Yeah, she's in America!'" Rasmina sings out the last two words, which sound ambiguously alluring.

Her mom went straight to Bara Bara to stay with relatives, all adults away from their children. That was her base, but like most of the other women, she did "living" as a live-in nanny (in New Jersey) and sent all her earnings back home, working toward the day when her husband and daughters could join her. Several years later it happened: Rasmina was eleven, flying to New York and expecting to live in a skyscraper. People back in Nepal still think she lives in one—doesn't everyone in New York?—and she can't be bothered to explain that it's not like the movies. The reality was a tiny apartment in Bara Bara, shared with a couple of families from Tsele, but at least now the whole family was living together for the first time. They soon moved to a one-bedroom of their own in 380, but it lasted only a year: her father had been sick for a long time in Nepal, and his condition had deteriorated soon after their arrival in Brooklyn. He died at Coney Island Hospital just as Rasmina was finishing her first year of school in New York.

For the next ten years, they lived in a studio, also in 380, with mom by the window and the sisters sharing a bed behind a curtain they put up. Kathmandu boarding school had prepared Rasmina surprisingly well for a public school in Brooklyn full of other recent immigrants: "People used to question me. 'How do you know English? Do you take class outside? Do you take tutoring? You're not telling us, you're lying.' I think it's because they didn't have it in their country." The ubiquity of English in South Asian cities, rooted in British colonialism and refigured today as a sign of class and modernity, means that many young immigrants from the region have at least a linguistic edge over those coming from Latin America, East Asia, or the Middle East.

Free time was for helping out at home or for working, first at a South Asian–owned 99 Cents store on Kings Highway, later at an Indian restaurant in Midtown and a Korean deli on Bleecker Street. No one in her family and few in the community had ever made it to college, but Rasmina pushed through an associate's in nursing at CUNY, then a bachelor's at SUNY. Like hundreds of other Himalayan women in New York, she was drawn to nursing by the good pay, steady work, and compassionate aims.

By now her English was fluent and professional, and she was even picking up some Spanish. Nepali remained the constant language of family, friends, and community. She could understand a good deal of Hindi and Urdu thanks to Bollywood, neighbors, and similarities to Nepali. It's common for Nepali speakers to "pick up" Hindi/Urdu, a case of what linguists call asymmetric mutual intelligibility where the smaller and less powerful group comes through heavy exposure or pressure to understand the larger group's related language, but not the other way around. She still has some Tibetan comprehension, mostly for Buddhist rituals, as well as a little Baragaon/Loke, depending on who's speaking.

With all these other languages, was there even room for Seke? Even a first language can slip away, like memories of a childhood on the other side of the world. Away from the village, there was just one time when Rasmina could always use her mother tongue: on the phone with her grandmother, before she passed away in 2021. Many languages without any other sphere or setting can at least survive on the phone as a link between relatives. Rasmina will sometimes speak with her mom, but usually only "to tell her something secret in public." Or with her mom's friends, though they instinctively address anyone younger in Nepali. "When I get spoken to in Seke, I respond in Seke," says Rasmina, "but if they're speaking Nepali to me, I automatically reply in Nepali. If there are words that I don't know, I'll switch to Nepali naturally."

What about in thirty or forty years, when the last Seke-speaking generation may be gone altogether? Already Rasmina has no one her own age to talk to. The Seke now used in New York isn't the same as what Rasmina's grandmother used to speak, which had less Nepali, almost no English, and more traditional, ritual, and polite vocabulary, including certain "secret" words specific to the village or the clan or the family, Rasmina isn't sure which. Tones, sounds, and grammar were all a little different. Sometimes she tries a phrase or greeting with her sister or cousins, but they always smile nervously and respond in Nepali. "I think they want to speak more, but can't," she explains. "Sometimes they try to learn from me." One girl a year younger still lives in the village. "I think she speaks pretty well," says Rasmina brightly. There are scattered others, like Bikas, a young Gurkha soldier in the British army who started helping us from afar when he had downtime at the base.

Neither Rasmina nor anyone else she knows writes in Seke, but at least the older generation is recording voice messages, the preferred medium in the WhatsApp and WeChat groups. "I hear my mom's group chat all the time and all the voice messages are in Seke," she says. "They're just leaving messages left and right." The billionaire lords of Facebook and Tencent, who could care less, are the only outsiders with fraught potential access to this accidental archive. In general the community is deeply enmeshed in its group chats, though whether and how Seke is used seems to vary according to age, location, and other factors, across groups that may be composed of friends, relatives, or everyone from a given village. There's even one, probably encompassing a majority of all Seke speakers, for the "four-village family" of Tshugsang, Tsangle, Gyugu, and Timi (with Tangbe, the fifth village, on its own).[18]

For speakers of traditionally oral languages, who may not be used to typing or writing in any language, voice messages are gold. It's another instance of phones, as devices designed for the voice, being better for smaller languages than many newer technologies with higher barriers to entry. At the same time, older men in the community who went to school in Nepal may choose to type out perfect paragraphs in Nepali. Whatever the medium, the message is about staying connected: a virtual village to go with the vertical one. Someone passes away and help is needed with repatriating the body and performing the proper rituals. Someone is sick and needs money. Someone sends info on how to prevent COVID, or a dharma talk, a funny video, a bit of news.

With all her languages, Rasmina is almost an unofficial, unpaid interpreter and ambassador between 380 and America, like so many "1.5 generation" kids in other communities.[19] "Any time my mom has an appointment, they'll call me," she says. "I'll just speak like I'm my mom." She took her whole extended family to vote in the last election. She helped supervise four Seke kids as they struggled with remote learning during the COVID-19 pandemic. For others, she fills out unemployment forms, deals with repairs, translates prescriptions, and goes to parent-teacher conferences either with or instead of the parents.

"It's what a lot of immigrants go through," she says. "Many take their kids to their appointments, and if their kids are not available, they'll reach out to me. Let's say a relative got a job out in New Jersey and they've never been there, you would go with them the first time, or two times, to show them." The obligation is unspoken, but these things add up. She draws the line when aunties, like aunties everywhere, try to follow their kids onto social media: "The social media is getting to them. They're very addicted now. Every day somebody's mom is like, 'Make me Instagram, make me TikTok,' and I say, 'No thank you!'"

With a splitter piping sound into our two pairs of headphones, we turn back to a three-minute video we recorded in Tshugsang about the village's eight-hundred-year-old temple and the way the phazen, a group of local families who connect their lineage and migration with its founding, continually maintain it. It takes us three hours just to clean up the Seke transcription and English translation we've already drafted before we can publish it online. Rasmina eats a croissant and sips an iced latte while I ask questions, often focusing on a word or morpheme I don't fully understand.

"This word seze, is that connected to sewa, as in *good*, or shepa, *to say*, or something else?"

"How to explain it? It's like nishu seze!"

"*Twenty* seze?"

"Yeah, when it's actually a hundred. Like, *how dare you say it's twenty*! Or *how silly of me to say that*."

We play it back a fourth time to catch more swallowed words: cha ghar muwa seze, dim druk muwa. *There are six households* (on rotation to look after the temple), but the speaker says *six households* first in Nepali, then corrects herself (seze!) and says it in Seke. So is seze an exclamation, stronger than *whoops* but weaker than *damn*? Can it be broken down literally, maybe into the Seke for *I'm saying*, which it certainly sounds like? Rasmina isn't sure. We're going to need more examples.

We do a few more lines, then spend the next half hour on a single phrase, due lhawa. Due is a *kind of spirit or demon*, and lhawa means *throw*, but *demon throwing* is a particular ritual with numerous variations that a literal translation can't begin to illuminate. The lama may tell you to do it if misfortune or ill will seems to be coming your way. On a plate, or potentially in any container, you place bits of bones and threads and lotus flowers and sometimes even a few small bills—tribute for a hopefully not too discerning demon. Though not exactly "thrown," it should be left in a particular way in particular places: there are four spots in Tshugsang which Rasmina thinks might correspond to the cardinal directions. No one can say what becomes of the offering. There are now also spots in Brooklyn. She saw once on Instagram that some girls in Bara Bara had done it, leaving the offering out on Newkirk Avenue. Every now and then, an elaborate plate of little bones and threads just appears on Cortelyou Road, unmistakable if you know what it is.

## 4

Rasmina had never heard or even conceived of anyone being interested in Seke, until I asked her to work with me. I was going to be teaching a class at Columbia called Linguistic Field Methods, where students learn to document a language from scratch by working directly and intensively with a speaker and so get tossed right into the linguistic deep end. In this case there would be a larger and more urgent purpose as well, with Columbia paying Rasmina so that together we could start actually documenting Seke. Associating the language with paid work at a famous university is one way to bolster its prestige within a community, though at the risk of raising unrealistic expectations. The class would last just four months, but real progress in documenting the language would take years. Every language is inexhaustible in its own way.

Students in a Field Methods class are not supposed to be familiar with the language or consult any existing research. This wouldn't be a problem with Seke. The only articles, by a Japanese linguist who worked briefly with a few speakers outside the region, were an overview of phonetics and phonology, a précis of one dialect, and an analysis of how Seke verbs meaning *go* and *come* have extended their range to cover certain grammatical functions.[20] The only accessible recording was a grainy eleven-minute video we at ELA had filmed ourselves with a man named Jamyang Gurung, then living in Bara Bara, who had hardly used the language in the last two decades.

I asked linguists familiar with the region, and no one knew of anyone who had worked in the Seke-speaking villages. If this sounds surprising, consider that a short word list, at most, is all the documentation that exists for a third of the world's languages. Aside from the difficulty of getting there, getting around, and working with speakers, Upper Mustang was closed to outsiders until 1992, and even today you need to obtain a special, costly permit of limited duration from the Nepali government.

We started class by working through a Swadesh list, a classic linguists' tool for eliciting the core vocabulary considered most likely to be present and least likely to change in any language, and thus particularly useful for making comparisons with related languages. There is debate about just how universal the 207 items on the standard Swadesh list are, but overall they do represent the essential and timeless things that people actually talk about across all the languages of the world: pronouns, core kinship roles, body parts, basic actions, essential qualities, and globally common animals, plant parts, and elements of the natural world.

The list has words like *float*, *rotten*, and *cold*, but the only unit of time is the year. Only five colors and the numbers *one* through *five* make the list, but absent are most abstract words like *color* or *number*.[21] Likewise nowhere to be found are *work*, *friend*, *happy*, *art*, *nation*, *garbage*, *love*, *god*, or *thank you*. However fundamental they may seem to those who have internalized them, such words are culture-specific concepts with at least partially traceable histories. They can be borrowed across languages, of course, although loanwords get transformed and incorporated in different ways, and some words to some speakers may always sound like foreign guests or unwelcome interlopers. "I don't think we have a word for that," Rasmina would often reply to the students, with a trace of shame that I would quickly move to dispel. Seke, like all languages, has the words that its speakers have needed. If speakers have new needs now, it's a question of how best to meet them.

A Swadesh list usually presumes translation via a common language, which was English with Rasmina, but you can't rely too much on the rough-and-ready, one-to-one equivalencies of translation, and even less on pointing. You might think that all languages just name the same world with different labels, but there are many ways of dividing up semantic space, and this makes eliciting vocabulary far from straightforward. Even something as universal and concrete as the human body can be construed and divided in different ways, with language-specific "partonomies" that break down the body in different ways. The word bale in Seke means *leg-foot*, just as the word yaa means *arm-hand*, and many other languages also quite reasonably treat human limbs as hard-to-differentiate wholes, as in Russian нога and рука, which seem to match bale and yaa, respectively.[22] In Seke, bale tsungma is *toe* and yaa tsungma is *finger*, a parallelism that reflects the much less colloquial English idea of *digit*, itself now most often heard thanks to its derivative *digital*, which has been through several stages of semantic extension.

A lexicon is not just one word after another, but a structured whole that reveals the time-tested preoccupations of its speakers. As the Field Methods class went on, we were continually expanding our lexical database—our dictionary in the making, using software designed by missionary linguists for the purpose—until it had grown to about one thousand entries, many (crucially) with examples and notes.[23] Unfortunately, according to Zipf's law, the most frequent word in a language occurs twice as often as the second most frequent, the second most frequent twice as often as the third most frequent, and so on. Which means that infrequent words, if remembered at all, might only come up once in a decade with a particular speaker or in a particular context.

Common words often raise the thorniest questions. Take the Seke verb pungba, which by itself seems to mean *put* or *hit*, but combines with all sorts of actions for which it's hard to find any unifying thread: kira pungba *swim*, gi pungba *sing*, thul pungba *conspire*, zi pungba *stab*, and dozens of others. Pungba is what linguists call a "light verb," as flexible as *do* or *make* in English, but with particular patterns all its own. That means speakers can create new pungba constructions, providing an easy opening for loanwords, which is why I've heard "vote pungba" and "fail pungba" (although Seke doesn't have the labiovelar fricative sounds /v/ or /f/, so to English ears these sound like *boat* and *pail*, respectively).

Editing a dictionary is a lifetime's work, and lexicographers understandably get obsessive about their word hoards. But collecting words has its limits. Early on, linguists start looking for and asking about "minimal pairs," pairs of words that differ only in terms of a single sonic segment. This is the way to ferret out phonemes, those consistently meaningful sounds that make up the sound system of any given language. You don't need many pairs, and sometimes not even an exact correspondence, to prove that speakers are making a crucial distinction. Based only on the initial sound, for instance, English speakers hear *vote* and *boat* as different words and can assign them different meanings. In other words, their constituting a minimal pair is proof enough that /v/ and /b/ are separate phonemes *throughout* English, a fact that our writing system also reflects. Seke doesn't make this particular distinction—nor do Spanish or many other languages—so speakers don't really hear it, although they hear and make all sorts of other distinctions that English doesn't.

Take aspiration, which is pronouncing a consonant with a little puff of air right after and written with a superscript $^{h}$ in the International Phonetic Alphabet, that periodic table for sounds. Put your hand a few inches from your mouth and you can feel it. In English, we unconsciously put a /$p^{h}$/ in *port*, but just a regular old /p/ in *sport*. Because there are no minimal pairs like *port* and *$p^{h}$ort*, aspiration is not meaningful in English or marked in writing. This in turn is why none of my students could hear it when Rasmina insisted on the difference between pawa *be thin* and $p^{h}$awa *pay*, towa *need* and $t^{h}$owa *be big or tall*, or ku *pot* and $k^{h}$u *which*. In other words, Seke has a whole series of aspirated consonants at its disposal: not just /p/, /t/, and /k/, but also /p$^{h}$/, /t$^{h}$/, and /k$^{h}$/. Even harder to hear for an English speaker are the retroflexes, a series of sounds in Seke (and many South Asian languages) where the tongue is bent back just a bit extra when pronouncing a consonant. In Seke you're dealing not just with /d/ and /t/, but also with /ɖ/ and /ʈ/, as those retroflex consonants are written in IPA.

Though we started by writing everything in IPA, as linguists do, Rasmina and other speakers were immediately interested in what linguists call a practical orthography, a writing system that speakers of a traditionally oral language can actually use. As we figured out the sound system, we gradually worked through possibilities. Writing always involves choices, even if it's meant only as a stepping stone, not definitive but intuitive enough for speakers to start reading and typing. Many Seke speakers are now literate to different degrees in Nepali, Tibetan, and English, but none of those three writing systems can cover everything that Seke does. We decided to use a Latin-based alphabet for starters, if only for the ease of typing and our immediate local audience in 380. That made some decisions easier, like writing aspirates with a regular *h*, but others more vexed, like writing /dr/ and /tr/ for /ɖ/ and /ʈ/, respectively, following Tibetan convention.

Even more challenging were the tones. With Rasmina overemphasizing to train our ears, it didn't take us long to hear the difference between a clear, high nga, meaning *I* or *me*, and a creakier nga with a bit of bass, meaning *five*. But such clear-cut minimal pairs for tone are rare in Seke. Judging by related languages, Seke might once have had a four-tone system, including fine-grained "pitch contours" that could have grown harder to hear over the centuries. Whether it's due to natural, gradual change or present-day endangerment, Seke seems to be moving with each generation toward a simpler system, with just high tone and low tone, and this would also track with a wider pattern, where tone systems get simpler and eventually peter out when moving west across the Himalaya.

Much more than core vocabulary, tones can come and go across the history of a language. The process of tonogenesis—how tones come into a toneless language—was first convincingly described for Vietnamese, by a linguist who posited that the language had developed three tones by the sixth century C.E. and six tones by the twelfth century.[24] In fact, the so-called Great Tone Split was unfolding across East Asia about a millennium ago, of course too slowly and subtly for anyone at the time to notice. Pairs of initial consonants like /b/ and /p/ that had once differed (minimal pair–style) in terms of "voicing" (whether the vocal cords are vibrating as they do in /b/ but not /p/) gradually no longer did. What remained and became meaningful was the associated natural difference in pitch, i.e., tone.

Similar processes must have played out in Seke, but now something quite different, not exactly the reverse, may be happening. Working with Rasmina we find that Seke does have that voicing distinction between /b/ and /p/, which many tonal languages like Mandarin lack, and that it's consistently bound up with tone. If tone goes away in Seke, a voicing distinction may be left as its only trace. Bawa *bring* is always low tone, while pawa *be thin* is always high tone.

Remarkably, speakers of tonal languages may be more likely to develop perfect pitch, but that doesn't mean they can consciously isolate or specify what they're doing. Nor are tones always crucial for Seke speakers to make themselves understood today. Trying to write them feels clumsy, confusing, unnecessary.[25]

Operating at an even more unconscious level than tones is grammar. A half-swallowed syllable that keeps appearing, at first barely noticed and hard to translate, is probably a grammatical morpheme. Only once we have seen it enough times in different contexts can we isolate it, analyze it, and test invented phrases with Rasmina. Maybe a similar form exists in a related language, or at least something that fulfills a similar function, but maybe neither. The more languages linguists work on, the more they find types of markers which only exist in one or a few languages. The Mwera language of Tanzania has "hodiernal" tense marking, just for things happening today. Some Tibeto-Burman languages, and apparently a few others, tag the speaker's surprise at unexpected information—so-called "mirative" marking.

Like every language, Seke has dozens of grammatical markers, from *indefinite plural* **-za** (as in nyukyuza *dogs*, but nyuku som *three dogs*, without **-za** because the number is specified) to the *prohibitive* tha-, as in thalao *Don't do it!* These morphemes morph too, depending on phonological rules: we found that the Seke imperative is formed by adding **-o** to the verb (as in thala**o**), but that it comes out **-ro**, **-go**, or plain **-o** depending on the verb stem, as in bi**ro** *Speak!* or jaa**go** *Look!* Why or how do those extra consonants /r/ and /g/ slip in there, but only after certain vowels?

Some grammatical markers come up constantly, at least in certain contexts, while others are so rare that they require what linguists call elicitation: specific, structured exercises to bring out how a language handles kinship, space, time, deixis, information structure, modality, and other wonderfully nerdy, quietly essential linguistic domains. Some words start as ordinary vocabulary and then become "grammaticalized," like the Seke verb truwa, which originally meant *sit* (or *stay* or *live*) and probably only across generations, in a classic case of semantic extension, also came to express a purely grammatical notion of duration. Here's an example that made Rasmina laugh as soon as she said it, where the subject doesn't literally have to be sitting. It's glossed in typical linguist tiers—just to give you an idea—with SEQ short for sequential and CONT for continuous (terms which of course no normal human being would use):

| | | | | |
|---|---|---|---|---|
| utterance | **the tsaze ke trum** | | | |
| morphemes | the | tsa-ze | ke | tru-m |
| morpheme glosses | 3SG | eat-SEQ | only | sit-CONT |
| free translation | 'he just keeps eating (and eating)' | | | |

Some grammatical features are little known only because they happen not to occur in dominant languages. Take the "evidential" systems seen in many languages of the Caucasus, the Americas, and the Himalaya.[26] Speakers of evidential languages have to be explicit, with the required grammar, about what kind of evidence they have to support what they're saying. It's something English speakers can do optionally with phrases like *maybe*, *probably*, *I think that*, as well as tone of voice. But in Seke, speakers will reliably use the suffix **-do** to flag an inference: theze pindo, *she might be able to give it*. In fact, many Himalayan languages have one marker for inferences, another for things seen firsthand, a third for speaking from hearsay, general knowledge, or general facts, and even a fourth for being noncommittal or secretive, or just having a hunch.[27] It's a wonderful but at this point unanswerable question what this might or might not mean for how speakers of Himalayan languages think about law, justice, and ethical behavior.

Seke syntax poses a different kind of challenge, given speakers' tendency to leave anything out, especially pronouns and direct objects, that might already be known to or assumed by the listener. Verbs come at the end of every utterance, except when they don't. Tense is rarely explicitly marked, but what is usually required is what linguists call "aspect"—a description of how the event unfolded over time, including whether it was completed (perfect) or not (imperfect), repeated or not. Adjectives, as in many Tibeto-Burman languages, are not a word class unto themselves, but essentially indistinguishable from verbs. Instead of red, Seke ola is always *is red*, *reds*, or *reddens*.

By class's end, we can just barely transcribe, translate, and analyze all the morphemes in a short, simple narrative from Rasmina, with her constant help. Her own relationship to the language has been changing, too: improving as she speaks more with her mother, badgers her uncle with our questions, and makes a point of using it with the aunties around 380. Newly conscious of the language's complexities, she puzzles over how four different words can seem to mean *very*, in subtly different contexts. We still haven't figured that one out. Afterwards the work moves over to ELA, where we keep at it with a few of the most dedicated students, always learning how much we have left to learn.

## 5

Even after twenty hours flying from New York, it takes almost a week to reach Seke country between paperwork and travel. Rasmina and I are working the tiny crowd in a dusty sort of plaza near the center of Timi while our videographer Nicole sets up. People come to fill their pots at the tap and then stay to chat, and we'll record anyone willing. The village is tiny but vertical and dense, half fortress and half maze. Banks of well-placed boulders serve as seating as free-range roosters strut around. Call it the Seke public sphere, a neutral space to get on your soapbox. It's the first time I've heard Seke spoken outside of Brooklyn.

One by one, half a dozen Timiten hold forth about the village temple, major religious festival, water resource issues, unique architecture, family lineages, and assorted other topics. The presence of a camera inspires appeals to those who have made it out of the village and may be watching in Kathmandu or Brooklyn. Shown in boldface below, loanwords acquired via Nepali (sometimes originating even farther afield, like English or arguably originally French *budget*) are the keywords of complaint, but the rest is all Seke.

"Taa lale **sahar** dri truwara, hase **kunakabja** taa tsam halagam."

*Whatever is done is only for the people who live in the **city**, nothing for people in the **rural areas**.*

"Soshe pinbe mi gi ya hayang, soshe bize **bazat** ra hare."

*There is no one to build or to improve things. Even if we want to build or improve things, we don't have any **budget**.*

"**Shree pach sarkar** yi **bikas** yi **karekram** yinle tsam, da cheda **pachadi** mum."

*As for the royal* ***government****, whether it's* ***development*** *or* ***programs****, we are always being* ***left behind****.*

"Kyu yi dukpa dena mum. Kri ge lawa yin. Shen ngi hami. Da tsung nu, tsung nu harewa yin. Da dhiduk ki, dukpa lawa hase, ra ra yi za jangze lawa hase."

*There are many water problems. We work in the fields. Otherwise we don't have anything. As for business, now we don't have any of that. The work is hard, even with domestic animals and rearing goats.*

"Timiten ra nyapse ke lam."

*Timi people are looked down upon.*

Timi is just a half-hour walk from Tshugsang, but it's not connected to the one main road that runs all the way up Mustang and is just now being fully paved, thanks to Chinese funding, all the way up to the border with Tibet.

Mustang is justly known for preserving Himalayan ways and worlds destroyed or endangered by the Chinese occupation in Tibet. For Tibetans, it's an ancient north-south corridor, a rare place to pass through the mountains and down to the plains of South Asia. The route became a different kind of lifeline after the Chinese invasion, a way station to exile. For decades, thousands escaped this way, coming hundreds of miles on foot and counting on local help before usually continuing on to Kathmandu or the exile capital of Dharamshala, India, though some remained in refugee camps here. At the turn of the millennium, the fourteen-year-old Karmapa Lama, a revered figure in Tibetan Buddhism, made his escape through Mustang, prompting China to tighten the border. Since 2017, the Karmapa has been in the New York area, like so many of his followers, with Woodstock the North American seat of his global movement.[28]

Being off the road, Timi is less developed, preserving more of what life was probably like for Seke speakers twenty or even two hundred years ago. Avowedly Buddhist and at the same time maintaining an annual cult of the yul lha, *local deities*, with twice-annual animal sacrifices, Timiten are above all fiercely and proudly involved in maintaining their village community.[29] Few tourists come here, and not as many Timiten seem to make it as far as Brooklyn, though I later learned that one was working in a sushi restaurant just a few blocks from ELA's office.

"**Kamau** lala mangba yin, **kamau** lazi haruma tara **kamau** lawaza, rang yi yul ri phayul biwa dri, kipa phayul keza yi yul biwaza dri **sahayog** lala mangbin."

[*Those who went abroad*] *should make their* ***earnings****, but after* ***earning*** *and* ***earning***—[*remember*] *that* **aid** *is needed in your own village, your own dear homeland, your birthplace!*

"Seke biwaza **maslap** pinba hatawin, tongla pinba hatawin, seke lopla mangbin."

*Seke should not be* ***abandoned****, do not let Seke die, Seke has to be learned.*

"Da seke harazi bili, napse 'Gya taa gyupa? Gya taa kharize khawa? Gyi ha hama khari? Gyi khe mom khari? Gya taa?' bize sheshe harewin."

*If you don't know Seke, then later when you're asked, 'What lineage are you from? Where do you come from? And your parents? Your grandparents?' you won't know what to say.*

Rasmina and I get most of it, but all kinds of things are new. In certain parts of certain words (but why not all?), we hear *a* instead of Tshugsang's *i*: khari instead of khiri, lala instead of lali. We hear an initial *h* where a Tshugsang speaker wouldn't have it: hale instead of ale.

Afterwards, one of the speakers by the tap takes us up into the older part of Timi, a densely packed labyrinth of high earthen walls shared among thirty-odd houses, accreted over centuries but now largely abandoned and in various stages of collapse. Accessed by a so-called sanggo, *secret door*, the main "street" is an extremely narrow alley, permanently and perhaps purposely in the eternal shadow of the crumbling buildings that line it. Even the zone where people still live, the yul, feels at once ancient and futuristically communal, as opaque to outsiders as Manhattan's numbered grid is meant to be transparent. Stopping in a house for butter tea, we climb almost straight up on a notched log ladder past livestock on the ground floor, latrines on the next one, then third-floor living quarters bathed in almost total darkness in the middle of the day, and finally a roof of stacked firewood garlanded by drying churpi, yak cheese strung up in marshmallow-like cubes. Cliffs and caves, including the one that housed a makeshift tavern for CIA-backed Tibetan guerrillas in the sixties, are all around us. The crumbling beige citadel feels like a single form. This high desert blooms with terraced fields of poplars, willows, and fruit trees thanks to an ingenious irrigation system of networked gullies and tunnels. Narshing Khola, a gravel-bedded tributary of the Kali Gandaki, twists through the territory. At a spot just out of sight, its waters can cure any gastric ailment.

In yul, you can at least sense how Seke survived. When Rasmina first used the word, I thought it just meant *village*. Besides yul lha, there was phayul, a broader Tibetan word for *fatherland*, and shöyul, a collective term for the five Seke-speaking villages that literally means *low-lying territory*, despite all of it being over ten thousand feet. Beyul are the hidden lands thought to exist in remote pockets of the Himalaya which only tertöns, discoverers of spiritual treasures, can reveal in mystic guidebooks, and which may have gaven rise to the much-muddled myth of Shangri-la. By itself, yul can mean *village*, *valley*, *settlement*, *nation*, *home*, *territory*, *zone*, or simply one's *native land*, because scale plays no part in it. What matters is the sense of place and the connection to it.

Where does Seke come from? When people ask where a language comes from and how old it is, as though it were a person with a birth certificate, it often means that political, historical, and ethnic territorial claims are at stake. The word *language* is usually shorthand for shared linguistic norms and practices that are always more varied, dynamic, and tangled than we can imagine, with deep roots in ancient language families and contact situations, themselves abstractions we can only theorize about and trace so far back. The way people name and conceive of languages changes too. Only in rare cases can the birth of a language be dated to any definitive past event and then it almost always takes a few generations. Whatever people were speaking earlier may endure at least as a substrate, whose traces linguistic archaeology can sometimes reveal. More typical for language is a gradual evolution, though perhaps rapid compared to biological evolution, which is usually only dimly perceptible to the speakers themselves, let alone outsiders.

Only in the rare cases where there is a written record can these developments be mapped with any certainty. Old English becomes Middle English and ultimately Modern English, according to a later periodization that serves both to explain the changes and to insist on a continuity. In practice, continuity starts to break down at a certain point. Middle-English-speaking editors start helpfully glossing in the margins of Old English manuscripts. Modern English speakers start footnoting Chaucer and full-on translating Beowulf. When will Postmodern English begin?

Seke speakers may not have even used the name Seke until recently. Today the Seke word for *language* is ke, which can also mean *word*, *speech*, *noise*, as in Tibetan, and Se seems to have been a Tibetan term for an ancient kingdom whose spatial and temporal coordinates can only be guessed at. First mentioned in the earliest Tibetan writings from over a thousand years ago, Se (or Se-rib) was probably located in the general vicinity of today's Seke-speaking villages but extended much further, coming at various times under the control of more powerful neighbors in Mustang and Tibet. Judging from place-names and ritual language, at least a few other villages in the area once spoke Seke but have shifted to Loke in just the last century or so, not to mention abandoned Seke-speaking settlements.[30] Today Seke speakers are about as likely to have heard of the Kingdom of Se as English speakers are of the Kingdom of Wessex (or the Angles, for that matter), but at least some trace their roots to another lost kingdom from a millennium back, called Zhangzhung and located in what is now western Tibet.[31] On the subject of ancient kingdoms, many speakers also find it irresistible to link Se to ser, a borrowed word via Baragaon/Loke or Tibetan (and ultimately from Persian) meaning *gold*, making Seke *the golden language*.

Panning out, Seke is one of over a thousand languages spoken across high-mountain Asia, one of the most linguistically diverse regions in the world. From northern Pakistan to northern Vietnam, speakers from several completely different language families coexist, often at different elevations on the same mountain and pursuing very different but sometimes complementary livelihoods. Speakers of Tai-Kadai languages with their rice paddies might reside in the valley while speakers of Austroasiatic languages live halfway up and practice swiddening with a different mix of crops. Speakers of Tibeto-Burman languages like Seke (or Trung) have traditionally lived highest of all, planting millet and buckwheat while raising goats, sheep, and sometimes yaks.

Topography is critical to the region's diversity, but so are history and politics. Today ten Asian nations, anchored in the lowlands and mostly meeting the world at colonial seaports, back up onto this fractured, extraordinary region roughly the size of Europe and sometimes described as Zomia, the last and largest "nonstate space" remaining in the world. At least such was the case until recently, for the lowland capitals have been tightening their grip on the highlands. Now rapid development and climate change are driving outmigration, secession movements, civil wars, and Indigenous rights struggles.[32]

Precisely where and how the Tibeto-Burman language family itself originated thousands of years ago is a topic of heated, arcane debate for linguists, but at least there is some agreement about its subfamilies. In the highest, coldest zones on and around the Tibetan Plateau live speakers of Tibetic languages, which includes all major forms of Tibetan as well as Loke, Baragaon, and several dozen other languages, almost all of which now have speakers in New York.[33] These are the people whose DNA adapted within just a few hundred generations, in the fastest known case of genetic evolution, to breathe thinner, high-altitude air.

The next closest Tibeto-Burman subfamily, a little lower down in the middle hills of central Nepal, is known as Tamangic, and almost all Tamangic languages are also represented in New York, including Tamang, Thakali, Chantyal, Gurung, and Seke. None was traditionally written, nor were any properly documented or recognized by outsiders until the past few decades.[34] Mountains and rivers form formidable barriers between these languages, but in theory they all once had a common ancestor (Proto-Tamangic, linguists call it) or perhaps even formed a dialect continuum, with speechways changing gradually from village to village rather than residing in discrete blocs of linguistic territory, much like the old West Germanic and Scandinavian dialect continua that used to cover much of northern Europe.

In historical linguistics terms, Seke sits wedged between the Tamangic and Tibetic worlds. So it makes sense that Seke speakers are masters of betweenness in other ways too. Tsengu, the two-part Seke New Year, falls in December/January right between the Tamang, Gurung, and other Tamangic New Years on the one hand, and Losar (Tibetan New Year) on the other—though it's just the latter that many people now celebrate, says Rasmina. Likewise, caste is partially honored here, in a nod to the subcontinent, and partially not, in a nod to the Tibetan Plateau. Just south, Thakali people maintain more caste distinctions, if only a fraction of those used among the Newars of the Kathmandu Valley, let alone by Hindus in India. In fact, Seke has just a few words related to caste, and these don't apply to other Seke speakers, which is not to say that certain prejudices aren't in effect.[35]

Seke's position at the edge of two worlds comes out most clearly in the language itself. Tibetan is the ultimate source for a whole host of Seke words related to religion, educaiton, and older kinds of specialist knowledge, including amchi *doctor*, chu *book*, loppa *study*, and tsamling *world*, as opposed to Nepali loanwords for more recently imported concepts like bikas *development*, ganta *hour*, safal *successful*, khyal *joke*. Traditional songs seem to be in Tibetan, which may have functioned as a "singua franca" (a shared language specifically for singing) across the region. Much of the number system has been Tibetanized, but the words for *seven* and *hundred* are two notable Tamangic holdouts. First names are traditionally given by a lama from a small set of mostly gender-neutral Tibetan names, with several of the most popular reflecting the day of the week one was born on: Nyima *Sunday*, Dawa *Monday*, Lhakpa *Wednesday*. Less formally, parents now also give Nepali names, like Rasmina.

As in much of the world, last names were unknown until recently, a technique of control introduced by governments before ID cards and biometric passports. Seke speakers in their fifties and sixties, like those we meet in Timi, still remember when Nepal's government directed everyone to take last names en masse based on their ethnic group. That's why many Tamang speakers now have the last name Tamang and most Sherpas have the last name Sherpa. The smaller groups got swept into the bigger ones, so most Seke, Loke, and Baragaon speakers have the last name Gurung, to their own mild amusement and to the mild consternation of the "real" ethnic Gurungs (who also got the surname Gurung).

# 6

Days of no internet, little signal, intermittent power, juniper incense, fields of flowering purple buckwheat under a steady sun. A glaze of golden dust settles over everything. Everyone we meet is tor yawa, *coming up*, or mar yuwa, *going down*—words that represent the constant circulation of Seke speakers, who have made small communities at each main place on the way, with New York now the furthest known endpoint. To come here is also to understand a small but integral part of the city. We pass temples, schools, and bridges funded by villagers now driving Ubers and delivering for Postmates.

Towering from a holy hillside is an enormous stone Buddha in a bright web of strung-up prayer flags, all gifted by a restaurant owner in Queens. Yankees hats pair frequently with traditional garb. A framed diploma from CUNY hangs next to the requisite portrait of Mustang's king and queen. Five of my eight children are in New York, says a mother over tea. Half-empty, expanding houses here are the eerie inverse of packed 380.

Rasmina makes arrangements, and we try to keep up. She hasn't been here in years, but everyone knows her, or knows of her. Trust enables everything. We meet and greet and eat with countless relatives, strategizing about who to talk to, what to ask about, where to go. Again and again we explain ourselves, ask permission, describe what YouTube is and what archives are, and take down basic metadata: all the information about the speaker and the session which is key for putting any recording in context.

With the small grant we came on, we give modest gifts of money or goods for the time that speakers spend working with us. We gradually get better at the art of chatting while setting up to ensure the best background, the best light, the most comfortable seating, white balance, room tone, sound check. Hopefully things become natural, though it's still a far cry from a real unfiltered conversation over dinner. Some speakers need little encouragement, while others require continual prompting and gentle guidance not to drop into Nepali or Baragaon. My Seke is getting better, good enough to do basic interviews with, or at least to perform for polite astonishment and then only half understand the compliments that follow.

One morning in Tshugsang, we start at Jamyang's. He was the one I first interviewed three years earlier on a sweltering New York summer day in Bara Bara, where he sat cross-legged on the floor of the combined living room/shrine room looking nervous and haggard, a lav mic pinned to the embroidered collar of his best traditional shirt. The deafening AC was off for better sound. The final cut showed him only above the knees, out of respect.

Jamyang left his family behind and arrived solo in New York on his own in 2000, a man in his mid-thirties ready to work, but he soon landed in Coney Island Hospital with serious back injuries from construction. Later he moved to Boston to work as a dishwasher, but then couldn't bend over and started getting rashes. Returning to New York, he worked for eighteen months at a Thai restaurant, making $320 a week grilling meats and only getting a small raise after more than a year of pushing for it. He quit that for a Chinese restaurant, which paid about the same at first, but at least they gave raises, until they didn't. His back got a little better, to the point where he could sit for an hour or two without much pain, so he went back to construction work as a day laborer. So it went for seventeen years, nothing personal to speak of, sending everything back besides the bare minimum he needed to live on. Even more than work and pain, Jamyang seemed dazed by a creeping sense of loss: "My son doesn't speak Seke. Now even I can't speak Seke fluently—I have all the dialects mixed up. After ten years, or after my own generation, our language will vanish." How he said it proved the point: only a few words in Seke, the rest in a halting mix of Nepali, Baragaon, and Tibetan.[36]

Now years later, in a setting radically different from Bara Bara, he looks years younger. He sits in everyday Western clothes, finishing breakfast, and at first I don't even recognize him. He went home, as many immigrants always intend to, especially those who set out as adults and still have land and family back in the village. Some never get their green card, others are deeply disappointed in American life, and still others just want to grow old in the village house that their struggles have built. It was sudden in Jamyang's case: the father he hadn't seen in nearly two decades was ill, so he flew right back. They had a little time together before the ICU. After the funeral, Jamyang just didn't go back to New York.

Even in the Bara Bara vertical village rooming with other Mustangis, life had been lonely and depressing: "Mar dri taa yinli paisa tsam meupa ni tsam. *Whatever it is, down there it's all about money*. Da sem mar dri kikpo hamang. *The heart can't be satisfied down there*."

Now he tell us that back here in the actual village it's the other way around, with satisfaction but little livelihood: "Hoti aali hakhawaze New York lema ne din ko din ge haruwa. *Money doesn't come like in New York. There is no day-to-day work*." Changes in the village take getting used to: the road, the cars, the way people use New York remittances to hire rongpa, *lowlanders*, to work their fields. The river is washing away the land, adds Jamyang, and one day the village itself is likely to get swept away. Climate change and glacier melt on the Tibetan Plateau are starting to have serious downstream effects here, with less snow in winter and swollen rivers in summer. Jamyang has a small piece of land where he grows apples, with one dzo, a *yak-cow hybrid*, to plow it. He fears the new machines are damaging the land. People aren't leading simple lives anymore, he says, and their characters are changing.

Just shy of fifty-five, he looks forward to his tharchang, a *retirement ceremony* and major life-cycle event that many in Mustang hold around the age of sixty, which is supposed to mean release from shared labor responsibilities in the village. He's in better health since returning: "Mar dri ti sha tsowa muwa kere ni dosong ni sha, kreli hakhamba tsam tam. *Down over there I'd gotten a bit fat. I felt like I couldn't climb any more*. Khawanada ti brali ti sha sha lawa. *When I first came back, if I walked a little, I would start panting*. Dosong taa nga drang dri yarli, khambim. *Now even if I go into the forest, I can do it*."

His Seke is also coming back, though Jamyang is no more optimistic than before about the fate of the language. When he was in school, through fifth grade in the village, everyone had to speak Nepali or else be fined a penny per lapse. Soon he dropped out and started going with his father to Butwal near the Indian border for the sweater trade, the annual wholesale buying and retail reselling of winter clothing. Like many in the village, he is still seasonally mobile, *going down* (mar yuwa) to spend the coldest time of year in the lower-altitude cities of Pokhara or Kathmandu.

"Seke mali taa tashe? *And so what if Seke disappears?*" asks Rasmina. Jamyang is matter-of-fact: "Da Seke mali taa dangba Seke hutsu shepin biwu mi gi ni khado. *If Seke disappears, maybe one or two people will come and say, Before, people spoke a language called Seke*."

After a few hours with Jamyang, we visit a woman who makes dhido, a *buckwheat mash* that is traditional across the region. Another day we interview a group of men gathering for a traditional miso (*archery*) competition, until Rasmina starts arguing that women should be allowed to participate. We record Karma, perhaps the only remaining Seke-speaking ritual practitioner, and the one they always call from Brooklyn for cases of poor health, bad luck, scary dreams, or misplaced valuables. Often the ritual has to be done at the family home in the village for things to get better in Brooklyn. Karma may have stayed in Mustang as a fifth-generation lama, but his sons migrated out. We record him for an hour. He passes away the following year.

We record a woman in her fields describing everything she grows, and a man in his pens on how he cares for his animals. We walk to Gyugu to record a wasted, wild-eyed singer chanting haunting songs about mothers and daughters in archaic-sounding Tibetan; we walk to Tsangle to record a storyteller who knows all about demons, place-names, and the bizarre foundation stories, shifting fortunes, and land claims of the different villages. We can only publish these with disclaimers, Rasmina says, because no topic could be more contentious, even with so many people now in New York, even if we say we're just recording the language.

We interview the one Seke-speaking teacher, who explains that only ten of the ninety-five students in the local school are from Seke families, so having classes in the language here wouldn't even make sense—better to do it in Brooklyn. One afternoon in her orchard, Rasmina's eighty-two-year-old grandmother receives us in her rock-star shades and resplendent kon thowa, *a kind of traditional robe*, patiently answering our questions. Her husband was the one here who started cultivating apples, she tells us, which are now the major cash crop for the entire region. She became the head of the village after he died. She stays here now even if, or perhaps because, everyone else is leaving. She waits for their return visits, and she weeps every time people leave: "Themi khali nga semza ningsang yam. *When they come, my heart is at peace.*"

These kinds of meetings can only happen here. Certain things can happen in 380, but these villages are the language's original and fundamental home, and no record of the language would be complete without this fieldwork. It's not just the elders who try to return at least part of the year, but the homes and temples, plants and animals, particular landscapes and specific sites—all the things that can only be spoken about, with ultimate rigor, in Seke. We ask about architecture, agriculture, animal husbandry, medical practices, religious ritual, life-cycle events, the natural environment, local history, and life histories. We jot down nyelam, *pithy maxims and exhortations*:

"Mi shili min hashiwin. A *person may die, but their reputation doesn't die.*"

"Ja shili phu hashiwin. *A bird may die, but the feather doesn't die.*"

"Phayul pangli, rang ke pangba hatawa. *You may leave your homeland, but you can't stop speaking your own language.*"

Sometimes the right questions bring special terminology tumbling out: tell us about gyawa, *the forty-nine-day bardo period and mourning cycle*. As in Hindi and some other languages, your na, *nose*, is also your character, inherited from family and disgraced when someone "cuts" it. The edited, archived Seke corpus will eventually grow up to forty hours long, will have to encompass as much of the speakers' knowledge, wisdom, and experience as possible. Years can be spent working on a corpus of this size, and properly transcribing even a single minute, not to mention translating and analyzing it, can take up to an hour.[37] Nor is it a trivial matter to make it all accessible whether in the form of a dictionary, subtitled recording, article, book, or other format. We hope to return, but we work with the knowledge that this may be our only chance: speakers pass away, borders close, funding dries up, everything changes. Nor is it likely that another linguist will make it here, given all the stars that have to align. Most languages are documented once, if at all.

So there is a desperate edge to all our asking. We have thousands of questions about the language itself, and they are continually multiplying: the connotations of a certain word, the different uses of a morpheme, the differences between dialects, allowable variation in word order. Some parts of the grammar, though completely unconscious and natural for speakers, are particularly nuanced, fearsomely complex, difficult to pin down.

Like the **ze** which sometimes comes after nouns and is totally different from the sequential **-ze** mentioned earlier which attaches to verbs. As in the following sentence: Ijo **ze** tsu umbaa lhazi. *The father threw the rock.*

"Oh, that's for emphasis," says Rasmina.

"So you can leave it out?"

"Sure," she replies, a little doubtfully.

Speakers chatting casually in the village do just that, but when we ask them directly they put **ze** right back in. This is what linguists call "careful speech," the kind of style one uses, for example, with a linguist.

At the same time, there are times where you definitely *can't* include it: *Ijo ze bitishe lam. *The father is about to fall.* The asterisk means the sentence is ungrammatical, or just plain wrong to any Seke speaker: you have to get rid of the **ze**.

We may think of subjects and objects as fundamental because they are in English, but other languages have different strategies for marking or organizing the various participants ("arguments" in linguistics) grouped around any given verb. For example, agents (the subjects of transitive verbs) may be marked differently from subjects of intransitive verbs. A significant minority of languages, many of them in the Himalaya, carefully track on how much agency anyone mentioned has in what they're doing. So the father throwing the rock has agency while the father about to fall doesn't, which is why the former gets a **ze** and the latter doesn't.

Does this mean that speakers of Seke and other so-called ergative languages are more exquisitely attuned to questions of agency, more broadly?[38] Most linguists would resist the question, but it's undeniable that speaking Seke well means rigorously, albeit unconsciously, marking agency in real time. What's more, ergative **ze** can also mark an instrument or some other "inanimate" cause of an action that is not a person, plant, animal, or spirit. This might seem like a reasonable case of semantic extension—the ergative, instrumental, and causal all clearly have to do with agency—but which came first, assuming these uses are distinct? In the following examples, both ja *tea* (the cause) and goza *knife* (the instrument) get the **ze**, in addition to being put at the start of the sentence for extra emphasis:

"Ja **ze** nga dri nukam. *Because of the tea, I am sleepy.*"

"Goza **ze** ra dri khira pungbin. *One goes hunting for goats with a knife.*"

Seke specializes in other nuances of emphasis, contrast, and focus, often through word order, little "discourse particles," or what linguists call information structure, which is the way we pack meaning into the split-second space of a phrase or an utterance, foregrounding and backgrounding, and signaling our opinion or state of mind with just the slightest variation.

On the day we leave Mustang, we have more questions than ever, just no time to ask them. Rasmina's aunt does the farewell, with prayers for long life in Tibetan and words of good wishes in Seke, pouring clear liquor into little cups, thumbing butter into our hair, and packing us off with dried zimbu, *a kind of wild onion*, and gifts for those in Brooklyn. She crowns our necks with khata. We tie them for luck to a bridge at the edge of the village, as people do when they leave. Dozens are always snapping there in the wind.

## 7

Everyone is dancing by the end. Empty Stellas bob around buckets of melted ice. Groups of dudes in leather jackets and girls in short skirts are going wild, holding their phones high for Instagram. When the three Kathmandu-style rockers on stage are done shattering our eardrums, the DJ starts blasting songs in Hindi, Nepali, Tibetan, and English even louder. The hip young Queens Himalayans aren't just singing along; they're wholeheartedly belting out Bollywood, Rihanna, Nepali pop. The bartenders and barbacks, all trim, goateed, and ponytailed, are just as into it but keep the drinks moving. An owner works the scene, same look but older, shaking hands and opening bottles.

"There's so much demand," says Nawang, who once considered opening a bar like this. Then it was going to be a nail salon. Then a brow bar, since you can do that in a smaller space. For a while he was talking about popularizing tsampa-based protein shakes with a friend working at Juice Generation, making roasted barley flour seem more like cookie dough for the inji palate. For years he had been saving everything he could from work as a server at a chic Indian restaurant in Tribeca, and now he is about to place his two big bets on a daycare in Queens run by his wife and a restaurant upstate.

I had never heard of Seke until Nawang first casually mentioned it, after we had worked together on other Himalayan languages for several years. "Rasmina is my nyetsang," he added. That meant we could trust her.

Nyetsang doesn't really translate, as Rasmina says, because it's a whole conception, a traditional relationship rooted in Mustang's migratory rhythms of tor yawa and mar yuwa. "There were no hotels back in the day, no restaurants, no lodges. It was like, if I come to your village, I'll stay in your house. If you decide to come to my area, you'll be staying at my place," she says. "It was a mutual understanding and respect, like sworn lifelong friendship where you don't give any money or goods."

The tie applied to and was passed down through entire families; it also had real commercial significance, entailing obligations to provide hay and fodder for the livestock of any nyetsang passing through.[39] Though now the coming of roads, cars, and hotels to Mustang ("straight travel" in Rasmina's words) has obviated the original logic, people still have nyetsang in New York. Because Nawang's family and Rasmina's family are nyetsang, a fundamental mutual bond still applies here, even if its origins are now half-forgotten.

Such bonds of trust underlie everything around us. This bar has six owners, explains Nawang, including two from Mustang and four from elsewhere in the Himalaya. They got a favorable lease because of the pandemic, so they'll make back their money quick. Never mind that it's on a deserted stretch of Roosevelt Avenue under the 7 train—it's billed as a bhatti, *a Nepali-style speakeasy* where people down high-proof raksi and munch on water buffalo snacks. It's named for Thamel, the old hippie/backpacker quarter of Kathmandu where raucous little bars abound, fusing Nepal and the West. From above the bar roars the massive mask of a fearsome god, a lhaba. It just opened, but it's already reservation only, packed every night of the week with Himalayan twentysomethings, Rasmina's generation. By day these revelers may be studying at LaGuardia Community College or slinging salads at Sweetgreen, but at night they have a place to party, a self-confident spot with its own scenesters and influencers.

There's never been anything like it in New York, but it also looks like any other bar, with backlit bottles of premium booze, Edison bulbs hanging from the ceiling, silent sports on TV, barstools around barrels.[40] The snacks range from Wai Wai to guac. The drinks name-check Nepal, but what's in them is more reminiscent of New York cocktail programs. It's not clear if there's off-menu tongba, *a fermented millet drink*, or secret jhaikatte, the *moonshine hot toddy* (alcohol made from puffed rice floating under a thin film of ghee) that a restaurant in Jackson Heights keeps quietly in the back. There is a proper-looking security team, all South Asian but for a balding, Irish American guy with a cross around his neck who seems completely at home. He moves chairs as people mingle, brandishes a helpful flashlight under tables, sings along to all the Bollywood hits, and hugs all the regulars.

The language all around us is known half-jokingly as ར་མ་ལུག་ Ramaluk, an ever-shifting mix of words from Tibetan, Nepali, Hindi, English, and sometimes even an endangered mother tongue like Seke or Loke. In Tibetan, the term Ramaluk literally means *half goat half sheep*, which is a phrase similar to but perhaps a little more damning than *neither fish nor fowl*. In this case, goats and sheep of the label are variables that can stand in for any language. In Tibetan areas occupied by China, Ramaluk usually means mixing different kinds of Tibetan with the Mandarin words for numbers, days of the week, places, institutions, and other nouns, but also some verbs and adjectives, sometimes even if there are long-standing Tibetan equivalents.[41] In diaspora settings in India, Nepal, and Queens, there are words from

Hindi, Nepali, and English instead of Mandarin. Especially for some members of the second or third generation born outside Tibet, Ramaluk is almost like a "first language", such that uttering a complete sentence in any of the component languages may feel unnatural or even impossible. As with some Indigenous Mexican New Yorkers who feel "caught" between Mixtec, Spanish, and English, Ramaluk speakers may face serious language barriers outside their immediate milieu.[42]

Many Himalayan elders, intellectuals, and community leaders are anxious that Ramaluk is a leading indicator of cultural loss, a reflection of rapid cultural change that ultimately severs young people from their languages and traditions. It may be fascinating to linguists, but it's not clear that anyone in the community wants Ramaluk to last or be remembered. Instead many are trying to unite around the so-called Standard Tibetan which is based on the speech of central Tibet but is inevitably developing differently in diaspora. In fact, "Tibetan" is a complex conception in the midst of an epochal reinvention—the name a convenient shorthand for that cluster of distinct languages that linguists call Tibetic, including Baragaon/Loke from Mustang (but not Seke). As with Arabic and Chinese, unity is emphasized for political and religious reasons. There may be literacy through a single writing system, but the ways people actually speak are extraordinarily diverse—and now virtually all of the varieties are in contact in Queens, no longer separated by mountain ranges and hundreds of miles but by a block or two.[43]

Nawang knows about goats and sheep, because he grew up herding them in Upper Mustang. Now he works the room, whether here at Thamel or the Dunkin Donuts on Roosevelt Avenue, like he's the mayor of Jackson Heights. He counts Loke as his mother tongue but routinely interprets in Nepali and Tibetan; gets by fine in Hindu, Urdu, and sometimes Bengali; can do anything he needs in his marvelous Kathmandu-style English; and even admits to a little Ramaluk.

As the eldest of nine children, only four of whom lived past childhood, Nawang was technically in line to succeed his father as a village leader and practitioner of Bön, the pre-Buddhist Tibetan religious tradition. Instead he finds himself doing a very different kind of cultural and community work thousands of miles away.

It was Nawang who first conceived Voices of the Himalaya, a project based at ELA that aimed to document the mass migration of the last few decades, of which he himself is a part. Tens of thousands of Himalayans have come to New York from Tibet, Nepal, India, and Bhutan, including everyone from rock stars to rinpoches, but mostly ordinary people fleeing marginalization and seeking new horizons—such that even tiny communities like the Seke villages have been swept up in it.[44]

For many, the Chinese invasion of Tibet beginning in the 1950s and subsequent repressions set in motion ongoing intergenerational displacements, leading first to Nepal and India and now New York. For others, Nepal's civil war from 1996 to 2006, Bhutan's expulsion of Lhotsampa people, and the unfolding impacts of climate change in the mountains have been catalysts. People come as students, tourists, monks, asylum seekers, and increasingly now as spouses and relatives, sometimes distant, fictitious, and paid for members. Until recently, most New Yorkers, including city officials, didn't even realize there was a Himalayan community, mistaking its members for South Asian, East Asian, or even Latin American, if they saw them at all. Yet New York is now the most important Himalayan hub outside South Asia, an emergent center in a growing global diaspora.

The whole idea of a Tibetan or Himalayan diaspora is new, and from the Dalai Lama on down there is considerable anxiety about how to survive as a people with unique religious, cultural, and linguistic traditions during what could be centuries of Chinese control of the homeland. Nawang is not only living this history, but intent on documenting and understanding it. For Voices of the Himalaya, we crisscrossed

Queens together over two years, recording and translating twenty-five video interviews in a dozen different languages, which have now been viewed hundreds of thousands of times.[45]

We met people like the Sherpa climber "Mr. Speed," who set the record for the fastest Everest ascent but now works at a Whole Foods in Manhattan. "Sherpa" may be synonymous with mountaineering, but is actually a Himalayan group from Nepal with its own language and culture. Their area includes what they call Chomolungma, known in English as *Mount Everest*, but there are probably more Sherpas now living in New York than in their home region. We recorded a Bhutanese singer and comedian who won his country's answer to *American Idol*, manages a Bhutanese bodega in Sunnyside and can mimic the sound of a zipper like no one else.

What made the series meaningful for its primary audience, the Himalayan diaspora itself, were the "ordinary" struggles of immigration, narrated with dignity in languages rarely heard outside of people's homes. Cooks and construction workers doing fourteen-hour days meticulously swapped their New York street clothes for their best traditional attire and dug deep into their memories to speak their mother tongues. A woman in her eighties explained her total isolation after immigrating, waiting all day at the window for her family to come home from work. A Queens-born Tibetan American radiated pride at making it to a top American college, while also remaining fluent in Tibetan.

As a follow-up, we tracked down sixteen Himalayan singers living in the city who are collectively keeping alive a tremendous range of vocal traditions in six different languages—from a Tibetan drokpa, or *nomad*, singer praising his horto, *a traditional slingshot*, to the self-proclaimed first Tibetan rapper in the world, who escaped Tibet via Everest, going forty days on foot to Kathmandu before ultimately making it to New York, where he now restores rugs for Iranian and Pakistani bosses. His rap is so radical, he claims, that only the New York branch of the militant Tibetan resistance group Chushi Gangdruk dares invite him to perform at their events.[46]

Some of the darker undercurrents inevitably remained off camera or had to be edited out. Suicide, domestic violence, caste discrimination, and mental illness are taboo subjects. Rumors of a Sherpa gang in Queens, though just another instance of the city's endless ethnic rivalries and formations, were mentioned only in a whisper. Likewise the shocking attempted murder of a Sherpa cabbie by the Chantyal cabbie with whom he had been leasing a medallion, allegedly with a traditional kukri dagger, which ended with the latter jumping to his death off the Triborough Bridge.[47]

Laboring in homes, restaurants, hospitals, and nail salons takes a quiet toll, leading some Tibetan speakers to pun off the similar sounds of "New York" (in Tibetan) and mi gyog, *slavery* or *servitude*, as in the Queens filmmaker Lhaksam's *New York ma red, mi gyog red* (*It's Not New York, It's Slavery*), or the sarcastic nickname mi gyog grong khyer, *the city of people's servants.* Some are stuck in poverty while others grow rich, like the man rumored to run one hundred hot dog carts plus one with momos. Rampant materialism is an increasing concern, reportedly leading the Sherpa community to ban ostentatious birthday celebrations, though hardly anyone had celebrated birthdays at all before coming to the US. In 2020, a Tibetan NYPD officer and former "cop of the month" was charged by federal prosecutors with spying for the Chinese government, at once shocking the community and confirming the belief that spies are everywhere.[48]

Holding all these communities together are the kyidug—a Tibetan word which literally means *joy-sorrow* but by extension *welfare* and by further extension *an organization of people from the same home area*, typically with the same language, who are there for each other during the joys and sorrows of life. Sometimes called hometown associations in English, they go by different names in different languages: club (de oriundo) in Spanish, società in Italian, *Σύλλογος* syllogos in Greek, לאַנדסמאַנשאַפֿט landsmanshaft in Yiddish, hemşerilik in Ladino and Turkish, 同鄉會 tóngxiānghuì in Chinese, समाज samaj in South Asian languages. Not every group creates them, but again and again they emerge out of solidarity and necessity as peoples migrate.

The unit of organization may vary, from hometown to region to province or even the entire ethnolinguistic group, which can be more or less coextensive with any of these. Italians may gather by town (Società Figli di Castello del Matese, *Society of the Sons of Castello del Matese*) while Nigerians stick to the state (Akwa-Ibom Association of New York), and Aegean Greeks go by the island (Pan-Lesvian Society). Hometown associations may have their own choruses, soccer teams, youth groups, beauty pageants, women's auxiliaries, and houses of worship. All sorts of related offshoots can flourish if there's a critical mass, like the Trinidad-Tobago Ex-Police Association in its house down a side street in Crown Heights, or the American Fuzhou Langqi Alumni Association behind a Chinatown storefront, for those who once attended certain schools on an island in a city eight thousand miles away.

There are probably thousands of hometown associations just in New York, forming the largely invisible bedrock of the immigrant city, based on mutual aid and translocal ties. Historically, many hometown associations have lasted only as long as the immigrant generation itself but they are essential spaces where mother tongues can hang on for a time. Many are officially registered as nonprofits but have no fixed address, besides listing someone's apartment for official purposes. Few leave any traces online, at least in English. Unaware of their existence, outsiders would in any case find even their names inscrutable, referencing distant geographies in insider terms. They operate in the shadows of the larger, more externally facing ethnic, national, or religious organizations, which tend to be established later in the scramble for resources and representation.[49]

Like Thamel, the dozens of kyidug in Himalayan Queens are a sign of something new, not just a level of population and prosperity but a phase where almost every group from the region has a critical mass here. A single run-down building on a side street in Jackson Heights—at first glance a print shop with a working astrologer, a store for religious goods and groceries, and a whole series of other "multiservice" offerings all in one—is also home to four of these organizations. Each represents a tiny endangered language group from Nepal and rents a room in this unlikely labyrinth. For big events and Losar celebrations, such kyidug often rent out ostentatious banquet halls, with members and allies purchasing tickets, creating an almost obligatory circuit for the community minded. Kids may tag along, but will the Queens-born generation, between the drive to assimilate and the centrifugal pressures of housing prices, keep it all going?

The wealthier kyidug are now trying to find permanent homes in Queens to preserve their languages, cultures, and identities while it's still possible. The Mustang Kyidug, which represents Baragaon speakers, bought a house in Richmond Hill, where some people are moving. Not to be outdone, the Lo Nyamship Association, representing Loke speakers, bought a Woodside auto body shop from its Pakistani owners for nearly $4 million (plus renovations), raised through both a one-time levy and ongoing monthly contributions from everyone in the community, where the pressure to contribute can be intense. Close by is the Tibetan Community Hall, which cost even more to buy, not to mention renovate, but is already becoming an essential hub for education, events, and services, and even a kind of embassy for local Green Book citizens of the Tibetan government-in-exile. The hope is to make these new centers self-sustaining between private events, after-school programs, and more, but the all-volunteer legwork involved is daunting.

The Sherpa Kyidug raised money from its members to purchase a former church on the border of Jackson Heights and Elmhurst, beautifully transforming the main hall into a big-city version of a village monastery with murals, prayer flags, thangka paintings, and statues.[50] Though officially a Sherpa-run space, the building quickly became a focal point for the entire Himalayan community, a new kind of religious and community center. People now even do the *ritual circumambulation* called kora around it—up Seventy-Fifth Street, right on Forty-First Avenue, right down Seventy-Sixth, left on Woodside—and so make sacred space in the street grid. The temple is being enlarged, but even then it won't be big enough. Down the street is the lapta, *learning center*, where there are weekend classes in Sherpa language, song, and dance as well as other spaces used by the kyidug. They also just purchased over sixty acres near an important Tibetan Buddhist temple upstate, apparently envisioning a whole Sherpa world in miniature that would be impossible within the confines of the city.[51]

For the much smaller Seke speakers' kyidug, with its WhatsApp group and periodic meetings in the basements of Pakistani restaurants on Coney Island Avenue, the goal is the same, but options are more limited. The older men used to run the kyidug in Seke, but the younger generation is taking over in Nepali. Getting time off on the same days is hard, but almost everyone comes to a three-day gathering around New Year's (usually in a rented room in Queens) and the Fourth of July picnic in Prospect Park.

Everyone contributes money and food. A few dedicated souls make it to the park at dawn, holding down a prime spot on the shady edge of Nethermead. They bring a dozen giant blue tarps, perfectly arranged to form a single seamless surface. Others follow with massive sweating coolers packed with juices, water, and beers at the bottom. By late morning, the whole sixth village is on the scene, at least a hundred people ready to stay until nightfall.

All across the meadow, filtered through clouds of barbecue smoke, I hear laughter and music in languages from all over the world. On the blue tarps I keep listening for Seke, but it's almost all in Nepali. A pitmaster chars ribs with a mischievous grin and loads them into gigantic aluminum-foil trays. We tuck into plates of jelly noodles and okra with spicy dabs of martsa, *a chili paste* as fiery as it is numbing. Single-sex clusters of six to ten adults sit around playing khiti, flash, marriage, and other card games that combine luck and skill, with little heaps of bills for bids in front of the players. “The more we ‘gamble’ the more donation accumulates,” says Rasmina, explaining the bisting, a pot that grows as each player contributes in each round, and which goes in the end to the kyidug to pay for the event.

The kids run around and explore. I stay mostly with the twenty- and thirtysomethings passing a volleyball around a circle, where whoever strikes it determines the next recipient. The casual rallies gradually turn epic, saved time and again with diving derring-do, though sometimes the ball lands perilously close to the card sharks or the pitmaster. “Nice, nice, nice, nice,” we all keep on saying, as if that one English word will keep the ball in the air.

# Husniya
## *X̌ik (Wakhi)*

### 1

At every stage of her life, Husniya has had to learn and live in a different language.

At home with her family it was Wakhi, an endangered Pamiri language spoken by around forty thousand people in the remote high-mountain region where Tajikistan, Pakistan, Afghanistan, and China converge. What Wakhi people actually call themselves and their language is X̌ik, which sounds a little like a Russian speaker saying the English word *hick*.

Growing up, she had to pick up Shughni, the much larger language that broadly unites Pamiri people, who are native to southeastern Tajikistan and live nestled in a dozen of its high-altitude valleys, each one home to a distinct language variety.

Two of those distinct varieties, Rushani and Bartangi, Husniya gradually came to understand from meeting enough speakers. (Although Wakhi is considered a Pamiri language, it stands very much apart from the others, to the point of mutual unintelligibility.[1])

Through high school, her formal education was all in Tajik, the national language.

Its close cousin Persian was important to grasp for its poetry, religious texts, and aura of high culture—and is now beamed into the country thanks to Iranian TV.[2]

From her neighbors she learned Kyrgyz, a Turkic language which is essential in Murghab, her hometown of several thousand people in the middle of a lunar-looking plateau near the border with Kyrgyzstan: once the highest place in the Soviet Union, now the highest in Tajikistan.

Then there was Russian, which is still everywhere thirty years after the fall of the Soviet Union. It's vital for higher education, white-collar work, or just living in Dushanbe, the capital city of Tajikistan.

Now it's English. After a decade of struggles in New York, Husniya finished a master's in early childhood education, entirely in her ninth language. (Not including the German she studied in college and the Turkish she's grasping via Kyrgyz during visits to her sister in Turkey.)

"But I have an accent in every language I speak, even in Wakhi," she says, blushing a little sadly. Her hair, makeup, and nails are shining. As usual, her style turns heads: big sunglasses, puffy jacket, cool shoes, and a trail of perfume.

"Everyone has an accent in every—" I start, but her look stops me. She doesn't need any high-minded sentiments from linguists. She is resigned to sounding foreign to everyone, even when she communicates perfectly. Monolinguals and even bilinguals don't know how easy they have it.

"You have to learn the languages if you want the opportunities," says Husniya simply. She knows how improbable this all is, and she is determined to enjoy it. We're sitting at ELA, deciding which of our recorded stories to include in a series of children's books, one in each of six Pamiri languages.[3]

"Tuwətk nə tuwətk . . . *There was and there was not* . . ." the story begins. This is the Wakhi version of *Once upon a time*, gently casting doubt on whatever is about to follow. It would be vuδj navuδj in Shughni, vij navij in Rushani, vaj navaj in Bartangi. Nor is this ancient story-starting phrase strictly Pamiri. Hungarians say egyszer volt, hol nem volt, *Once where it was, where it was not*, while in Western Armenian it's gar u chgar, *There was and there was not.*

The sounds may be radically different, but the idea has been calqued with subtle variations into the native words of languages from completely different families, regardless of religious, political, or linguistic borders. It's even the same idea in Basque and Catalan, Maltese and Georgian. It's bir varmış, bir yokmuş in Turkish; yeki bood, yeki nabood in Persian; kân yâ mâ kân in Arabic—and a reasonable guess that the phrase conquered half of Eurasia thanks to those three major, mutually influencing languages of the Islamic world.[4]

Opening formula aside, there is a particular dreamlike vividness to the Wakhi fairy tales we have been documenting. In the story of two lovers sampled below, the daunting-looking draft transcription uses a combination of Latin letters, more or less as used in English, as well as characters from the IPA. Two are vowels: /ə/, which linguists call schwa and which sounds like the unstressed *a* in *about*, and /ɨ/, which is produced in the center of the mouth and sounds a little like how an Alabaman might say the vowel in *good*. The other four are consonants: /ʃ/ (a handy single character for *sh*) and three of those far-back-in-the-mouth sounds with which Wakhi is so richly endowed: /ç/, /ʐ/, and /ʂ/.

> jan toʃxon tavalud wost adzi xɨʃruj, adzi xɨʃruj ki jaw sɨrat ʃɨlak pə diwol dəʃtək. jan jaw tat naniʃ gon tʃil ɨdʒrai dərunət aram dəst jaw kaʈən. jan arangəv tavalid kərk . . . jətəv də tʃil odʒrai dərɨn kʈətkət lekin ara boɣət bustonəv kɨ taʃkil kərk. ara dəstəv jaw didɣətk. jan oxiron jan, ki sol rasidagi wostək jan tʃiz goçt jan "çand niçvəv maʐi" . . . jan tsart qar çə jan tʂit tər kuj ʂar gɨlqɨrbon ʂar tʂit. jan tʂitət jan jaw siwɨ dɨ dona tʃiziʃ danən jaw amroiʃ dan tʂawən. jan çatər goçt tʃiz jan kiʃti çatər goçt.

> *Toshkhon was born so extremely handsome that the reflection of his face would go right into the wall. His parents built forty houses, each one inside another, and put him in there. They built forty rooms, each one inside of another, and around him they made a big garden full of flowers. He was kept inside that place. Later when he grew up, he said, "Get me out of here" . . . One day Gulqurbon saw* [*Toshkhon*] *in her dream, and he saw* [*Gulqurbon*] *in his dream. The next morning, he left where he was and went to the city where Gulqurbon was. Thirty-two friends of his left with him. Together they built a boat.*

Arriving in his would-be lover's city, Toshkhon and his friends just happen to bed down at the house of an older woman who produces a miraculous soup that feeds them all. She also turns out to be Gulqurbon's official hair washer, which gives Toshkhon the opportunity to "drop his picture" into the bowl of water she uses, which leads to a meeting where the two lovers both faint on the spot.

"Some part of the story I've forgotten," the storyteller admits at this point in the recording, and the fragments that come next are more psychoanalytically suggestive than happily-ever-after. Toshkhon misses his parents, so the lovers go back together to see them, arriving to revive them just as they're about to die and, mysteriously restoring Mom and Dad . . . to their twelve-year-old selves. The ending is open ended. This isn't going to work for the book, I can tell from Husniya's face.

Husniya and I have recorded and worked on dozens of stories like "Toshkhon and Gulqurbon," trying to make them make sense—linguistically, logistically (who did what to whom where?), and in English—without losing what makes them so Wakhi. The storytellers rarely comment either on the action or their source. "Tuwətk nə tuwətk" is often the first and final verdict on veracity or anything else. Some stories explain crumbling local Zoroastrian fortresses, the ancient names of villages, or the reasons for certain landscape features in the region. Others are nominally about animals but really about human behavior. Sometimes it seems like anything can happen and then just as quickly be reversed or forgotten. It could also be the limits of our imaginations, the storyteller's rusty memories, or the gradual crumbling of the oral tradition itself.

There is also a distinctly Wakhi way of storytelling, with a trance-like pattern of rhythm and sound revolving around that opening axis of doubt and occasionally self-interrupting to confirm the listeners' comprehension. Wakhi storytellers glory in the telling: Nikbakht with her gold teeth and Soviet medals pinned to her traditional dress; Sultonali in his camo fatigues, swaying with sparkling eyes in the darkest corner of his house; Jumakhon in his dandyish hat, hands rising and falling with every twist of the plot.

So much evaporates as soon as it touches the page, and linguists have a knack for burying even the most riveting action in impenetrable transcriptions and fusty, overly literal translations, in monographs that are later impossible to locate. Besides recording new stories, we've been trying to breathe new life into several flawed, forgotten collections of Wakhi stories made by Soviet linguists starting in the 1930s. This is not always easy going.

"At least there would be a lot of interesting things to illustrate," I say of "Toshkhon and Gulqurbon."

Husniya frowns. "We need a simple story with a good moral."

Her heart is set on creating clear, practical, and beautiful language materials for kids, especially the very first Pamiri Americans, who are just now being born. "This is something very, very new," she says of these kids' existence. How will they see themselves, and what languages will they speak? It's hard enough to balance national, religious, or even broader pan-ethnic or racial identities with being American; it's far from clear how a little-known label like Pamiri or even Wakhi can manage.

One of the Pakistani Wakhi grandmothers we interview sees it as only natural that the new grandson she is trying to raise in Wakhi, in hyperdiverse Bensonhurst, will continue speaking the language:

"trəm amrika adzəng tʃiz ki, kɨ taniʂ tsəj çɨ woriʂ jod tsarən, istemol tsarən. tʃajnizeʂ be çɨ zik, tʃiz tsart, istmol tsart. kum zik be tsəj, raʃjan da zik be ki, tsəj, har xalg çɨ, speniʃ çɨ zik."

*Here in America, everyone speaks their own languages. The Chinese are also using their language, and the Russians their language. Everyone, the Spanish and their language too.*[5]

What if it really were completely natural to keep speaking and passing on your language in America? Husniya is not so hopeful, even about Bensonhurst. Though the community is barely a decade old, most Pamiri New Yorkers, like Husniya, are already living more and more of their lives in English, a language that connects them not only to American society, but to other Ismailis and the wider world. Russian and Tajik may still be crucial for work and for life, at least in Brooklyn, and Shughni is a potent symbol of Pamiri identity, but there seems to be little room for much smaller mother tongues like Wakhi, Rushani, and Bartangi. As with other languages in New York that are doubly or even triply embedded within larger communities, speakers might use them, if at all, only on the phone with a handful of older relatives.

Storybooks for children, very few of which exist in any Pamiri language, will be a step and a symbol, believes Husniya, but also a powerful tool for Pamiri parents. Studying early childhood development, she saw the benefits of something as small but profound as a mother singing a lullaby to her child in a native language. "Do you have lullabies in your language?" she now eagerly asks anyone she meets at ELA.

I'm thinking about how we can find the funding to publish the books, while she makes plans to shuttle copies in her luggage past suspicious border guards on her next visit home. A Pamiri animator living in Dushanbe is doing the illustrations, which Husniya declares will be both traditional and modern, with hip kids in hoodies and toki (*skull-caps*) playing on their phones and kicking soccer balls. When finished, the books will be whimsical and wild, bringing touches of Disney and anime to Wakhi tradition.

As for which stories to choose, the pressure is serious, particularly since Husniya's language work has inadvertently made her a kind of social media star across the plugged-in Pamiri diaspora. People will be sensitive about everything: the dialect, the spelling, the speakers, the morals, the age level. Though she probably could do most of it herself, Husniya will be checking and rechecking everything with speakers of all six languages. None of the Pamiri languages were traditionally written, but in recent years people have started using both Cyrillic- and Latin-based systems, so we decide to have both, with the needed variations for each language, plus English translation. Nothing is straightforward.

"There is no way to make everyone happy," says Husniya calmly, and we keep working.

## 2

Most speakers of unrelated languages work separately at ELA, getting to know each other only in passing unless there are specific points of connection. But there are parallels and affinities between Husniya and Rasmina, two young women from high-mountain Asia striving to make their way in the city while boosting their languages. They admire each other's efforts, hearing similar sounds and seeing similar faces in the videos each is recording. They marvel at the occasional word in common, which usually comes via Persian, Hindi, or Urdu. They bond just as easily over salty tea and a basic understanding of goats and sheep as they do over the latest New York fashions. They follow each other on Instagram.

Today, mountain peoples the world over are coming down to the plains, driven by necessity and desire.[6] In geological and ecological terms, high-mountain Asia can be seen as a single enormous region at the heart of the Eurasian supercontinent, the planet's "third pole" which people are fleeing fast. Three of the world's major language families (Indo-European, Tibeto-Burman, and Turkic) come together at the Pamir Knot, a junction of the Himalaya, Hindu Kush, Karakoram, and several other mountain ranges.[7] Politically speaking, the Great Game between the British and Russian Empires left divisions that deepened during Soviet times, proving at least as consequential for the peoples of this region as the Iron Curtain was during a shorter period in Europe. Pamiris and Himalayans ended up in different linguistic worlds, with English ruling one and Russian the other, which explains why so many Hindi- and English-speaking Himalayans head south to India and then ultimately the US, while most Russian-speaking Pamiris head northwest to Moscow and other Russian cities.

Central Asia was once substantially Buddhist and the Himalaya, for centuries, had a meaningful Muslim presence. But now religious divides echo political and linguistic ones. Like most Central Asians, Pamiris follow Islam, but as Ismailis who acknowledge a supreme religious authority: Aga Khan IV, who is considered the forty-ninth imam and thus a direct descendant of the Prophet Muhammad and his son-in-law Ali.

Like the Dalai Lama, the Aga Khan is a global religious leader who synthesizes tradition and modernity for an ever more diasporized following. He holds British and Portuguese citizenship, skied for Iran in the 1964 Olympics, manages an extensive business and philanthropic empire, and takes a special interest in historic preservation and modern Islamic architecture. Because of Soviet rule, Pamiris for generations had little contact with the commander of their faith, until recently.

Isolation, and a desire for the wider world, defined Husniya's childhood. She grew up on Murghab's Russian army base, a world unto itself where her mother managed the guesthouse for visiting dignitaries.

Her father was a driver who shuttled goods from Kyrgyzstan, essential work since almost all food has to be brought in. “Soviet, right?” she said when she showed me the one black-and-white photo that exists of her as a child, though it looked more like Tsarist-era sepia to me.

Luckily she was too young to remember the end of the Soviet Union and the ensuing civil war. It’s said that Tajik speakers pulled suspected Pamiris off buses and made them pronounce the word hasht, *eight*, a shibboleth because Pamiris speaking Tajik say the word without an initial *h* sound.[8] Thousands were killed, while others hid or fled. The Pamir region was completely cut off from the world, and people were beginning to starve when the Aga Khan intervened.

What Husniya does remember are the sacks of flour that followed, marked USA in blue or else with the stars and stripes. When the crisis passed, the Aga Khan came to the region for a first-ever didar (*seeing, meeting, visit* in Persian), and it’s said that every Pamiri man, woman, and child went to hear him speak (in English, with interpretation in Tajik). Husniya remembers all nine siblings getting a shower, putting on new clothing, and driving out into the desert outside town with eighty, ninety, even one hundred people on every giant flatbed truck available. Just to lay eyes on the Mawla, the Imam of the Time, was beyond belief. The world was cracking open. Except that life since, for many, has only gotten worse.

“All I wanted was to go at least one time out of the country,” says Husniya. By then she was studying and working full time in Dushanbe, and at the same time volunteering as the teacher of a religious class from 9 p.m. to midnight. Only after would she start her homework, working silently until 4 a.m. so she wouldn’t wake her two sisters in the room they all shared.

“Ба осмон на рав, ба замин биё. Ba osmon na rav, ba zamin biyo,” one sister warned her at the time, proverbially in Tajik: *Don’t go up into the sky, come down to the earth*. And: “You’re eating with ten fingers in your mouth, eat with two!”

Husniya countered with a Russian expression: "Кто не рискует, тот шампанского не пьёт. Kto ne riskuet, tot shampanskogo ne p'ёt. *If you don't take a risk, then you never drink champagne*."

She borrowed from a relative to cover travel expenses and got help from a company in Dushanbe that arranged short-term J-1 "exchange visitor" visas for limited study and work in the States. Then she borrowed more to go say good-bye to her mother and still have $500 in her pocket when she landed. "I said I would go only one time and come back." But her mother kept weeping. America, she knew, was the name of another planet.

Husniya was among the first Pamiris to venture so far. Ismailism reinforces the Soviet legacy of stressing education and gender equality, which can raise tensions with (mostly Sunni) Tajiks. Even so, Husniya radiated a rare ambition: other twenty-one-year-old girls didn't just move to the other side of the world on their own.

The "cultural and educational exchange opportunity" arranged by the J-1 visa company was work at a Dairy Queen in North Carolina for $7.25 an hour. For a while Husniya became Hasina. Food was free, so she ate an enormous number of double cheeseburgers and banana splits. Just a few weeks in, she wanted to send at least something back, so she started with $200 of the $500 she had brought with her.

After that, desperate to make money faster, she spent five months in Arkansas, working seven days a week as a cashier at an Ismaili-owned gas station and staying at a hotel nearby. When the overwork and alienation were too much, she came back to New York, where she had landed briefly at first and where at least she could buy fresh naan from a tandoor oven.

It was the one place, too, where she had contacts. For several months she stayed in a bedroom in Queens with five other Pamiri girls, while two Pamiri guys slept in the second room. The nearby jamatkhana, an Ismaili religious and community center, was an essential point of entry. There on Woodhaven Boulevard an established, entrepreneurial community of Indian Ismailis—many of them Gujaratis driven out of East Africa in the 1970s—has continually helped the Pamiri Ismailis find jobs, loans, and other opportunities. In the 2010s, a small community of a few hundred Pamiris began settling, perfectly positioned within walking distance both of the jamatkhana and of Russian-speaking Rego Park.

Husniya was almost down to her last dollar, asking for a subway swipe from strangers, when she found work as a hostess and later waitress at an Ismaili-owned restaurant in South Street Seaport. "I would go to work, and they would give me only a few hours and I would cry so much, I need to make money!"

This was the bind. She could only stay by enrolling in one of the city's countless private English-language schools, which would enable her to change her status to an F-1 student visa. But that cost money she didn't have and at the same time legally limited the number of hours she could work. Which of course made it hard to make any money and actually afford to stay in the country. "I was too afraid to be illegal," she says, almost sighing.

For years Husniya continually struggled to balance her dream of studying with the need to make money, send money home, keep her immigration status, and work toward a green card, which was the only thing that would allow her both to stay in the US and travel freely and see her family again.

"Eighty percent of my friends are immigrants and deal with this," says Husniya, "so we learn from each other." All the ways are hard. The employers who sponsor are few and far between and may hold it over anyone they sponsor, penalizing them with years of low wages. Some find love, and real marriages happen, but the majority are fake, a whole economy of well-documented fictions. The immigrant may pay their citizen "spouse" tens of thousands of dollars plus ongoing payments to ensure that they keep up with the process and don't run off too soon—not to mention money for the special Russian lawyers, the expert photographers, the various certificates. As for asylum, that routinely takes over a decade, is often unsuccessful, and means living in total uncertainty in the meantime.

With all this strategizing to navigate the immigration bureaucracy, was there any room for self-discovery? Like many people in their twenties, Husniya didn't actually know what she wanted to do. As her English improved, she learned to navigate the higher education system, trying business management, accounting, liberal arts, international affairs, and early childhood education. Community colleges and language schools provided a precarious foothold and at least a sense of momentum. In addition to classes, she was working full days at a Russian daycare and evenings at a Staten Island restaurant. Any free time she spent volunteering at the jamatkhana, helping new arrivals apply to schools and planning community celebrations.

"Sometimes I don't know where I am, like Marco Polo," says Husniya with a laugh, knowing that the thirteenth-century Venetian traveler wrote of passing through a land called "Vokhan," where the people "have a peculiar language", in one of the few written records about Wakhi until modern times.

But it's one thing to travel far and something else to live with a permanent sense of dislocation. Husniya constantly carries a language and culture that no one around her can remotely understand.

Wakhis are a minority within a minority within a minority, exotic even to other Pamiris. They sound different, too, speaking with no fewer than fourteen fricative consonants, seven voiced and seven voiceless, including retroflex and uvular pairs which even other Pamiri languages don't have—and which to English ears sound impossibly, athletically far back in the mouth, if they can be distinguished at all. Commenters on ELA's Wakh videos (from all over the world) reach for ever-wilder comparisons: "Sounds like old english mix with Persian, Urdu, Pashto, Greek, more Turkish and when Harry Potter speak to the snake in Chamber of secret."

"I used to say I'm from Murghab, as if they know, right? If you say Tajikistan they don't know anyway, so I would say Persian, just not to make the conversation long. But in the US, if you say Persian that means Iranian. They would never think that Central Asians can be Persian." Given negative perceptions of Iran, she often says "more Russian," but sometimes now "Russian" doesn't get a good reaction either. People mistake her for Latina and speak to her in Spanish all the time. Others assume she's Jewish.

Her Albanian super is always coming over, friendly but insistent, trying to convince her with various YouTube videos that all Wakhis and other "white people" of Central Asia are actually Albanians, thanks to Alexander the Great. She makes friends and gets freebies from the Afghan- and Uzbek-run breakfast carts near ELA's office, who say sweet things in Persian and promise her that the bacon in their bacon, egg, and cheese is strictly halal.

An identity is not always fluid and situational as a matter of choice. When you're from the smallest and least-known group, but at least somewhat connected to so many larger ones, it can be a survival strategy—a constant negotiation from moment to moment that goes well beyond the traditional idea of assimilation. This is how Pamiri New Yorkers live, says Husniya, making their way by plugging into Ismaili, Tajik, Russian, Central Asian, and other networks, but at the same time trying hard to keep up a little world of their own.

Like Husniya, many Pamiri girls find work in restaurants and many of the guys become drivers, first with Uber and then in long-haul trucking if possible. Their Viber group keeps growing. Some people are starting families and moving to Atlanta, Chicago, Dallas, and elsewhere, where life is cheaper. One Rushani guy opened a small restaurant in Brighton Beach offering Central Asian and Mexican food, plus halal breakfasts, wraps, and burgers. When that went bust, he opened a Tajik-focused restaurant in Bensonhurst, with elaborately embroidered chairs and a giant screen playing bizarre Russian hip-hop videos—for now, the preferred spot for Pamiri celebrations, with Tuesday nights quietly kept for the community.

At times Husniya has been the only Wakhi from Tajikistan in the city, and her mom had long been the only person she could consistently speak to in the language, on the phone. Then through the jamatkhana she met Nazir, a Pakistani Wakhi, and through him half a dozen Wakhi families originally from Pakistan and now mostly settled in Brooklyn. Despite dialect differences, she could actually understand them. The fascination was mutual. They could never have met "over there," given the century-long border restrictions between the two countries.

One day Nazir brought her to ELA. He had first been brought by Rustam and Nanish, a Shughni-speaking couple who saw ELA mentioned in the newspaper and started working with us.

Husniya was incredulous during that first visit to Eighteenth Street: "I could never ever think of coming to the States and working on my own language. For the Wakhis, it's shocking: they're trying to forget it, because they don't need it. But now someone in the US is learning that? It's like they must have nothing else to do! Slowly, slowly I developed the desire to work on the language." She started barraging her mom with audio messages with our thorniest questions about the grammar, the vocabulary, the folklore. Every day they talked or texted, always ending with Husniya's promise: they would see each other soon.

## 3

The summer we finally make it to Tajikistan, the goal is to both see her mother and to do a linguistic survey—not a deep dive into documenting a single language like with Seke in Nepal, but a sweeping overview of the current state of Pamiri languages. In the Pamir region, the language may change from one rugged valley to the next, but there are no monolinguals: everyone knows Shughni, Tajik, and Russian, and even elders, encouraged by the Aga Khan, are now proudly trying to learn English in free classes. We visit every community we can, building relationships, fostering potential collaborations, and getting the lay of the languages. The end point is western China, where we cross the border at fourteen thousand feet and Husniya miraculously manages to make a few recordings in the "Tajik" (i.e., Pamiri) corner of a Xinjiang under occupation.

By summer's end, we have forty hours of video with seventy different speakers of a dozen languages. There are hundreds of powerful individual narratives it will take years to work through. A Rushani elder describes being blind her entire life in the village. A Bartangi man shares stories of the supernatural. A father-son team details years of work on a Shughni dictionary. An Iskhashimi man, apron-clad with a neat silver mustache, speaks of his love of crafting tools and toys. Wakhi storytellers spin their classic tales of foolish kings, headstrong queens, clever viziers, and simple farmers.

And then there are uncanny moments like this one in the Khorog bazaar. By mid-afternoon, the place is almost empty. The flies are as bored as the traders who swat them. We pass a hundred stalls before something stops us.

Our interest is fading fast when the trader asks where we're from.

"New York? My niece is there," she says.

Husniya catches up, and the two women almost scream on their way to an embrace.

"Ganjina's aunt!" says Husniya.

It's a genuine coincidence, because Khorog is no village. It's "the Paris of Pamir," a regional microcapital and worldly little oasis for thirty thousand people. Afghanistan is just across the river, keeping drug smugglers and small-time gangsters employed. Fine buildings line the two main streets, Gagarin and Lenin. Chorbogh City Park is full of poplars and people chatting in Shughni, Tajik, and Russian. The University of Central Asia, which operates in English, sparkles on a hilltop campus. Most Pamiri New Yorkers come from, or at least via, Khorog.

Ganjina is a Shughni speaker with a beautiful voice, originally from here, who waitresses at a Bukharian-owned restaurant in Queens. She sings karaoke with others in the basement after hours, usually in Russian and English, and religious songs in Persian during celebrations at the jamatkhana. One day Husniya brought her to the office, and she quickly swapped her jeans for a kurta, touching up with her phone as a mirror and singing an emotional Shughni lullaby for the camera. Thousands of Pamiris shared, liked, and commented on the video.

"Ganjina just got married," says her aunt, "but no one in the family could get a visa to go. The groom's side did." Husniya nods because such things are common.

Then the aunt is onto something else, suddenly animated in Shughni, a language I've learned only a few words of. The woman in the next stall joins in. It's clearly not their first discussion about this, but our presence is sparking something. Suddenly we're off to a whole other part of the bazaar, halting in a huff at the stall of the DVD man.

All three women go off at once: "Show us!"

He finds a disc among hundreds and slides it into the player. An image comes up on the monitor overhead: our recording of Ganjina in New York. The music is different: some poppier, peppier Shughni song dubbed over the original. No carefully wrought bilingual subtitles. Other pretty Shughni girls are spliced in. But still it's unmistakably an ELA video.

"Someone in Russia sent it to me," says the DVD man, pulling nervously on a smoke. "I don't know where it came from. It sells okay." He does the editing, the packaging, the merchandising. From YouTube to the bazaar in less than twenty-four hours. His stall is a marvel, the internet of things but actually. He has plenty of Hollywood, Bollywood, and other knockoffs, but it's apparently worth carrying some Shughni songs too. Our research is just fodder for the remix.

Husniya makes him give us a free one, so we can't manage any actual outrage, and we're secretly a little thrilled that ELA's work has made it back here unaided, even in such a bowdlerized form. The internet is still slow, expensive, and often busted even here in Khorog, let alone in the villages. We had actually burned DVDs with some of our videos in New York to distribute on this trip, so we hand one now to Ganjina's aunt, but there's no way we can compete with the bazaar DVD man.

You know a cultural revival is succeeding when people are just doing it, buying it, wanting it. The bazaar DVD man deals in mercantile realities mightier and murkier than pieties or platitudes about preserving language and culture. Behind the sales are the politics: the Pamiris are becoming a people. Physical, religious, linguistic, and other differences are all long-standing, but only in the last thirty years have the fall of the Soviet Union, civil war, opening to the world, and other factors sparked a kind of ethnogenesis, a whole new sense of group identity around the word "Pamiri." Sometimes the name is equated with Shughni, because of their numbers, which risks upsetting Wakhis, Rushanis, Bartangis, and others who have no desire to be junior partners.

Call it infinite ethnic regress, but it's the dangerous dream of sovereignty and self-determination, that little kernel of micronationalism, that often saves an endangered language. A language needs at least one full-blown setting, one self-contained world, that runs on it, or at least the possibility of establishing one. No one here can speak openly of independence, but the sense of autonomy is real, and Pamiris have risen up several times in the last decade in small but deadly clashes with the Tajik government. New houses are rising in the old Pamiri style. Traditional Pamiri clothing is back in fashion. Even the 04 on local license plates is a point of pride shading into separatism.

Driving for weeks in the region, we spend dozens of grinding hours in the jeep with Shogun, Husniya's brother, one of those master drivers of the world's unpaved mountain places who casually navigates landslides, floods, and thousand-foot drops. Any tension goes straight to his cigarette. Every treacherous mile is set to his soundtrack of locally produced music videos in half a dozen languages and styles: Afghan crooners channeling Bollywood, Tajik pop stars channeling Russian ones, Russian contestants in TV song competitions channeling American ones, love songs set to scenes from Turkish movies, synthy Pamiri pop full of yamaha (the local word for *any keyboard instrument*). But above all there are the soul-stirring, electronically enhanced, neo-folk Pamiri anthems, full of religious devotion and longing for the homeland. All stylized to the max, often with beautiful young Pamiri couples in traditional dress chastely cavorting in CGI-type settings. Nor is this just a Pamiri thing: locally produced music videos like these, sometimes even in endangered languages, are spreading across the Himalaya, Asia, and beyond.

Our recordings are blandly realistic by comparison, but they too are bound up in performance. As long as there's language, we always say. We just want people to talk. It rarely works to insist on "real" situations or conversations; people change into their traditional best and try to speak "pure" regardless. Anyone on social media is already performing, of course. Linguists may like it raw and decry any tampering with the evidence, but the speakers themselves always assume that we'll do a respectful, even enhancing edit: cut the interrupting phone call, smooth over words forgotten or misspoken, delete a sensitive comment someone might later regret. Speakers are not just speaking, they are representing the language, which is always an unreasonable burden. Particularly for groups on the margins and with fewer resources, putting the language in the best possible light for the most general audience requires an affirmative and idealized authenticity, however different from the unedited everyday version.

In our recording, it was actually a bunched-up blanket that Ganjina was lulling to sleep, standing in for a nonexistent baby. And her traditional-sounding Shughni lullaby was in fact written in the 1980s as a vehicle for the magnetic late-Soviet Tajik pop star Nargis Bandishoeva, who made it a massive nationwide hit before her tragic death in a car crash right at the outbreak of the civil war.[9] These layers of lost innocence would probably be even more lost on the bazaar DVD man, but it's what Ganjina wanted to record.

## 4

For Husniya, coming home like this carries purpose and prestige, but also implies distance, self-consciousness, a new way of relating to her roots. "It's helping me preserve the language in myself," she says. "When I was growing up or would go back home, I would never just sit like this with someone while they tell me stories." Preservation starts inside a single person, and Husniya is herself now an essential carrier of the tradition.

If this research trip works, it's only because of her hundreds of phone calls and text threads, deep networks, months of preparation, and knowledge of all the languages. She has built a small team for each of the six main Pamiri languages: people who are not just speakers but activists and organizers who understand the goals, identify speakers, and guide us around their valleys.

Everything works through these ever-lengthening chains of relationships, with everyone bringing you as far as they can. Sometimes you have to go five levels down to find exactly the right person in one particular house deep inside one village, while other encounters are completely serendipitous. Here, unlike in New York or Moscow, the whole context for these languages can make itself heard, down to the buzz of a local fly right into the mic.

For hundreds of miles, we follow a road along a river: the muddy Panj, whose meandering course is dotted with wild and grassy little islands. The Afghan side is a tan and stony landscape with scattered clumps of low unpainted houses, people and their animals, small fields green with wheat. At a roadside samsa stand, we hear muffled booms, and the owner warns that rocks could come flying any minute, but it's not the war, he says reassuringly, they're just building a road on the other side. Everything's okay as long as you can see lights or people, he assures us.

We think of crossing, for there are speakers of almost all the Pamiri languages in Afghanistan too, and also of the related languages Munji, Yidgha, and Sanglechi, of whom almost nothing is known after decades of war. In retrospect, there was a rare window of relative peace and quiet in the 2010s, now closed, but even as we work the Taliban is getting closer. People wounded in recent fighting are being brought over for treatment, the last cross-border bazaar is being closed, and the few Tajik banks here are sending all their cash back to Dushanbe. Not that Tajikistan itself is entirely safe: on this same road just a few days behind us, four cyclists on their way around the world were murdered by five men pledging allegiance to ISIS.

We're equally concerned about Tajik officials and police, but we feel secure in Pamiri hands—with Husniya, who can talk her way out of any situation, and Shogun, who has a knack for sharing the strategic cigarette with sleazy guard types and a winking way of suddenly disappearing and returning with fresh-picked sea buckthorn berries for all. Besides having the swagger of a quieter, Pamiri version of The Fonz, Shogun is invited annually by many families to be the first to enter their newly cleaned houses at Nowruz, because of what local tradition calls his "lucky footstep." (In Wakhi, the name Shogun actually means Nowruz, the Persian world's New Year.)

Almost everywhere we stay with extended family, sleeping on stepped platforms in the one main room, which always resembles an inner courtyard surrounded by five carved wooden columns (said to represent the Five Pillars of Islam) and topped by a chorkhona, *a skylight of four concentric squares* (said to represent the Zoroastrian elements of earth, water, air, and fire).

We take breaks at local hot springs, more than fifty in this corner of the country bottled into a string of Soviet-era sanatoriums that function as an alternate medical system, each famed for helping with a particular ailment. At a spring for skin conditions, we float in sulfurous water under white lime rock deposits, surrounded by naked bodies devastated by burns and boils or mapped by psoriasis. At night, we see fields of stars as if our eyes were being cleaned to the bottom, so far is this place from any light-polluting population center.

By day we visit homes, with Nicole recording wherever the light and sound are good and the speakers are comfortable, which is usually the topchan, the *raised and cushioned platform* in the garden, where people hang out and entertain as sun pours down throughout the day. However much we demur, whatever the time, the dastarkhan is laid out, a tablecloth spread with bowls and plates which brim with apricots and mulberries plucked from the surrounding trees as well as Russian-style wrapped candies, packaged cookies, and circles of naan marked with the baker's stamp.[10] Giant thermoses of tea and bottles of RC Cola wash it all down. Meals center on Central Asian staples: heaps of the great greasy rice dish plov and steaming bowls of shurpa, *a meat and vegetable soup*. But a few times we taste dishes like noshkhukhpa, *dried apricot soup*, and Wakhi-style osh, *a noodle soup made from a mix of different flours*—endangered foodways which bend words widely used in the region to hyperlocal tastes.

Summer is wedding season, so we end up on the sidelines, if not at the center, of five different ones. Weddings mean music, and everywhere we meet singers and musicians whose art is both completely local and thoroughly cosmopolitan, no contradiction, just as speakers of the smallest languages are always the most multilingual. Poetry and song are one and the same for Pamiris, with musical form inseparable from poetic structure, as if the world of medieval minstrels had continued developing through the age of DVDs.[11]

Even instruments have remained largely unstandardized, one master musician explains, showing us all the varieties of rubob, the *six-stringed unfretted longnecked lute*; the similar but larger tanbur; the ghizhak, or *spike fiddle*; and the *circular frame drum* called daf. Each individual instrument is different—he is handcrafting a rubob as he says this—but there are also continuities, gradations, and variations on these all across Eurasia. Which is not to say that pop isn't popular. "I used to think it was grandparents' music," says Husniya, now repentant, of the rubob's subtle stylings. Rubob has long been a male domain, but a Pamiri woman in New York now dares to play.

All who can sing can sing in Tajik, joining a tradition of high-culture, classical Persian poetry based on Rumi, Hafez, and others. Just as people do in far-off Kabul, Bukhara, and Shiraz, Pamiris recite the poetic quatrains called ruboi. Like people from Morocco to Indonesia, Pamiris sing qasida, *a kind of sacred praise poem*. There are masters of maddo, the spellbinding soundtrack of funerals and healing ceremonies, and of falak, which means *heaven*, *fate*, or *universe*—a fitting name for mystic music that shakes the soul and reaches for the divine.

In recent years, Pamiris have also started writing for these genres in their own local languages, reflecting the ongoing cultural renaissance. In their notebooks, new masters carefully compose bayd, *modern Wakhi poem-songs*, and one musician even offered to whip up a Wakhi qasida about ELA. Certain poetic and musical genres exist only in Pamiri languages, including lalajik, *lullabies*, where the mother may fondly address her infant as "your mother's gravedigger." In Rushani, there is even a funeral lalajik, lulling the departed to eternal rest.

Only Wakhi women sing bɨlbɨlik, *nightingale songs*, traditionally half-improvised according to a certain formula, a cappella, while out in the ayloq, *the upper pasture*.[12] "It's always sad when they sing these songs," says Husniya when we wrap up recording one night. "I guess being happy was not in fashion. There's no man singing bɨlbɨlik. I feel like *they* were having a good time! I'm so glad for the century I live in."

The bayd composer Qurbonsho agrees, with a difference. He says bɨlbɨlik are about human longing, "a lament from the depth of the soul," and that the women singing them today are just memorizing, not feeling it. "Because today you can get anything you want," says Qurbonsho, a little optimistically.[13]

Below are a few lines from a bɨlbɨlik we recorded:

jəm bi nanvən jav ɟaʂ wəsk e
*Those without mothers are thirsty.*

bɨlbɨl tar noləm e lol
*I wail for you like a nightingale, o dear brother.*

ʐ̜ɨmakək bə dəm ti jortʃ
*The moon is reflected on your floor.*

ʐ̜ɨ solək dzɨqlaj tuje e lol
*I was at a very young age, o dear brother.*

ti fikrək maʐ̜ kərk ʂɨkortʃ e lol,
*Thinking of you turned me into ashes, o dear brother.*

ti fikrək maʐ̜ kərk ʂɨkortʃ e
*Thinking of you turned me into ashes.*

ar bor ki çɨ pətər jodəme e lol
*Every time I remember my son, o dear brother.*

aft boron arəm ʐ̜ɨ ruj e lol
*The tears on my face are like seven lines of rain, o dear brother.*

## 5

A few years later, we're celebrating Husniya's graduation at the city's only Tajik restaurant, deep in post-Soviet Brooklyn. Even her ancient-looking, kerchiefed mother is here, brought with difficulty by her daughter to America for the first time to celebrate the milestone. Husniya is detailing their adventures all over the city, and ten Instagram smiles later her mother is clearly exhausted: unused to all of it, unable to understand or communicate, disgusted by all the food except cheeseburgers and fries, which delight her.

At least the neighborhood feels familiar, and here among the salient elements of a traditional chaykhana, a Central Asian teahouse restaurant, she can play the role of detached, benevolent elder. The truth is that she just wants get back to the apartment and watch the new fifty-five-inch TV with all the Russian channels, which Husniya set up and subscribed to just in time for her visit. This is what makes a Wakhi matriarch feel at home, nine children later, after a lifetime in a remote settlement twelve thousand feet up.

Linguistically, it's a typically extraordinary gathering. Beside Husniya sits her closest friend, the Turkmen girl she's gone through the whole drama of immigration and integration with. With each other they speak Russian. They used to have a Turkish roommate, though they kept things professional by speaking to her in English.

In the corner, their Ukrainian friend is purring to her baby in Ukrainian. Husniya used to talk to her in Russian, but they switched to English several years ago. Next to her is a Kosovar friend comfortable in all the Balkan languages. Husniya's mother quietly asks her daughter, in Wakhi, if she can go take a nap. The waiters juggle orders in English, Russian, and Tajik, the last of which a motley crew of boxers, bruisers, and groupies are booming out at a nearby table. Our own conversation turns to "Runglish," the Ramaluk-like Russian-English mixing that passes for a common language at the daycare where Husniya used to work, and in southern Brooklyn more generally, and apparently also on the International Space Station, or at least the Soyuz rocket that visits it, two hundred miles up in the sky.

Like many Pamiris, Husniya strongly identifies with Russian culture and is grateful to the Soviet Union for modernizing the region. "It was always one boy, one girl, one boy, one girl," she says of mixed-gender seating at school, "otherwise we would be like Afghans," explaining that she means covered up, illiterate, uneducated, married off, unable to count or maybe even know their own birthday. Tajik Wakhis can see with their own eyes that for their Afghan cousins across the Panj the infrastructure is null, the poverty worse, and the options severely limited, even to leave.

"It was normal back at that time to have nine children," says Husniya, who was the seventh. She has more nieces, nephews, and cousins than she can count. She looks tenderly, a little apologetically, at her expressionless mother. Today, most people are having only three or five, she adds.

"Is the power on in Murghab now?" I ask Husniya's mother, who shakes her head. She moved to Dushanbe when Husniya's youngest sister was entering university, got used to the lower altitude, and had a blood pressure spike as soon as she tried to go back home. She even sold off the family's flock of goats and sheep, which a Kyrgyz shepherd had been tending for them, and split the money among her children. But two of Husniya's brothers have stayed up there at that surreal crossroads for Pamiri workers, Kyrgyz nomads, Tajik officials, Russian soldiers, and Chinese traders.

Without power for the last two years, the people of Murghab make do with little battery-powered LEDs, but mostly the nights pass in total darkness. By day, the light is clear and pitiless. No trees can grow there, so they burn animal dung mixed with teresken, a dwarf shrub of otherworldly appearance, itself in ever shorter supply. The bazaar is a jumble of repurposed shipping containers, impossibly far from the ships they once rode on. The only little library in town is devoted to Rahmon studies, with the dictator's memoir *World-Famous Tajik* prominently displayed. This is what an outpost on the new Silk Road looks like.

"Men die younger there and no one knows why," says Husniya. "I want my brothers to leave."

Leaving is what people do now. With large families and no work, it can seem like the only option. The poorest country in a poor region, Tajikistan without Soviet subsidies has become more dependent on remittances than just about any other country in the world. Only four of Husniya's eight siblings have stayed in the region; the others are in Dushanbe, Turkey, and Malta, with children in Moscow and Dubai.

"If the country was rich, we would never leave," said Husniya at one point, but now the political situation is deteriorating too. For an ethnolinguistic and religious minority like the Pamiris, who make up just 3 percent of Tajikistan's population, the political marginalization laid bare by the civil war only adds to the sense that the future must be elsewhere. Now Pamiris are being locked up if there's any suspicion that they support independence, a recent arrival tells us, which can include speaking Pamiri languages.

"Nine young Pamiri guys just crossed over from Mexico, and more keep coming," says Husniya in a lowered voice. "And they say Mexico is like a second Uzbekistan."

Everyone is trying different routes, she adds. For a while you could fly from Turkey to Mexico and pay $8,000 a head to a Mexican woman who would take people through a "corridor" across the border. Or Panama, but that was more than double the cost. Now it depends on having a Schengen visa, so you might have to go from Russia to Spain to Colombia and only then start the dangerous trek through Panama and Central America. Whatever the route, Pamiris are aiming for New York because there are other Pamiris here who can help them, including a lawyer with experience in asylum and immigration cases. Even as the threats mounted under Trump and even during the worst days of the COVID-19 pandemic, Pamiris have kept trying to come.

Husniya has been helping her nephew make it over. He had been working in Moscow, unpaid and in miserable conditions for months. Then the Russian invasion of Ukraine spelled economic disaster and even the threat of conscription for millions of Tajik migrant laborers, Pamiris among them. He's a tough guy, she tells me, who dreams like many young Central Asian men of glory as a UFC fighter, but even for him it was a hellish four-month journey. After flying to Turkey and then Ecuador, he went by boat, then overland, and finally on foot across the US-Mexico border, only to spend two months shunted among three different detention centers. Finally reaching Brooklyn, he stayed with Husniya to find his feet.

"I'll be a sister to you here, not a mother," she told him, advising him to focus first on paying off the debts from his journey and paying the lawyer to start the asylum process. She helped him get work right away, initially at a Georgian restaurant in Midtown and now on a construction site in Pennsylvania.

"It's good for me," she says, matter-of-factly, of having someone else who can send money and support family back home. With dozens of nieces and nephews and even more cousins, there is bottomless need, and Husniya has long been the backstop. Another nephew and niece are also on the way here. She hopes that eventually her mother will also come for good, so Husniya can take care of her.

Wakhi seems far away, Murghab unimaginable.

Husniya feeds off the city: "New York opened my eyes. It shapes you to be a human being, not dividing based on religion, face, or race, or anything. It has that energy, the power that tells you: you can do it, you can do anything, you're unstoppable. You know that's how I believe."

The deeper she goes into her language, Husniya tells me, the more her perspective actually broadens. She was supposed to marry young and start having kids with a Pamiri guy, but she kept her independence instead. Her Instagram DMs and Facebook messages are full of flirters from back home, whose intentions she find confusing. Some Pamiri New Yorkers may go back to find a match, looking for a "pure village girl" or boy. Meanwhile in Muslim Brooklyn, Husniya has encountered guys from Pakistan, Morocco, Egypt, and Iran, but everyone has to work as an immigrant, she says, and that changes the gender dynamics. Now she wants both traditional courtship and equal partnership. In her thirties, she still hopes to marry, but she believes that happiness is within—you shouldn't expect a partner to make you happy.

What happiness does require is money. "I'm done being poor!" she blurts out with a smile.

Self-realization is Husniya's latest language. A picture of a BMW was on her dream board, and then she got it. The same inner force that drives her to document her language is driving her to succeed on American terms. With the master's degree barely behind her, she is already getting her real estate license. With the car she started crisscrossing Brooklyn to show listings, got promoted, then turned around and sold it for a profit in the off-season. She tried a house-flipping operation, cold-calling people in foreclosure or short-sale situations, also all on commission. It wasn't fun, with only one in a thousand bites, but she's still hustling. When real estate turned sluggish, she started learning to be a QA engineer. She's paying off the student debt and the credit card debt, laying off the traveling and shopping.

But she takes these risks because she wants to drink champagne. "Everything is advertising," as she says. "If I'm just sitting in my apartment in Bay Ridge, who knows me? It's nothing. You have to put yourself out there." When business is slow, like now, we work on the language.

For over a decade, Husniya has been pushing toward citizenship against every imaginable bureaucratic, financial, and personal obstacle. A few months later she is finally doing it, taking her oath as a US citizen in a large anonymous room at 26 Federal Plaza, the local headquarters of ICE and USCIS. The room is crammed with over four hundred joyful people from all over the world, herded in and out quickly and a bit roughly in federal fashion to make way for the arriving 10 a.m. batch. There's a very different scene on the other side of the building: hundreds of recent arrivals direct from the border, lined up for appointments and clutching blankets against the cold.

"Any time it just depends on me, I've got it," says Husniya as we celebrate over pancakes, with the strength of a hundred inspiring TED talks, podcasts from motivational speakers, and the Classical Persian poetry on YouTube she listens to before bed. She has always dreamed of writing to Ellen DeGeneres and going on the show, which was her favorite. Maybe Ellen will do something for Wakhi? Will I help her write the letter?

# Boris
## ייִדיש (*Yiddish*)

### 1

Boris, sipping from a slim-waisted glass of Turkish tea on Emmons Avenue, insists that he is not the last major Yiddish writer.

He acknowledges that Jewish Bessarabia, the world of his childhood, has completely disappeared. The same with its successor Soviet Moldova, where he raised a family and stood at the center of cultural life. He admits that the *Forward*, the last great Yiddish newspaper which he edited for eighteen years, is nothing like what it was.

When Boris wants to emphasize a finished thought, he flexes what I can only call his jowl, which has the effect of extending his mustache, changing the shape of his lips, and expressing more honestly than any words—at least this is how I understand it—a bottomless ambivalence. He's been doing it all afternoon, telegraphing something I'll never quite understand.

Of course Yiddish is not dying, he says in Yiddish, the language we've always spoken in the fourteen years we've known each other. Almost everyone now knows this. "But when people say there's a renaissance," says Boris, "a nekhtiker tog."[1]

A nekhtiker tog is *a yesterday day*, an impossibility and a contradiction in terms out of step with time itself. The expression may be enunciated with an almost audible snort.

“There are enthusiasts doing this or that,” he says of the scattered Yiddishists. “They’re constantly making new lists of neologisms you can break your head on.”

“And there is a tiny elite of academics,” he adds, though in fairness they don’t exactly live it up like God in Odessa. “They research and write books in English or other languages *about* Yiddish, digging just deep enough into the language or culture to get a doctorate. They have subsidies, they go to conferences. They’re deep in the old times. But here’s a new Yiddish book, write about its meaning, in Yiddish! How many read their academic books in English?”

As for the Hasidim who now constitute around 99.9 percent of day-to-day speakers, the largest number of whom anywhere in the world live here in Brooklyn: “I’ve never thought they were the future of Yiddish, kholile (*G-d forbid*). Of the language, yes, but not of the culture. Some few will cross over, but in general they are cultural amoratsim.” This phrase originally from Biblical Hebrew (am ha’aretz) is literally *person of the land*, but here pluralized in Yiddish it means *ignoramuses*, especially about matters Jewish, who think they have knowledge, nebekh—the nebbishes.

But somehow Boris is still bullish on Yiddish, and his whole life attests to it. If no longer for a whole people, he says, then let it be “a language of faithful individuals, not just a connection between yesterday and today, but a mission to tomorrow, and nobody knows what might happen tomorrow.” The twentieth-century revival of Hebrew as a spoken language in Israel—though it came at the expense of other Jewish languages and unwittingly drew on Yiddish in countless ways (as the mother tongue of a majority of the revitalizers)—gives credence to this mildly messianic hope.[2] So, in a certain sense, does the twenty-first-century expansion of Hasidic Yiddish in New York.

Like the great Yiddish writers of the past, Boris feels the imperative to write for children: “A literature without children is not a literature, just like a literature without criticism." Isaac Bashevis Singer, accepting his Nobel Prize, said he had five hundred reasons to write for children. As for why he wrote in a dying language, Singer claimed he did it for the ghosts ("The deader the language the more alive is the ghost. Ghosts love Yiddish") and the Yiddish-speaking corpses who will ask on resurrection day: "Is there any new Yiddish book to read?"[3]

Boris and I meet at the newsstand under the Q train, with its papers in half a dozen languages, before passing in quick succession the Dungan Lagman House, Hohhot Coffee, Georgian Bakery, and the fanciful Belarusian Xata (*Cottage*) restaurant, where every rough-hewn table really looks like a cottage surrounded by its own rustic fence. We walk under the Belt Parkway, passing Cafe Dushanbe, Baku Palace, Randazzo's, and faces from half of Eurasia. We sit at this Turkish café, which is wrapped in Istanbul nostalgia but with Russian pop blasting, almost in sight of the sea.

A glezl tey in Yiddish is more an invitation to talk than an actual glass of tea. I hear a wavering in the usual steadiness of Boris's voice: "Nisht bashert iz nisht bashert. *Not destined is not destined*. Azoy hot di pandemye gebrakht azoy fil 'korektsyes' af undzere lebn, abi me lebt. *So it is that the pandemic brought many 'corrections' to our lives, but as long as we're alive*." Good friends died. His two sons and seven grandchildren are in New York, but it didn't feel safe to see them. The war in Ukraine has been tearing what little fabric remains of Jewish life in Eastern Europe, perhaps for good.

"Now that's something I love: catching fish," says Boris, brightening with a wave toward the dock where the half-day party boats launch out into international waters with their fish-seeking radar. "Last time we caught fifteen kilos of sea bass, porgy, fluke. We were eating for months."

In the morning, he usually works on a novel, a play, a poem, an article, or a children's book—if he's not editing someone else's book, finishing a short film, or putting out *Yiddish Branzhe*, the free online monthly journal he created after "retiring," which is now on its fifty-seventh issue all in Yiddish with a thousand subscribers. He cajoles his neighbor on East Twenty-Ninth Street, not far from here just off Avenue U, into volunteer tech and layout.

In the afternoon, he rests or reads or walks; in the evening, when possible, a concert. Sometimes the gym, where he sees the old Soviet types he knows too well, whose children are fleeing Brooklyn and the Russian language as fast as they can. He has his violin, though he no longer plays: "It takes revenge, sending me more than a few dreams."

Boris has no svive, no *scene*. As the infrastructure of Yiddish literature collapses, he himself is becoming the infrastructure. To my mind, there is no one left like him, no one else consistently producing and publishing major literary work in Yiddish. He contests this, citing two younger writers he mentors, one of whom is Evgeny Kissin.[4] Already a world-famous classical pianist, Kissin learned the language as an adult and sought out Boris to become his Yiddish guru. He now recites Yiddish poetry at some of his performances and publishes original work under the Yiddish Branzhe imprint (which he sponsors). He and Boris even collaborated on a Yiddish musical for children that premiered in Birobidzhan, the bizarre Jewish (and originally officially Yiddish-speaking) Autonomous Oblast created by Stalin in Siberia. It was all set to play New York, on Boris's seventieth birthday, when the COVID-19 pandemic hit. "We have to have a little vision, a little fantasy," he says, "even in the current negligible state of things."

Being a Yiddish writer is a shtekn mit tsvey ekn, he adds, *a stick with two ends*. You can't just write in the language, you have to work for its very survival. You have to be a klal-tuer or kultur-tuer, a *community* or *culture doer* committed to developing and supporting a whole infrastructure. The idea is similar to, but not the same as, the English term *cultural activist*, which tellingly denotes a minority culture.[5] Specialization is a luxury that smaller cultures can't afford, so everyone has to lend a hand. Without government support or a consumer market, those building small-scale, stateless cultures are effectively on their own. A kultur-tuer has to be on the ground, engaged in all the day-to-day moments that materially and intellectually extend a tradition. Creating a "modern culture" complete with publications, organizations, events, education, and more requires an enormous amount of work, often unpaid and always precarious.

Nor can one turn away from the dominant culture entirely, as articulated by Jacob Glatstein, who brought Yiddish poetry to its zenith in interwar New York: "What does it mean to be a poet of an abandoned culture? It means that I have to be aware of Auden but Auden need never have heard of me."[6] This may be true for anyone writing in a minority or endangered language, and it may explain why, apart from all the personal, practical, political, and economic considerations, so many native speakers of Yiddish have chosen to write in other, national languages: Appelfeld in Hebrew, Wiesel in French and later English, Kanovich in Lithuanian and later Russian, to name just a few.

Though there is a fragmentary written record of Yiddish going back at least as far as the thirteenth century, its status has always been politically and religiously marginal, associated for centuries with women. As for its genesis, medieval Jewish communities in Germanic-speaking lands along the Rhine forged something new from the speech of their neighbors, transforming it with infusions of loshn koydesh (*the holy language*—a mix of Hebrew and Aramaic) as well as the multiple Slavic languages they encountered on later migrations east.[7]

For example: **דער** זיידע **האָט געבענטשט** גומל / **Der** zeyde **hot ge**bentsh**t** goyml / *Grandpa said the prayer* (i.e., *was grateful*) *for having made it out of danger*. The overall framework is Germanic, including all the grammatical bits in bold: the masculine definite article **der**, past tense form **hot ge—t**, and the order of elements itself. But zeyde, *grandpa*, is Slavic; bentsh, *pray*, is a Romance word (in fact cognate with English *benediction*), and goyml is loshn koydesh, the truncated name for the prayer of thanksgiving (birkat hagomel) said after safely escaping danger.[8]

A "fusion language" which has grown immensely rich, varied, and particular and whose name simply means *Jewish*, Yiddish is written in a modified alefbeys, the Hebrew alphabet that Jews have taken with them around the world. As with Ramaluk, speaking Yiddish well can feel like speaking two or three languages at once. But only in the late nineteenth century, thanks to a massive, quasi national awakening, did Yiddish begin to take its place among the world's supposedly respectable languages. At some point, each of those has been declared worthy by its own speakers with an arsenal of respectable signifiers including standardization, dictionaries, grammars, textbooks, and literature.

At its peak in the 1920s and '30s, some ten million people spoke Yiddish from Brooklyn to Buenos Aires, from Warsaw to Winnipeg. Not only pogroms like the one in Kishinev (the city Boris long called home) but daily persecution and grinding poverty were driving them out of Eastern Europe—just as a unique combination of cheap steerage fares, open borders, and economic opportunities were drawing them westward and above all to the United States. Thus New York, where around a million-plus Yiddish speakers settled between 1882 and 1924, became the nerve center of the global Yiddish diaspora, with the mass media, theater, and other institutions to match, almost giving the stateless language the semblance of a capital.

At first it was the Lower East Side, which suddenly became both the most densely populated place on the planet and the most Jewish. Following German (including German Jewish) settlement in the mid-nineteenth century, Yiddish speakers from across central and Eastern Europe poured into the streets from Canal to Fourteenth, even forming somewhat distinct zones for Jews from the Russian Empire, Galician Jews, Hungarian Jews, and so on. Some 2,500 different hometowns were represented by New York landsmanshaftn, mutual-aid organizations similar to the Himalayan kyidug. After the Holocaust, these groups were also largely responsible for creating and publishing the extraordinary yizkor books that memorialized the lost communities across the ocean to which Jewish New Yorkers had once been linked.[9]

Though most of the immigrants spoke at least three or four languages, depending on where exactly they came from, Yiddish united them and flourished in ways which had been impossible or restricted in Europe. Its dominance initially continued even as people left the Lower East Side en masse for more salubrious conditions in Harlem, Williamsburg, Brownsville, and many other parts of the city and the country. Yet a deep shame persisted around Yiddish, and many speakers never saw it as more than a jargon, a broken form of German indelibly linked to the shtetl. Grudging tolerance in New York didn't add up to real support or acceptance, even within the Jewish world. Wholesale second-generation shift to English both drove and was driven by a wider Americanization, with New York's public schools at the center of the story. At the same time, the community was cut off from its source, with only a trickle of new speakers arriving after the immigration restrictions of 1924.

Still, no one could have predicted the suddenness with which Yiddish collapsed globally. At least half of all speakers were killed in the Holocaust, known in Yiddish as the khurbn, *the destruction*. Most of the remaining speakers were dramatically uprooted. Hundreds of thousands arrived in Israel, which nonetheless gained its independence as a firmly Hebrew-speaking nation and confined Yiddish to the margins.[10] Some 140,000 survivors came to the US, mostly New York, where Yiddish played a crucial role in their initial resettlement, but by then hardly anywhere in the city was it still a widespread language of daily life.

The language had lost its eastern European homeland, except for the Soviet Union, but there a postwar crackdown on the language was followed by intensive Russification. In the 1970s, Soviet Jews boldly asserted their right to emigrate, backed by a movement of American

Jews. Yiddish, however fast it was fading, again played an important role in the resulting process of resettlement and reunion.

Long past their peak as summer getaways for the city's masses, Brighton Beach, Coney Island, and the surrounding neighborhoods, including where I'm sitting with Boris, were transformed. This is Boris's world, and he has built his home and many of his books, however warily, on what he calls as "a threshold, dividing the old world from the new," as he describes in *Lamed-vovnikes fun mayn zikorn* (*The Hidden Righteous Ones in My Memory*), in my translation:[11]

> ס׳רובֿ פֿון [די רוסישע יידן] האָבן זיך באַזעצט אין פֿאַרשיידענע ערטער פֿון ברוקלין, אָבער אַ היפּשע צאָל, בדרך-כּלל געקומענע פֿון אָדעס, האָבן זיך געצויגן נעענטער צום וואַסער, צום ברײַטאָן ביטש. די זאַמדיקע פּלאַזשע, פֿאַרפֿלייצט מיט חוצפּהדיקע מעווען, דער רעש פֿון כוואַליעס, וואָס וועקט און ווייטיקט, און וויגט אײַן; די לופֿט, אָנגעזעטיקט מיט ריחות פֿון פֿיש, שרצים, ים-געוויקסן און איז באַשטראַלט מיט זון—דאָס אַלץ און דערצו נאָך פֿאַרמישט מיט טויזנט אַנדערע אינגרעדיענטן פֿון מענטשלעכע געפֿילן, געדאַנקען, וויצן, זשעסטן, טרערן האָבן געשאַפֿן דאָ דעם זעלטענעם אייגנאַרטיקן באַלזאַם, וואָס פֿאַר קיין שום ״גרינע״ און אין קיין שום אַפּטייק אין אַמעריקע קאָן מען נישט קריגן.

> S'rov [fun di rusishe yidn] hobn zikh bazetst in farsheydene erter fun Bruklin, ober a hipshe tsol, bderekh-klal gekumene fun Odes, hobn zikh getsoygn neenter tsum vaser, tsum Brayton Bitsh. Di zamdike plazhe, farfleytst mit khutspedike meves, der resh fun khvalies, vos vekt un veytikt, un vigt ayn; di luft, ongezetikt mit rikhes fun fish, shrotsim, yam-geviksn un iz bashtralt mit zun —dos alts un dertsu nokh farmisht mit toyznt andere ingredyentn fun mentshlekhe gefiln, gedanken, vitsn, zhestn, trern hobn geshafn do dem zeltenem eygnartikn balzam, vos far keyn shum "grine" un in keyn shum apteyk in Amerike kon men nisht krign.

> *Most [of the Soviet Jews] settled in different parts of Brooklyn, but a considerable number, in general those coming from Odessa, were drawn nearer to the water, to Brighton Beach. The sandy beach covered with gulls full of chutzpah, the rush of waves which wake and ache and rock you, the air filled with stenches of fish, critters, and sea plants and irradiated with sun—all this, mixed besides with thousands of other ingredients of human feelings, thoughts, jokes, gestures, and tears, had created here the rare and distinctive balm which no greenhorn could find in any pharmacy in America.*

Boris has just handed me the book, along with its recently published sequel *Mit a shlikhes keyn Moskve* (*With a Mission to Moscow*). It's emotional to hold a fresh Yiddish book, as with any new publication in an embattled language. Though the inside says Forverts Oysgabe (*Forward Edition*), Boris says the newspaper played little role—it was a one-man publishing house, run by Boris with his neighbor's help, as surely as Yiddish Branzhe now is. With so few readers scattered all over the world, printing and shipping costs are becoming prohibitive, so he's ready just to distribute them for free as e-books: "What's important to me is that someone reads them, then I'll send them. I have a lot of email addresses. I can send it and whoever wants to read can read, maybe at least people will take a look. Otherwise they'll sit in packages with me at home, which takes away the desire to write anything at all." He flexes his jowl.

This duology is his most personal work yet ("90 percent true, all biographical, a memoir but not a memoir"), tracing the demise of Yiddish literature and journalism through its passionate, eccentric caretakers, as Boris witnessed it across three lands: the last improbable "little blooming" of the Soviet eighties, the twilight of the Israeli nineties, and the shambolic finale of the American aughts. *The Hidden Righteous Ones* of the title is an attempt to translate the untranslatable lamed-vovnik, *thirty-sixer*, which refers to the Yiddish folk belief that there are thirty-six holy people, hidden and unbeknownst both to themselves and each other, whose existence can save the world and justify humanity in the eyes of God.[12]

Boris's characters, from all the different waves and wavelets of Jewish immigration, can neither stay nor build on the Brighton Beach threshold. As he writes:

> *Even in Israel it happened more than once that I heard: Brighton is not Brooklyn, Brooklyn is not New York, and New York is not America. Then imagine going from Brighton to the rest of America. . . . Human memory is short, especially once one bundles oneself over from immigrant Brighton further—via the Brooklyn Bridge, on all four sides—so that one occasionally forgets completely from where one began the journey.*

One series of stories follows a Brooklyn private detective, who first turned Orthodox in the late Soviet religious underground led by Chabad and later entered yeshiva in Flatbush. The novella "Karolino-Bugaz" is about an aging couple who meet in the low-key beach town of that name outside Odessa and emigrate together to Brooklyn, where a marital crisis threatens to capsize everything. In the novella "Royte shikhlekh far Reytshl" ("Red Shoes for Rachel"), a recent Jewish immigrant from Moldova and a Brooklynite daughter of Holocaust survivors fall in love on the Brighton Beach boardwalk, drawn together by their Yiddish-inflected traumas. It's a kosher update of Bashevis Singer's 1966 Coney Island novel of trauma and adultery, *Sonim, di geshikhte fun a libe* (*Enemies, A Love Story*), which, like much of both Bashevis and Boris's work, was first serialized in the Yiddish *Forward*.[13]

As for translation, a potential lifeline, "you have to live two lifetimes, the second to translate your own work." Besides "thousands of articles," he counts twenty-seven books to his name, including translations of his own work in which he is always closely involved. He has an easier time with Russian, supervising and paying translators out of his own pocket. A few of his books have been translated into German and English, but it can be overwhelming to explain or convey everything to American readers who "live in another world, don't even know the concepts." His main English translator was Barney Zumoff, a retired Brooklyn physician and brigadier general in the Air Force Reserve, who in his spare time was also a kultur-tuer and translator of dozens of Yiddish books, until his recent death at the age of ninety-four.

Even the story of Brighton Beach as Little Odessa, which Boris has captured as well as anyone, is fast becoming the memory of a memory. With the collapse of the Soviet Union, other Russians followed that initial Jewish wave and later so did people from every major ethnolinguistic group in the former Soviet Union.[14] With Russian the essential lingua franca, and late Soviet culture the glue, these neighborhoods became home to Lezgis and Avars from the Caucasus, Turkmen and Kyrgyz from Central Asia, Buryats and Yakuts from Siberia. There are an estimated one thousand Koryo-saram, ethnic Koreans from Uzbekistan, who may still remember their distinct Koryo-Mar variety of Korean. Large communities like the Uzbeks and Georgians each now number in the thousands, establishing separate neighborhoods near, if not necessarily in, Brighton Beach.[15] Among so many other languages jostling for airtime on these sandy and sun-bleached blocks where the city meets the ocean, there are also many speakers of Turkish, Uighur, Urdu, Arabic, Mandarin, Cantonese, Spanish, and Sicilian all around us.

## 2

Postwar Moldova was one of the last places in the world where non-Hasidic children grew up speaking Yiddish. Though it lasted barely a decade, this moment of linguistic transition shaped Boris forever: "Until

I was five, I spoke only Yiddish, no Russian. My sister, eight years younger, could understand Yiddish but always answered in Russian."

"My home is not connected to a piece of land," he insists. "Everything I write about, I may call it Belz, but it's not the Belz where I lived, it's my dreamed-up Belz." Maybe so, but the city of Belz, now known as Bălți, the second-biggest city in Moldova, was a very particular place in the years directly after the Holocaust.[16]

It's no exaggeration to say that in just the past century ten different flags have flown over different parts of Moldova, today often considered the poorest country in Europe. And that's just where the complexity begins, for the earlier Principality of Moldavia, which became an Ottoman vassal in the sixteenth century, corresponds only inexactly to the current nation-state. Passing under Russian control in the nineteenth century, the name Moldavia vanished and most of the territory became the Governorate of Bessarabia, a name that remains resonant in Yiddish to this day (and has nothing to do with Arabia).

In Bessarabia, between the Prut and Dniester rivers, a substantial Yiddish-speaking Jewish community took root among ethnic Romanians, Ukrainians, Russians, Gagauz, Bulgarians, and Roma, to name just the main groups. Even now Boris speaks a juicy Bessarabian Yiddish that differs meaningfully from the so-called klal, or *standard*, that I learned, itself based largely on the Lithuanian variety.[17] Where I would say *un*, he says *in*. Where I would say *of*, he has *uf*. For *mayn*, he has *maan* (with a single long *a*). And this is just a quick tour of the vowels, which differ more or less systematically, but there can be differences too in the grammar and vocabulary, in one's whole mode of expression. Offhand he mentions words like kesl for *bucket* (which would be a *kettle* elsewhere) and ashozat, a Romanian loanword meaning *arrange*. Boris includes an entire glossary in the back of *Hidden Saints* just to help other Yiddish readers grasp his dialect.

Today very few people speak the particular way Boris does, though there are similarities with the so-called "Polish" and

"Hungarian" dialects of Yiddish which most Hasidim use and which as a result are now just about the only dialects remaining. His own dialect is "a little ruined," admits Boris, because of his immersion in the wider Yiddish world, including the more standardized literary language. But he believes that "a writer's identity card is their language" and his mission as a writer has been to tell and preserve the story of Jewish Bessarabia in all its particularity, as well as of the people who emerged from it, just as the masterful Yiddish novelist Chaim Grade, living in the north Bronx for decades, set himself the task of patiently reconstructing the shattered world of Jewish Vilna, "the Jerusalem of Lithuania."

After the First World War, Bessarabia as an official entity was no more, split between independent Romania and the Moldavian Autonomous Soviet Socialist Republic (part of the Ukrainian Soviet Socialist Republic, itself part of the broader USSR). Though both his parents grew up speaking Yiddish at home, Boris's mother was in the former, in a more traditionally observant Jewish household, and also learned Romanian. His father, in the latter, became more "Sovietized" and knew Russian.[18]

Then came the Soviet invasion of 1940 and the German-Romanian counterinvasion the following year. At fourteen, Boris's father was trapped with his family in one of the Transnistrian ghettoes to which some seventy-five thousand Jews were deported, but he escaped and eventually entered the Red Army. Meanwhile, Boris's mother was evacuated with her family deep into the Soviet Union, where she was totally immersed in Russian.

The two met in Belz after the war, a time of profound dislocation when the new "independent" Moldovan Soviet Socialist Republic was just solidifying with Soviet backing. Of Bessarabia's more than two hundred thousand Jews, the majority had been massacred, and in general only those who managed to evacuate to the Soviet Union had survived.[19] Many of the characters in Boris's novels are "haunted by the horrors of the Transnistrian ghettoes and camps," writes Mikhail Krutikov, whom Boris considers the only literary critic working in Yiddish today. "Their stories are barely familiar to a Western audience, for whom the Holocaust means Auschwitz and Treblinka, or the ghettoes of Warsaw and Vilna." Few have heard of the Tulchyn ghetto and the Pechora labor camp.[20]

Cities like Belz, which lost virtually their entire Jewish communities, were repopulated by people like Boris's parents, evacuees and survivors with roots in the surrounding countryside. "Everyone came with their own shtetl," says Boris. "With their foolishness and their wisdom and their language, they made a kind of shtetl in the city, and this was my access to the shtetl in general, though in going from shtetl to shtot something was altered." A shtetl was a market town, literally a *little city*, as formed linguistically by changing the vowel in shtot and adding the diminutive suffix -l, which along with the other Yiddish diminutives -ele, -enyu, -ik, -chik, and -inke (among others), is all about affection, though sometimes with a sprinkle of derision.

"The *idea* of the shtetl was formed by Yiddish literature," says Boris, "by writers like Peretz and Sholem Aleichem who had gotten out and were living in the big cities." Whether transmuted through a Chagall painting or a high school production of *Fiddler on the Roof*, the shtetl has come to stand in for the whole vanished world of traditional Jewish life in Eastern Europe, shrunk down to the scale of a folklorized village. More fundamental, according to Boris, is "the metaphysical shtetl, the spiritual baggage carried inside oneself from the grandparents." With all its virtues and faults, it has remained operative in the great Jewish metropolises of Kiev, Odessa, Warsaw, and New York today, even among many who see themselves as modern and assimilated. "Every generation has its nigun," says Boris, quoting Peretz, a nigun being a *devotional Hasidic melody*, usually wordless and improvised and often haunting—"but people are a continuation, in essence they haven't changed."

Belz, if the name is recognized at all by Jews today, is known from "Mayn Shtetele Belz (*My Shtetl Belz*)," a now nostalgic Yiddish theater megahit composed in New York in 1928 to honor a famous singer, who was born there but by then was basking in the bright lights of Second Avenue. "*My* little city Belz, overgrown with my own dreams, visions, and experiences, became with time an idea, which wanders around with me above life," writes Boris in *Hidden Saints*. He describes meeting an old New York Jew, also a Belzer, who asks him again and again about certain people and places long gone even by Boris's time: "With my every 'No' or confused shrug of the shoulders, the fire in his eyes was more and more extinguished." Finally, writes Boris, using first the ordinary Yiddish word for *question* and then the one for *question with no simple answer*, "I answered his frage with my kashe, as true Belzers do, shouting to him in his big deaf ear: 'When was the last time you were in your Belz?' 'In . . . 1918 my parents escaped from the pogrom . . . I was seven years old at the time.'"[21]

It was and it wasn't the same city, but Boris's 1950s Belz was still a Jewish, Yiddish-speaking world, especially the mahallah where Boris lived together with his parents, his maternal grandparents, and his younger sister. The word mahallah itself, originally from Arabic via Turkish and indicating a special unit of community somewhat like a *neighborhood*, gives voice to the lingering Balkan, post-Ottoman influence on local Jewish life, where baklava was more familiar than babka and coffee was made Turkish-style in a long-handled finjan, with a few dashes of salt.

At home, he was not Boris, but Bore or Berele (that diminutive again). Children played in the streets openly speaking Yiddish. He was one of the few with living grandparents: "We didn't understand anything about tradition with a capital *T*, it was just what one did, a part of us. My grandfather was a kosher butcher and a mohel, so there was a religious element which wasn't in other homes." Despite official

Soviet atheism, a modicum of observance was initially permitted in Moldova, perhaps because certain officials came from a Jewish background: "Purim was Purim and Passover was Passover, but not everything could be done openly. Matzah was produced illegally. There remained just one synagogue after the war, and even that was closed in the early sixties."

Russian came at school, but at first thirty of the thirty-five students were Jewish, and the teacher, who was also Jewish, would explain in Yiddish anything they didn't understand. "As Soviet children, it was truly a golden age with 'pioneer palaces,' programs, dancing, and music," says Boris. Being closed off from the rest of the world hardly mattered. Ethnic tensions stayed beneath the surface, though there remained "an inner border, an us and a them," and Jewish students had to go "a head higher" than their classmates to avoid the quotas restricting them from advancement in higher education and official employment.

Between the passing of a generation and a changing way of life, Yiddish seemed to be fading inexorably into the background, as in Israel and the US during the same period. In truth it had been brutally suppressed: on August 12, 1952, now known as the Night of the Murdered Poets, thirteen of the leading lights of Yiddish culture in the Soviet Union were secretly murdered on Stalin's orders in the basement of Moscow's Lubyanka Prison.[22] The Soviet Union's once considerable infrastructure of Yiddish schools, newspapers, publishers, and so on was erased virtually overnight.

One way Jewish identity continued was through music. "In those years, there wasn't a Jewish home in which a kid didn't learn to play music," remembers Boris. "A survivor wanted their child to grow up to be a mensch, and that meant a cultured person."[23] He started on the accordion when he was five and on the violin when he was seven. At the age of fifteen, he entered a full-time music school and soon after a conservatory in the capital city of Kishinev, now known in Moldovan as Chişinău. This is arguably the city where the Jewish twentieth century began, on April 19–20, 1903, with a shocking pogrom in which forty-nine Jews were killed, many Jewish women raped, and 1,500 Jewish homes destroyed or damaged. More than with any previous attack, news of Kishinev spread around the world, including rumors of the Russian imperial government's involvement. Many European Jews concluded that the only solution was emigration to Palestine or the US. Many American Jews were galvanized into making the connection between the pogroms in Europe and anti-Black violence in the US.[24] In his 2004 historical novel *Ven der goylem hot farmakht di oygn* (*Stones Don't Bear Witness*), Boris unpacks the events in deeply researched, almost Tolstoyan detail, including large sections from the killers' perspective, whose antisemitic harangues of course are all deliciously delivered in Yiddish.

Boris spent most of the next three decades in Kishinev as a violinist. He married and had two sons. He briefly tried writing in Russian, which felt deeply unnatural, until he met Yehiel Shraybman, one of the few Yiddish writers to survive the purges: "He saw it all, lived through it, lost his mind, and wanted to take his own life."[25] At a time when Boris didn't even know the alefbeys, Shraybman became his vegvayzer, his *way-shower*, not only editing his first stories but "beginning the conversation with me about what literature is," as Boris puts it.[26]

In 1981, thanks to Shraybman's recommendation, Boris was one of five Yiddish intellectuals invited to study within the Maxim Gorky Literature Institute in Moscow for a kind of PhD under the auspices of the journal *Sovetish Heymland* (Soviet Homeland). It was the first time in four decades that there had been any opportunity remotely like this. Besides *Der Birobidzhaner Shtern* (*The Birobidzhan Star*), published in the dwindling Siberian Yiddishland, *Sovetish Heymland* had been the only Yiddish-language publication permitted after the Night of the Murdered Poets. Indeed, this remarkably high quality and generously state supported journal was at least partly intended as Cold War propaganda for Yiddish readers overseas. Uniquely self-censoring (since its editor was a trusted party member) and in a language few could read, "it was the only publication in the USSR," says Boris, "where for example one could find material about ghettoes and concentration camps, with images, and about the killing of Jews, not just 'Soviet citizens.'"

During those two years in Moscow immersed in both Yiddish and Russian literature, he learned how to edit a Yiddish journal and wrote his debut story collection *Treplekh aroyf tsu a nes* (*Stairway to a Miracle*). The miracle of the title was the new experience of being able to read in Yiddish at all: "as I recognized it sentence by sentence, something came to life in me, as at an archaeological dig with its strata, digging through the sand and clay until you come upon something living: an image, a mosaic."

Back in Moldova, with glasnost and perestroika underway, he plunged into projects that would have been impossible just a few years earlier: creating and teaching Yiddish classes, establishing a Jewish library in Kishinev, launching a television program, and publishing a new newspaper half in Yiddish and half in Russian. For the latter, he jettisoned the so-called Soviet Yiddish orthography, which spells out the loshn koydesh words phonetically, and re-taught himself how to spell in the traditional, more difficult way.[27]

Both in Moldova and across the collapsing Soviet Union, suppressed ethnolinguistic impulses and buried histories were now returning with a vengeance. "It was an overloaded life, and no one knew how it would end," says Boris, but by the late 1980s "every night train cars full of people were leaving for Israel," whose official representatives were on the ground encouraging emigration. "There was a battle among us: should we just let it all burn? I was against it." The war in Transnistria not only drove Jews from the eastern side of the Dniester but also hastened the mass exodus from Kishinev and Belz. Because of Russian support for the breakaway Transnistrian republic, the conflict is still "frozen" today.[28] Boris documented it all in real time in the haunting documentary *Vu iz mayn heym?* (*Where Is My Home?*), which is dedicated "in Memory of Bessarabian Jewry" and opens with a valedictory flip through the uniquely Bessarabian Jewish names in the Kishinev phone book.[29]

In 1991, in the middle of all this, Boris was invited by longtime Yiddish activists to come to New York for the first time. He stayed for a month in their tiny Yiddish-speaking enclave on Bainbridge Avenue in the Bronx, for he knew hardly any English and they didn't speak much Russian: "I tore myself away once and went into the subway alone, but came back soon after." For someone used to the "art palace" of the Moscow metro, he remembers, it was shocking to encounter "the schmutz and blood of that thieves' den" known as the New York City subway.

Another time he set off all the way to Brighton Beach, to find two of the last old Yiddish-speaking communists, not recent émigrés, who wanted to meet him. "On the phone they said they would be waiting on a certain corner holding a copy of *Birobidzhaner Shtern*," remembers Boris. "They must have subscribed. We met at some kind of Cuban or Mexican pizzeria, which is there to this day. They were both retired, one was a carpenter and the other also some kind of worker. We met for two hours, but they didn't really eat. Imagine: for me it was something wild. I had only read about Jewish communists, but here it was: a living example! It was something phantasmagoric. There were communists in the Soviet Union, but not true and faithful ones."

## 3

Bainbridge Avenue, that little street in the Bronx where Boris first touched down, was a radical experiment. Here in the 1960s, even as Jews and so many white New Yorkers were dissolving their communities and leaving the city in droves, three families decided to buy houses next to each other and raise their children together in Yiddish.[30] Only

Hasidim, with very different aims not so directly linked to the language, were doing that.

On Bainbridge Avenue, the Fishmans, Shechters, and Gottesmans, a mix of survivors and the American-born, set out to create their own Yiddish-speaking island. They believed that even a few committed families could maintain a fast-fading language in the middle of the city, starting with their own homes on a single block, while still participating in the broader society. A few years later, five Irish-speaking families on Shaw's Road in Belfast would do something similar, ultimately establishing Northern Ireland's first Irish-medium primary school and growing into a community of over twenty families—the hub of a language movement that made rapid progress, especially among imprisoned fighters during the Troubles.[31]

The New York Yiddishists focused on keeping the language and culture alive and in some ways even "purifying" it.[32] Though they drew on previous movements, especially in Eastern Europe, they were less overtly political. They respected Jewish religious practice as part of a broader, holistic Yiddishkayt, or *Jewishness*, but they were distinctly fray (*secular*) compared to the frum (*pious*) Hasidim. They called their experiment Bainbridgivke, a play on Sholem Aleichem's idealized fictional shtetl Kasrilevke, where the -ivke/-evke ending is yet another diminutive that entered Yiddish from Ukrainian, evoking someplace small and cozy.[33]

Initially there were still other, older Yiddish speakers in the north Bronx, as well as an existing secular Yiddish day school on the same block.[34] But the three couples, with their nine young children, created a Yiddish world of their own, establishing small cultural funds, publishing journals for children and adults, and organizing a children's group called Enge-Benge for whom Van Cortlandt Park was a Yiddish-saturated Enge-Benge Land.[35] When the day school later closed, the families purchased the building and turned it into the small but heymish Sholem Aleichem Cultural Center, where occasional events are held to this day. Until her death in 2013 at the age of ninety-three, Beyle Schaechter-Gottesman, a living archive of Yiddish song who published eight books of her own poetry, would host regular zinger-ayen, *community sing-alongs*, at home at 3338 Bainbridge Avenue, where Yiddish speakers and researchers from all over the world would gather and stay.

Meanwhile, Beyle's brother Mordkhe Schaechter, a "one-man Yiddish empire" also born in Chernowitz (now Ukraine), was filling his house two doors down with his kartotek, a personal archive consisting of hundreds of shoeboxes with hundreds of thousands of note cards on which he had scrawled over a million words, expressions, and "linguistic observations," gleaned from all possible sources and covering hundreds of topics in unsparing terminological detail.

For those swept up in a language movement, lexicography is mania with a purpose, and linguists, however improbably, can be heroes.[36] Schaechter was an avowed territorialist who believed, like others in that movement, that Yiddish speakers needed to flourish in a territory of their own, somewhere in the world but not necessarily Israel. This "Bronx Suriname" was the closest he ever came.[37] He published relentlessly on Yiddish *in* Yiddish, from his 1991 טראָגן, האָבן, און פֿרײַקע קינדער-יאָרן: אַן ענגליש-ייִדיש ווערטערביכל (*Pregnancy, Childbirth and Early Childhood: An English-Yiddish Dictionary*) to his four-hundred-page די געוויקסן-וועלט אין יידיש (*Plant Names in Yiddish: A Handbook of Botanical Terminology*), finally released in 2005.

At once a teacher, writer, editor, and activist, Schaechter founded the Committee for the Implementation of the Standardized Yiddish Orthography at the very moment when people were ceasing to write any Yiddish at all. He spent the 1980s laboring as an editor of the exhaustive, all-in-Yiddish *Great Dictionary of the Yiddish Language*, which never advanced beyond four volumes dedicated to aleph, the first letter of the alphabet—but what an aleph section it is![38]

With time running out and the prospects for transmission in America diminishing, Schaechter was not the only New York Yiddishist conceiving ever more monumental projects to salvage what remained of the language.[39] When Ben Stonehill of Queens, whose living was installing carpets and linoleum floors, learned that the former Hotel Marseilles on 103rd and Broadway on the Upper West Side had been transformed into temporary housing for Holocaust survivors arriving in America, he set up in the lobby and recorded over one thousand now mostly forgotten songs.[40] Just north at Columbia, the well-funded and linguist-directed *Language and Culture Atlas of Ashkenazic Jewry* set out to map Yiddish dialects in all their local complexity, gathering 5,755 hours of recorded interviews, conducted mostly by Shaechter with Yiddish speakers originally from six hundred different communities across Europe. In the 1970s, as the Yiddish-reading public was dying off, heaps of books were being discarded by their illiterate inheritors. A desperate operation, which later grew into the National Yiddish Book Center, took shape: one day the zamlers (*collectors*) would be racing "in the freezing rain to rescue 8,000 books from a garbage dumpster"; another they would be forming "a 'bucket brigade' to recover a 15,000-volume Jewish library from the basement of a demolished building in the Bronx."[41]

Joshua Fishman, who was part of the Bainbridgivke experiment and whose sociolinguistics library now lives at ELA, gave these struggles a wider resonance beyond Yiddish. He recognized that soon only "poets, professors, and pietists" ("pietists" meaning Hasidim) would be using the language. The scope for cultural or ethnic autonomy was so narrow in America, even in New York, and that was assuming enough Jews even wanted it. He reasoned that religious movements stood a better chance. A pioneering sociolinguist who lived his work, Fishman helped establish the new study of language endangerment and revitalization, arming communities to defend themselves. He was so venerated among language activists worldwide that Māori dancers came to

New York to honor him with a thundering haka just before his death in 2015, which was the last time I saw him.

What about the children of Bainbridgivke? Fishman's wife Gella, also an activist, admitted that some were lonely and disappointed when they discovered that there were virtually no other Yiddish-speaking children like them anywhere.[42] Almost everyone else had abandoned the language, entering a profound amnesia while the Bainbridgivke kids were off in Enge-Benge Land.[43] They left the avenue, but they did become Yiddish poets, musicians, journalists, folklorists, academics, activists, and above all *speakers*, often moved to pass down the language to their children in turn. Schaechter spoke only Yiddish with all sixteen of his grandchildren. The children of Bainbridgivke have been instrumental in maintaining much of the remaining, once-massive secular Yiddish infrastructure in the city.

When my own grandfather died in 1998, he was the last Yiddish speaker in any branch of our extended family tree. He had no one to speak to, so he rarely spoke it, and all I remember is the low gravelly rumble of his Lower East Side English. Only a decade later, when I came to understand that Yiddish was a language with a grammar and a literature—not just a broken jargon good for punch lines—did I start to learn it and seek out people to talk to. I found at least a partially networked archipelago of scattered native speakers, semispeakers, heritage speakers, rememberers, enthusiasts, and students. New York was still the center, the only place with a constant, in-person critical mass, and of course no shortage of rivalries resulting. I worked for a while at the Folksbiene, the one surviving century-old Yiddish theater. I met just enough Yiddishist descendants, self-taught ideologues, straight-up oddballs, grad students, retirees, and international types passing through that there was something to do in Yiddish and a chance to speak the language every week, if not more: a klezmer concert, a theater performance, or a svive (in this case, not just *a scene*, but specifically one of the roving Yiddish-only parties at apartments around the city).[44] Here people would speak knowingly with forgotten turns of phrase about Soviet Yiddish poets and lost radical movements of the 1920s like Doikayt (*Hereness*). Many were moved by the dream of creating or recreating a radical Jewish culture that was leftist, diasporic, and queer.

Every summer, several hundred people, including many families with children, gather at a camp or bungalow colony upstate. Call it a "metalinguistic community," for almost all speak English and few are native or day-to-day speakers of Yiddish. But for a week they choose to try to speak the language, everywhere from the swimming pool to the dance floor, giving it a curious postvernacular afterlife.[45]

At other Yiddish-related festivals and gatherings with fewer serious speakers, the language was clearly surviving more as seasoning than substance. A vanishing language can become symbolically and emotionally charged, more bound up in ritual and performance than practical communication. No longer viable enough to pose a threat, its authenticity can be celebrated and its stigma forgotten in the rush to reclaim roots. The post-sixties embrace of heritage, genealogy, identity, ethnicity, and multiculturalism—anything beyond the assimilationist paradigm—has put a puff of wind in the sails of sinking secular Yiddish. The Yiddishist gatherings were usually warm and joyous, but at some level seemed deeply unnatural. Reality, it was hard not to feel, was still always in English.

It took a long time to grasp that something much more important and profound was happening just a few miles away from some of these gatherings, in what might as well be another world. Yiddish was being reborn in Brooklyn, as a Hasidic language.

Though before they had largely shunned immigration to America, dozens of distinct, decimated Hasidic communities regrouped in Brooklyn after the Holocaust, quietly and tenaciously maintaining and reviving the language against all expectations.[46] Enormous Hasidic courts are presided over by king-like rebbes, whose movements at least still resoundingly reference faraway towns like Satu Mare, Romania (Satmar); Pápa, Hungary (Pupa); Bobowa, Poland (Bobov); and Vyzhnytsia, Ukraine (Vizhnitz). This is no archaic sliver of shtetl just off the J train, but the conscious attempt of Holocaust survivors with meshugene koyekh, *crazy force of will*. Immigrant languages in America rarely last beyond the third generation, but the Hasidim are now passing on Yiddish to a fifth right in the middle of the city. They are achieving what arguably only the rural Old Order Amish and Mennonites have achieved with Pennsylvania Dutch.

In Williamsburg—which became the world center for the Satmar dynasty, with its grand rebbe Joel Teitelbaum playing a pivotal role—Yiddish became even stronger than it had been in prewar Europe, moving into new spheres and reversing the shift to Hungarian that had been underway in the community.[47] In Williamsburg and subsequently in Borough Park, Far Rockaway, parts of Rockland and Orange Counties, and elsewhere, all the way to other centers in Israel, Europe, and Canada, a global Hasidic population now in the hundreds of thousands has been rebuilding a new community from the ruins of the old. Given the Hasidic birthrate, Yiddish is now growing at a ferocious rate, with half of all New York speakers under the age of eighteen. Recently passing some invisible inflection point, it has gone from one of the city's "oldest" languages, demographically speaking, to one of the youngest.

This extreme youthfulness is part of why Hasidic Yiddish is a language in the making, the as yet little-studied product of speakers converging from various parts of Eastern Europe on a few Brooklyn neighborhoods while absorbing and parrying influences from English, Hebrew, and elsewhere. Most influential because of Satmar, however, is the Eastern Transcarpathian dialect from the Unterland region in what is today mostly Hungary. For debated reasons, unusually rapid change is occurring, including the loss of gender and case distinctions across the language.[48]

In a different sense, language use itself has actually become gendered, with women more likely to use more English, especially among themselves, and men more Yiddish.[49] Though in a sense sanctified by tradition and the losses of the Holocaust, Yiddish is "just" the day-to-day language, hardly at the holy level of Hebrew or Aramaic. Part of its role today is to keep Hasidim separate from both secular Hebrew-speaking Israel and the hopelessly goyish world of English. It's actually convenient that no one else, not even other Jews, can speak it.

For a secular Yiddishist, the Hasidic revival can be supremely ironic, fascinating, and frustrating.[50] The secular "standard" Yiddish is so different that those few who learn it can hardly communicate with 99 percent of the people they should in theory be able to talk to. Because of religious prohibitions, Hasidic Yiddish speakers are supposed to be unaware of, uninterested in, or actively opposed to secular literary or cultural achievements. Secularist disdain for the "broken" language of "fanatics" can be no less potent.

But in twenty-first-century New York, probably more than anywhere else, there is now some back and forth between frum and fray. Like so many others, the language itself in its kishkes, *the guts*, can seem almost impossible to disentangle from traditional belief and practice, immediately embroiling the speaker in religious terminology.[51] From the traditional greeting "Sholem aleykhem" (*Peace be upon you*) to the all-purpose "Baruch hashem" (*Blessed be the name*) and much deeper into the language, lexical choices signal religious commitment. Does saying "Gut shabes" on the Sabbath imply that you yourself observe it? Unlike in English—where "Bless you," "Good-bye" (God be with you), and various King James phrases (bottomless pit, den of thieves, law unto themselves, etc.) now signal exactly nothing religious—the secularization of Yiddish is an unfinished project.

There are more and more OTD'ers, Hasidic dropouts and true countercultural badasses trying hard to deprogram,[52] and even some who stay in the community now discovering and developing the wider

Yiddish cultural inheritance as writers, linguists, and translators. This raises hopes for at least a modest new haskole, or *enlightenment*, and an associated cultural flowering. "Sosneh is a pine; osineh, an aspen; berezeh, a birch; klion, a maple; topolieh, a poplar, and lindeh, a linden tree," writes one, with a certain sadness. "But the only word I, a native Yiddish speaker from Brooklyn, New York, had ever known for all these wonderfully specific classes of trees was boym: a tree."[53]

On the flipside, there are Yiddishists who want to be more than mere tourists among the Hasidim and have started living on the conveniently gentrifying edges of ungentrifiable Hasidic neighborhoods like Williamsburg and Crown Heights. Overcoming secular prejudices, a few become enthralled by the limits and the rituals, by the chance to join a tribe and gain a manual for living, all folded into an ancestral language. Before hardening into a total system widely seen as traditional and conservative, Hasidism started in the eighteenth century as a viral movement stressing joy, inner light, and the ordinary person's capacity for mystical experience. Some neo-Hasidic seekers try to graft these qualities onto the decaying wood of secular Jewish life. Yiddish can be just one of many routes to becoming a bal-tshuve, literally *master of return*, but figuratively a secular Jew who returns repentant to God and traditional Judaism.[54] Chabad Lubavitch, the global Hasidic movement based in Crown Heights, has been the main bal-tshuve magnet, to the point where Anglophone bal-tshuves may have tipped that particular community away from its distinctive "Lithuanian" Yiddish toward English (and Hebrew).

But what makes Hasidic Yiddish an ever more dynamic presence in twenty-first-century New York is not just demographics or the appeal of the religious life. It's a powerful network of institutions and the will to sustain them. An entire school system educates Hasidic children in Yiddish, with controversially little concern for English or secular studies.[55] Housing stays in the community. Shomrim security forces patrol Hasidic neighborhoods in cooperation with the NYPD. Hatzolah sends an ambulance when you need to go to the hopsital and bikur holim societies visit you when you're there. There is a vibrant, shlocky Hasidic press—where photos of women, among other things, cannot be printed—and even a growing "kosher" literature. As many Hasidim as possible are either engaged in full-time study or work within the community, whether in real estate, the Diamond District, at B&H Electronics, or elsewhere. Relations with the outside world, especially and most crucially the New York City and State governments, are carefully managed for community benefit and autonomy. Large numbers mobilize against threats like the unkosher internet, which I joined a crowd of over sixty thousand mostly Hasidim in protesting with mass gatherings and speeches at two Queens stadiums in 2013. So nearly total is the complex of all-in-Yiddish institutions for Hasidic New Yorkers that some in fact speak little English.

This is unlike anything seen before in New York or any American city, though perhaps it bears comparison with the extraordinary and much larger-scale survival and growth of African American English across the US since the Great Migration. However hard to replicate, the Hasidic Yiddish revival is a potential model that at the same time is troublingly tied up with separatism and superiority, an us versus them, the erecting of walls between peoples. It's not simply a language movement, but the historic mission of a people set apart by the will of der eybershter, a Germanic word for *uppermost* which came to mean *G-d* in Yiddish, as communicated through holy scripture and the rebbes. Maybe reform will come before more conflict does, but it may be that every successful language movement has this secessionist drive inside it, that sometimes vicious little kernel of chauvinism or nationalism, and in some cases a literally religious zeal. Is it worth the price?

## 4

I make it just in time for the farewell speeches, which are all in English. When it's Boris's turn, he too speaks in English, his fourth language, trying hard to be clear in that unmistakable Brighton Beach accent. I've never heard him speak more than a few words of the language before, though he uses it with his grandkids. It feels like 80 percent of him is missing.

Of course it has to be English. Of the several dozen people gathered here to celebrate his retirement, most work for the *Forward*, the English edition which started in 1990. *Forverts*, the Yiddish edition which started in 1897 and built up all the power and funding, was progressively marginalized to the point where Boris was doing much of the editorial work single-handedly, with fewer and fewer colleagues. I greet them in Yiddish, and they smile nervously, speaking in low voices.

Little differentiates this from any other Manhattan office, though the rent here two blocks from Wall Street is surprisingly a bit cheaper. When Boris started, the paper was on Thirty-Third Street, in an impressive citadel for multiple Yiddishist institutions that's now a Hilton Garden Inn. Before that, it was at 175 East Broadway: a ten-story Beaux Arts building, now full of multimillion-dollar condos, which at its 1912 opening symbolized Jewish arrival in New York and towered over the Lower East Side with its marble columns and stained-glass windows and bas-relief carvings of Marx and Engels.

For at least its first four decades, *Forverts* was a proudly socialist paper, in step with the working-class immigrants who ran it and read it, the yidn fun a gants yor, the regular-guy *Jews of a whole year* who believed in social democracy, solidarity, and justice and would pick up a copy at the corner candy store, the bodega of another era. Under the legendary editor and novelist Abraham Cahan, it became a major player in Jewish life and left politics, remaining fiercely independent but working with powerful organizations like the United Hebrew Trades federation, the Jewish Socialist Federation, and the Arbeter Ring, a Jewish labor fraternal order.[56]

At its height, *Forverts* was a daily paper with editions in cities across the country and a circulation over 275,000.[57] Did Cahan undermine the conditions of his own success by encouraging his readers to switch to English? Columns like the famous Bintel Brief (*Bundle of Letters*)—where griner (*greenhorn*) immigrants wrote in with their frages (*questions*), kashes (*questions with no simple answer*), and even shayles (*religious questions*)—proved so effective at teaching American and English-speaking ways that many walked right off into the non-Jewish world.[58]

Such is the permanent dilemma of the so-called ethnic media, most of it in languages other than English, which has played such a central but underappreciated role not only in specific communities, but in the history of New York and many other cities. To mention just a few examples: the German *New Yorker Staats-Zeitung* goes back to 1834 and at last sighting was possibly still hanging on in some form at the editor's Florida home. In the 2010s, a new crop of Nepali newspapers were doing well thanks to advertising from Nepali businesses in Queens.[59] New York's first Czech paper, *Lucerna*, was hand written and lasted only a single issue, but it set the precedent for *New Yorske* and *Delnicke Listy*. Many groups forbidden or otherwise unable to publish "back home" first developed modern media, in their own languages and often with radical political agendas, in the media capital of New York. Besides *An Gaodhal*, that first-ever Irish-language periodical produced in Brooklyn, consider the early twentieth-century flowering of Arabic newspapers in Little Syria, or those founded on the run by Lithuanian activist Jonas Šliūpas like *Lietuviškasis balsas* and *Unija*, or others in Aromanian or Rusyn. Today a very partial directory of the city's ethnic media lists over 350 newspapers, magazines, websites, and radio and television channels operating in a few dozen languages. But this is just part of the story of how communities in the city have shared vital information in their own languages, well before YouTube, Facebook pages, and WhatsApp groups.[60]

Forcefully for such a sedate gathering, Boris makes the case for the Yiddish paper. He's been giving this stump speech for the last eighteen years, but to the fray third- and fourth-generation American Jews in the room, mostly monolingual English speakers with at most a little Hebrew, Spanish, or French, Yiddish is irretrievably something of the past. Between the Yiddish and English editions there was in essence no common language. Yiddish may deserve polite acknowledgment as heritage—a people's, the paper's—but the mission here is to be the American Jewish newspaper of record, a miniature Jewish *New York Times* for what remains of a progressive secular community.

In 1992, Boris and his family finally left Moldova: not enthusiastically, he says, but "understanding that I had to leave because Jewish life was ending there." Like almost everyone they knew, they went to Israel, where Boris had met some of the remaining Yiddish intellectuals on previous visits. His wife, Raisa, an engineer trained in Siberia because the Jewish quotas were lax there, reinvented herself in Jerusalem as she later would again in New York. Boris was immediately drafted into teaching Yiddish to Israelis, though he spoke only a smattering of Hebrew. Then he took a library job creating an exhaustive digital catalog for the interwar Yiddish press from Warsaw. "It was the whole history of Jews, day by day, from 1919 to 1939," he says. "For me the whole world opened up. I didn't feel like I was in Jerusalem." He spent the rest of his time recording the country's last Yiddish writers ("a ghetto, a tiny clique, but also an entire literature"), who had managed to produce newspapers, novels, and theater in the land of Hebrew, despite the overt bans and the covert stigma that started with the "language wars" of 1913.

In 1998, he came to New York to work at *Forverts*, by then down to a weekly with a circulation of several thousand and falling, around half of them Holocaust survivors then in their seventies and eighties.[61] Among those who even knew it still existed, the paper was seen as too far gone. "In truth," admits Boris, "the whole paper was being written and put out by one person, Mordkhe Strigler, zikhroyne livrocho, *of blessed memory*. And he was a universal person, a great knower of both Yiddishkayt and worldly things who had survived Buchenwald, a huge person. He thought there were no writers left. The joke was that Strigler wrote one long, long article and cut it into pieces and put each under a different pseudonym—and this was actually true, except for a few other things."[62]

Strigler died just a few months after Boris's arrival, taking all his pseudonyms with him. Boris was immediately asked to take over. In *Righteous Ones*, he very thinly fictionalizes the antiquated scene at what he calls *Foroys* (using the actual word for *forward* in Yiddish, with *Forverts* a borrowing from German vorwärts).[63] The paper was a shmate, a *rag* with no pictures or images, he says, and he quickly set about transforming the design and somehow finding and recruiting seventy writers from around the world, which was just about everyone still alive and writing in Yiddish at that point. The paper brimmed with recipes, reviews, folklore, klezmer reviews, and Boris's own serialized novels, as well as a relentless catalog of deaths, anniversaries, and yahrzeits, or *death anniversaries*.

Boris commissioned what was perhaps the first real Yiddish website from two of the techier Yiddishists. He would sometimes lend a hand with the short-lived but ambitious Russian *Forward*, launched in 1995 for the newly arrived Soviet Jewish immigrants.[64] He put out dozens of books, CDs, and DVDs; started printing an edition called *Vayter* (*Further*) for younger readers learning the language; and even featured online radio dispatches from daily correspondents in Buenos Aires, Paris, Warsaw, Moscow, and Melbourne. He was constantly shooting videos ("It was a bad studio, but it was a studio") and even attempted to attract a Hasidic audience. For them, the paper with its secular, socialist history is never going to be kosher—but at times can be "a guilty pleasure."[65]

I was also drafted into this last-minute renaissance. Boris overrode my protest that I was still just learning the language: in a smaller culture, every reader is needed immediately as a writer. He convinced me to start filing video dispatches from China in Yiddish under the moniker "A New York Jew in China." Viewed online hundreds of thousands of times, this unlikely series proved Boris's hunch: all kinds of people were still hungry for the sound and sense and style of Yiddish, especially if it was something new, even if they could understand it through the subtitles. Even when I came back from China, he wouldn't let me stop, and for a while I made him videos wherever I went, including Birobidzhan, Singapore, Hawai'i, and Zuccotti Park.

Boris describes all this, still flexing those jowls. Everything was done on the most minimal budget, he says, and it was continually being cut, though sold-off real estate and radio assets left over from the glory days have bankrolled an extended twilight for the larger organization. The paper's traditional subscriber base was also continually falling, but ultimately tens of thousands of new readers have started coming to the Yiddish website every month.[66]

People are fidgeting and checking the time, eager to get back to Scarsdale or Teaneck or Roslyn. Drinks and bites are running low. But Boris refuses to hurry up, or play only in the key of nostalgia. He gazes out on the pileup of the past, but he is propelled to work as if there were a future for his newspaper and his novels, his poetry and his publishing ventures—for the language and literature he has devoted half his life to.

It reminds me of how the Book of Life closes on Yom Kippur, sealing one's fate at least for another year, although for the few days before you can rush to get a last word in. A gut kvitl! some say in Yiddish during this time. *A good little note*, referring to a hasty scrap of prayer or petition like those stuck in the cracks between stones at the Wailing Wall in Jerusalem. Is there still time to add a gut kvitl to the canon of Yiddish?

If that feels too pious, Yiddish has another expression. Trepverter, literally *words on the staircase*, are a last blast of wit, a final retort, as you head for the exit.[67]

# Ibrahima
## ߒߞߏ (*N'ko*)

### 1

Try running a website in a new alphabet that few people have ever heard of. You need a font that fits, which is not just a matter of taste resolved by scrolling through a list of hundreds of funky options. At best, there may be one font actually designed to render the alphabet's characters, ligatures, diacritics, and other elements correctly. Typing in that font then requires a keyboard, although luckily now not a physical one but a piece of software called a keyboard layout, which inventively maps the alphabet onto the QWERTY standard or the few others available. Then there's rendering it in whatever software, running on whatever system, on whatever device. But above all, you need readers and writers.

Sitting here in a little room in a century-old house in a New Jersey suburb, Ibrahima is the eternal beta tester, working out constant kinks as he emails, texts, tweets, reads, blogs, and runs his website all in N'ko, the West African alphabet created in 1949 to which he has devoted himself for the last fifteen years. An N'ko-mɔɔ ߒߞߏ ߡߐ߮ (*N'koist*) like Ibrahima (the letter ɔ is pronounced like the vowel in *thought*) puts his faith in the power of African writing for African languages, for an African future. For complex reasons, nowhere in the past two centuries has the push for new writing systems been stronger than in West Africa, with over twenty different scripts invented. None has spread as successfully as N'ko.

The N'ko alphabet was first revealed in Bingerville, Ivory Coast, on April 14, 1949, by a young teacher of the Quran who was also starting to trade in kola nuts. Souleymane Kanté was a Maninka speaker from Kankan in Guinea, not far from Ibrahima's village. Writing had been on Kanté's mind for at least five years, ever since a traumatic encounter that he later described, here in Coleman Donaldson's transliteration and translation:[1]

[illegible]

> Ń tó dá Bɔ̀kɛ́ lón' dó sìinén' lɔ́ɔfɛ' dɔ́, ń kà lɛ́ra' dó sàntá' yé fàdafín' ná kùn-n-tánya' sɛ́bɛn'ò dɔ́, ò sɛ́bɛbaa' bɔ́nɛn Líban kó Kámal Máruwa. Ń k'o máɲininka mɛ́nkɛ̌' àlu kán kó bi m'à wá, o lé' kán' kó fàdafín' ná kùnfinyá' tɛ́ bán fɔ́ lá, i fɔ́lɔ́' mɛ́n' dí àlu kán' fén tɛ́ sé sɛ́bɛ lá, kó: à dén' bánbannɛn tɛ́ kángbɛ síla' màkó sɛ́bɛli fén' tɛ́ kó kán gbɛ́nɛ fãn' tɛ́ fàdafín' bólo fó kánbolo' dàmá', hákilima' t'à míri mɛ́n' sɛ́bɛ̨ kó' mà, kó tùbabu lɔ́nninna síyaman' nè bád'àlu soolá fàdafin kán' nù sɛ́bɛ lá, konin ɲá sí sɔ̀dɔnɛn t'o kóɲa' lá', k'o dɔ́ án kàran fàdagbɛ kán' ná o lé' nɔ̀ɔmán ǹ kàrán' dí ǹ jɛ̀dɛ̀ kán' ná.

> *One day, sitting at the marketplace in Bouaké, I saw some book for sale with something about African stupidity on it.*

> *Its writer was from Lebanon and named Kamal Maruwa. He was saying that African ignorance never ends. He said, first, none of their languages can be written; they aren't made according to any grammar. They aren't meant for writing; they were made for speaking only. They don't actually have a true language, just dialects that no intelligent person would waste their time thinking about writing. Lots of Europeans have become interested in writing African languages, but there is just no way. He said, teaching us European languages is easier than teaching us our own languages.*

Shocked and insulted, Kanté tried to contact Maruwa to rebut his claim that African languages were "like those of birds," in other words incapable of being written down, but the journalist had already returned to Lebanon.[2] Kanté could read *these* words because he was a fluent reader and writer of Arabic from attending the well-known Quranic school run by his father. It's possibly he was also exposed to Ajami, the practice of writing West African languages with Arabic letters, of which there is evidence going back at least to the seventeenth century, when an unknown scholar north of Lake Chad wrote glosses in Kanuri (using Arabic letters) inside a copy of the Quran. By the early twentieth century, full-length works were being composed in Wolof, Fulani, and Hausa using Arabic letters. Some may have been doing this with Maninka when Kanté was growing up, but he couldn't read what they wrote, and his uncle told him that Ajami served mainly as an aid to memory. Long before encountering Maruwa, Kanté himself had been wondering whether "African languages are worthless because God has not allowed for them to be written."[3]

For two years, Kanté experimented in his spare time with writing his mother tongue in Arabic letters, but found no way to indicate certain sounds, let alone the tones which are crucial for so many West African languages. He also threw himself into learning French and tried writing Maninka in Latin letters.[4] He tested a group of children and adults unfamiliar with both the Arabic and Latin scripts and discovered that a majority spontaneously started drawing from the right—so he decided that his new script, like Arabic, would go right to left. According to one account, a dream may have served as pivotal inspiration, as with many new writing systems around the world.[5]

N'ko was not just a new alphabet, but in some ways also a new language. Though anchored in the Maninka of Kankan, the mother tongue of Kanté (and Ibrahima), it also standardizes and encompasses the whole Manding language group spoken by as many as forty million people in West Africa, as well as a growing global diaspora that includes thousands of people in New York. Just as forms of Danish, Swedish, and Norwegian form a tight-knit group within Indo-European, Manding is a subgroup within the larger Mande family, which has around eighty million speakers across nine countries. Just as variations on the names Rome and Latin are used for some Romance languages (Romansh, Romanian, Ladin, Ladino, etc.), the names Manding, Mande, Manden, Maninka, Mandingo, Mandinka, Malinké, and Mali are used today in different ways in different languages—but they all point to the Mali Empire, one of Africa's mightiest until the seventeenth century.

N'ko is primarily designed for and unites Manding-language speakers from the core area of the old empire in what is today Guinea, Mali, and Ivory Coast. The most widely spoken Manding languages here go by the names Bambara (Mali), Jula (Ivory Coast and Burkina Faso), Mandinka (Gambia), and Maninka (Guinea). In the languages themselves, these are called Bamanan/Bamanakan, Julakan, Mandinkakan, and Maninkakan, respectively, names which are formed by simply adding the suffix -kan, meaning *language*, *dialect*, or *speech*, to the name of any place or people.

As in so much of the world before nation-states and recording technologies, it may be impossible to unravel all the intricacies of exactly who spoke what where. Language names are convenient but rarely precise abstractions, given that no one besides linguists wants to talk about "subcontinua flowing smoothly into each other," as one describes the Manding situation. For instance, western Manding languages typically have five vowels while eastern varieties like Ibrahima's have seven. People generally have no problem understanding each other from one town to another, but it gets trickier and more interesting in the Bronx when a Mandinka speaker from Gambia may be neighbors with a Maninka speaker from Burkina, a thousand miles to the east. N'ko provides a written and potentially even a spoken standard for all.

The name N'ko itself—whether applied to the alphabet alone, a way of speaking based on it, or the movement as a whole—means *I say* in all Manding languages. No less a figure than the Mali Empire's legendary thirteenth-century ruler Sundiata Keita is said to have addressed himself "to all men, women and children of Manden, and to all my brothers who say N'ko."[6] In one creation myth, N'ko is said to have been the first word spoken on earth.[7] Naming a script-language *I say* is also brilliantly recursive, reinscribing a first-person act of speaking into every mention.

N'koists like Ibrahima argue that only a standard like N'ko can address how colonial nation-state borders continue to deepen divisions and sow confusion. Today Bambara, Jula, Mandinka, and Maninka are the major spoken languages of Mali, Ivory Coast, Gambia, and Guinea (respectively), with different language policies applying in each country. At the same time, all remain dramatically subordinate to French, which is still the sole official language in countries like Mali and Burkina Faso (or likewise English, in the case of Gambia). French remains essential for anyone in the region trying to get ahead through higher education or the civil service. Perhaps nowhere in the world does language policy remain so overtly colonial as in formerly French West Africa, and nowhere in the world are official literacy rates lower, typically just above 30 percent.

Even when its days were numbered in the 1940s, French colonial policy forbade the use of African languages in schools. The constant postcolonial meddling of Françafrique since then has done its best to keep things that way. With all its resources, French continues to spread rapidly, although there is some debate about whether it's French or some of the larger West African languages that represents the ultimate threat to the region's smaller languages.

It's evening in Montclair, and we're eating Ibrahima's grilled chicken stewed with carrots and peppers, drinking nonalcoholic beers. His wife Greta is on the phone with their son, who's on summer break and needs a pickup at Six Flags. Their other son is in Philly, interning for a major bank. Bowie, a five-year-old rescue dog named for the singer, does circles in the darkening yard. Ibrahima and Greta have gradually been fixing up the house, rewiring and reinsulating. "This guy is from Israel, this guy is from Norway, this guy is from Morocco, Argentina," Ibrahima says proudly, pointing to the other houses. He's a man who genuinely likes his neighbors. The New Jersey Transit rumbles by.

"Let's get this out of the way," starts Ibrahima, "polygamy is not like a big orgy. It can be culturally and socially beneficial."

His father Kelety had four wives and twenty-two children. At first his mother Fadima had been married to Kelety's older brother Djoume. Djoume and Fadima were a young couple living with their children in the coastal city of Abidjan when Djoume suddenly died, and so Fadima made the journey eight hundred miles inland to the village of Kiniebakoro to see her father-in-law Bamba, Ibrahima's grandfather. She had nowhere else to go. "I lost your son," said Fadima when she reached the village and saw her father-in-law. "I have the kids. What do you want me to do?"

"You're staying here," was Bamba's reply. "His younger brother Kelety is going to take care of you."

That was how Fadima moved in and became Kelety's third wife, as a way of protecting her and her children. Anthropologists call it levirate marriage, but it goes under different names in societies around the world: the commonsense custom that a brother of the deceased should marry his widowed sister-in-law.

Ibrahima was born in Kiniebakoro to Kelety and Fadima. "I say I was born in 1959, but when I was born there was no electricity, no doctor, nobody's wearing a watch, no calendar on the wall, so basically that was a guess. When I put the numbers together, I feel like that's the right age. To my life experience."

Would he still be alive if he had stayed in the village? Current life expectancy for men in Guinea is sixty-one, one of the lowest rates in the world. When he reached exactly that age, Ibrahima, then working at Amazon, came home one day and collapsed here in the kitchen.

It was the first time he had ever had serious health issues. Language is often affected in such cases, but Ibrahima kept chatting away in three languages in the hospital, delighted to find a custodian from the Ivory Coast he could speak French with and doctors originally from Egypt and Sudan he could speak Arabic with.

At first he even tried to keep up his language work, coming out soon after for ELA's five-hour International Mother Language Day Marathon, where speakers of dozens of languages shared stories, songs, and speeches—one of many annual celebrations we have held over the years on that sole linguistic holiday, which falls on February 21. Ibrahima looked deeply shaken, his eyes almost lifeless, but he still went onstage to read a poem and talk about N'ko. We had arranged a field methods class at Columbia, like we had done for Seke, but that would have to wait.

Now two years later, I recognize him again: shaved head, salt-and-pepper stubble, steady smile, warm eyes, muscles from workouts on the elliptical, stories at the ready.

Until he was six, Ibrahima lived in Kiniebakoro, the ancestral village. Maninka was the language, but he never saw it written. Like him, almost everyone there was a Traoré, except for a small number of Kouyatés, a line of bards, and Kamaras, a line of fishermen. Livelihood was traditionally linked with lineage, and the Traorés were hunters and fighters.

October 2, 1958—within a year of Ibrahima's birth, give or take—was when life started changing. Guinea declared its independence and became the first new nation to emerge out of colonial French West Africa: "Before, there was no Mali, no Ivory Coast, no Guinea, there was no border. The French said, Okay, if you're going to break up the relationship, we'll leave and we'll take everything from here." Under its new leader Sékou Touré, Guinea turned toward communism and the Soviet Union, China, and Cuba. For a while Touré embarked on a radical program to use and teach African languages, but it failed like so much else under his government.

Ibrahima and his mother were among the estimated 1.5 million Guineans who left the country. "It got to a point where you had plants growing in the middle of the street in Conakry," he says of Guinea's capital, "because no one was there, just like Cuba. And like Scarface, when you're exiled from a communist country, you just want to make ends meet. Every other country called us different things: drug dealers, cockroaches, all kinds of stuff." Desperate Guineans were selling whatever they could, including medicines produced in other communist countries, which they smuggled out to buyers across the region. Recent and ridiculous though they may have been, West Africa's nation-state borders were hardening into something real.

Ibrahima moved with his mother and two sisters to Bouaké, the Ivorian city where his brother was already living and where Kanté had his revelation a few decades earlier. At home his mother always spoke Maninka, which corresponds closely though not exactly to Dyula, the lingua franca of Ivory Coast, so Ibrahima picked up the latter quickly. Almost as prevalent was the distinctive local French patois: "If you come from Paris and land in Ivory Coast, you'll get lost!" promises Ibrahima. There was even a French-Dyula mix called Nouchi, meaning *mustache* and associated mostly with gangsters—Ibrahima shyly admits to knowing a few choice expressions. But knowing an African language wouldn't get you ahead in Ivory Coast.

At school, Ibrahima had to master both standard metropolitan French and Arabic, which many study for religious education in this overwhelmingly Muslim part of West Africa. So-called "Franco-Arabic" schools were just becoming popular, meeting parents' demand that their children learn both the lingering colonial language and the holy language of the Quran. More to the point, says Ibrahima, "the French part was supported by the French Academy, while the Arab countries were supporting the Arab teachers and sending tickets and scholarships for African students to go to Egypt, Syria, Lebanon, Iraq."

Beginning in the 1970s, many were also able to find work in an Arab world newly flush with oil money. After finishing school, Ibrahima, with all his languages, made his way to Saudi Arabia to become a fixer for West African groups on the hajj to Mecca and Medina.

It was a decent living, but inherently temporary; as a guest worker, Ibrahima had to renew his visa constantly. On his time off, he would wander the outdoor cassette markets in Jeddah and Medina, hunting for the music of Black America, especially Charlie Pryor, James Brown, and Michael Jackson. He dreamed of going to the States.

One day during the hajj, he saw a man resting in the shade, "really beat down" because his passport had been taken and his entire pilgrimage was at risk.

Within a few days, Ibrahima had helped him figure things out.

"You saved my pilgrimage!" said the man, who turned out to be an Ivorian named Kamara living in New York.

"Actually, I really want to go to America," Ibrahima told him frankly.

"I'll help you," Kamara promised.

## 2

On the strength of that chance encounter, Ibrahima left his job in Saudi Arabia, went back to Guinea to see family one last time, and got his things together. The year was 1988, and he had just turned thirty.

Kamara turned out to be a driver for Ivory Coast's UN mission, and he proved to be as good as his word when Ibrahima landed in New York and headed straight to crash at his apartment.

"Every day before he went to work, he put some change on my desk and said: 'Go walk around, no pressure, see New York.'" Ibrahima had just one school year's worth of English, plus the lyrics of Charlie Pryor.

He had been exploring New York for about four months when the nudge finally came. His room was needed for a politician who came every year from Ivory Coast to New York to watch a boxing match. "Go look for a hotel anywhere, and I'll pay for it," said Kamara, but Ibrahima wandered Midtown and couldn't get a hotel room. So Kamara gave him the address of a gas station where another Ivorian worked, where he would take the Mission's car for maintenance or an oil change. The man there gave Ibrahima another address: 110th and Lenox.

This was the Park View, a single-room occupancy hotel right on the northern edge of Central Park, colloquially known as Le Cent Dix. At the time, "doing the 110" was a byword for immigrant hustle, as were the similar "Cinquante" (on Fiftieth Street) in Midtown and the Belleclaire on the Upper West Side.[8] Le Cent Dix could be rough—new arrivals packed into rooms, code violations everywhere, crackheads and prostitutes in residence—but in the eighties and nineties it was a place where Francophone Africans in New York could get settled cheaply and connect with one another. Many new arrivals were advised to find a West African cabbie as soon as they landed at JFK, who would take them directly to Le Cent Dix. It helped to be right in the middle of African American Harlem.

From Francophone West Africa, it was the Senegalese who came first, mostly thanks to the Murids, one of the highly organized Sufi Muslim brotherhoods which have been major political and economic forces in the region since the late nineteenth century. From their headquarters in the city of Touba, the Murids actively equipped their young male traders for immigration, initial settlement, and street vending in New York, as they had done before in Paris and Milan. These traders were speakers of French and Wolof but also the broadly related Atlantic-Congo languages Serer, Jola, Mandjak, Baïnounk, among others. Across the city, they organized dozens of dahiras, prayer circles for the disciples of particular marabouts, or saints, where not just religious devotion but social, economic, and political influence were at stake.[9] Soon 116th between Malcom X and Frederick Douglass became the symbolic commercial center of Le Petit Senegal, but the Brotherhood selected 137th to be its spiritual heart. There they are reimagining the former Edgecombe Sanitarium, a pioneering institution established by Black physicians, as the central Murid mosque, complete with a red-brick minaret and dazzlingly ornamented portals.

Soon after Senegalese networks paved the way, significant communities from Guinea, Ivory Coast, Mali, Burkina Faso, Togo, Benin, and Niger followed. Cross-border ethnolinguistic ties, however, are usually more telling than national origin. Those who came were Manding, Fulani, and Soninke as much as they were Guinean, Senegalese, or Malian. Thanks to the amnesty law of 1986, the diversity lottery, and tightening immigration restrictions in France, the US was becoming a more attractive and achievable destination. Then came the 1990 devaluation of West Africa's regional currency, the CFA franc, when many lost their life savings overnight.[10]

Earlier arrivals in New York, like Ibrahima, often had connections with UN support staff or their family members. After taking a room at the Cent Dix, Ibrahima got a job at the Amoco gas station around the corner. "I was coming from Saudi Arabia and Africa, and this was winter," he remembers. "You hold that pump, and it feels like a cold fire, but I loved it, and there was money." They set him up with someone else's Social Security number, so taxes were taken out, but he would never see any of the benefits. This is how immigrants without papers, and without complaints, pay billions in taxes.

After a year Ibrahima was starting to hate the gas station, so again he followed local advice: "There was a Senegalese guy, very very smart but a crackhead, living in the hallway at the Cent Dix. If any African had a paper problem, he had a way to send them to a job. His name was Issa, and I went to the crack house to see him. He said, Call this number."

That led to a job at Lehman Brothers' corporate cafeteria downtown, which was run by Marriott, again on someone else's Social. Suddenly he was learning how to handle and cook food, working with ingredients he had never seen before. Soon after, he moved to the Lower East Side, then a disaster zone full of junkies, where he was drawn by the underground dance clubs playing house and techno. He made friends with the DJs and was soon working the decks himself. One night he walked into the legendary bar Max Fish and picked up Greta, a white girl from Texas and the daughter of a Lutheran minister, who had moved to the city to do modern dance. They shot pool, went dancing, and ended up making a life together.

Almost on a whim, they opened an African bistro in Harlem, where Ibrahima did the cooking and ran a little club with live music in the basement. He also became a kind of social worker for the African immigrants who had no other place to go and would gather there to share their woes and worries. It wasn't great for business, says Ibrahima, laughing, that they would rearrange the chairs to form a circle, and that one person would order a meal while three or four others then asked for spoons and shared it. It was the nineties, before gentrification had brought the stroller brigades. Many of the immigrants were merchants, hustling to extend the long-standing ethnicity- and lineage-based trade networks of West Africa one extralong but logical step further, thanks to growing American interest in African arts, antiquities, and other products, as well as African demand for American goods like cars and electronics.

Not far from the bistro on 125th was the city's great African market, organized in part by the merchants' country of origin and specialization: Malians selling cloth on the Lenox Avenue sidewalk; Senegalese and Gambians with beads, incense, and bracelets at the northwest corner of 125th; Nigeriens (from Niger) farther west with handbags from Korea, straw hats from China, and straw bags from Kenya; as well as Jamaican and African American vendors.[11]

Downtown in Chelsea, the Warehouse was an extension of this scene for a higher-end clientele, where Songhai- and Hausa-speaking dealers, among others, would store and sell artifacts and jewelry to American, often African American, collectors.[12] New York more generally came to serve as a kind of headquarters or clearinghouse for merchants following the African American expo circuit across the US, with one of the biggest sellers being the kente cloth produced by Korean and Chinese wholesalers in New Jersey, with the aura of African authenticity provided by the immigrants who sold it.[13]

Though many never intended to settle in the US, a growing number of these African traders ultimately ended up bringing their families over. Like the Songhai-speaking art dealer Yaya, one of the prosperous "New Yorkais" admired in Niamey's Great Market, whose story is told by anthropologist Paul Stoller. Yaya returned home to Niger to die after three years of chemotherapy at East Harlem's Metropolitan Hospital.

Ibrahima's restaurant went under after a few tumultuous and exhausting years, while Greta studied business and got a corporate job. They married, had two boys, and made the move to Montclair. Ibrahima often watched the kids during the day and hustled for work at night: catering, cooking, DJing.

One day Greta suggested they visit Kiniebakoro, where Ibrahima hadn't been in nearly twenty years. Before cell phones came in the early 2000s, it could take two months to get a message to or from the village. When his father died, the news went first by bus to cousins in Ivory Coast, who then wrote Ibrahima a letter.

It was only on this trip, back in the house where he was born, that Ibrahima came across books he'd never seen in a script he couldn't read. It turned out that a much younger brother of his was even studying at a pioneering N'ko school. Not only could Ibrahima's language be written, it could be taught as well. That was the moment something inside Ibrahima shifted.

## 3

The Bronx, 170th and Grand Concourse: a patch of green where vendors vend, people clump for buses, and old heads blast music into the summer heat. Cars attack from every side, but I don't see his yet. I trace letters in Baba Mamadi Diané's *Original Selection of N'ko Syllables*, a textbook with the Brooklyn Bridge and Lower Manhattan on the cover. A logo shines in the top left corner: a balafon with mallets inside a hut topped with a three-tiered roof and crowned by a full-ray sun—the light of Manding knowledge.

This seventy-two-page booklet was printed in Cairo, but for teaching N'ko in the US "to Manding and non-Manding people." Ibrahima is credited on the back as an "N'ko advocate in New York City," "son of Laji Kelety Traoré and Fadima Doumbia," and one of "the three misters" who "contributed to the expenses of this book." The other two, whose parents are also listed (with the titles El-hajd and Hadja to acknowlege their pilgrimages to Mecca), are originally from Kankan and Bamako but now living in Ann Arbor.

Besides a few English words on the cover, everything is in N'ko, down to the page numbers with N'ko numerals. It's very DIY, as teaching materials for less-common languages usually are, with an inch of image or clip art for every newly introduced word: wheels, elephants, pineapples, tractors, and hundreds of others. I'm working my way through, poring over tables that show the proper forms for each letter, filling in the empty lines for each exercise with endless versions of the first three letters: ߊ, ߋ, ߌ. Typing, with the newly installed N'ko keyboard layout on my laptop, is easier.

The twenty-seven letters of N'ko look like no other writing system, despite a few appearing superficially Latin-like and all running right to left and connecting at the base as in Arabic. There is a single symbol for labial-velar *gb*, indeed a single sound doubly articulated at the lips and the velum which is rare outside West Africa—and who wouldn't prefer just writing ߜ to the awkward digraph *gb*? There are even a few original punctuation marks (߸ for commas and ߹ for exclamation points) and distinctive numerals for one through nine, also written right to left (unlike in Arabic, which left-to-rights them). But the crowning feature from a linguistic standpoint are the seven diacritics used for marking vowels in terms of four tones (high, low, rising, falling) and length (long and short). There's no eighth accent because the short falling tone, considered the default, doesn't have to be marked.

## LETTERS

| ߐ | ߏ | ߎ | ߍ | ߌ | ߋ | ߊ |
|---|---|---|---|---|---|---|
| ɔ | o | u | ɛ | i | e | a |
| ߙ | ߘ | ߗ | ߖ | ߕ | ߔ | ߓ |
| r | d | c | j | t | p | b |
| ߡ | ߟ | ߞ | ߝ | ߜ | ߛ | ߚ |
| m | l | k | f | gb | s | rr |
|  | ߦ | ߥ | ߤ | ߣ | ߒ | ߢ |
|  | y | w | h | n | n' | ny |

## NUMERALS

| ߀ | ߁ | ߂ | ߃ | ߄ | ߅ | ߆ | ߇ | ߈ | ߉ |
|---|---|---|---|---|---|---|---|---|---|
| 0 | 1 | 2 | 3 | 4 | 5 | 6 | 7 | 8 | 9 |

## TONES and VOWEL LENGTH

| | **VOWEL LENGTH** | |
|---|---|---|
| **TONES** | **short** | **long** |
| **high** | o߫ | o߯ |
| **low** | o߬ | o߰ |
| **rising** | o߭ | o߱ |
| **falling** | | o߮ |

Ibrahima pulls up in an SUV. He's just back from Guinea, where he went for a sister's funeral. Travel is easier now, but the language work is only getting harder because of Guinean politics, he says as I climb in. Only a few people now listen to his podcast, and he's slowing down with the videos, the website, the social media activity. People are fearful ever since a reformer in Kankan started praying in N'ko/Manding in the mosque and landed in jail. The mosque was burned down. "Like Martin Luther, but too soon," says Ibrahima sadly, making the connection between religious reform and vernacular language. Just a few months later, there is a coup in the capital.

We ride down the Concourse, turning by the old Sephardic Jewish Center, where Ladino, Greek, and Turkish were still spoken into the 1970s, before the congregation moved to Forest Hills and a Black Baptist church from Harlem moved in. Yankee Stadium is just a few blocks down the hill. Given the major African American, Puerto Rican, and Dominican worlds here, it can take a while for "mini–West Africa," as

Ibrahima calls it, to come into focus. As in Africa, African languages are for the most part invisible while colonial languages remain dominant: French in both its official and local West African forms, English both as imposed by the British and as it has evolved in Nigeria, Ghana, Sierra Leone, and elsewhere. Muslim West Africans like Ibrahima also know classical and contemporary Arabic to varying degrees.

"There was just one mosque when I first came here, but now there are forty or fifty," he says, meaning just the West African ones. "It's for the afterlife. If you give to the mosque, and people are praying in it, your place in heaven is assured." The mosques are open to all believers, but in practice are often connected to particular languages, hometowns, and networks. There are four predominantly Manding mosques in just these few blocks. And just from the Baté ("between the rivers") region of northeastern Guinea, which is mostly Manding, there are hometown associations here with hundreds of people each from Kouroussa, Kankan, and Siguiri, the market town to which Ibrahima's village is closest.

We pull up and park by Mosque Loogman, in a converted brick-and-vinyl townhouse on East 169th Street. An open hydrant feeds an urban river draining fast through the grill of a sewer. We head inside and make our way up to the second floor, where the committee is waiting.

Here above the mosque is the official headquarters of N'ko USA Inc., which has a mission to promote the writing system on American soil. For practical purposes that means primarily here in the Manding melting pot of the Bronx, where the Mali Empire lives on culturally, linguistically, musically, and in many other ways.

The first person to teach N'ko in New York was Ibrahima, starting with his two sons at home, where he installed a chalkboard. Then for ten years he would drive here every Sunday to teach what was sometimes just a handful of students, ranging in age from five to twenty. For years he would also drive to teach a small group at a mosque on Sutphin Boulevard in Jamaica, home of the N'ko Association of Queens, and another in Philly, because N'ko USA tries to send a teacher anywhere with five willing students. Classes are always free.

Now Djibrila, a devout imam and the general secretary of N'ko USA, takes on more of the work. He welcomes me formally in his light blue boubou, a loose full-length robe. I shake hands with the other officers: seven men in their forties and fifties, wearing either boubous or button-down shirts, some covering their heads with kufis. In this little space not unlike ELA's, N'ko USA has squeezed in an office, a classroom, and a vision. They keep close ties with other N'koists and associations in Guinea, Mali, Ivory Coast, and Burkina Faso, including an active group on the social network Telegram. Ibrahima would like to see more ties with different kinds of organizations in the US, so he recently took it upon himself to represent the group and hand out free T-shirts at a climate change march. Little English may be spoken here, but the officers move easily between N'ko, French, and Arabic. Ibrahima later tells me, delicately, that there can be differences in terms of mentality and religious observance. Not to mention the expectation to attend every wedding and funeral in the community, which is only possible if you're living in the Bronx but can become a serious burden in terms of money, time, and energy.

We take our seats on red chairs around pushed-together tables. Business cards and bottled waters make the rounds. Giant maps of Guinea, Mali, and the whole African continent fill the walls, with every number, place-name, and legend in N'ko. To see this is to believe in the script, not only the passion of its users but its ability to name the world. Around the image of a compass radiate sixteen words for every fine-grained direction. There are framed certificates of appreciation, completion, and outstanding service. From stacks on a bookshelf, Djibrila pulls out two dictionaries: one N'ko-French and the other entirely in N'ko, packed with one hundred thousand entries, if I understand him right, which would be enormous. Work has already started on an N'ko-English dictionary, he says, but it is paused for the moment.

None of this was a given when Souleymane Kanté envisioned this system, within a broader philosophy of writing he explored in his ߒߞߏ ߞߊ߲ߜߍ ߞߎ߲ߓߊߓߊ N'ko Kangbè Kùnbába' *(Big Book of N'ko Grammar)*:[14]

> *The part of the body in which a thing's sign is seen is called the mind. The mind's container is the brain. The thing in which the mind looks for signs is thought, consciousness or one's spirit. The process of identifying things' signs in thought, that process is called reasoning. Expressing reasoning so that someone else can understand it, that is communication. Yet, there are three kinds of communication: gesture, speech, and writing . . .*
>
> *Writing is putting the signs of speech on paper with pen and ink. The individual signs' names are letters. An alphabet is all of one language's letters put together. Almost every language has a particular alphabet. But, nowadays many languages are grouped together under one alphabet. Writing clarifies language, supports thought, and promotes knowledge. For this reason, no intelligent person thrives without writing nowadays . . .*
>
> *If writing is honey in terms of sweetness, then writing one's own language is ambrosia. If writing is sauce, then writing one's own language is the seasoning* [*salt*]. *If reading is work, then reading one's own language is its respite.* (Translated by Coleman Donaldson.)

Kanté was also a natural linguist, masterfully analyzing the sounds that Manding speakers needed to represent in the first place. N'ko has other handy features, like its convention of dropping the first instance of a vowel-accent combination if it's repeated in the following syllable.[15] Kanté also adapted or coined detailed terminology for talking *about* both his script and the grammar of Manding languages, including keywords like ߞߊ߲ߡߊߛߍߙߍ kánmasere, which is sometimes translated as *phonetics* but refers specifically both to the seven accent marks and the linguistic phenomena of contrastive tone and length that they mark.[16] Compare the words ߓߟߊߝߐ߲ *balafon* (a kind of xylophone, traditionally made of rosewood keys with different-sized calabashes hung underneath as resonators), and ߓߊ߬ߟߊ *porcupine*, both pronounced "bala," but the first *a* left unwritten as redundant in the former and the ◌߬ making a short low tone on the latter. Tonal complexities go deep into the grammar of Manding languages, too. A "floating tone" untethered to any particular syllable marks definiteness, for example, which is the difference between *a* balafon and *the* balafon.

I ask the committee about ߞߊ߲ߜߍ kangbè, one of Kanté's most important innovations. It means *clear language*, says Djibrila, but also grammar. It describes the way we try to speak and write, a standard. Its frequent alignment with Kanté's own dialect, everyone is quick to stress, is not a matter of geographic bias, but of historical accuracy, rooted in Manding language history as Kanté understood it. Kangbè also avoids French or Arabic loanwords, trying to use more "pure" Manding roots instead, including in many neologisms.[17]

What kangbè means in practice is that a Bamanan speaker from Mali, for example, will learn while studying N'ko that the /g/ (or sometimes /j/ or /w/) in their dialect is equivalent to the historically more correct form, labial-velar /gb/. They may start writing ߜ *gb* and even saying it. Speakers from Guinea like Ibrahima may already say /gb/ and not need to adjust. Likewise, people whose dialects have different plural endings like **-u** or **-w** may switch over to the N'ko ending **-lu** ߟߎ߬.[18]

The same goes for the possessive marker—speakers whose dialects have **ka** or **ta** for this will start writing and maybe even saying the

**la** or **na** instead. But usage is trickier to standardize than pronunciation. There is a wonderfully complex distinction across Manding languages between alienable and inalienable possession. Many languages around the world distinguish between things that are possessed and can't be given away (like family members and body parts—this is inalienable possession) versus things that can be given away (alienable possession). So Ibrahima says n fa, *my father*, but n na gbelengbelen, *my cell phone*—where **na** marks the phone as being "alienable" (and gbelengbelen is classic ringtone onomatapoeia). It quickly gets more complicated, to different degrees in different Manding languages, depending not just on the nature of what's possessed, but on the perceived animacy (i.e., aliveness) of any would-be possessor.

Like any standard, N'ko tries to curb variation in the name of unity, a dilemma faced by linguists and language activists everywhere. How much standardization is necessary to defend diversity, to make a language maximally clear and useful so that it can hold its own against larger languages? If N'ko were to unify forty million Manding speakers and gain status wherever they live, it could hardly be counted as an endangered language. There is even a distant risk that one day it could erode the distinctive features of Bamanan or Jula or especially smaller Manding languages, just as the standardization of French and Mandarin has erased many of their related "dialects."

Within the movement, N'ko and the clear language of kangbè are not just about literacy or even Manding unity, but about molding and educating citizens pursuing ߞߏߟߐ߲ ߓߍ߲ ߓߊ߯ߙߊ kólɔn, bɛ́n, báara (*Knowledge, Harmony, Work*). This is the slogan across the banner that dominates the N'ko USA office, emblazoned on the logo of an open book flanked by a pen and a hoe.[19] In other words, N'ko is not just a writing system and a standard language, but an ethical path and a way of life for those who adopt it.

From the time he revealed the script until his death in 1987, Kanté presented N'ko as a vehicle for enlightenment, with a lit lantern as one of its symbols. His own encyclopedic output of over a hundred books runs the gamut from histories (of Bamako, of Arabs in the Sudan, of the Kaba family of Kankan, etc.) to the poems, songs, proverbs, and collections of medical knowledge he gathered, including treatments for 317 tropical diseases.

Perhaps the most important and controversial N'ko book of all was the Quran, translated by Kanté at the very outset along with other key Islamic texts. Before publication, Kanté's N'ko Quran had to go through an exhaustive check involving Islamic scholars in both Guinea and Saudi Arabia.[20] Kanté wanted Manding speakers, many of whom memorize the Quran in Arabic without understanding it, to have a version in their own language. Members of Kanté's own family opposed him, Ibrahima told me, because they made their living from teaching Arabic.

Sitting here with the committee, despite these tensions, it's clear that N'ko still embodies an anticolonial, proudly African, and also devoutly religious project.[21] Merchants have adopted it for (confidential) correspondence and recordkeeping. Healers used it to store and transmit traditional medicinal knowledge. Students developed a method of learning it over four months through memorization and imitation, partly by copying Kanté's manuscripts by hand with carbon paper since texts were so rare and precious.[22] N'ko has grown into a genuinely grassroots movement for literacy, spreading person-to-person wherever there were Manding speakers.[23]

Those who know at least a little N'ko may now number in the hundreds of thousands. A much smaller number are intensely dedicated N'koists like the men of N'ko USA Inc., who continue Kanté's enlightenment project with translations and original works on history, science, medicine, mathematics, and so on, for a total N'ko library of over four hundred books and counting, as well as numerous periodicals and a growing presence online.[24] They are opening N'ko schools, academies, bookshops, and associations wherever their migrations take them.

# 4

In the history of writing, there have been only three confirmed cases of completely independent invention, all ancient: Sumerian cuneiform, Chinese 甲骨文 jiǎgǔwén (*oracle bone script*), and Olmec writing, which seems to have combined hieroglyphic and syllabic elements.

Olmec fed into the earliest Nahuatl writing but has no living successors, and the spread of Chinese characters was mostly limited to East Asia, but long, complex lines of descent from Sumerian cuneiform connect scripts as disparate as Syriac and Manchu, Bengali and Balinese. Even systems that look unique, from Egyptian hieroglyphs to the Phoenician alphabet that ultimately conquered Europe,[25] owe at least something in their conception or design to other existing systems ultimately traceable to Cuneiform.

Writing, after all, was historically confined to tiny elites in a small number of societies. Or as Ibrahima says, "If the world was born in the morning, writing came in the evening." Remember that oral language is always primary, linguistically speaking, and writing an adaptation, if not a distortion, though it may take on a life of its own. Verbatim transcripts of natural speech look strange on the page if they include all the ums, ahs, and repetitions, just as toasting with a written text usually sounds stiff and stilted.

Oral communication has sufficed for most societies most of the time, but the ability to fix words on a page (stone, scroll, etc.) does have practical advantages when it comes to communication across time and space, commercial recordkeeping, and the spread of dogmatic diktats not meant to be altered. Bias against the unlettered is rife in every literate society, where "history" is traditionally defined as starting when written records begin. A writing system is now often mistakenly equated with the language itself. Illiteracy has become a byword for ignorance, instead of indicating or being weighed against someone's oral abilities. Some have posited a fundamental cognitive divide between literate and nonliterate societies, or even individuals.[26]

It might seem unthinkable to create and promote a new writing system today, but throughout history there have been individuals, with at least the powerful ones being renumbered and getting the credit who have done it. Think of the brothers Cyril and Methodius, those Byzantine missionaries to the Slavs who devised the alphabet later known as Cyrillic, or how Korean hangul were reportedly created by King Sejong the Great. Aware of and literate in other systems, they pioneered their own.

Yet perhaps even more extraordinary are the cases of essentially ordinary people who themselves were not literate in any language, but were inspired just by hearing about writing to reverse engineer the idea for their own languages. The Hmong peasant spiritual leader Shong Lue Yang created, taught, and continually refined his Pahawh Hmong demisyllabic alphabet from 1959 until his assassination by military leaders in 1971.[27] Shong Lue is not known to have been literate in any other language, but he would have heard stories about writing, and he was likely aware of both local religious pseudowriting (a kind of glossolalia on the page) and writing systems for other languages, as well as emerging alternatives for Hmong. The initial revelation came in a dream, but over successive versions Shong Lue reduced his inventory of characters from 151 to 81 and evolved a sophisticated system that fully and elegantly represents two different dialects, marks eight tones with diacritics (much as N'ko does), and takes the very original step of treating the vowel as the nucleus of the syllable. All this he accomplished despite, but perhaps also because of, the continual displacement and violence of the Vietnam War. Shong Lue's dedication was matched by a core group of followers as they moved between last rebel holdouts, refugee camps, and ultimately diaspora in California and Minnesota.[28]

Are there any broader conclusions to draw about the history and evolution of writing from such recent, well-documented cases as

Pahawh Hmong and N'ko? Do scripts naturally evolve in the direction of ever greater abstraction, from the logographic to the syllabic to the alphabetic? N'ko was an alphabet from the get-go, and Shong Lue seemed to move that way, but elsewhere the evidence is equivocal. One plausible conclusion is that people create scripts and embrace writing most readily when threatened by other societies where literacy has already taken hold.[29] Even more recent than Pahawh Hmong are the Naasioi Otomaung script, revealed during the Bougainville Civil War of the 1990s, and the Osage script created in Oklahoma in 2006 as a spur to revitalization, following the death of the last native speaker.

Conflict and endangerment may explain the unparalleled creative outburst of new Indigenous writing systems across West Africa. Over the past two centuries, not only N'ko but some twenty other highly distinctive scripts have been invented for a range of languages in the sub-Saharan region stretching from Senegal to Cameroon. In general, they have little in common with one another, and the circumstances of their creation have varied greatly, but in a sense they are all responses to Maruwa's challenge. Even as colonial powers were invading the region and disparaging if not destroying local knowledge systems, these scripts stood as proof that African languages could stand with any other. In West Africa, as in many parts of Asia, the idea has been spreading that every language group should have its own iconic form of writing, unlike in Europe, where just a few scripts dominate and were adapted for diverse languages.

The earliest was Vai, dream-discovered by Momolu Duwalu Bukele in 1832/33 possibly in response to the new, nearby coastal colonies for American freedmen that would shortly become Liberia. Bukele's left-to-right script contained 212 symbols representing most but not all of the language's sound combinations, and it didn't mark tone. But his ingenious and useful invention caught on, serving as an inspiration for several later West African scripts, including the right-to-left Mende, Loma, and Kpelle scripts (which may also have drawn on existing pictorial and notation traditions)[30] and even the royally mandated Bamun in far-off Cameroon. Unlike many others, Vai writing remains in use today, including on phones, on computers, and in Bible translations. Outside of Africa, Staten Island's Little Liberia is one of the only places where the Vai and Bassa scripts, at least to some extent, are being used.[31] Even more extraordinary is a possible link between Vai, the oldest sub-Saharan script, and Cherokee, the oldest North American one, invented by Sequoya in 1821 at a time when white settlers were pushing deep into Cherokee lands. As different as they look, both are syllabaries, where the characters represent whole syllables rather than just individual sounds (as they do in alphabets). If a Cherokee-Vai connection is proven, nothing could illustrate more dramatically how new scripts have grown up along global networks of anticolonial resistance.[32]

Besides his experiments with Arabic and Latin letters, Souleymane Kanté at least knew of Vai and possibly other African writing systems. At the same time, he anchored N'ko in Manding oral tradition. The verb ko itself has resonances beyond *saying*, becoming in many Manding languages a so-called quotative marker that functions just like an oral quotation mark and introduces reported speech.

Also indirectly invoked with the name N'ko are the great sayers of Manding culture, known in European languages as griot (etymology unknown) but in Manding as jeliw (the plural of jeli). This hereditary caste of epic poets, genealogists, musicians, oral historians, and orators has no exact equivalent outside West Africa, though oral cultures worldwide gave rise to extraordinary bardic traditions before the advent of mass literacy. Like the Homeric singers of tales, jeliw feats of memory depend on set structures, familiar themes, linguistic formulas, and other mnemonic devices, often involving intricate tonal and prosodic changes from everyday spoken Manding languages, always set to music.[33] They in turn trace their origin to the court of Sundiata Keita, hero of the most famous West African epic of all, and they have maintained a vital role in Manding societies down to the present. Souleymane Kanté's own story has itself taken on some of the qualities of a modern-day jeli epic.

In Manding terms, the jeliw sing of badenya and fadenya. Badenya is literally *motherchildness*: ba *mother*, den *child*, and ya, a Manding suffix for forming abstract nouns. Representing "social cohesion and equilibrium: love, respect, trust, faithfulness, etc.," badenya is sometimes seen as yin to the yang of fadenya, *fatherchildness*, "that set of forces which could be interpreted as contributing to social disintegration and disequilibrium: injustice, envy, jealousy, hate, distrust, etc." But badenya and fadenya unfold and entangle in a dialectic more complex than any binary opposition or clear complementarity. Jeliw evoke the fadenya of past rebellious heroes in order to inspire their descendants to similar deeds, but those often destructive exploits should serve only to strengthen and ultimately be absorbed into the continuous bonds of badenya, which begin with mother and child but unify all of Manding society. ߥߊߣߊ߫ ߡߊ߲߬ ߘߌ߫ ߝߏ߫ ߞߏ߫ ߖߎ߯ ߟߏ߲. Wana man di fo kojuulon. *The hero is welcome but on troubled days*, goes the jeli expression—not all times are right for fadenya exploits. "Where are the heroes of yesteryear?" they also sing. "Ah! The world has cooled down!"[34]

Many jeliw are master musicians, accompanying their praise singing and tale telling on the kora, an ethereal-sounding harp-lute made from half a calabash covered with cow skin, its twenty-odd strings strung down from a long wooden neck. Or the balafon, of which the sacred eight-hundred-year-old original, known as the Sosso Bala and linked to Sundiata Keita's chief jeli, is enshrined today in a village not far from Ibrahima's and still played ceremonially by a Kouyaté family.

"Everybody has a jeli—it's like they're assigned to you naturally," says Ibrahima, meaning that the ties between particular jeli families and their patron families run so deep that no one remembers how it all started. "I can walk in somewhere in the Bronx and say 'I'm a Traoré,' and someone else will say 'I'm a Kouyaté' and start telling me my lineage—my grandfather, my great-grandfather—and I have to give him some money. I can be on the subway, and someone says, What's your name? I say I'm Traoré. He says I'm Kouyaté, pay my fare, so you have to give him." Like Mustang's nyetsang, the tie is still operative in New York, and these complete strangers may know more about his family than Ibrahima does, though Traorés and Kouyatés would never marry. "Don't work, don't hunt, do nothing, sit around and tell me about my ancestors," so Ibrahima summarizes the jeli's function from a Traoré perspective—though he quickly adds that they also play music, make peace, hold ceremonies, and serve as messengers and representatives.

In New York, jeliw almost always have to work other jobs. Rather than wait around for a Traoré's Metrocard swipe, some jeliw busk in the subway, usually soloing on a kora with quiet dignity on the platform, unlike the mariachi guitar and squeeze-box trios who move bravely from car to car or the Kichwa-speaking troubadour troupes in ponchos who would play pan flutes in the middle of busy stations.[35] Other jeliw refuse to bring their lofty tradition down into the city's tunnels.

There may now be hundreds of Manding New Yorkers from jeliw backgrounds, raising the question of how oral tradition is surviving in the city, which in a certain sense is the reverse mirror image of the efforts around N'ko. How many jeliw families will be able to transmit the full range of traditional and musical chops in cramped apartments off the Grand Concourse? Place-based knowledge may fade fastest, including the mapping of local landscapes, sometimes down to individual trees, that jeliw sometimes do when they sing.[36] Besides, their roles have changed considerably in West Africa itself. During the postcolonial Authenticité movement of the 1960s, many talented jeliw were drafted into national ensembles and became quasi-classical musicians. When the groups went on tour, many stayed on in New York (or Paris or London) rather than return.[37]

One result is extraordinary innovation as jeliw from across West Africa coming to New York find both each other and a range of musicians from other traditions to collaborate with.[38] A handful, like Salif Keïta and Toumani Diabaté, become famous as professional touring musicians, redefining African music for global audiences. Others like Alhaji Papa Susso, who splits his time between Gambia and the Bronx, carve out flexible contemporary roles as roving performers, educators, and ambassadors for Manding culture—Papa even writes original compositions celebrating astronauts and mocking Trump. In 2011, more than twenty New York–based jeliw from eight West African countries performed at a "Griot Summit" at Wave Hill Garden in the Bronx.[39]

Performing for outsiders has its benefits and drawbacks, and most still make some of their living from the gatherings and life-cycle events of Manding immigrants, including baby namings, weddings, and funerals. "I wouldn't even have a celebration without inviting them," says Ibrahima, "but they will come even if you don't invite them, because that's their bread and butter. When you don't give something, they'll say you're a cheap bastard, not your father's son." And then there are the stylish, deafening all-night concerts held in rented auditoriums and churches in Harlem and the Bronx, where big bands back big-name jelimusow, *female jeliw singers*, as they praise female patrons who literally shower them with money.[40]

## 5

"We want to have a liaison between N'ko and the city government," say the leaders of N'ko USA. They ask about getting N'ko into hospitals, the subway, any official signage: "How do we get it in the system?" I can't express how impossible this sounds, when even major languages like Spanish and Mandarin are not always well supported. I talk about how ELA worked with Ibrahima and Djibrila to have N'ko included in a PSA campaign filmed the year before at City Hall in twenty different languages—probably the first time N'ko was used in any official government message anywhere. But this is just one message in one campaign in one city.

I suggest starting small by contacting a local city council member, or a school in the Bronx with a critical mass of kids from the community. I try to temper expectations. So far no one can say how widely N'ko is known in the US, but the committee says there are N'koists teaching and using it in Philadelphia, DC, Atlanta, Ohio, and Michigan. They gather every year for a conference on N'ko Day, April 14.

"People are losing their languages," says one man in a psychedelic green boubou. "We don't want to lose them, Americans don't want us to lose them. How to make our children come?" Can these men, who all grew up in West Africa and settled in New York as adults, convince their Bronx-born children to join the movement and invest themselves in all it represents? We talk about making videos, children's books, cartoons, new forms of media and entertainment, but it's far from clear how the kangbè ideal will play out in the Bronx. "Not having writing," says Ibrahima, "we can say our language is endangered even if we don't know it's endangered."

Ibrahima pushes the committee to think about technology, understanding that diaspora activists and organizations can have an impact because of their proximity to the places where tech standards and products are made. Users of larger languages can blithely assume that all the new updates, devices, platforms, and applications will support them from the get-go or soon after. We live in a time when just a handful of writing systems—Arabic, Chinese, Devanagari, and Latin above all—increasingly dominate everything.

Kanté struggled to get a few N'ko typewriters made through Second-World connections. His disciple Baba Mamadi Diané (author of *Original Selection of N'ko Syllables*) created his own font by hand with colleagues at Cairo University in the early 1990s, though he was the only person then in a position to use it. If speakers in Mali or Manhattan can now type N'ko on their phones, it's because of two decades of work by speakers, linguists, librarians, and computer scientists. The action often goes down at small, deeply geeky workshops like the one Ibrahima and I attended with the Script Encoding Initiative, which works to get all the world's writing systems into Unicode, the global body which determines all standards for representing text on digital devices. In 2005, Vai made it in after a workshop at NYU involving speakers, linguists, and typographers. After years of petitioning, N'koists secured approval the following year. Other African scripts have followed.

The effort is considerable, which is part of why so many communities opt for Latin-based orthographies. Besides all the technology designed around Latin characters, there is the fact that so many people are already familiar with them. In fact, N'ko is up against a jumble of Latin-based systems designed or promoted for Manding languages since the 1950s by different West African governments. "In Mali alone," writes Coleman Donaldson, "Bamanan speakers may opt to write their language in any number of ways: with post-1982 International Phonetic Alphabet (IPA) characters, with the pre-1982 Latin system, with French spelling conventions or with or without tonal diacritics."[41] Yet none of these systems has been particularly popular, and Malians pick and choose informally from a spectrum of styles, if they use Latin letters to write their Bamanan at all.[42]

N'koists know they have to keep checking, lobbying, and volunteering their time to make their letters appear at all. In 2009, responding to the appeals of Ibrahima and others, Microsoft started supporting N'ko natively with its Ebrima font, which in theory meant that at least you could type it and see it in all Microsoft products. N'ko came to Macs soon after, as well as Apple and Android cell phones and tablets.

This is not about fancy tools or interfaces in the language, just about ensuring the alphabet's survival. It's about users writing hundreds of comments on Microsoft's feedback portal, mostly in N'ko, to request proofing tools like spell-check for Word. It's about patiently building the one-thousand-plus-article N'ko Wikipedia. A complete digital world in N'ko, as with 95 percent of the world's languages, is still a long way off, and it may always be a game of catch-up.

The biggest challenge of all, says Ibrahima, is convincing people to read and write N'ko in the first place, given so few digital tools and little support from any government. With literacy in larger languages now essential for survival, speakers of thousands of smaller ones are wondering if it's even possible to document, teach, or transmit a language today without writing it down. But transitioning to the strange technology of writing and the host of technologies that come with it can be every bit as daunting as keeping a spoken language alive.

The committee stresses that N'ko is iconic and distinctive, fitting the structure of the languages it is supposed to represent. The Latin-based systems might seem easy, but they are in fact divisive, colonial, and simply not as good at representing the language.

N'ko also seems to have set a precedent for a literacy movement taking hold in another large, linguistically diverse West African community in New York. ADLaM—an acronym for the phrase Alkule Dandayɗe Leñol Mulugol, *the alphabet that keeps a people from vanishing*—aims to unite Fulani speakers as N'ko does Manding speakers. In 1990, two teenage brothers, also originally from Guinea but now living in Portland, Oregon, started designing their right-to-left alphabet with thirty-four original letters and ten distinctive numerals.[43] They haven't stopped since: as university students in Conakry, they launched an organization, published books and pamphlets, and asked everyone they taught to teach others in turn, until they were hounded out of the country by the government. Now they say ADLaM is spreading in twenty-four countries across West Africa, Europe, and the Middle East, with an active presence in New York, where the new alphabet is discussed and disseminated at Fulani mosques and community gatherings. ADLaM entered Unicode in 2015.

The muezzin's voice from downstairs is filtering into the office. We finish without hurrying, shaking hands and taking pictures. Someone offers a Manding proverb: *One finger can't pick up a pebble.* Even the smallest undertaking requires collaboration. At least we are in touch. In the small inner room, its whiteboard filled with letters, Djibrila shows me a copy of a letter typed in English on their official letterhead—enclosed, it reads, is a $500 donation from N'ko USA to the City of New York on April 10, 2020, to help with the COVID-19 pandemic. I hope it was never cashed.

I wait out in the street, beside a taped-up notice with dial-in numbers for Manden Radio, an internet station run by local imams, where Ibrahima used to spread the gospel of N'ko. The storefront next door, half-hidden behind a light blue steel gate, at first looks no different from the thousand other multiservice places which dot the immigrant world of the outer boroughs, though there are fewer and fewer of them each year. The awning is printed in both N'ko and English, advertising Money Transfer, Flight Tickets, Pure Honey, Apparels, Phone Accessories & Other Stuff. All six services are symbolized on the leaves of a tree, which instead of roots resolves into the tip of a pencil writing in an open book: ߟߐ߲ߠߌ߲ ߣߌ߫ ߓߍ߲ ߣߌ߫ ߢߍߕߊ߯ *Knowledge, Harmony, Development.*

As the officers of N'ko USA pray, I return to a frequent thought: how hard it is for even the most dedicated activist to keep a language alive in their own home. "That's the battle I'm losing, which is very saddening for me," Ibrahima had admitted over dinner in Montclair. Unquestionably American, his sons row crew, do finance internships, go to Six Flags. Striking a balance between Greta's Lutheran background and Ibrahima's Muslim one has been hard enough.

"They can choose how they want to go from there," says Greta. "Having a spiritual life is important to both of us. Being a good person and a moral person is important. With kids whatever you give them first—you can make them and make them and make them, and they'll run far away from it."

Some eventually return. Now that Ibrahima is one of the elders in his family, with all the responsibilities that implies, he wants to be back in Kiniẹbakoro, which is also near the center of the N'ko movement.

On his most recent visit, he showed up with a delivery: a wheelchair for a relative, solar panels, over-the-counter medicines, and hundreds of John Lennon–style and other classic New York T-shirts produced and donated by his Norwegian neighbor in Montclair. All of this Ibrahima shipped in a container from the US to the port in Conakry, then drove hundreds of miles to the village. He also brought a large generator for the school, where one day he would like to teach, since the teacher now can come only once a week. He planted sixty citrus trees and secured the well on the land where he hopes to spend part of every year, speaking and growing the language he was born to.

# Irwin
## *Nahuatl*

### 1

One of the first poems Irwin ever wrote in Nahuatl was a declaration of love to Juanita, scribbled while riding the Metro-North Railroad on a freezing ten-degree day from Grand Central to Mamaroneck:

> Tlen nimachilia axa, tla nechkokohua nimopachohua
> inahuak noichpokato itek iyolohtzin, nin cihuatzintli i
> toka "JUANITA."
>
> Nechnapalohua.
> Nechtema noyolotzin, noielihtzi uan notonaltzintli
> mokahua chipahuak uan ihki kuali nimahmachiliz tlen
> ka itek noihtek.
>
> Nima nikita kualtzi no chichilohtlitzin,
> tlen notonalamatzin kihtohua ninehnemiz.
>
> Nimoyehuatlali ipan nopetlatl
> uan nitlahtlachia, nokuentla.
> Nokuentlahtzin za zeka kate.
> Nehua amo nika, nika zan nomahuizotzin.

We sit at ELA grappling with each word. Some seem straightforward, but others have depths that only keep deepening. It takes time just to pinpoint the roots, slough off the prefixes and suffixes, disassemble each bit to see how it works, and then put it all back together again. Not that short words are any easier. But Irwin is patient.

"What's kuentla?"

"Like *outside*," says Irwin.

"*My dear little outside?*" Nokuentla has to be *my* kuentla, and nokuentlahtzin *my dear little* kuentla, because **-tzin** is the Nahuatl "caressive" suffix, a verbal caress conveying fondness and devotion. Maybe *outside* is not such a simple idea. Outside of what? Can all of us have our very own *dear little outside*?

Irwin grins. "No, it's like space—but time also has space, from start to finish, so the universe."

Einsteinian space-time, meet Nahuatl time-space. Sometimes there's not much dictionaries can do.

"Okay, tonal?" I'm asking about what must be the root inside both notonaltzintli and notonalamatzin.

"Tonalli!" he says, excited on my behalf, using what linguists call citation form, the one that seems most basic and dictionary-like to a speaker, like the infinitive form of the verb in many European languages.

Tonalli is the kind of word that crystallizes a whole theory of body and spirit and then spins a widening web of semantic associations—a little like Chinese qi or Greek pneuma, which also link *breath*, *life*, *soul*, and *character*. But tonalli is distinctly Nahuatl: it's *the heat of the sun* and it's *summertime*. It's *human sweat* and it's *the bodily heat of being alive*, which should always be kept in equilibrium. As notonal, with that possessive prefix **no-**, it can mean one's *soul* or ultimately one's *destiny*, *fate*, or *fortune*, as assigned at birth by a diviner from an *almanac of day signs* called tonalamatl. The tonalpohualli was a *sacred 260-day count*, a calendrical cycle based on that same almanac, which may have fundamentally structured people's concept of time.[1]

Lonely and frigid on the train to work in Westchester, Irwin dreams of Juanita's heat as both his soul and his destiny. By going inside her, he gets outside of himself—until that self itself melts away in the heat:

> *If what I feel now causes me pain, I enter the heart of my woman.*
> *This woman is called "JUANITA."*
>
> *I bathe.*
> *The heart, emotions, my soul, all become clean and I can feel what is inside me.*
>
> *I can see clearly my red path,*
> *which my destiny tells me to follow.*
>
> *I sit on my mat*
> *and start looking at my time-space.*
> *My time-space and I are together.*
> *I'm not here. Here only lies my essence.*[2]

Irwin shows me Juanita on his phone: a squat stone igloo, off-white, with a petate (*woven mat*) just barely visible inside. Juanita is the name that Irwin's great-great-grandparents gave their temazcal, the last one left in the little town of La Resurrección in the state of Puebla. Irwin firmly believes that a temazcal, a traditional Indigenous Mexican *sauna* or *sweat lodge*, can "save your mind." When he was growing up, every house in town had one, and everyone went in once a week to sweat and get clean: "I remember every Saturday around 3 p.m. you could see smoke everywhere."

"My grandfather told me how they used to speak with the stones" until fear of the Catholic Church made it a silent ceremony. But Irwin's family continued to consider Juanita the temazcal a living relative, and Irwin got to know her early on: "Whenever there's a newborn in the house, we make up the temazcal and put flowers around, and we introduce the baby to the temazcal."

At first, it wasn't all caresses. Irwin's aunt would impose Juanita's scorching heat as a form of discipline. "I struggled with school," admits Irwin. "I was always distracted." Sent on an errand to get cilantro, he might spend half an hour staring at bugs on the side of the road. In the temazcal, his aunt would pour more water over the volcanic rocks for every class he wasn't doing well in. Dried corn husks or the branches of the capulín, a Mexican cherry tree, were deployed for curative striking, like doing platza with a broom of oak leaves in an eastern European–style banya.

Irwin couldn't take it at first, but "after a while it feels good, you feel the heat inside your bones. If I think about the heat, it's impossible to survive. I'm going to scream or just run away, so I have to relax and focus on myself, kind of like meditation." His aunt would send steam to his glands, seeking out nodes similar to acupuncture points, balancing his tonalli while keeping his grades up. "For all the anxiety and fear and emotions," he says, "I learned how to control myself."

"Then suddenly the smoke started disappearing, and eventually it was only us, one house," remembers Irwin. The city of Puebla was expanding rapidly in the 1980s and '90s, especially after a catastrophic earthquake in Mexico City pushed many people to move there. All the new development engulfed La Resurrección: the road was widened, new concrete houses went up with indoor plumbing and showers, and Spanish speakers started moving in. The older residents replaced their own tepetate houses, swapping adobe for concrete and tearing down their temazcals to make showers.

"The shower is fast," admits Irwin, "but they forget about something important with temazcal. I told my mother, Don't touch the temazcal. If you take it out, you won't see me again. Now people know we still have the temazcal, and they ask to use medicine there, because it's the last place."

Irwin himself hasn't seen Juanita in over twenty years, which is all the more reason to send her a love poem, in the proper language, even or especially as everything around her is changing.

Irwin's family has been in La Resurrección since pre-Hispanic times. After the sixteenth-century arrival of the Caxtilteca, *the Castilians*, "a priest came and got a property, so he gathered all the Indigenous there," says Irwin, though most of them simply moved from a preexisting settlement on the other side of the hill.[3] Despite the awe-inspiring Catholic name, La Resurrección was just one of several sleepy Nahuatl-speaking towns on the lower slopes of the Malinche volcano, which rises over fourteen thousand feet.

Glittering fields of corn still surrounded the volcano when Irwin was growing up, even as more and more people were turning to wage labor, like his taxi-driving father. Traditional life largely continued in La Resurrección until the 1980s, says Irwin. Then almost overnight it became a suburb of Puebla, Mexico's fourth-largest city, now just a ten-minute drive away.

"Everybody was speaking Nahuatl," says Irwin of his childhood, before correcting himself: "Well, like here, how everybody speaks Spanish and the kids speak English, something similar happened there. They struggled to be Indigenous. Nobody wants to be like that. They didn't want to speak Nahuatl." His parents usually spoke Nahuatl with each other, but Spanish with the kids.

Crucially for Irwin, he went to stay for several years with his grandfather, who lived alone nearby, didn't speak much Spanish, and needed a little help with his pigs and turkeys. "So every afternoon I was with him, just watching the sun coming down and the sky red behind Popocatépetl," says Irwin, referring to another famous, more distant volcano. "He had a little grocery store, so people were just sitting down and talking in Nahuatl. There were so many stories he had about all the adventures when he was a kid."

Forms of Nahuatl—the last two letters add up to a voiceless alveolar lateral affricate, a single sound that's rare outside the Americas—were spoken first by the ancient Toltecs and later by the Aztecs, Tlaxcalans, and many other Indigenous peoples of the region, as far south as El Salvador. Today there are over 1.6 million people across central Mexico speaking what linguists group as six closely related languages, comprising around thirty definable dialects.[4] Nahuatl is just the most widely spoken of the country's estimated 282 Indigenous languages.

Life was local, and Irwin remembers little dialect differences from town to town—like how he would say tlátzihui for *lazy* while people in San Miguel Canoa, one town away, would say tlatzíhuiki. Many people called the language Mexicano, the language of the Mexica (i.e., Aztecs), but also fundamentally of Mexico itself.[5]

Almost everyone who spoke it when Irwin was growing up also spoke the local Mexican Spanish. For all of the twentieth century, in fact, this part of Puebla was a special kind of bilingual zone, where there was constant contact and intricate mixing on almost every linguistic level between the two languages.

"Spanish is used in most public functions and is in general a more 'formal' language, while Mexicano is usually the language of the domestic and informal sphere," reported the linguists Jane and Kenneth Hill in their classic linguistic study of the region, conducted exactly when Irwin was growing up there. "Spanish is the language of transactions, of relatively impersonal dealings between people, as in markets, government, and the public religion. Mexicano is the language of emotional commitment, of respect for ritual kin, and of aspects of the sacred which are particularly associated with life in the towns, as opposed to life in the cities."[6]

This is classic diglossia, the functioning of two languages in different spheres of life, but in reality there were always subtle and complex forms of overlap and mutual influence. Like anyone who grew up under the volcano, Irwin can tell you the local Spanish verbs for the all-important successive stages of the corn plant's growth: xilotear (*first flowering*), elotear (*the first tender ears appear*), and pixcar (*harvest*).[7] Only the **-ar** here is Spanish, an infinitive ending tacked onto Nahuatl words.

Much more common are cases of Nahuatl incorporating Spanish. To talk about loanwords or code-switching doesn't go far enough, because Nahuatl speakers from a place like La Resurrección can make total creative use of almost any Spanish vocabulary and still be understood. Almost any Spanish verb, for instance, can get stamped with a Nahuatl suffix like the *intransitive* **-(i)hui**—as in **De** tlen **tratar**ihui? *What it is about?* where the bold-faced bits are Spanish and the rest is Nahuatl. Just about any Spanish noun could take either the typical Spanish plural **-s/-es**, or the Nahuatl plural **-tin**, or even both, as in camión-es-tin *trucks*.[8] Changes went deep into the syntax: adjectives, which traditionally come before the noun, started going after it, as in Spanish.

Meanwhile, distinctively Nahuatl grammatical features have become rarer, like noun incorporation, where the direct object is folded into the verb, as in ni**tlaxcal**chīhua, *I-tortilla-make, I am making tortillas*.[9] (Tlaxcal is the Nahuatl word that *taco* comes from.) Even more compressed and idiomatic meaning-making is possible, as in ōnicihuāmic, literally *already-I-woman-died*, but really *I have become a widower*. But here the English and the Nahuatl may contain quite different assumptions and connotations, which an informational translation can hardly hope to capture.[10]

Irwin wrestles with these issues as a speaker, teacher, and poet. He is not a purist, but like many language activists he worries about any obvious inroads made by the dominant language. Linguists can admire with more detachment the utterly natural and practical ways that speakers in the region have been combining the two languages, discerning vital evidence for how language use can be active, conscious, and creative, not just inherent or mechanical. Are these hybrid, syncretic forms a way of resisting Spanish and keeping Nahuatl alive, or do they foreshadow wholesale shift?

The linguistic trend lines, especially since Irwin's childhood, are not promising. This corner of Puebla was a holdout, but communities in the surrounding region that once spoke Nahuatl have been shifting to Spanish for over a century. Language is changing along with the way people dress, eat, live, work, and travel. The Mexican government may call it mestizaje, *mixing*, with the aim of producing a united mestizo nation, but in practice very few people considered mestizos actually learn Indigenous languages. Instead the influence is almost all one way, toward Spanish—a process of desindianización, *de-Indianization*, or cultural and linguistic assimilation and loss.[11]

La Resurrección and the surrounding towns seem likely to lose Nahuatl in the next generation, although a degree of Indigenous identification may continue. Already in the 1980s, it was becoming "a language of passwords, a secret language which people use exclusively to validate identity and their right to walk in the towns and on their lands."[12] Even in other, more remote areas where different varieties of Nahuatl are spoken, there is relentless pressure. A study of Coatepec Nahuatl, with an estimated 1,400 speakers on the border of Guerrero and México states, found that "development" and migration in the 1990s marked a turning point.[13]

Whenever Indigenous people go to a larger town or city, especially at moments of vulnerability, they still risk encountering discrimination or feeling ashamed for looking or dressing a certain way, let alone speaking an Indigenous language. "My sister-in-law was at the hospital one time getting information from someone, and there was a woman waiting there in traditional dress," says Irwin. "The person there didn't say anything to her, just kept working. So my sister-in-law asks, Why don't you pay attention to her? Because 'es una india sucia.' *She's a dirty Indian.*"

Besides that period spent with his grandfather, Irwin was living almost entirely in Spanish: education, radio, TV, and just about every interaction. At school, even a hint of Indigenous influence meant that his Spanish could be considered inferior: "They said, You speak different. Why don't you speak well? Like you have an accent." And there were many Spanish words he didn't understand. "I remember one of the teachers said, You should go work, you're no good in school."

Thanks to that kind of encouragement, Irwin was at loose ends, hanging out on the street and strumming a guitar when a passing priest recruited him for a kind of seminary. He went along and took in the conquerors' perspective for a few years: "Mostly I liked the architecture, sixteenth century, learned a lot of history, the other side, the Spanish story, baroque painting," he says, laughing. "When I came back, my head changed, and the way I walked changed." Asked to minister to a poor and dangerous area where cars couldn't go because of the mud, Irwin would cheerfully bike over to visit drug addicts and alcoholics who affectionately called him padrecito, *little father*. But he didn't want to be a priest. With the church covering his fees, he finished high school and decided to try construction.

It was the 1990s, and people were leaving Puebla in droves for New York. Many in La Resurreción itself actually preferred to stay and work in nearby factories, but that wasn't for Irwin.[14] By then his father, following a friend, had ditched his cab and was doing landscaping work as a day laborer in Freehold, New Jersey. Four years in, he sent for Irwin's brother, who decided at the last minute that he didn't want to go. Did Irwin want to instead, since everything was ready?

"Sure, I'll go," he said, without thinking about it too much, "I have nothing else to do right now."

## 2

"It was April 11, 2002, when the airplane landed in Islip," remembers Irwin, "because if we go to big airports it's Immigration there, they'll catch you. So you transfer. You take a taxi. I said, Taxi, let's go to Freehold, New Jersey." It was an expensive hundred-mile ride, but he had no idea about buses or trains, and this was the way to make it safely to where his father was staying. For the next four years, Irwin would sit with his father and Freehold's other jornaleros on street corners, waiting to pick up landscaping, construction, and other jobs from local contractors, companies, and homeowners.

All of them, without exception, were recent undocumented immigrants from Mexico and Central America, trying to save and send money home—part of a major new migration which was dramatically accelerating in the 1990s and would more than triple the Mexican-born population in New York City to over three hundred thousand, not to mention the surrounding area. Almost all of the new arrivals were undocumented, with half estimated to be between the ages of twelve and twenty-four, like Irwin.[15]

Irwin makes it sound like he came almost on a whim, but the chain of events behind his decision reflected a much deeper history. An important factor was the booming US economy, including a massive expansion of mostly informal service-sector and construction jobs in the New York area. At the same time, a series of social and economic shocks were detonating in Mexico. NAFTA brought the price of corn and other crops crashing down, forcing farmers off their land; the ensuing peso crisis of 1994 spelled economic depression; then came drugs, cartels, and violence.

The much older and larger Mexican communities in California, Texas, and the southwest were originally formed by people from central and northern states like Jalisco, Michoacán, and Guanajuato, where few Indigenous languages are spoken. In New York, however, an estimated 70 percent of Mexicans were coming from Irwin's home state of Puebla, where substantial Indigenous communities speak forms of Nahuatl, Mixtec, and many other languages, though many are shifting under pressure to Spanish. Especially in the state's southern and western reaches, in the towns and villages around Atlixco, Matamoros, Acatlán, and Tulcingo, the logic and momentum of the migration toward "Puebla York" became so powerful that whole towns were drawn in. Today at least a dozen bakeries, restaurants, bodegas, and other businesses around New York are named for Tulcingo alone—but before opening a business, you had to spend years looking for work on street corners.

Freehold was one of many suburban towns where homeowners, fearing for their property values even as they needed the men's work, started going after day laborers. They called the town police, who were more than happy to break up the already desperate and dehumanizing search for work. "You stand up when the police point the lights, you freeze and you've got to move, otherwise you're going to get a ticket," remembers Irwin. "Officer discretion, they called it." The mayor started hinting darkly that Mexicans had no place at all in Freehold.

The day laborers started organizing in response, but their leaders soon faced relentless harassment from the police: "Everywhere they went, there was a car in the back with the lights just following them around, even outside their house. They stopped feeling safe because they had families, so they just ran away from town." Irwin became a leader by default: "I was alone, so I was free, nothing to lose."

He learned on the fly how to be an organizer and started representing the workers at meetings with lawyers and politicians. The National Day Laborers Organizing Network lent its support. So did the local Black, Jewish, Quaker, and gay communities, says Irwin, "because they understand discrimination." For recent arrivals who spoke little English and sometimes even Spanish as a second language, it was a crash course in American-style coalition building and local politics.

Eventually, the day laborers and their allies sued the mayor of Freehold personally, and they won.

It was a major victory, but Irwin didn't want to stay in town after everything that had happened. The same pattern of anti–day laborer discrimination was unfolding in the New York suburb of Mamaroneck, and through the organizing network Irwin was hired to move there. "I knew how the police were going to act, so I was ready with my camera and my journal every day, taking notes on the police, taking pictures." He knew how to hold his ground in front of an officer, showing he wasn't afraid and shielding the other workers. He sang psalms in the local Catholic church, gaining allies. Again, Irwin and his fellow organizers slowly built their case, the mayor was sued, and the day laborers won.

"This situation was happening in every part of the country," says Irwin of the mid-2000s. "Every town had day laborers struggling to make a living, because they didn't let you work peacefully. So somebody said let's do some cross-country protests for day laborer rights and Indigenous rights."

At the time, there was little awareness about Indigenous immigrants from Latin America, many of them day laborers. Nowhere was this more the case than in New York, where by the 2000s the largest number of arrivals were coming specifically from La Mixteca, an arid and rugged region that includes parts of Puebla, Guerrero, and Oaxaca. One of the poorest and most marginalized areas in Mexico, La Mixteca is even more heavily Indigenous than the parts of Puebla people had been coming from a decade earlier.

The dynamics of day laborer migration meant that Indigenous Mexicans and Central Americans from particular towns were now coming not just to the inner city but to particular towns in the greater New York metropolitan area: Zapotec speakers from the town of San Agustín formed a community in Poughkeepsie;[16] Triqui speakers from around San Juan Copala made it to Albany; Tacuate (Zacatepec Mixtec) speakers gathered in New Brunswick; and other Zapotecs found farmwork in New Jersey's southern agricultural belt around Bridgeton. The Mixtec-speaking towns of San Marcos Natividad (Oaxaca) and San Jerónimo Xayacatlán (Puebla) re-established themselves through day laborer work in Staten Island's Port Richmond neighborhood.

Irwin's cross-country campaign acknowledged this reality, pointing out that Indigenous people were suffering disproportionately from the harassment and mistreatment of day laborers. In the coming years, the number of day laborers on the streets would dwindle substantially—between the economic downturn, reduced immigration, and the creation of safer new spaces and services for finding work—but the connection between justice for immigrants and Indigenous rights would only become more urgent. In recent years, more people crossing the border than ever before have been speakers of Indigenous languages, especially from Mexico and Guatemala. People whose families have been in the Americas for millennia are suddenly being called "illegal aliens" by recent European settlers.

Irwin was asked by the National Day Laborers Organizing Network to be one of twelve activists running a relay race starting in Santa Monica on March 4 and ending on Cinco de Mayo in Coney Island. Together the runners logged a total of seventy or more miles per day, holding events for supporters and media along the way—cheered on wherever there were larger Mexican communities, but facing stony silence or worse in some of the places in between.

Irwin was still happy to see the country, especially the Native reservations in the Southwest that welcomed the runners. "That's when my Nahuatl started coming back again," he says, as he was invited into sweat lodges and ceremonies that reminded him of Juanita back home. "If I'm going there, I look normal," he says of being on the San Carlos Apache Reservation in Arizona. When a border guard in the area asked him if he spoke Spanish, the person next to him whispered, "Don't speak Spanish, or they're going to take you." Irwin didn't feel comfortable in English, so he responded in Nahuatl. It worked, possibly because the guard took it for Apache. "Have a nice day, sir," he said, waving Irwin on. Apache is not related to Nahuatl, but a number of other Native languages in the American Southwest are, including Hopi, O'odham, and Paiute—part of the same Uto-Aztecan language family that stretches all the way from El Salvador to Idaho.

Back in New York, Irwin moved to Jackson Heights, which was fast becoming an epicenter of the new Indigenous city, along with neighboring Elmhurst and Corona. Not that it was easy for him to find any of the thousands of other people from Nahuatl-speaking backgrounds in New York. Indigenous New Yorkers everywhere remain largely invisible to outsiders, living almost hidden among other Spanish speakers. Many work long hours at difficult jobs, keeping quiet to avoid deportation and the stigma of being seen as Indigenous. At the time no explicitly Indigenous community organizations or institutions existed in the city, only small networks of families, friends, and people from the same town.

The opportunities to use Indigenous languages were (and still are) few and far between. The degree of linguistic diversity even just among Indigenous Mexican New Yorkers makes it a challenge to connect, requiring people to improve their Spanish or even learn it in New York. Entirely different from Uto-Aztecan languages like Nahuatl are the languages of the Otomanguean family, which spans much of central and southern Mexico and includes Mixtec, probably the most widely used Indigenous Mexican language in New York. Over half a million people speak it in Mexico, often calling themselves Ñuu Savi, *people of the rain/clouds*, and their language Tu'un Savi.[17] Because of how diverse Mixtec is, linguists talk about "Mixtecan" as a whole subfamily comprising dozens of different languages that are little documented and vary greatly from pueblo to pueblo—similar to the Tibetic situation. All forms of Mixtec are tonal, with tone used not only for distinguishing words (as in Chinese) but also for core parts of the grammar. Tense, aspect, mood, and person may all depend on it.

Today a Mixtec archipelago tens of thousands of people strong stretches across Latino neighborhoods in every borough.[18] Within the Mixteca region, many have come from La Montaña, an arc of rugged villages around the regional commercial center Tlapa de Comonfort in Guerrero. Depending on their specific background, they may have little or no Spanish, only a few years of formal education, and not necessarily any experience of the world beyond Tlapa—until they make their harrowing journey to the border, cross on foot with a coyote, and board a bus to New York.[19]

Beyond anecdotes, there was no reliable information on the extent of Indigenous Mexican languages in New York, no statistics, and no official recognition. The closest indication was an informal but telling 2013 survey of those seeking services at the local Mexican consulate. Seventeen percent reported speaking an Indigenous language, nearly three times the rate in Mexico, with Mixtec and Nahuatl by far the most common but fourteen other languages also listed. In other words, there were potentially over a hundred thousand speakers of Indigenous Mexican languages in the metropolitan area.

It was only at ELA that Irwin finally met others like himself, who feel increasingly emboldened, despite centuries of discrimination, to speak, teach, and even write in their languages.

## 3

Irwin is making mixiotes, moles, tamales, and tacos served with chipotle and guacamole. To him, these are more than just names. He knows the flavor of each word. He cooks each one with a theory of its meaning and origin.

"A French menu should be in French," he says, "and a Nahuatl menu should be in Nahuatl."

His shirt says WILL COOK FOR BEER, like he's that cheerful uncle at a barbecue, but the toque signals a serious chef. His kitchen here at Under the Volcano, a slick bar in Midtown Manhattan, is the size of a closet with two electric burners, a toaster oven, and a few small surfaces for prep. Every condo on this block has something better. One assistant helps. Even as he's earning rave reviews, Irwin is cooking with both hands tied behind his apron.

Yet Irwin, who hides melancholy with a smile, is looking genuinely happy. His culinary and linguistic vision is coming into view and being put into practice on people's plates. (At least until this place goes belly up a few months from now, in classic New York restaurant fashion—though Irwin will land on his feet, slinging barbacoa tacos at a new spot in Brooklyn.) He won't eat, but he watches me with evident pleasure and won't say no to a little mezcal.

When I was little, he says, the kitchen was the safe place and the sacred place. There was no gas or electricity, just tletl, the *open fire*. "Every day you want to eat, you got to put the fire," which explains why he can still build one anywhere easily. A giant comal, *an earthenware griddle for making tortillas*, sat balanced on stones in the hearth. No food processor: you used the traditional metate, *a stone grinding tool*. (Now Irwin's family home has both a traditional open-air kitchen and a modern indoor one with a stove.)

Indigenous rituals, stamped out by the Inquisition in other spaces, could still quietly be practiced in the kitchen, like the traditional blessing for a newlywed couple. You could process grief there: if you were crying and someone noticed, you would just say you were making tortillas and that the tears were from the smoke. "If I fell down playing outside," says Irwin, "I'd come in and somebody would always be doing tortillas and saying, Don't cry, have a tortilla with salsa."

That tortilla was made of masa dough, and masa required the molino, the local neighborhood mill where people would bring giant buckets of nixtamalized corn for milling under two volcanic stone blades. Nixtamalization itself—based on the Nahuatl word for the soaking and cooking of kernels in limewater to loosen the hulls and release essential nutrients—is an ancient process which spread far across the Americas, together with corn, and remains at the heart of Mexican cooking. The creator god Quetzalcoatl—a Nahuatl name which combines quetzal, a bird species known for its splendid feathers, with the word for serpent—is said to have made the original masa for making people with nixtamalized corn, ground-up bones, and his own blood.

Machismo was a force in both the kitchen and the mill. Women handled food, and men rarely lifted a finger. Typically a man wouldn't even enter the mill after helping his wife, sister, or mother carry the bucket up to the entrance. But Irwin didn't care, walking right in one hungover morning, and soon other men in town were doing the same. Likewise, he started learning from his mom how to make tortillas and cook with avocado leaves, epazote, and herbs like pipicha and pápalo. His aunt, a nun who came home on holidays, taught him to prepare tamales and recipes full of cloves and cinnamon.

I dip into a little bowl of ayocotes, a type of runner bean which a Nahuatl dictionary describes as medically useful for "fighting animalejos (*little animals*) that descend to the abdomen of men."[20] The little stomach animals really do seem to retreat as the umami richness of the beans, stewed simply with avocado leaves and salt, washes down my throat. Next up mixiotes: sacks painstakingly assembled and steamed with their enclosed juicy bundles of lamb, garlic, and salsa with avocado leaves and nopales (*fried cactus leaves*). "It's an old recipe, pre-Hispanic probably," explains Irwin, "because we use the skin of the maguey to wrap it," though in the States he has to substitute parchment paper and sprinkle mezcal into the salsa to conjure the flavor of the missing maguey.

It was an accident that got Irwin started cooking professionally. The day laborer work was done, and he was commuting from Queens to Westchester to do landscaping full-time for a company. One day he fell while holding a trimmer, badly cutting two of his fingers and ending up in the hospital. He wasn't going to be working again any time soon.

It happened that a community organization in Westchester, in conjunction with the Restaurant Opportunity Center, an organization for workers, was holding free cooking classes. For the next three months, Irwin learned at least the basics of baking, sauce-making, food safety, and a whole range of cooking techniques far removed from his mother's tletl.

He found his first few jobs at various Mexican restaurants around the city, but soon became curious about all the different cuisines around him. "I had the idea to learn more about spices, so I went to work in a big Pakistani warehouse," he says. He started cooking at a Vietnamese place because his son loved pho. There he also mastered the art of running a busy kitchen without a ticketing system, keeping all the orders in his head.

The kitchens of New York are home to thousands of unsung Irwins: young men from Puebla and Guerrero, many of them speakers of Mixtec, Nahuatl, and other Indigenous languages who have come to the city and learned, in a very short time with little formal training, to cook food from all over the world. Today they run everything from Greek diners to ramen shops to burger joints to neighborhood trattorias. Anyone for Mexican-Vietnamese, Mexican-Italian, Mexican-Indian, or maybe Mexican–New American? There may be only occasional signs of fusion on the menu, but in New York that indescribably authentic moussaka or bouillabaisse you just ate was very likely made by a Mexican immigrant.

It raises the question of how exactly the city's famously diverse food culture actually reflects the cultural and linguistic roots of its peoples. Given culinary hierarchies, diners still expect to pay three times more for items on a French menu versus a Nahuatl one. In some ways it's fundamentally misleading to categorize restaurants in terms of "national" cuisines, a shorthand which is often unavoidable for owners and which Google, Yelp, and endless food blogs are perpetuating. The very idea of a shiny, packaged cuisine complete with recipes and restaurants is not unlike a standardized national language. In reality, traditional foodways are often much more local, like languages, while ingredients, like words, can reflect origins, migrations, and connections much older and broader than the nation-state map. How else could the Nahuatl xitomatl have become the *tomato* so central to Italian cooking, or the beverage chocolatl been transformed into Swiss *chocolate*?[21]

Food work of all kinds has been an economic mainstay for Mexican New Yorkers at least since the 1990s. Many have advanced from washing dishes or bussing tables to becoming waiters, chefs, and restaurant owners. Some like Irwin have a long-standing interest in food, but for many Mexican men it's a radical reversal of gender roles, a creative adaptation to a city with a massive, fast-growing food service industry—including not only restaurants but all kinds of cafeteria, catering, import-export, and other food-related jobs.[22] Once the occupational niche was established, Mexicans also started finding adjacent lines of work as fruit, vegetable, and flower vendors, grocery store stockers and clerks, and most recently deliveristas.[23]

Such niches have long been crucial for hundreds of ethnolinguistic communities in New York. They may reflect troubling racial, ethnic, and linguistic pecking orders, with starkly unequal valuations on different types of labor, but they also draw on the heterogenous skill sets and preferences brought by many different groups and provide an economic foothold on arrival.[24] Even within New York's food world there is an extraordinary range—and not only the well-known Greek diners, Chinese takeout spots, Italian (now often Albanian- or Mexican-run) pizza joints, and Egyptian halal carts.[25] Nor is "one's own" food necessarily the point: witness the Yemeni bodegas, the Afghan-run fried chicken places, the Bangladeshi-run Subway and Dunkin' franchises. Bretons, Galicians, and Istrians have run many of the city's French, Spanish, and northern Italian restaurants, respectively. Countless other New York niches operate as much through language as on any national or racial basis, like the Bukharian barbers, Garifuna home attendants, Malayali health-care workers, and Kichwa nail technicians, among many others.[26]

Irwin ultimately found his own niche partly thanks to the COVID-19 pandemic. The stressful cycle of restaurant jobs was going nowhere, with one bright spot: a series of cooking and language classes in his apartment, where he led a handful of students in uncompromising labor for hours, doing everything by hand with the metate to make a mole poblano, for example. Little by little, as the students chopped and ground, Irwin also fed them Nahuatl.

Recently divorced, he lost his job cooking at an Irish bar at the start of the pandemic. Then one day at the height of the pandemic in the summer of 2020, he walked by a shuttered cevicheria in the shadow of the elevated train tracks above Jackson Heights. He took a chance and scraped together four months' rent to start a pop-up called Tlaxcal Kitchen, recreating his teenage memories of the multiethnic city of Puebla.

That meant cemitas, a classic poblano sandwich which fuses European elements (bread, olive oil, and cheese) with Mexican essentials (avocado, chipotle, pápalo, and beans).[27] Irwin combed New York in vain for the proper bread, so in the end he got a recipe from his brother-in-law's brother-in-law in Puebla and started baking it himself in small batches several times a day. His other specialty was tacos árabes, the *Arab tacos* first introduced to Puebla a century ago by Lebanese immigrants, whose use of spit-roasted, spice-marinaded lamb shawarma inspired tacos al pastor. The classic recipe had long been a closely guarded secret, but Irwin's son's Lebanese music teacher turned out to have just the right spices.

The pop-up closed with winter coming, but not before the owners of Under the Volcano had come to see him and made an offer: "Do the menu and let's see what happens." Pandemic regulations meant that the bar needed food.

As Irwin talks, I polish off a plate of his cochinita pibil, a Mayan slow-roasted pork dish from Yucatán. Pib is an *underground pit oven* in the Yucatec Maya language, he says, and that part unfortunately can't be recreated, but he does make the achiote seed paste from scratch and sources just the right kind of cinnamon, which is skinnier and sweeter than what's common in the States.

Yucatán is not really close to Puebla, but in the last few years Irwin has gradually been exploring the whole gamut of Mexican cooking, particularly Indigenous foodways.

"The original diet was more vegetables, beans, tortillas, chiles, salsas. Meat was very rare," says Irwin. "Something is going on here." He sees the same amnesia around food and language whenever he shares recipes with Mexican American kids at his local community garden: "They don't know how to cook, and they don't even recognize the ingredients that are still staples for their grandparents."

The vast majority of Mexican restaurants, he says, "taste nothing like Mexican," lacking proper salsa, spices, or chiles, and "even the meat has no flavor because of the way they grow the animals too fast." As for the tortillas, because of citric acid they can keep for years in the fridge: "It's like an immortal tortilla, that's why they taste so bad." Like many Mexican immigrants, Irwin felt his health enter a downward spiral as his diet became more American between too much meat and too many preservatives. He was gaining weight every year and had to take medicine for inflammation and change his diet. Now he hears about the same soda, meat, fast food, and cheap, low-quality corn flooding into Mexico itself.

On the other hand, Indigenous ingredients are looked down on. "Things like alaches are getting lost," says Irwin of a fibrous plant whose name comes from the Nahuatl word for *slippery*, ahalactli. "The people buying alaches in Queens are from Mexico, and they used to eat it there, so they remember, but the second generation don't have the same love of the ingredients, or the memories. Because they eat it in our communities, people think it's low quality. Nobody wants to eat alaches in the restaurant, because this is for the poor." The same goes for huauzontle (from Nahuatl *hairy amaranth*), a plant full of proteins, calcium, and fiber, as well as pipián, *pumpkin seeds*, which have so much protein they can substitute for meat: "I want people to see and taste them."

"The information is in the word," Irwin says, and there is no Mexican cooking without the Nahuatl language. Even a contested etymology is a vision: "If you say mole, it means *movement*, so it has to cook very slow, stir constantly." Where sauce meets clay, a tiny bit of flavorful crust can form at the bottom, but you can't let it burn: "Don't stop. You have to move, that's the key. It doesn't mean you have to have certain main ingredients. Sometimes they're important, but each town has their own recipe. Don't forget what it's named after."[28]

## 4

What prompted Irwin to write that poem to Juanita on the Metro-North was his grandfather's death back in La Resurrección. With that, memories came flooding back—getting a haircut together or selling cheese at his store—and with them whispers of a language that Irwin had hardly thought about, let alone used, in fifteen years. He found himself reaching for the kind of Nahuatl that his grandfather and the other elders had spoken, which was very different even from what Irwin's parents used. Irwin had only rarely spoken the language with his father, who in any case had been deported, then started working again as a driver in Puebla, and eventually returned to New Jersey to keep doing the landscaping work he liked best.

Irwin himself has thus far never been able to go back to Mexico, but he hopes to soon. His turning back to the language later in life is not without precedent. As Nahuatl comes to be associated with elders, like so many other endangered languages, some believe that proficiency comes with age: "I'll speak it later."[29] Some people do relearn or reactivate Nahuatl as adults, without classes, even if they were raised in Spanish, such is its importance as "a badge of community membership."[30]

There was something else: Irwin had just had a son and he dreamed of passing on the language that was almost entirely in his head, that he had only just started writing. One day when he was flipping through the *Astoria Post*, a neighborhood newspaper, he saw an article about ELA and got in touch.

The challenge was that Irwin, like the vast majority of Nahuatl speakers, had never formally studied his language. Nor, growing up, had he ever seen or read anything written in it, except a few famous fragments (a line from which appears on Mexico's one-hundred-peso bill) from the Aztec emperor-poet Nezahualcóyotl, whose work was transcribed in the sixteenth century. Beyond that, all Irwin knew were a few tidbits from a nineteenth-century author who wrote in Spanish but came from a Nahuatl-speaking background.[31]

Yet Nahuatl, almost uniquely for the Americas, has a long and extraordinary history as a written language. Though sometimes associated with the Aztec Empire, of which it was a kind of capital, Tenochtitlán was in fact just one of hundreds of semiautonomous, Nahuatl-speaking altepetl—literally *water and mountains*, by extension *city-state*—that once spread across the entire Valley of Mexico. At first the other altepetl, some of which were allied with the conquistadors, weathered the Spanish conquest of Tenochtitlán in 1521. It was not some caricature of a clash of civilizations, and Indigenous Mexicans were not shocked, overwhelmed, and driven to extinction. Despite Spanish aggression and demographic disaster, there existed for centuries a degree of cultural and linguistic stability that allowed for, as one scholar puts it, "the preservation of indigenous structures of all kinds while intercultural ferment went on gradually, hardly attaining the level of consciousness."[32]

In contrast to the more immediate suppression of Native languages by English settlers on the Atlantic seaboard, the Spanish had no choice but to rule through Nahuatl for much of the sixteenth century, and it continued significantly longer as the lingua franca for much of Mexico. Mexican Spanish filled up with Nahuatl words, reflecting just how fundamentally the language was filtering European understandings of the land. This is why almost every well-known Mexican dish gets its name from Nahuatl, not to mention chocolate, tomato, avocado, chile, mesquite, mezcal, peyote, and coyote—and why other Indigenous groups like the Mixtec came to be known in Spanish by their originally Nahuatl names, rather than by what they called themselves. As they spread the gospel, Spanish priests not only learned Nahuatl, but devised a way of writing it with Latin letters that rapidly replaced the former Aztec system, which consisted largely of pictographs which today are incompletely understood.

An extraordinary Nahuatl literature using the Latin system flourished in many genres, including poetry, chronicles, and a vast number of administrative records, especially in the sixteenth and seventeenth centuries. In 1536, the first European college founded in the Americas was established in the altepetl of Tlatelolco for the purpose for educating young Nahuatl-speaking elites in Nahuatl, Spanish, and Latin. It was here with a team of graduates that the Franciscan friar Bernardino de Sahagún compiled a twelve-volume encyclopedia of Nahuatl culture, in Nahuatl with Spanish translation, known today as the Florentine Codex.

Of special interest is Book 12, an Indigenous account of the conquest based directly on oral tradition and differing in a number of respects from Spanish accounts.[33] It begins with the first of eight omens said to have heralded the arrival of Cortés:

> In aiamo vallaci españoles, oc madacxivitl, centlamātli tetzavitl achto nez, ilhuicatitech, iuhqui in tlemiiaoatl, iuhqui

in tlecueçalutl, iuhquin tlavizcalli, pipixauhticaca inic necia; iuhqn ilhuicatl quiçoticac: tzimpatlaoac, quapitzaoac: vel inepantla in ilhuicatl; vel yiollo . . .

*Ten years before the arrival of the Spaniards an omen first appeared in the sky, like a flame or tongue of fire, like the light of dawn. It appeared to be throwing off* [*sparks*] *and seemed to pierce the sky. It was wide at the bottom and narrow at the top. It looked as though it reached the very middle of the sky—its very heart and center . . .*[34]

Today this is considered Classical Nahuatl, but Irwin can read at least some of it. Despite changes in the language, the sixteenth-century writing system using Latin letters is fairly intuitive for him, with a few exceptions. Likewise accessible, if not exactly easy to read, are the Nahuatl dictionaries, grammars, and textbooks subsequently published by other teams of priests and native speakers, which still stand as landmarks of language documentation and analysis—some of the first such works anywhere in the world.

The standout is Jesuit priest Horacio Carochi's *Arte de la lengua Mexicana* (*Grammar of the Mexican Language*), compiled in 1645. Not only does it show the language at a unique moment, absorbing many Spanish nouns but not yet taking on verbs or prepositions, it actually presents thousands of real examples of courtly rhetoric as well as idiomatic, everyday speech as used in Nahuatl homes and families. It also delves deep into features like the so-called reverential mood and applicative voice, which transforms verbs ending in **-oa** with the ending **-huia** when an action is "applied" to someone, as Carochi copiously illustrates:

Nitlapoloa, [*to lose something*]; Nimitztlapolhuia, *I lose something of yours*. Nitlapòpoloa, *to erase, waste, or destroy*

> *something*; Nitētlapòpolhuia, *to destroy something of someone else's, or pardon him his offense, as if erasing it for him.* Nitlapōloa, *I make mud or clay;* Nitētlapōlhuia, *I knead clay or mud for someone.* Nitlaxeloa, *to split or divide something;* Nitētlaxelhuia, *I share something with someone, or divide it for him.*[35]

Soon after Carochi's *Arte*, the record goes dark. Spain's colonial language policies varied, but the pressure to shift to Spanish mounted over time, only increasing after Mexican independence in 1821. By then, few were literate in Nahuatl; by the twentieth century, even fewer.

Only in the last few decades have attitudes shifted. Precisely when Irwin and so many poblanos were setting out for New York, the political and cultural situation in Mexico was being dramatically upended. The 1994 Indigenous-led Zapatista uprising in Chiapas paved the way for the constitutional reform of 2001, which in principle significantly strengthened Indigenous rights. "Now everybody wants to be an Indigenous," says Irwin, half joking. "I was one of the first with the language. Now I see the younger generation on Instagram: Nahuatl classes, Nahuatl poetry contests in school, Nahuatl this and that, because now there's money." Stereotypes die hard, but he at least sees less overt discrimination, more awareness, and sometimes even meaningful official support for Indigenous languages in schools.

With hardly any support, Irwin wanted to do something for Nahuatl in New York. Backed by ELA and Mano a Mano, a Mexican arts organization in the city, he taught himself to teach the language and led three years of classes. Soon he was being called on to interpret for Nahuatl speakers caught up in the courts, in relay with a Spanish interpreter because he still wasn't comfortable with English, especially the formal, high-stakes kind.

Besides family court in the Bronx and Staten Island, he remembers interpreting for a criminal case in Manhattan and working with the deeply frightened defendant for two weeks straight, all day: "He didn't understand what was going on, because his Mexican Spanish is not good and anyway the first interpreter was Puerto Rican. He was getting confused, like, 'Yes, no, yes, no, maybe, like, what's going on?' 'Do you speak another language?' 'Yes, Nahuatl.' He was from Guerrero, so it's a different [Nahuatl] language, but at least he could understand me better than the Boricua Spanish."

Irwin also started posting in Nahuatl on social media to a growing number of followers, sometimes under the Spanish name Rescatando al Idioma Nahuatl, *Rescuing the Nahuatl Language*. He started posting poems too, which he continued to write and recite at ELA events around the city. "At first I was just trying to speak," he says of his poetry, "but now the structure is getting better." One of his most recent, "Ome Poali Uan Yei" (*Forty-Three*), takes on an explosive political topic: the abduction and murder of forty-three mostly Indigenous students from Guerrero's Ayotzinapa Normal School in 2014—likely by local police in cahoots with a cartel, though justice has yet to be served.[36]

In another, "Tlaxcal Kitchen," he captures a moment in miniature from one of his cooking classes:

Kuentla tlapakiahui, tlatekuinia, ipan nohtli mochihua ze huei ahueyatl.
Uan tehuanti timokololohua kalihtek, timotlakualchihua uan tichihua zeki memelas uan zeki atoltzin.

*Outside, thunder and lightning, the street forms a great river.*
*And we stay together inside, making corn flour cakes and a drink of hot corn porridge.*

Several of the poems call on Aztec gods, reference the divine, or speak of Miktlan, *the Land of the Dead*. Irwin is watching with interest the growing number of efforts to revive Indigenous religion, including in New York, from the performances and recreations of the Mexica and neo-Aztec dance groups to the work of curanderos, *healers*. "But nobody has a place," he says, so everything is transient and scattered, "just keeping things alive, but not growing." Catholicism is losing its hold on Indigenous people, he believes, but so far charismatic evangelical movements are filling the gap. There are several evangelical services around the city conducted at least partly in Garifuna, K'iche', Kichwa, and Mixtec.

Irwin hopes for something different: "There needs to be a place for us, where everybody can gather and share the knowledge with whoever wants to learn. And it's a good idea to use Nahuatl for the religion, but we need it outside the city, because part of the culture is in nature." He dreams of a kitchen like the one he grew up in, with no gas, just tletl, equipped only with metates and molcajetes, *the mortar and pestle*. "The food would be delicious, like what I ate in Mexico. And when I have the kitchen there, we can start a community, a place to stay, a destination, and we can develop schools for Nahuatl, and for dancers, and a little farm with our own herbs from Mexico. And on the same land have a church and a priest." He just needs the investors.

## 5

Suddenly out of the humid grit and grime of a Bronx summer evening Irwin bursts in, with his flowery shirt and backwards cap. He and two helpers carry stacks of steaming aluminum trays full of ribs, rice, potatoes, and salad. Good smells fill up the room, and the focus cracks just a little as stomachs rumble. Irwin grins, warning that the salsa may be extra spicy, and then as one the collective is on its feet, lining up at the little counter and plunging into the feast.

The thirty or so people here are deliveristas for Uber, DoorDash, Grubhub-Seamless, and Relay. They are jornaleros, cooks, and stay-at-home moms with children on their laps who look bored or serious.

Usually these people are the ones feeding others. They are New Yorkers who speak Nahuatl, Mixtec, Me'phaa, Totonac, Triqui, Mixe, Garifuna, Kichwa, and K'iche'. In fact, they are just about the only people around who have experience interpreting and translating in these languages.

The place is an unmarked brick building, where a Nahuatl-speaking upholsterer named Esteban has his business and lets La Red de los Pueblos Trasnacionales, *the Network of Transnational Villages*—La Red, or *the Network*, for short—hold its meetings. Next door is a lounge that doesn't open until 10 p.m., a storefront church, and a standard bodega, with Spanish names that promise salsa, salvation, and a fire to sit by, respectively. A few blocks away is La Morada, a Mott Haven restaurant run by a Mixtec-speaking family from San Miguel Ahuehuetitlán in Oaxaca, famous for its moles and its activism.

At Esteban's place, a steel gate is rolled down where the shop window would be, but the door on the side, with a little rolled-up steel gate of its own, is unlocked. Inside, the world of the Network opens up. Here many of the most isolated and vulnerable Mexican immigrants in New York, particularly those from rural and Indigenous backgrounds, are organizing themselves. The Network functions as a coalition of hometown associations from at least seven different towns in Puebla, Guerrero, and Tlaxcala that now have communities in specific neighborhoods around the five boroughs. At least three of the groups include Nahuatl speakers: people from Teopantlán, like Esteban, in different parts of Queens; those from Necoxtla (Puebla) mostly in Corona; many from San Francisco de Tetlanohcan (Tlaxcala) who have moved to Coney Island and New Haven. In others, some speak Mixtec.

Passing through a narrow corridor, there is a large windowless room of whitewashed brick walls and exposed pipes under a high scalloped ceiling. Strings of beer-garden lights and a rainbow's worth of papel picado, those elaborate chains of Mexican papercuts made from perforated tissue paper, crisscross the space. Half a wall is a mural of an Indigenous woman weaving a volcanic landscape of creatures and flowers into being. Posters deliver Zapatista common sense: Tierra y Libertad (*Land and Liberty*), El Maíz Es Nuestro (*Corn Is Ours*). A handmade map and chart track femicides across Latin America, while a Day of the Dead skeleton dangles between the bulbs of a two-headed emergency light. Movies, movements, meetings, and parties have all left their traces. In a corner is a counter, with just enough space for a fridge and a fire extinguisher, plus plates and cups.

It's Sunday evening, the only time everyone can gather, given working hours. I sit next to Zenaida, a speaker of Me'phaa, which outsiders call Tlapanec, from the mountainous zone outside Tlapa in Guerrero. Like Irwin, Zenaida has taught herself to write poetry in the language in New York, and she interprets for fellow speakers caught up in the courts or with Immigration as far away as California and Arizona. In the different WhatsApp groups where the organizing happens, Zenaida is always first with a kind word. She is brave enough to wear her colorful Tlapanec blouses on the streets of the Bronx. She works a restaurant job, mostly. On her lap is one of her three sons, playing on Mom's phone. She hasn't seen her own mother in fourteen years, when she migrated—though they talk often, except during rainy season in the village, when sometimes there may be no signal for months.

The purpose of this meeting is to forge something entirely new: an Indigenous Interpreters Collective with speakers not just of Nahuatl, Mixtec, and Tlapanec but also K'iche', Mam, Garifuna, and potentially any Indigenous language now spoken in New York.

Digging into Irwin's dinner, the assembled interpreters talk about the dignity and difficulty of translation and the importance of countering the shame around Indigenous languages. Little by little, courts, hospitals, and city agencies are realizing how essential it is to translate materials, hire interpreters, and, most importantly, engage with the communities of tens of thousands in the city that speak these languages. The big, for-profit "language services" companies tout their reach and convenience, profiting by hiring the cheapest translators they can find working as remote freelancers from anywhere in the world. This exploitative model is not only nasty but ineffective when it comes to Indigenous languages in all their orality and complexity. With the Collective, the money will go straight to the interpreters, who are actual members of the local community. The dream is to bundle enough work for deliveristas, jornaleros, and street vendors who have language skills to become, in effect, ambassadors for their communities in New York, helping those members who need it most.

But the Collective has to build almost everything from scratch. For most Indigenous languages, dictionaries, textbooks, and other resources are hard to come by. There are no interpreter training or certification programs, nor any history of professional interpreting, nor any standards, procedures, or precedents for translating the legal, medical, and other terms that frequently come up in interpretation settings. In Latin America itself, provision is piecemeal, although grassroots Indigenous-led interpreting is a little further along in California. A team of Zapotec and Mixtec activists from Los Angeles recently held a two-day training here in Esteban's workshop for many of the people in this room.[37]

Over the past four months, the Collective completed its first major project, providing interpretation in seventeen mostly Indigenous languages of the Americas, Asia, and Africa for a series of conversations held by the New York City Department of Health about the COVID-19 vaccine. Holding all these events virtually with so many different communities was challenging enough without all the linguistic conundrums. ELA coordinated, handling paperwork, logistics, funding, and discussions with the Health Department. Many of the people here interpreted, but the series would never have happened if not for a Department of Health staffer, herself half Zapotec, who is determined to bring visibility and resources to Indigenous New Yorkers, even when it means battling her colleagues.

As recently as the mid-2010s, ELA was one of the only places in the city where speakers could meet and use Indigenous languages, whether teaching them, doing research, hosting radio shows, or reciting poetry. Despite their large numbers and especially vulnerable place in the city's labor market, schools, and hospitals, there was virtually no information available at the time about these communities. The Department of Health approached ELA to fill the gap, resulting in a fifty-page report, based on dozens of hours of interviews conducted by speakers themselves in six major languages.[38]

What we found was that the communities are large and growing but dispersed, invisible, and without access to basic services including translation and interpretation.[39] Many were still using their languages in very limited settings, especially on the phone with older relatives back home, but the stigma of centuries of colonialism, including discrimination from their non-Indigenous neighbors, had followed them to New York. Even in this relatively young population, with few people over forty, these conditions were taking a serious toll, with reports of diabetes, alcoholism, deteriorating diets, and a sense of being excluded from the medical system.

It wasn't easy to get anyone at the department besides our one contact to read the report, let alone make it public or act on its recommendations. But she kept pushing and finding small creative ways to fund small research projects and programs for the Indigenous community: programs on food and language, with Irwin cooking; then weaving workshops for Indigenous women, connecting craft with livelihood and mental health. Only with COVID, for the first time, was there a more substantial, though circumscribed, grant, focused on getting critical public health information to Indigenous New Yorkers, in at least some of their languages.

It was no coincidence that this was happening, and a few other city agencies starting to take notice, at a time when there were other signs of Indigenous organizing across the city. Among the first was

New Yorktlan (**-tlan** being the Nahuatl suffix for place-names), the Network's annual cultural festival which has moved year to year from the basement of a Bronx church to a Queens park to a cultural center in East Harlem. There is nothing else like it: an explosion of music, dance, costumes, and crafts that comes as close as possible to capturing in the big city what a village fiesta in Puebla or Guerrero is like. But the gathering is also electric for very personal reasons: it's a legal way every year for dozens of people from different villages to obtain cultural exchange visas, bringing their traditional knowledge to New York while visiting with their families.

By focusing on the transnational dimension—translocal might be even more apt, reflecting the deep ties between villages, valleys, etc., that often bypass any recognizably national level—the Network is tapping into a fundamental logic that governs how the immigrant city functions.[40] As with the Himalayan kyidug, many communities in New York have stronger connections to places five thousand miles away than to anywhere in the US. Towns like Esteban's hometown of Teopantlán should be considered New York's real sister cities, in a deeper sense than most of the famous official ones.

Everyday translocalism is everywhere in the city but tends to go almost unnoticed, like a passing van from the bakery Pasteles Capy that says *Smile, Be Happy, and Eat Tres Leches*, with cakes which they sell in a dozen flavors from piña colada to choco-caramel at ten locations across four different boroughs. "From Atlixco to New York" is the Capy slogan, though only a poblano will know the town in question, and fewer still that the Moctezuma family with nine brothers in Mexico and New York has run this thoroughly translocal business since 1984.

Growing out of both ELA and the Network, more explicitly Indigenous-led formations are now finally coming to the fore. The Concejo de Pueblos Originarios, *Council of Original Peoples* (preferring that term to Indigenous), not only articulates radical demands for justice in both Mexico and New York City but has started doing so proudly and publicly in Indigenous languages in places like Union Square and Times Square, not to mention East Harlem and the South Bronx. They have even started meeting with officials at the Mexican consulate in Manhattan, something unthinkable until a change of government in Mexico City a few years ago.

In tandem has been the rise of the city's deliveristas, estimated at sixty-five thousand strong and overwhelmingly made up of young Indigenous Mexican and Guatemalan men. The Manhattan side of the Willis Avenue Bridge, once a dangerous choke point where deliveristas were attacked, is now a rallying ground complete with a guardia civil, a security patrol inspired by the ones that some Indigenous villages have, but with e-bike escorts. A lot of the action is also on social media, where accounts like El Diario de los Deliveryboys en la Gran Manzana (*The Deliveryboys in the Big Apple Daily*)—run by a squad of Tlapanec brothers (and their nephew)—chronicle chronic bike thefts, reveal working conditions, and post calls to action.[41]

Deliveristas feeding the stricken city were dying of COVID-19, and when deliverista Francisco Villalva Vitinio, from the Indigenous village of Xalpatláhuac in Guerrero, was shot dead in East Harlem in 2021, it lit a spark under the movement. One group, Los Deliveristas Unidos, gained support from a major union, the attention of major politicians, and eventually something closer to a living wage mandated by the city. With so much of the movement's inspiration and leadership being Indigenous, the rallies were not only in Spanish but sometimes included Mixtec, Tlapanec, or K'iche'.

The people in this room are the ones sparking this Indigenous awakening across the city, which is still in its early days. There is a confidence and conviction in the voices as we go around now, saying who we are and what we're doing here. No one is ashamed of speaking their language.

# Karen
## *Lunaape (Lenape)*

### 1

It's a ten-hour drive, with barely a stop, from rural southwestern Ontario to *the place where we get bows*.

Retracing in part the path of forced migration endured by her ancestors, Karen comes to Manhattan to teach Lenape, the language of the land the city is built on. She's the first, as far as anyone knows, to bring the language back to the city in this way.[1] Piled high with cargo for class, her minivan pulls up once a month to Eighteenth Street and idles until 6 p.m., when noncommercial vehicles can park. One time she got a ticket and we laughed about fighting it in court—"It's just their ancestral land, your honor!"—as we clicked through the website and paid.

Upstairs in the office, her classroom for the night, Karen arranges handouts, worksheets, and laminated cards. Towering and joking, her husband Michael totes a tub full of raffle tickets and a giant bag full of purple marshmallow Peeps, half off at Walmart after Easter. Her frail but unflappable mother Heather settles in, ramrod straight in her foldable wheelchair, sipping instant noodles from the bodega across the street and quietly watching over us all. They greet the regulars, passing out pouches of ginger snaps and cranberry-flax omega-3 cookies. Iris the dog, known as Isis until the short-lived caliphate, is bounding under the table, responding to commands in Lenape.

We smudge with Karen's smudge kit, doors closed and hoping the smoke alarm won't go off as we repeat a prayer to the Lenape Creator, Kíisheelŭmúkweengw, *the one who thought us into existence*. (I use the Munsee variety of Lenape here and throughout; in the Unami variety, the Creator's name is Kishelëmukong.) There is a way of doing introductions: your name, where you're from, whether you're Lenape or not, your clan (the animal whose ways you follow), and how you're feeling. Karen is Waapeetkwuchukahkuyaxkweew, *White Buffalo Woman*. She is from Nalahii, the Lenape name for the Munsee reserve in Canada. Like others there, she follows the ways of the Turtle. She is feeling fine. Mehch ngiish aaptonee, *I'm done talking now*. This is how you put down the talking stick.

Karen takes us through it one by one, gently laughing through all our mistakes. She believes in teaching anyone who wants to learn.

"Nii noonjiyayi Lenapehoking," I try saying when I'm up, a grateful guest among powerful words. "*I'm from the place of the Lenape*."

I try thinking and feeling it, letting it break my brain a little.

"Nii mata ndulunaapeewi. Nii naawalootamun . . . *I am not Lenape. I follow the ways of . . .* "

"If you don't have a clan, just pick one from the list," says Karen to set everyone at ease.

"Atoh. Noolamalsi. Mehch ngiish aaptonee. *Deer. I am feeling fine. I'm done talking now*."

Like Native words, Native names were erased because Native places and Native peoples were. Across the region, over three hundred Lenape place-names have at least been recorded—unique, substantial traces of the language and how it mapped onto the land—but most are disfigured, "corrupted," and barely recognizable.[2] While the language itself moved on, the settlers who recorded, repeated, and adopted Lenape names rarely had any knowledge of the language. A likely case in point is "Mannahatta," a spelling adapted by Walt Whitman from "Manna-hata" (from the logbook of one of Henry Hudson's officers) and still often repeated down today. The desire for a distinctly Indigenous name with its own "exotic" sound ends up obscuring the fact that "Manhattan" itself is likely closer to the Lenape.[3]

Few invaders can completely destroy the names that preceded them. Languages otherwise gone can live on, little recognized, in place-names. Manhattan, Gowanus, Rockaway, Maspeth, and Canarsie are all unquestionably Lenape, however twisted their forms and uncertain their etymologies. But for all the names that remain in the city, an untold number have vanished. Expediency and accident can help some persist, as fossils of a time when reality was defined unthinkingly, at least there, in the original language. Names should fit with nature, and to old names and old paths there can cling something fit and proper. Names become second nature, like infrastructure. Changing names that are anchored deep within us can be an act of symbolic violence, colonial or revolutionary, toponymic cleansing in the extreme.

Even when the names remain, their original meanings and referents fade. Manhattan, one of the first Native American place-names ever recorded by European settlers, has been debated ever since its appearance on a map and in a logbook from Henry Hudson's voyage of 1609. Among the shaky explanations advanced are *island of* (*many?*) *hills*, *place of general intoxication*, or simply *island*, in an impossibly tangled game of Telephone usually made worse by supposed records and experts. As for *the place where we get bows*, it seems both to fit how Lenape actually works and to match rare testimony from an actual Lenape speaker named Albert Anthony (or Shiikwáhkwunund, *Lone Pine*), who was born in Canada in 1839. A prominent priest, farmer, and interpreter, Anthony was visiting Buffalo in 1884 for a ceremony honoring a Seneca chief and happened to give an interview to the city's historical society, breaking down *Manhattan* and mentioning the oral tradition about those hickory trees "of peculiar strength and toughness."[4]

Most original Lenape names probably marked out very specific sites with actionable information, but Lenapehoking was a later attempt to fit a Lenape name onto the vast abstraction of a lost homeland. In one form or another, the ending **-ing** or **-ink** is everywhere on Lenape land, from Mantalok**ing** on the Jersey shore to Nevers**ink** upstate, from the Shawang**unk** Mountains to Wyom**ing** (originally in Pennsylvania, the name later transposed to the distant west) and Manhatt**an** itself. Linguists call it a locative suffix, meaning *the place of/where*, like Nahuatl **-tlan**. The name Lenapehok**ing**, *the place of Lenape land*, was coined by Weenjipahkihelexkwe (*Touching Leaves Woman*), also known as Nora Thompson Dean, who died in Oklahoma in 1984. One of the last masters of the language, she was also apparently one of the first in centuries to make return visits to where her people had lived. In 1970, she went with the linguist Jim Rementer to the Jersey Shore, where he took a photo of her in regal profile, offering tobacco with an extended arm to the ocean, which before she had seen only on TV.[5] In 1981, she was introduced to then-Mayor Ed Koch at City Hall, who proffered nothing more than a perfunctory politico handshake.[6]

Pressured piecemeal into hundreds of land deals, Native people who survived the initial impact of European settlement were almost all driven out or drawn away over the course of the seventeenth and eighteenth centuries. Disease and violence killed thousands, bringing the population to a fraction of its former level. At the same time, contact with the settlers was forever transforming the Lenape way of life. Resistance, evasion, accommodation, assimilation: every strategy was attempted. Hundreds of Lenape individuals are named in land deeds and other sources, making it almost possible, through painstaking reconstruction, to get a sense of who leaders like Tackapousha, Teedyuscung, and Tamanend (Tammany) actually were. (Tammany Hall, which was founded as a political organization in New York in 1786 and remained powerful for nearly two centuries, supposedly honored this Native leader known for wisdom and peace, though perhaps the name is better seen as an example of "playing Indian" like the Boston Tea Party.)[7]

No one knows when the language was last spoken in New York City itself, though it may have been in use at the edges as late as the early nineteenth century, or even later in remote sections of western Long Island, up in the Hudson Highlands, or in the New Jersey Pine Barrens. Small groups continued to live off the land by moving seasonally, camping in out of the way places, and avoiding a settler population by then in the hundreds of thousands but still overwhelmingly on the coast. For many, the upper reaches of the Delaware River around the impregnable island of Minisink were a final refuge within Lenapehoking. Only with the Treaty of Easton in 1758, a dubious series of wartime bargains between the British and thirteen different Native nations, did Lenape representatives under enormous pressure sell off that last stronghold of their homeland.

Even then, pushed and pulled and splitting and joining down through a dozen generations, a few Lenape groups remarkably stayed together and headed west, founding dozens of settlements across the future states of Pennsylvania and Ohio, sometimes for just a few years before moving on. Other tribes, calling them the grandfathers, provided shelter. It was a fluid age, with the British, French, Americans, Iroquois, and other Native groups all converging on the Ohio Valley. All kinds of North American futures were still possible and expected. One Lenape group, coming to the three rivers of Pittsburgh, became the first Native nation to sign a treaty with the newly declared, still revolting United States of America in 1778.

"That all offences or acts of hostility by one, or either of the contracting parties against the other, be mutually forgiven," read Article I of the treaty, "and buried in the depth of oblivion, never more to be had in remembrance." This is formulaic nonsense, but we don't have the Lenape version. There would be forty-seven more treaties between Lenape groups and the United States, the new nation which the Lenape dubbed xwanzhíikan, *Long Knives*, extending a moniker the Iroquois had originally given to the Governor of Virginia in 1684 and which other Native peoples then applied to the various and ever-multiplying groups of settler-invaders.[8]

In 1782, just after this pledge of eternal friendship, Pennsylvania militiamen slaughtered ninety-six Lenape people then living at Gnadenhütten in Ohio with missionaries from the Moravian Church of central Europe, itself in exile. The horror and treachery of the massacre were recognized even then, particularly because these Lenape were Christians, and a century later no less a Manhattan frontiersman than Theodore Roosevelt called it "a stain on frontier character that the lapse of time cannot wash away."[9]

The 151 survivors turned north toward Canada, obtaining permission to settle on Chippewa land. For those Lenape groups that remained in the US, the story was "this is your home from now on, until we want it," as Rementer describes the series of expulsions and rotten land deals across Indiana, Kansas, and elsewhere that stopped only in mid-nineteenth-century Oklahoma—itself a prison of peoples to rival Stalin's Kazakhstan, where more insidious policies promptly began.[10]

New Lenape homelands, squeezed in among other tribes, were finally established. Today, they are in Ontario: three officially recognized Lenape clusters at Moraviantown, Munsee, and the Six Nations Reserve. They are in Oklahoma: two federally recognized Lenape tribes in the west and the east of the state. They are at the Stockbridge-Munsee reservation in Wisconsin. Each setting has its story and its specifics, but gradually the Lenape diaspora is being knit together again despite the continuing legacy of genocide and displacement. Tribal enrollments are booming. In 1992 a North American Grand Council was formed, uniting over twenty-five thousand members of the formally recognized Lenape tribes.

Meanwhile, other groups have emerged in New Jersey, Delaware, Pennsylvania, and elsewhere in the last few decades, seeking formal government recognition as Lenape tribes. Their tradition is that they hid and mixed and stayed behind, and at present their claims are accepted or not to different degrees by tribal, state, and federal governments. All now connect more local names and identities to the word Lenape, which once meant *human being*, then *Indian*, and finally this miraculously surviving and multiply reconstituted group of people and their ways of speaking.

Across Lenapehoking there must have been dozens of closely related language varieties, which gradually merged as the remaining speakers banded together and went into exile. Written records of the language begin with Dutch, Swedish, and English travelers and chroniclers. Only a small number of them ever mastered it, mostly Moravian missionaries. But along the lower Delaware River for much of the seventeenth century, an early wave of settlers found at least rudimentary knowledge of the language to be essential for living, getting around, and doing business, leading to a contact language called Pidgin Delaware.[11] It was not the only case where Native power and an interethnic "middle ground" of exchange and interaction led to new language formation in North America. From Mobilian Trade Language around the Gulf of Mexico to Chinuk Wawa in the Pacific Northwest, these "jargons" reflected little worlds of Native/settler coexistence that appeared, for a time, to be in balance.

Over the eighteenth and nineteenth centuries, the dialects originally spoken in the southern part of Lenapehoking coalesced into the language that came to be known as Unami, meaning *downriver*. A presumed Northern Unami is gone, but Southern Unami was later brought to Oklahoma, where Nora Thompson Dean and her brother Edward Thompson, who died in 2002, were among the last to speak it.[12]

Likewise "Munsee," named for that last refuge at Minisink, was the term later applied to all the dialects from the north of Lenapehoking, including what is now New York City, as well as the people who spoke them. It was the Munsee who later made it to southwestern Ontario and gave Karen's reserve its name, not to mention Monsey (New York), Muncie (Indiana), and several other places.

Call it Munsee, Delaware, or Lenape—there are people who use each term—but just one person alive today is thought to be a native speaker of the language: a woman now in her eighties named Dianne Snake in Moraviantown, Ontario.

## 2

Growing up, Karen only caught echoes of the language. "I remember my mom's mom speaking the language when her friends came over from Moraviantown," she told me. "That's the only time I remember that, and I know my aunt would say a couple of phrases when she was joking around."

Only recently did Karen learn that her dad's dad had been the last fluent speaker on the Munsee reserve (Canadian English for *reservation*), but she never heard him speak a word. "I had this dream after he passed away that he came to me, and he said that he was going to help me learn the language, and I thought, that's bizarre, how would he help me?"

The reason Edward Dolson still spoke fluent Lenape, growing up in the early twentieth century. Unlike most other children from Munsee in that era, he avoided being sent to the nearby Mt. Elgin Residential School, where students could be punished for speaking a Native language. This, not the "purchase" of Manhattan or any of the dozens of expulsions, is where Karen focused her story of language loss: "Because of the residential schools we lost our language and our culture."

One lost generation can break a language. "Education" at the boarding schools, as they were called in the US, began with forced forgetting. "Kill the Indian, and save the man" was notoriously the ethos. After hounding Native languages out of their youngest speakers and forcing English in, it became that much easier to instill Christianity, farming, private property, and other settler values. Only now with the unearthing of mass graves is it becoming terrifyingly clear how many Native children died at these schools due to neglect, abuse, and terror.

Because most of his generation went through the residential schools, Edward Dolson ultimately had no one else to speak the language to. Karen remembered him being both a committed traditionalist and a serious Christian. She remembered how he would take his headdress and regalia everywhere even before he was chief, going to church meetings all over and drawing connections between the colors of the beads and the meanings in the Bible.

She remembered certain mysterious things he used to do around their home: "He would walk the perimeter of the land and put medicines down. I was a kid. It was in the evening, you know, and I'd be peeking out the window wondering what he was doing out there, and I would just watch him walk around, and I never asked anybody. Now I understand that he was probably taking care of the land and protecting us." Though church was one thing and ceremony another, the big outdoor "camp meetings," in Karen's mind, seemed to rhyme with older ways of Native spirituality. Of course, many things were never discussed.

Karen was still living on the land where Edward Dolson used to place his offerings. "I know that my great-grandparents lived here," she said, "but I'm sure it went way further back. We were lucky that there must have been enough sons and grandsons to pass the land down to, so that it stayed in our family." Canada's Indian Act of 1876 made it effectively impossible for Native women to own or inherit land.

"Any woman who married a Native man became whatever tribe he was from, so if there was a Munsee woman who married an Oneida man she became Oneida," explained Karen. "She couldn't retain her Munsee status and she had to leave, she had to move to Oneida. Also, if a Native woman married a non-Native man, she totally lost her status and had to move off of Munsee. The other thing is if a Native man married a non-Native woman, she became Native." Everything went through the husband. As intermarriage between tribes and with settlers became more common, the whole calculus of Native belonging became ever more scrambled under pressure from the state.

Karen, too, would have lost her status if the Canadian Parliament hadn't finally amended the Indian Act with Bill C31 in 1985. "I went to school with a girl who is about two years older than me. She's non-Native, and she married someone from Munsee and she has Munsee status. My first marriage was in 1989, and I married a non-Native man, but I kept my status, so it was that quick that it changed over."

Consider the complexity of Karen's family. The Munsee who escaped to Canada became one of the smaller Native nations in southwestern Ontario, clustered among larger ones. They took refuge among the Chippewa, as described by Karen, using the older local term for the several hundred thousand people living across southern Canada and the Upper Midwest now generally referred to as Anishinaabe. Of her noohumak, *maternal grandparents*, Karen's mom's dad was Chippewa, so when her (Munsee) mom's mom got married, she lost her Munsee status and transferred to the Chippewa. When the two got divorced, she went back to Munsee. Heather, Karen's mom, tried to honor both, while living at Munsee.

At the same time, according to Karen, "we're all on the same land base, so like the house beside us on the left is Chippewa and we're Munsee the next house; on our right is Munsee and the next one's Chippewa. Some Munsee people know more Chippewa than they do Munsee."

As for the numoxoomsak, Karen's *paternal grandparents*, her dad's dad Edward Dolson—chief, medicine planter, and last fluent speaker on the reserve—married a Potawatomi lady from Walpole. "I didn't know what she was saying, but we used to say she sounded real Indian-y. She talked like the old, old Indian fluent speakers. She passed away when I was probably eight or nine. I don't really remember much about her except for hearing her speak in the language, and even when she spoke English, it was like broken English."

Karen left home at sixteen and moved to London, Ontario, the city just thirty miles from the reserve that many move to, because housing at Munsee is tight and jobs are scarce. After high school and college in London, she worked there as a bookkeeper for fifteen years.

In those years, Karen quite literally didn't know her own strength. One day a mechanic, a friend of her husband's, was fixing their car and talking about powerlifting. Her husband quickly caught the bug. "And I was like, I have no idea what that is, I've never worked out in my life," remembered Karen. She went to watch them bench-press and do dead lifts in the mechanic's basement, and it turned out that his sister, a Royal Canadian Mountie, was also a powerlifter.

"He said he was open to any woman that wanted to do it. Right then, he asked me if I wanted to try it and I was like, yeah okay, why not?" The mechanic demonstrated. The setup was safe, with a catch for the bar, though Karen didn't have knee wraps, wrist wraps, a belt, or anything else. "So he put some weight on there, and I had no idea how much it was. I got under the bar, and I took a step back, and I squatted down, back up, and I walked back forward and put it on the rack. And they were all standing there looking at me with their mouths wide open. I said, 'What did I do wrong?' and they said nothing." She had just lifted 250 pounds.

Karen started working out with them three times a week, and soon she had broken every Ontario record for her weight class, and then the Canadian record, and was regularly lifting over four hundred pounds. People started calling her Wchetak, *Muscles*. "I think being short really helped, lower center of gravity, and when I squat I don't have as far to go," she put it modestly, "and when I dead-lift you know I don't have as far to stand up." Within a year of that first lift, Karen was a top contender for the women's World Powerlifting Competition in New Zealand, with her employer raising the money for the trip. The sexism was fierce, whether from old ladies in the community or from the immigration officer who thought it must be her husband who was competing.

For Karen, lifting was less about showing physical strength and more about focusing an inner power. One time she tried closing her eyes and visualizing the lift first, not worrying about weight: "Then I opened my eyes and walked up to the bar, lifted it, put it down, and it felt like I was lifting up a pencil. It freaked me out and I never did it again." She stopped lifting soon after, both because "things in life happen," as she put it, and because she had done what she wanted to do.

Language, even with Karen's gentle intensity and force of will, has been a longer and harder lift. "I remember when I was thirteen, I had a summer job at Munsee cleaning up people's yards, painting their houses and their porches. There was a lady that was teaching the language, and they said do you want to work outside, or do you want to come into this air-conditioned building every afternoon and learn language? We were like, air conditioning! So she taught us some words, and I remembered the words for *dog* and *cat* from back then, but I didn't really remember too much else." Life was always in Canadian English, and Lenape felt distant.

Only many years later did that change, after she moved back to Munsee to be closer to her mom. Another class was starting up, taught by someone who would come up from Moraviantown, the reserve considered to be Munsee's "sister nation" and the place where Lenape has survived longest.

In the 1960s, the linguist Ives Goddard found only a handful of speakers left at Munsee, but learned that around forty of Moraviantown's four hundred residents could still speak. Over the years he ended up working closely with fourteen of them and documenting significant variation just among them, including entirely different words for certain things and even some grammatical differences. Some speakers would mention forms they knew but would never use themselves.[13] Was this a reflection of different migration pathways, or layers in the history of the language? Or just the kind of thing that happens in oral language communities, where there's no authority to standardize speech? Variation and diversity within small language communities, perhaps especially those on the brink, can go deep.

Karen was drawn into the class by accident, unless it was all a quiet plan of her mom's: "She just had surgery on her eyes so she couldn't drive at night, and she asked me if I would take her to the classes, and I said, Sure, you know, no problem, so I'd drive her up there. So we went in the building, and I sat in the back of the room, and everybody else sat around the council chambers [the seat of tribal government] and they were learning. The teacher would say a word or a phrase and have everybody repeat it, and then have each person say it individually. He came over to me in the back of the room, and he asked me to repeat it, and I said, No, no, I'm just her ride."

The teacher wasn't having it: "If you're in this room, you're learning this language, he said, and I remember thinking: Crap, I should have stayed in the car!"

## 3

For over a decade, Karen taught at least a little Lenape to hundreds of people in New York, New Jersey, and Canada, and online. She made almost nothing from it—in fact, she spent a lot of her own money on gas, snacks, prizes, and printouts, not even thinking about her time. She taught anyone willing to learn, anywhere she could get to, with Michael and Iris always by her side. She brought the language into spaces where it has rarely if ever been, from universities to YouTube, and started training so that one day she could teach it as a second language in local schools.

Karen would call herself a language keeper, forthright about her limitations as both a speaker and a teacher. A class is a conversation, a chance to keep the language breathing, to elevate its status and take the sting out of its stigma. She was always getting people laughing with newly coined words like kshi-miichuwaakan *fast food* and malamwusuw kshaxun *online shopping* and little mnemonics linking English and Lenape. Any of her students would remember the beautifully illustrated Lenape calendars she made every year—and that *May* is called Ehahkiiheet ("A hockey hat!") Niipáahum, *Planting Moon*.

To the slightly desperate den of the ELA office, Karen's class brought something different: the easygoing ways of Native visiting, now mostly unknown in Manhattan. Curious non-Natives would drop in from time to time to learn or at least hear a little of the language, but the regulars had a deeper reason to be there. People of all appearances and walks of life, they traced their descent from remaining and reviving Native groups across the region. Their own languages might be almost impossible even to reconstruct, but Lenape is the closest living cousin. Friday nights with Karen on Eighteenth Street were as close as they could get to how their ancestors sounded.[14]

There was the architect from Staten Island with the thickest New York accent, who only discovered he was Native in his late twenties, the first time he met his father.

There was the punk rock drummer in the Destructive Bastards T-shirt, with a black ski hat pulled over his mullet and his muscles rippling with tats. He talks in one big breath about the great warriors Pontiac and Tecumseh and all the money he just lost in Vegas. The Lenape dictionary he pulls from his bag is well thumbed and heavily marked up.

There was the extremely motivated young woman who started putting up posters advertising the class in the subway. Then she spotted the mayor on his treadmill at the Y and insisted he come and learn the language of his city. Or so we learned when an official email arrived in ELA's inbox, informing us that the mayor could not attend, but wishing us a successful event and asking that we keep hizzoner in mind for the future.

Some regulars would come from the Ramapough Lenape Nation in New Jersey, which claims over five thousand members in and around the highlands near Mahwah, just thirty miles from the city. There a half-hidden community of extended families of mixed Dutch, Black, and Native descent has survived centuries of misunderstanding, misclassification, and acts of hostility from their white neighbors. Where once they may have used Jersey Dutch, now they were learning Lenape. "My grandmother's house growing up on Wednesdays there'd be twenty people there," says Chief Vincent Mann, describing how the Ramapough have always stuck together, "and we'd be eating two pounds of spaghetti in a yellow Pyrex bowl and hockey-puck hamburgers, and it would feed us all."[15]

Chief Mann doesn't need to go back to the seventeenth century to talk about the threats his community has faced down. From 1967 to 1971, Ford dumped untold tons of toxic paint sludge from what had been the largest auto assembly plant in the nation into abandoned mines nearby. Alleging pervasive health problems, the Ramapough have been fighting Ford and the EPA for decades. More recently, an oil company has been trying to build a pipeline across Ramapough land. New Jersey has officially recognized the tribe after years of battles, but so far neither New York State nor the federal government has.

Native Long Islanders, likewise excavating buried identities, were also among Karen's most dedicated students. Where exactly Lenape ended and the languages of Long Island began is impossible to say. Old settler sources named thirteen Native nations on the island, but that was probably a fantasy or a misunderstanding, unconnected to the social, cultural, or political self-conception of the groups themselves, of which limited evidence remains. Several Native groups persist today, with just the Unkechaug and the Shinnecock having reservations and the latter only federally recognized in 2010 after decades in the courts. Others, like the Matinecock and the Montaukett, are still fighting.

One of Karen's regulars was Reggie, a retired shiatsu master, herbologist, and massage therapist, now absorbed in his work as Turkey Clan chief for the Matinecock, whose traditional territory stretches east from Queens along the north shore of Long Island. "My mother's generation abandoned everything," he says, "but now we're trying to revive Nunowa, our version of Thanksgiving, which had almost disappeared."

Reggie describes his ancestry as Matinecock, Dutch, African, and Blackfoot, and that's the simplified version, but like many others with Native forebears on the East Coast, he may be seen by strangers simply as Black. He grew up in Queens, aware that his family was different but not sure how or why. Only later did he understand that they were part of a tight-knit mixed-race group with Matinecock roots, who stayed in the region despite all the changes and waves of immigration.[16]

Bushy gray facial hair flourishes all over Reggie's sparkling face. "My language is in pieces," he says. "Lenape is the closest I can get." But there is something "gratifying and intense" about speaking even a single word—the only way to "get the essence of what the ancestors knew . . . how they felt when they walked on the earth, their connection."

Reggie thinks the last native speaker of Matinecock might have been his great-grand-uncle James E. Waters, or Chief Wild Pigeon, a poetry-writing postal worker in Manhattan who had Native ties across Long Island, or what Reggie calls Sewanhacky.[17] Wild Pigeon spent his final years trying to stop the obliteration of a Matinecock burial ground in what is now Little Neck, Queens, caused by the widening of Northern Boulevard into a four-lane highway.

The work went forward in 1931, and the remains were moved to the nearby Zion Church, where today a giant split rock marks the spot, and an old inscription reads, "Here rest the last of the Matinecoc." No sooner proclaimed than countered: in 1958, a woman named Ann Harding, also known as Princess Sun Tama, had a vision and put out a call in a local newspaper for all Matinecock descendants to come forward. Around two hundred eventually did.

Another regular was Leala, who is Montaukett from Queens and a dependably warm presence at many of the city's powwows. Like Reggie, Leala learns Lenape to get closer to a language of which little can be known for certain. The Montaukett people were proclaimed extinct in the early twentieth century, directly to their faces by a New York Supreme Court judge—in a case (again under appeal today) involving the popular weekend vacation spot at the eastern tip of Long Island known today as Montauk. The Montaukett language was embattled even in 1798, when John Lyon Gardiner, seventh Lord of the Manor on Gardiner's Island (just off East Hampton), reported that there were only seven speakers left. One of them, sixty-six-year-old George Pharaoh, provided "a specimen of their language," which Gardiner transcribed "as near as he pronounced as I can with the English alphabet."[18]

Just a few years earlier in 1791, Thomas Jefferson, who was concerned by the disappearance of Native American languages, went to the Unkechaug near Mastic and recorded 202 words from three old ladies, said to be among the few who still remembered the language.[19] With the few hours he had, the future president did his best with nouns—*whippoorwill* is whácorees, *rainbow* papuhmúncsunc, *belly* cráckish—but managed only a handful of verbs and virtually nothing of the grammar.

From bare-bones word lists like these, it looks like Unkechaug, Montaukett, Matinecock, and Shinnecock were not entirely different languages separated by clear boundaries, but part of a now-vanished linguistic continuum that stretched across Sewanhacky. Their closest ties were probably not with Lenape, but with the Native languages of southern New England just on the other side of Long Island Sound. Linguistically speaking, however, all of these languages belong to a single subgroup, Eastern Algonquian, which once climbed the coast from North Carolina to Nova Scotia—itself just one branch of the larger Algic family, which reaches deep into Canada and even northern California.

It was the peoples of the north Atlantic coast, speaking at least seventeen distinct Eastern Algonquian languages, who first faced European settlers in the seventeenth century. Even when they survived, their languages came under enormous pressure. Yet of all Native American languages, these gave the most to English before their speakers were pushed out and hunted down. In those initial years of the intercontinental invasion, English speakers needed names for many unfamiliar animals (moose, skunk, raccoon, possum, chipmunk) and foods (squash, succotash, hickory, hominy, persimmon) that were critical for survival, not to mention all the place-names.

Besides Lenape, which survived by retreating a thousand miles inland, no other native language south of Maine continued to have living native speakers into the twentieth century. Only in the far north did Mi'kmaq, Abenaki, and Maliseet-Passamaquoddy endure, at a distance from the main colonial centers. The survival of these languages down to the present, even in the mouths of just a few native-speaker elders, is a linguistic miracle. Likewise, today something is stirring in the wider world of Eastern Algonquian, thanks to Karen's regulars and dozens of other language activists like them, despite the enormous challenge of reassembling, let alone speaking, these languages.

On Long Island, the Algonquian Language Revitalization Project based at Stony Brook is patiently rebuilding Unkechaug, Shinnecock, and Montaukett, through both dictionary work and classes for tribal members and local students. In Connecticut, the linguist Stephanie Fielding is reconstructing her Mohegan language, not to be confused with Mohican of the Hudson Valley, by using materials from her great-great-great aunt, Fidelia Fielding (a.k.a. Jits Bodunaxa), who died in 1908 and was widely considered the last speaker.[20]

In Rhode Island, the linguist Frank Waabu Brown of the Aquidneck Native Council has worked for decades as a "lone wolf" on Narragansett, drawing on *A Key into the Language of America* by the colony's founding figure Roger Williams, which was the first description of any Native North American language, published in 1643. The *Key* shows that Narragansett, among other things, was the source of the word powwow, which originally meant *healer* or *spiritual leader* before it was generalized across North America to mean the kind of public dance or gathering that is now so central to Native life.[21]

In Massachusetts, Jessie "Little Doe" Baird, a member of the Wampanoag tribe who studied linguistics at MIT, has been a leader in reclaiming the very first language the Pilgrims encountered. By the eighteenth century, Wampanoag was not just unusually well documented but in use as a written language by many Wampanoag people themselves in legal documents, land deeds, and letters. Based on these, but especially an early Bible translation, Baird and others have been publishing materials, launching programs, and producing actual new speakers for over thirty years—bringing the language back to life after nearly two centuries of silence.[22]

## 4

There is no reason, linguistically speaking, why we shouldn't all be speaking Lenape here in Lenapehoking. Of course it would now take a magical justice. But no feature of any language, other than the power of the people who use it, makes it any more or less adaptable to the life of a great city, any more or less fit to spread in the mouths of children. Any language can add vocabulary; any language is more likely to simplify as more people use it; any society can run in any language. Some languages are harder to learn as second languages, depending on your first language, but with enough exposure every first language is learned by children with equivalent ease. Someday English, too, will be down to its last speaker.

Yet with few resources, only monthly meetings, no one to speak to, and no sense of urgent practical need, Lenape class had the feeling of starting again from scratch with every session. Karen would take us through the sounds, and we would take turns chanting a string of syllables which the whole group then repeats: pi, po, pa, pe . . . pii, poo, paa, pee.

The first set are short vowels and the second are long ones, for in Lenape (as in many languages) you can extend the duration of a vowel, even just a little, and create a distinctive sound, written as two identical vowels but pronounced as one long one. So the /a/ in the Lenape word máxkw, *bear*, is pronounced like the /o/ in English *other*, but /aa/ in áanay, *road*, lasts longer and comes out like the /a/ in *amen*. (The accent indicates stress.)

As for that intimidating cluster *xkw*, Karen showed us how to cough up what linguists call a "velar fricative" and she called "a catch in the throat"—that phlegmy little vibration familiar from German or Hebrew, which is spelled in Lenape with an /x/. But neither German nor Hebrew can have a velar fricative immediately followed by a labiovelar, in this case like the /qu/ in English *quick*.

For anyone raised speaking English, the Lenape sound system is a serious challenge, with its unfamiliar consonant clusters. Lenape syllables have no problem starting with /ng/, /nd/, /mb/ (which can come only at the end of a syllable in English), where the first letter means just the gentlest hit of initial nasal noise. And there's no way to avoid these clusters even in the most basic phrases, but Karen is completely encouraging as we all go around trying to say nii ndushiinzi . . . , *I am named* . . . , where /nd/ is a first-person prefix on the verb shíinzuw, *to be named*. On the other hand, /f/, /v/, and /r/ are found only in English loanwords. The /r/ sound does exist in the Unami variety of Lenape, where it corresponds to the Munsee /l/, which is probably why Swedish sources from the southern part of Lenapehoking recorded the name as Renapi.

Karen would school us in Lenape writing, a system adapted from the Roman alphabet that is relatively new but already playing an important role in revitalization efforts. Like all Native North American languages before Europeans came, Lenape was traditionally an oral language. The Walam Olum (*Red Record*) was allegedly a collection of pictographs notched on birch bark or cedar tablets, an ancient American epic describing in soaring Lenape the creation of the universe, the first people, the flood, and the original settlement of North America.[23] It turned out to be an elaborate hoax, perpetrated with the unimaginably measly motive of winning an international linguistics contest. Its supposed discoverer, the erratic Constantine Samuel Rafinesque-Schmaltz (his real name), born in Istanbul to a French father and a German mother, was actually its manic inventor. Twice rejected by Lewis and Clark for their expedition team, he crashed for a summer with John James Audubon while ranging around the new United States looking for things to discover and name. He left an indomitable paper trail claiming thousands of newly discovered plant species, but only a few are still recognized today. For a while he professed botany and languages at Transylvania University in Kentucky, where he is still ritually remembered every year around Halloween during "Rafinesque Week," where students compete to sleep in what is said to be his tomb.

Lenape people seem not to have been fooled, but it took decades for scholars to doubt the Walam Olum. Today's actual Lenape writing, shaped by linguists working with the last speakers in Moraviantown, is generally clear and consistent. It uses the Latin alphabet in ways that are both keyboard friendly and far more consistent than how things work in English, though Lenape writing does often conform to English-speaker expectations as to what a letter should sound like. Which of course is not always possible, since the phonetics of Lenape are very different. For instance, there is no English-style /u/ sound in Lenape, Karen explained, so that letter has been repurposed to stand for that important little unstressed vowel, schwa. This—together with the fact that the second vowel in the word is long—is why *Lenape* is actually spelled Lunaape. Then there's the whole group of consonants which linguists call voiced obstruents, because the vocal chord vibrates and airflow is obstructed: /b/, /d/, /g/, /j/, /z/, and /zh/. Strictly speaking, the letters shouldn't be needed, because these sounds don't actually occur by themselves in Lenape, only their voiceless counterparts: /p/, /t/, /k/, /ch/, /s/, /sh/. But they do occur in one very specific situation, after the initial nasal consonants m- and n-, by an ironclad rule, which is why you get n**d**ushiinzi, m**b**úy *water*, n**z**ukíhleew *turn black*. Only there will you meet those letters.

There are other consonant clusters that seem terrifying at first, in words like ktahtakíleew, *run outside*, psakohkwéepŭwak, *sit close together*, or its equally chunky synonym kchukohkwéepŭwak, but Karen would steer us through one syllable at a time. Repeating after her, we fall into a rhythm every time she says Weemu aween. *Everyone*.

Lenape is also a classic agglutinative language, where the words get long quickly, with four or five morpehemes per word not uncommon. German compounds like Minderwertigkeitskomplex, *inferiority complex*, or Unabhängigkeitserklärung, *independence declaration*, are just long fussy nouns with transparent building blocks, compared to what goes on in Algic languages, which agglutinate every bit as hard as Quechua or Turkish.

Kŭwíingunéewalohmwa! was Karen's hearty way of greeting the group, *I'm glad to see you all!* She would belt it out in an instant, but it breaks down into kŭ- (*1st > 2nd person prefix*), wíingu (*like to*), néewul (*see*), -ohmwa (*verbal plural*).

Or take a sentence like Noolasnániin kŭlooshliihiiwáakanal (*I carried the groceries*), where *I-carried* is in the first word (wŭlásanuw is the verb in its most basic form, before it morphs almost unrecognizably into noolasnániin) and the groceries are handled in the second (kŭlooshliihii is an English loanword adapted for Lenape phonology). The suffix -wáakan marks the groceries as a plural direct object but the final -al clinches that it's both plural and inanimate, because groceries are understandably not considered to be alive. *Bears* would be mákwx**ak**, never mákwx**al**.

This animate/inanimate distinction is pervasive in Lenape. Any inanimate noun is made plural with **-al**, while any animate one (people, animals, and certain other things) pluralizes with **-ak**. Of course, "all grammars leak," as the linguist Edward Sapir puts it. Lenape treats *spoons* as animate, but feathers and branches as inanimate, and what does it mean to be alive anyway? "Animate" is a linguistic category, but do nouns that take **-ak** actually seem more alive to speakers? Does *the table*, la mesa in Spanish, seem at least a little bit feminine—however deeply buried the mental representation—while *the bridge*, el puente, is just a little bit masculine?[24] The evidence is suggestive, but hotly debated. In fact, Spanish and other European languages that divide up their nouns by gender seem to have started long ago with animacy—the animates later splitting into "masculine" and "feminine," while the inanimates in some languages became "neuter."

Animacy in Lenape, which doesn't gender nouns, is for more than just making plurals. Instead it goes deep into the verbal morphology, the way verbs are shaped, conjugated, and transformed. Lenape verbs are deeply enmeshed with their subjects and objects, conveying all the nitty gritty of exactly who or what is doing what to whom or what.[25] Distinct prefixes encode the "person" (first, second, or third) of both the subject and the object, as in the kŭ of kŭwiinginéewalohmwa above, which marks a first-person subject relating to a second-person object. Even a seemingly simple verb like *bring* has two different stems depending on whether the object being brought is animate or inanimate, which is why you say "Peetoow!" (*Bring it!*) for a grocery item, but "Peeshuweew!" if it's a bear you want brought.

Tense, which seems so fundamental to an English speaker, doesn't really exist in Lenape. What matters instead and is marked with any action are person, animacy, and transitivity (whether the verb takes an object or not). In other words, Lenape verbs come in four flavors: intransitive inanimate, intransitive animate, transitive inanimate, and transitive animate. They usually come so packed with information that neither the subject nor the object needs to be mentioned separately, as in the ordinary sentence nduloohumawaaw, *I show something to someone*.

Even a basic pronoun requires a little extra consideration. Say *Let's go* and picture the situation. Is everyone present included in your invitation, or do you have to be a little clearer about the particular people you want to go with? Lenape, like many languages, makes a distinction which English doesn't. Niiloona is *we* or *our*, including whoever you're speaking to, but kiiloona is *we* or *our*, excluding the addressee ("No, not you—the rest of us!").

These are what linguists call inclusive and exclusive pronouns. Mandarin, like Lenape, makes the same distinction with inclusive zánmen versus exclusive wǒmen, possibly having gotten it, centuries back, from either Manchu or Mongolian—because Cantonese, Fujianese, and other southern Chinese varieties don't do this. Does this mean that Lenape and Mandarin speakers have a special awareness of *we*-ness, or is having two ways to say *we* an almost arbitrary linguistic fact? At least at some point in the history of Lenape (and Mandarin), this "clusivity" distinction must have done useful, social work, while speakers of English (or Cantonese) have managed to ignore it, talk around it, or figure things out from context.

As in any language, many words are stories in themselves, "fossil poetry" that at least seems to give a glimpse of how an ancestor might have seen things. Psakwŭlúnjeew, meaning *squirrel*, is literally *he who has sticky fingers*. Wteéhiim, *strawberry*, is linked to *the essence of life*—reportedly because the first strawberry came into being when the trickster hero Nanabozhoo pulled out a piece of his heart and planted it.

A whole gaggle of verbs start with **mih**-, a widespread ancient root that some guess meant openness, exposure, or extension. But what exactly links mihloossuw (*to be an old man*), mihtukw (*tree*), mihtapuw (*to be born / to be visible*), mihkoomeew (*to remind someone*), mihtaandpeew (*to be bare-headed*), and a dozen others? There may be no pinning it down, but every lexicon has these structures and resonances, just as English, somewhat mysteriously, has all those sn- words for nose-related things: snout, snort, snore, snot, sneeze, snivel, and others.

If one thing was clear to all of us sitting around the table with Karen, it was the challenge of making an adult English-speaking brain adjust to the Lenape way of saying things. It's not just about memorizing all the forms, although there's plenty of that required; it's a whole different way of planning and plotting speech, a whole other set of unfamiliar categories to pay attention to. Of course, any kid in Lenapehoking could have learned it without any problems. Even Kíisheelŭmúkweengw, the Creator to whom our prayer is directed, is less a name than a verb—third-person singular conjunct, if you're curious—that never stops thinking us into existence.

## 5

It was Karen's mom Heather who thought to use the gas station.

It was right on the reserve, with a little store attached that was standing empty. The cousin who owned it said sure, so they just set up shop teaching bits of the language to anyone who stopped by. You filled up your tank and learned a word of Lenape.

"She thought we might as well teach what we know. So she sat there and said 'Koolamalsi? [*How are you?*]' to everyone that came in," remembered Karen. "They would ask questions, and she'd give them a word to say or a phrase as they were going out. Everybody liked her. They didn't even need gas. They just came to see Mom. It was just her classroom."

Heather and Karen had themselves barely started learning the language. After that initial class Karen got dragged into, they had gone together to the Lunaapeewiixsiitiht Sheshkoolhalluweesak Eehakehkiingeewanikaan, *the Lenape learners' language camp*, led by Glen Jacobs, also known as Chohkalihle, *Red-Wing Blackbird*. There they met dozens of like-minded people from across the Lenape diaspora—the stirrings of a movement.

On that first day of camp, Karen went off to her car alone and cried in frustration at the difficulty of the language and the pressure she felt to learn it. Then she went back to the group and kept at it.

Glen was born in Moraviantown in 1950. By then, even there the language was no longer being passed to children, but he picked up everything he could from his grandfather and the other elders who could still speak. "When he was a little boy, his dad's friends would come over, and it's not the best of circumstances but they would come over and drink," said Karen, "and that's when they would feel comfortable speaking in the language because they let their guard down. That's when they would teach him the language."

Years later, Glen would organize annual camps rotating between Moraviantown, Munsee, and Stockbridge-Munsee in Wisconsin, with a dedicated group of followers that always included Karen and Heather. The camps might seem relaxed and social, but they could also be intense as people came closer to the language with all its painful and powerful associations. The camps were the closest thing left to a Lenape-speaking space, a real-life context for the language—even just three or four days at a time.

Glen liked to work one word at a time. He made his own learning materials by drawing on the work of linguists, especially the one modern dictionary that exists, published in 1996 by John O'Meara and based on his work with Moraviantown speakers.[26] After training at a nearby university, Glen got certified as an Ontario Provincial Native Language Teacher, able to work for both the tribe and the local elementary school. He became the first person to teach the language in school.

"He just had this way of making you feel comfortable with making mistakes," said Karen. "He would stay there until he made sure that you said it perfectly. He would come over and visit and have coffee with us and just talk about life and everything. If we wanted to know anything about the language, he would teach it to us."

One of Glen's less typical students was the actor Daniel Day Lewis, preparing for his role as Hawkeye, a (fictional) child of white parents raised among Lenape speakers in the 1992 movie *The Last of the Mohicans*. "He taught him in two-syllable chunks, so if it was *Mother Earth*, which is Kukuna Áhkuy, then it was kuh-kun a-key. It kind of makes some sense when he's talking in the movie," said Karen, laughing.

On the Munsee reserve, Heather and Karen were the ones who kept it going. They soon outgrew the gas station, so the tribe let them use the council chambers, where the tribal council meets. The teachers from the tribal daycare center started coming to learn words and songs to share with the kids.

For a few years, Karen was the sidekick quietly helping her mom from the corner. Then one day Heather suggested they teach something together, which started them splitting the lesson, always Heather first and then Karen.

"Karen, do you want to start the class out with your lesson and then, you know, I'll go after you?" asked Heather eventually, at the beginning of a class. Karen agreed, but then fifteen minutes in, while Karen was still going, Heather suddenly packed up her stuff and moved over to sit with the students.

"Out of the corner of my mouth I was like, What are you doing?" Karen hissed. "You're ready, she said. So I taught the entire class and I was so nervous, but she pushed me, you know, she pushed me to do it. And she was at every class that I taught up until the last couple of years."

Then Glen passed away, and Karen felt a new level of urgency: "Oh my god, I thought, I can never ask him another question about language. It hit home: how are we going to carry this on?" His students started pooling their knowledge and contributing what they could remember, hosting camps and classes of their own.

"I believe that Glen has passed us messages in the spirit world," said Karen. "About a month after he passed away, I kept hearing this word, miiltuwáakin, and I had no idea what it meant and I tried looking it up in the dictionary. I tried everything I could, looking through my notes, and it just felt so familiar, but I could not figure out what it meant."

There was no Glen to ask. It was only later, one zoned-out day when she was coteaching with another of Glen's students, that she suddenly heard the students repeating miiltuwáakin, miiltuwáakin, miiltuwáakin, and her coteacher explaining that the word means *gift*. "I had to leave the room and I got really emotional. I believe that was Glen passing on a message to me that our language is a gift. I never forgot that."

Just as Karen was feeling the call to bring the gift to new places, an invitation came from Collegiate Church, the oldest "corporation" in America, founded in 1628 in New Amsterdam. Collegiate was hosting its Healing Turtle Island Ceremony at the foot of Lower Manhattan, near the place where we get bows. The church wanted to apologize for its historic role in what happened to the Lenape people. It was Karen's first time in the city, driving a vanload of people down from Ontario. From that trip, everything else followed.

"I felt so comfortable, like I didn't even have any problems driving in Manhattan," is how she put it to me, laughing. "I slept like a baby when we were there. I felt like I was home, you know. Oddly everywhere I've ever lived, I never felt like I was at home. At that point it didn't even occur to me that we were on our ancestors' land, even though that's why we were there. I didn't put it together until later—that's why I felt so comfortable. It was almost like being welcomed home."

## 6

It takes me ten hours driving, with barely a stop, to trace Karen's route in the opposite direction. It's an unsettling journey, knowing the path of Lenape exile. The map shows places called Albion, Antwerp,

Alexandria; Bethlehem, Berlin, Bombay; Cairo, Canaan, and Cuba. As if every age of human history and every region of the world had to be raided to name this landscape—as if the words of its original people had not been enough.

The bar at the Canadian border lifts, and soon I'm speeding along the Queen Elizabeth Way, no cars or settlements in sight.

After two years of Karen's classes, I'm here to see the last stronghold of the language.

At first, Moraviantown seems no different from any other place in rural southwestern Ontario. It's a flat tract of land five square miles in size, a rectangle on all sides but one, where it borders the meandering Thames—Asiiskusiipuw, or *muddy river* in Lenape. Moraviantown is called Náahi, *Downriver*, as opposed to Munsee, which is Nalahii, *Upriver*. The Delaware and its tributaries may be hundreds of miles from here, but a river remains central, the very basis of names.

This is where that one group of Lenape came at the end of the eighteenth century after the massacre at Gnadenhütten. Canada—the Chippewa, really—provided refuge. Again the Lenape rebuilt, until two decades later the Long Knives struck again.

How did the language endure here? A memorial at the edge of the reserve suggests a partial answer. On a tranquil field stands a stainless dome in the shape of a turtle, open to the air. On the elliptical bands of its back are the outlines of ten clan animals, gaining their colors from the sky. Fifty different species of grass surround it, and two lines of land that draw apart and then close again, a symbol of the Two Row Wampum Pathway. The idea of the pathway—a lost vision of coexistence, or at least a separate togetherness—dates from one of the very earliest treaties, signed by the Dutch and the Iroquois at a time when Manhattan was still Lenape.

What all this cryptically marks is the Battle of the Thames, a pivotal moment during the American invasion of Canada. Here in 1813 the Shawnee leader Tecumseh, who forged one of the great Native confederacies with supporters from Alabama to Minnesota, died together with many of his warriors, in alliance with the British. Another memorial tells a different version of this story: the trompe l'oeil carving on the Capitol rotunda in Washington, DC The death of Tecumseh became the crowning glory of the young republic.

But it was hardly a victory for the Americans. They soon retreated, though not before burning the first Lenape village here to the ground. Canada remained unconquered, and the Lenape survived in their new home. Two centuries later, Moraviantown is still their sovereign territory, "known for its pickerel fishing and its fastball teams" (as the tribe puts it). There are 457 registered residents and 587 band members living off the reserve. Non-Lenape can live on the reservation, but they have to pay an annual fee and they can't own property.

So few cars pass that I see locals looking up at each one, likely to see a relation, and it's how people seem to visit with each other too, cars side by side idling in front of yards. Nine names appear over and over in the graveyard: Jacobs, Peters, Snake, Timothy, Logan, Stonefish, Hopkins, Whiteye, and Huff. These are the extended families that kept the language going for generations.

Other Lenape may be from the Wolf, Turkey, or Deer clans, but this is Turtle country. Older sources don't mention the Lenape having animal-based clans, so they may have evolved later, as a way of reacting and regrouping under the catastrophic impact of European invasion. In Moraviantown today the image of the turtle is painted or posted almost everywhere, besides shining in steel from Tecumseh's battlefield. It was a Lenape speaker in what is now New Jersey who was first recorded mentioning Turtle Island—a name and notion that later spread across North America, meaning sometimes the continent and sometimes the entire world, resting on the back of a turtle.[27]

I stop at a standard red stop sign that says NGIHLAAL, wondering about the form of the verb. A water tower rises like a stunted minaret above ordinary houses. There are places to buy cartons of tax-free cigarettes, and the soft horn and rumble of a passing train are always somewhere nearby. The tribe runs health and education and other programs, as well as a gas station and a grocery store, with many bare shelves but a tiny Tim Horton's tucked in the back.

On one family's land stands Nmaachihna, a recreated traditional village whose name means *We are going home*. It's a cluster of structures in a clearing, including magnificent wigwams hand-built from giant panels of bark. A cookhouse, a fish hatchery, and a deer hide–tanning station will eventually be part of this "living village," surrounded by fields of corn, beans, and squash.

"I learn the language so I can talk to my ancestors, so I can talk to the trees, in the language they would understand," one of its founders tells me.

"I like your sweatshirt," I say to a woman in a New York City sweatshirt.

"That's my homeland!" comes the cheerful reply.

"I think I'll keep going till I'm eighty," says Dianne Snake, "and then the rest is history. That'll be it."

People generally agree that Dianne is the last native speaker of Lenape. She looks indestructible, but very soon she'll be eighty.

There are two houses on the Moraviantown property to which I turn up unannounced, having found no other way to get in touch with her. I come first to the one with a carved wooden sign on a giant easel: Laaweewiikiipush Wshiixay, *Pheasant Nest*. A bleary, understandably miffed lady in a robe (Dianne's daughter) shakes her head and indicates the house further back.

I start tapping out a series of hopeless, hurried knocks. A minute passes and I'm scribbling a note half in Lenape, which I'm about to shove under the door. Then a woman appears, fully dressed for the day and peering skeptically out of her glasses. I'm either a door-to-door salesman or some kind of criminal, judging by how she keeps her distance, mulling confrontation or retreat. My introduction tumbles out, begging her for the briefest chat, and by then she is incredulous, annoyed, or at best vaguely amused that a linguist has turned up at her door, at nine in the morning, hoping to meet her.

We don't know much about last speakers—beginning with who they are and what they speak, let alone how it feels—but they are becoming singular symbols of linguistic loss, a complex process otherwise hard to fathom. Though always multilingual, they are equal parts ordinary and extraordinary, and they seem often to be women. Like Dianne, many end up dedicating their later years to documenting and teaching their languages, whether or not they have any formal education. Their singular example can jump-start a movement. Their passing can mark a moment, a human-interest hook to hang a story on, a touch of "Indigenous celebrity."[28] Fidelia Fielding, the Mohegan speaker, kept a four-volume diary in her language. Marie Wilcox, who spoke Wukchumni, compiled a dictionary with thousands of entries before she passed away in California in 2021, inspiring her two daughters and dozens of grandchildren, great-grandchildren, and great-great-grandchildren to vow that they would carry on the language.

Focusing on or fetishizing last speakers obscures a stranger reality. The concept itself can be problematic.[29] Who does a last speaker speak to? Before he died in 1983 in California, Arthur Anderson, the last speaker of Yuki, said that he hadn't actually spoken Yuki since 1908.[30] Dianne is not having natural Lenape conversations the kind we take for granted every day, with anyone. And what is "last" anyway? Previously "undiscovered" speakers are sometimes found, as has happened with Cornish in England, Kusunda in Nepal, and Laghu in the Solomon Islands.[31] There are almost always scattered people, often just out of view, who might remember certain things under certain circumstances. Languages can "sleep" and "reawaken" from both memories and archives, living several lives and several afterlives, as long as there is someone to keep them going. Languages may need keepers as much as speakers.

Dianne fends me off, yielding nothing. On the purgatory of her deck, my bare-bones Lenape all but vanishes. In English, the only language we really share, I say that we're trying to learn the language in New York.

"You should!" she says, amused, with a challenge in her voice.

I mention the regulars, the people who come to Karen's classes.

"Who are they? I wouldn't teach them," she says firmly.

Karen's willingness to teach the language to anyone interested, I suddenly remember, is not universally shared. A few leaders of an unrecognized Lenape group in Pennsylvania had learned the language well, with one even writing a textbook, but a blogger went after their genealogies. The Oklahoma tribe publicly labeled them impostors, and another person lost a senior position at a famous college.

On the one hand, the long history of appropriation is undeniable. On the other, especially with East Coast Native groups, many people are or believe they are one-eighth or one-sixteenth Native, the legacy of a still unacknowledged mestizo North America. People claiming Lenape descent today may look "Indian," Black, or shwaanuk, which literally means *salty* and, by extension, *white*. DNA testing, online genealogy, and the notion of "blood quantum" (with one-eighth Lenape descent required, for instance, by the Oklahoma tribe) lend themselves to a concept of identity based on biological descent, but language, at least in theory, is learnable for anyone committed enough. On the other hand, some groups reeling from centuries of dispossession consider their languages theirs to do with what they wish—not for outsiders to observe, preserve, or dabble in.

"The reason I still have the language is that my grandparents raised me, and my grandmother lived a long time," says Dianne. "When

O'Meara was making the dictionary back in the eighties, I would go with him and listen while he recorded the last group of elders, six of them, all dead now in the last ten to fifteen years."

Lenape is *her* language, in a fundamental way that makes every kind of sense.

"Now there's nowhere to hear the language outside the walls of my head," she continues. "There is another speaker who knows a fair bit, but she lives in a nursing home, she's not in good shape. O'Meara is always sending questions, and sometimes I talk to Goddard from the Smithsonian. You know them?"

She looks at me hard.

There are so few people anywhere who can hold even a basic conversation in Lenape, but not all those people are on speaking terms with one another. Some of it is personal history. Some of it is generational. Given all the pressures, it's ultimately not surprising that people might go their own ways: to the ancestors, to outsiders, to a select group of disciples.

When a language is down to just a few speakers, the challenges are not just linguistic and educational, but logistical, social, and profoundly interpersonal. Two Wanyi-speaking cousins located by linguists in far-flung parts of northern Australia were brought together for a week in a Cunnamulla RV park. Of only three speakers of Mati Ke, another Australian language, two were brother and sister, forbidden by tribal custom from speaking to one another since puberty, while the third lived far away and spoke very differently. In Mexico, Manuel Segovia and Isidro Velazquez were said to be the feuding last two speakers of Ayapaneco, but this turned out to be a trumped-up trope exploited by the mobile phone company Vodafone, which staged a flashy and ineffectual attempt to "save" the language. Outside interest can make things worse.

A language is learned not by memorizing words, but by sharing life with those who speak it. That might mean the same people, your entire life, in a place like Moraviantown. A stranger even with the strongest interest—even a linguist—may not be welcome. Either way, you have to want to talk to *specific people*. Those people have to want to talk to you, and to each other. The same is true when it comes to revitalizing a language. It's a life's work that depends on the lives of others.

Dianne says that for the last three years, with the tribe's support, she has been training five Moraviantown women, three days a week, in an old stone homesteader house in the woods here. All five are teachers in the local schools, where the kids are starting to get Lenape as a second language, at least a few hours a week. They're getting good, says Dianne of the teachers she teaches.

For now Dianne is the authority. She doesn't say how things will go without her, when "the rest is history." Will one of the five teachers be seen as the expert, or will they compete for authority? Defer to the dictionary, or the recordings? Will the language become purely symbolic, used mainly on signs and in names? Will there ever again be children raised in the language?

Dianne's daughter is coming over.

"You lasted longer than the last guy," she says, grinning at me. "He ended up in the pool."

Dianne growls something to her dog in Lenape, which I don't catch, and he dashes off. Soon I leave too.

## 7

In-person classes with the regulars on Eighteenth Street go "on pause" during the pandemic. Karen is undaunted, teaching up to four sessions a week remotely with different groups, not to mention all the videos and messages she puts out on Facebook and YouTube. She is planting seeds, serving as the connector, sharing language with anyone anywhere who wants to learn. She is still pushing to become an accredited teacher in the Canadian school system, hoping eventually to establish a curriculum beyond Moraviantown, at the three schools at Munsee and in London. Karen knows these kids and sees them as the future of the language.

These are her plans, but somewhere behind her voice on this phone call I hear exhaustion. Reluctantly she tells me that Michael has just had heart surgery; next they'll be putting in a pacemaker. She admits, almost as an afterthought, that she herself recently had to have bariatric surgery. Then she was diagnosed with cirrhosis of the liver, nothing to do with drinking. She was in and out of the emergency room for a week. When word finally gets out, a GoFundMe goes out in minutes among her far-flung family of students.

But a week later it's Michael that I hear from: "Karen passed." Double pneumonia, sepsis. She was fifty-four years old. He takes her back to the reserve, where the Munsee-Delaware Nation live streams her funeral, the tribal drummers sounding rhythms into her open casket.

A language keeper named Ian, who had started working closely with Karen, reads these words in the language they have to be in, which is also the one she'll soon be needing:

Anushiik Karen.
*Thank you, Karen.*

Kii kmsooxwi kwiichkune naxpii huluniixsuwaakan.
*You travel all over, help others with language.*

Niloona ktawalohmwa kweek leew "Koolamalsi," naxpii ihuluniixsiitak.
*We love you, say "how are you" to all the speakers.*

Niloona kwiiloomeewohnwa, kii kaakuluksuwiingweexiin, kii keelkusiit.
*We will miss you, your smile, your laugh.*

Kii kwiichkune naxpii huluniixsuwaakan.
*You help others with language.*

Niiloona kwchi eelohkeet koonjulunumun.
*We try (and) do the work you do.*

Laapii uch knewul nijoos.
*See you, my friend.*

# IV. Future

Is this peak linguistic diversity?

On the four hundredth anniversary of its colonial founding, with the arrival of those Walloon settlers in 1624, New York is the consummate Babel, the privileged recipient of ever more global flows of migration that continue to enhance and enrich it immeasurably. But the most linguistically diverse city in the history of the world could diminish fast, before there has even been a chance to recognize, document, or protect it.

Urban linguistic diversity, like urban biodiversity, is a fact that no one planned for. Even less so the large-scale arrival of endangered-language speakers in the last few decades.[1] Cities like today's New York do little to cultivate or sustain even a fraction of what comes to them. When acknowledged at all, linguistic difference is often seen as a problem, the curse of Babel. The experiment is under threat, and the most immediate threats are political.

The expansive era for immigration that started in 1965, which set a model for the world and led to today's diversity, may be coming to a close. Fiercely anti-immigrant politics of a sort not seen in a century drove the rise of Donald Trump, a Queens-born grandson of immigrants whose administration tried a host of measures, including over four hundred executive orders, to roll back the world that 1965 made.[2] On the one hundredth anniversary of the 1924 Immigration Act that closed America's doors, the possibility that the door will once again be slammed shut is very real. Is this a replay of the midnight races, as people gamble on a last chance to get in?

Though it failed to pass, the 2017 RAISE Act provided a brutal blueprint for the new anti-immigrant agenda, combining a drastic reduction in numbers with a new points-based system that heavily favors skilled English-speaking workers. For the first time ever, language would play an explicit and central role in who even gets a chance to become American, in keeping with the English-only movement which started gaining ground in many states in the 1980s.

Net annual legal immigration, which peaked in the 1990s and remained over a million as recently as 2015, collapsed to 247,000 in 2021, its lowest level in four decades, though the COVID pandemic was certainly a factor.[3] The record-breaking backlog in the US's legal immigration system is leaving in limbo millions who are already in the country, many of whom may have no choice but to give up.[4] Meanwhile, without any standing orders to the contrary, the estimated eleven-million-plus undocumented immigrants in the US, including over half a million people in New York City, are more vulnerable to arrest and deportation than ever.[5] Record numbers of people are still trying to cross the US-Mexico border, suggesting that the US retains its appeal as a destination and that the need to migrate has never been greater. This is also abundantly clear from the mass migrations ongoing elsewhere in the world—a planetary-level demographic reality very much like the major migrations of the nineteenth century, only pushing and pulling in different directions.

In particular, the resource-starved refugee and asylum systems are broken precisely when they are needed most.[6] While refugees are typically channeled by resettlement agencies to less expensive cities like Atlanta, Buffalo, and Houston, New York has remained the undisputed capital of asylum. Asylees often have to wait years for a hearing, if they can get one, barely getting by in the meantime. But the city's immigration judges make some 40 percent of all asylum grants nationwide, and asylum seekers are up to ten times more likely to win their cases in New York than in Atlanta, for instance.

The small number of politically appointed judges responsible for this may well be New Yorkers who grasp, or themselves are part of, the city of survivors.[7]

At the national level, only 11,411 refugees were admitted in 2021, the lowest annual figure on record since the passage of the Refugee Act of 1980. In 2022, the rapid admission of one hundred thousand Ukrainians, while showing what might be possible, offered most of them only temporary permission to stay in the country, via other channels. At the same time a new and unprecedented "migrant crisis" has brought over 100,000 people and counting to New York, many of them Ecuadorian, Colombian, Venezuelan, Russian, and African asylum seekers. Some were being bused north from other states by Republican officials in a deliberate attempt to break the ultimate sanctuary city, with its unique "right to shelter" and capacity for integration. Throughout the city's history, that capacity has fundamentally depended on immigrant communities themselves, whether the help has come from friends, family, hometown associations, or speakers of the same language. It's happening now too—explaining why New York has been far and away the migrants' top destination, and overwhelmingly so for certain groups from Asia and Latin America. By comparison, the city's official response, coordinated through the newly created Office of Asylum Seeker Operations, is bound to be of limited impact.

If 2024 becomes the new 1924, closing the country and cutting off the city, there will be untold ramifications for both, and for peoples and languages around the world. Even for those already here, the string of emergencies that began with Trump's election in 2016 is far from over—a frightening new time with tragic consequences not only for many of the city's communities, but for the city itself. Where white nationalists may fear the Great Replacement, New York has long depended, in quite literal demographic terms, on what could be called the Great Replenishment, the continual infusion of newcomers into the lifeblood of the city.

American cities are inconceivable without immigrants, who have played a historic role in building, maintaining, and reviving them at every level. Yet gentrification and the spiraling cost of housing are now putting large parts of cities like New York out of reach, raising the prospect that linguistically diverse Queens and Brooklyn could go the way of Manhattan. On the other hand, certain other large cities around the country and many satellite cities, suburbs, and even small towns in the New York area are becoming increasingly linguistically diverse. You can hear Mòoré in Newark, Kabardian in Paterson, Telugu in Edison, Guarani in White Plains, Kaqchikel in Riverhead. The outskirts may be the future, but the longer-term consequences of less diverse major cities are hard to predict.

At the same time, many of the city's recent tragedies have disproportionately befallen immigrants, like the fire that took seventeen lives, including eight children, in Touray Tower, a vertical village of mostly Soninke-speaking Gambians in the Bronx given that informal name for an immigrant pioneer who spoke nine languages and was the first from his community to move in.[8] Of the thirteen New Yorkers who died during Hurricane Ida, eleven were Asian immigrants who drowned in mostly unregulated basement apartments in Brooklyn and Queens, the tenements of today that are likely home to hundreds of thousands.

When New York became the global epicenter of COVID-19, minority, immigrant, and Indigenous language communities of the outer boroughs were suddenly at "the epicenter of the epicenter." While whole neighborhoods of Manhattan fled to the safety of second homes, hundreds were dying and thousands falling sick every day in neighborhoods like Jackson Heights, Elmhurst, and Corona. The real numbers in the city's most "invisible" communities were impossible to fathom, with so many dying at home untested and unreported. Countless others were thrown out of work and ineligible for or unable to access government support.

Fundamental inequalities around income, housing, and health were exposed, as well as the fact that so many immigrants are essential workers in health care, food service, and transportation and thus unable to quarantine. Layering the Department of Health's case data over ELA's language map revealed an additional, less recognized factor: language. In a public-health emergency like COVID, with constant and sometimes contradictory messaging full of new terms like "social distancing" and "community transmission," the translation of new directives and interpretation for the sick and the hospitalized take on a critical importance. It isn't just a matter of translating a single sign or poster, but of having flexible, accessible channels with video or audio, featuring trusted voices using community languages on an ongoing basis. For the poor and undocumented, there are basic fears around trying to access medical care. No public health system in the world was prepared for this, but nowhere was the need more pressing than New York in March 2020. A few days could make a difference, and speakers of less common languages were suddenly at a life-or-death disadvantage.

Though less immediate than these fundamentally political dangers to life and livelihood, there are also dire threats to the languages themselves. With language loss now operative almost everywhere, cities like New York can no longer count on tapping reserves of linguistic diversity elsewhere.

Rasmina wonders whether another child will ever be raised the way she was, surrounded by Seke. Husniya sees more and more Wakhi speakers migrating, with little chance of maintaining their language in diaspora. Even if Yiddish lives on among Hasidic speakers, the secular and literary languages championed by Boris are in full retreat. Ibrahima sees hope in N'ko, but reaching the young and keeping current is a constant battle. Irwin fears that Nahuatl, however much people now claim to value it, is actually being used less and less every day. With

Karen's passing, a chapter in the Lenape language movement has come to a close. So much depends on a few people.

ELA is still ELA, though it's a scramble every year to raise the organization's very modest budget. Only a handful of funders have heard of or will consider supporting endangered languages, and this pittance goes primarily toward academic fieldwork. Though vital, this does little to support communities or speakers, like the six in this book, who are trying to maintain or revitalize their languages.

Cities present resources and opportunities, beginning with the better livelihoods and concentrated public and private resources that speakers are seeking when they move to them in the first place. But the long-term viability of minority and Indigenous languages in urban environments has always been in doubt. A city is still a profoundly challenging place to document, maintain, transmit, or revitalize a language.

Though many do have rural backgrounds and associated environmental and agricultural knowledge, New York, to a significant degree, is "a city of people from other cities."[9] That means language loss usually starts well before people even get here, as they come via towns, cities, businesses, schools, or networks in their home country, making continual linguistic adjustments along the way. Then there's the sense of profound downward mobility on arrival: cabbies with advanced degrees, waiters with a hundred acres or a hundred sheep in the village (now looked after by someone worse off). It's a nonstop hustle to survive. Many speakers feel their languages perpetually slipping away, and it can seem downright strange to speak it at all in the radically different, often profoundly hostile context of the city. Outside of traditional territories and environments, many parts of a language may feel impossible to access, from the terms for local plants and animals to all the narratives and lifeways linked to the land. Linguistic churn in the city is constant: mixing, shift, loss.

Are new languages emerging in New York and similar cities? Phenomena like Ramaluk are so fluid and flexibly defined that they are generally never enumerated, written, or documented. Speakers themselves may not be aware, let alone proud, of what they're doing, although there may sometimes be a little communicative cachet, not just ease or necessity, to the right kind of mixing. In the end Ramaluk is less a "language" than an ever-evolving, contextual practice forged in the white heat of particular multilingual contact situations and thus likely to fade away within a generation or two. Though many languages have emerged from mixing, including English, it's rare that hybrid speechways are actually embraced, stabilized, and passed on—though there are examples like Sri Lankan Malay and Michif (a combination of French, Cree, and other elements spoken by people of mixed European and First Nations ancestry primarily in Canada).

A remarkable number of New Yorkers do live *between* languages—translanguaging, as the linguist Ofelia García and other scholars call it.[10] Languages sharing space in a city exert a relentless pull on one another, which always means more than mere coexistence. Like Ramaluk, what people call Spanglish, as studied by García and others, is not a fixed "language" but a linguistic pas de deux that can take many forms and even become a point of pride, as for the Nuyorican poets, soaring above the constant pressure to "choose" either Spanish or English.[11]

Likewise the many mixed English-based languages of New York, whose speakers move seamlessly between registers and repertoires, the different levels of speech appropriate to different situations. Yet shame, stigma, and racialization often apply, with language attitudes and policies from "back home" continuing to exert pressure. How else to explain why so few Jamaican New Yorkers claim to be Patwa speakers on the census, not to mention the absence of African American English from the census altogether? New York has also been the crucial birthplace for new English-based "ethnolects" like Italian American English and Jewish English, which bear a New York stamp even when they're spoken in Miami or LA.

The city's most diverse neighborhoods may even be incubating *multi*ethnolects, recently described in European cities, which come about when several different groups are in contact with each other and "adolescents are left as it were in a strange place without a map, and are invited on a quest through a landscape with all kinds of linguistic and cultural possibilities and challenges."[12] Though vital for social identity, the mixed codes that emerge may be detected only as "microvariation": the realization of a vowel, the metathesis of a consonant cluster (*aks* for *ask*), or the use of uninflected *be* (by Puerto Rican New Yorkers, among others, who have been in contact with speakers of African American English).[13]

At the same time, even setting aside the many ways that language plays into the city's social and ethnic conflicts, there is no end of subtle and overt linguicism, as many are now calling linguistic discrimination and intolerance.[14] A hierarchy of languages, with Dominant American English at the top, still rules communication.

Threats to the city's languages and those who speak them ultimately threaten the city itself, which depends on all its diversities. With diverse peoples and their languages comes a diversity of skills, procedures, methods, ideas, contacts, and goods. It's especially evident in realms like food, music, dance, and the arts, where the city's knack for crossbreeding and popularizing different linguistic and cultural traditions has played a decisive role in shaping global culture.[15] Fashion people, finance people, restaurant people, sports people, tech people, not to mention chess people, jazz people, whiskey people, and a thousand others, have their own sectors of the city, their "ecosystems," spots, lingos, and perhaps even lifeways.[16] The future of the city's professional and subcultural diversity may seem comparatively assured, given its compatibility with capitalism, specialization, and individual choice, but this too ultimately relies on the city's linguistic and cultural diversity.[17]

Even if few things stick, some argue, won't something new always make its way to the city? Or are too many traces the same as oblivion, rendering New York a palimpsest beyond all possible deciphering? "Every place you ever go, you leave something of yourself, however small or intangible," writes László Krasznahorkai, in John Batki's translation.[18] "If every such exchange were marked by a small dot on an imaginary map of the world, some places, like the oceans, would be barely marked, while others would be unimaginably dense. In this map, Manhattan is a black hole." Or, as Jean-Paul Sartre said of the city, "Nowhere more than here can you feel the simultaneity of human lives."[19]

In reality, the city that results from all this, but is now under threat, is a great center of hybrids, a theater of combinations and conjunctures that could happen nowhere else, though other cities may have their own equivalents.[20] It's evident even in the lexical tendrils of a humble local institution like the bodega. This essential Caribbean Spanish loanword into New York City English reflects the stores' predominantly Cuban, Puerto Rican, and Dominican owners from the 1950s on.[21] The word is all the more useful for being hard to pin down: usually (but not always) on a corner, (almost always) independently owned, (traditionally) in the New York metropolitan area, and (definitely) containing everything necessary for protracted human survival. Etymologically, its roots branch even further: from ancient Greek apotheke, *storehouse*, to Latin apotheca, *store*, and then later into French (boutique, *any small shop*), Italian (bottega, more of an *artisanal workshop*), Polish and Russian (apteka, *pharmacy*), and even the bodegas (*wineries*) and bodegóns (*family-style restaurants*) of Argentina. In today's New York, boutiques and bodegas sit side by side, not to mention New Age apothecaries, Polish and Russian aptekas, and the high-end fashion brand Bottega Veneta. We may see only the differences between them, but the words suggest otherwise.

Polish-, Indian-, Chinese-, Colombian-, and Mexican-owned bodegas have much in common, not to mention the sole Seke-speaking one, but today Palestinian and especially Yemeni immigrants run most of them. Around half of the city's ten thousand bodegas are thought to be Yemeni owned, and the owners have become ever more of a political force since the Yemeni bodega strike of 2017, which protested the Muslim travel ban.[22] And while the word bodega is sticking, the word ock is now coming in. Originally akhi, or *brother* in Arabic, ock is now affectionately used (as *brother* itself might be) to mean *local bodega guy*.

How was this Arabic word transformed, in both sound and sense, and adopted especially by so many African American, Caribbean, and Latino New Yorkers?[23] Arabic-speaking bodega workers were able to get a word in, literally, with a set of their (mostly) English-speaking customers, because of frequent personal interactions in hundreds of neighborhood bodegas, year after year. The spelling now on bodega awnings and Instagram accounts has been Englished to look like *dock*, *rock*, etc. Hip-hop and social media have played a role too. Ocks and their bodegas embody the city of hybrids.

Embodying it at an even more intimate level are the many mixed families where multiple cultural and linguistic legacies come together in a single person who is "half this," "a quarter that." Arguably where hybrid linguistic and cultural forms thrive most is the "world of the second generation": the children of the speakers featured in this book—who in general are familiar with, but do not speak, the languages that their parents are working so hard to sustain.[24]

It's often the second generation that starts identifying less as Fulani or Fujianese and perhaps not quite as American, but above all with New York. Among them, "friendships develop in schools, colleges, playgrounds, and workplaces, and political alliances are formed on certain issues and electoral campaigns."[25] Arguably they are not so much assimilating as "creating a new kind of multiculturalism . . . of hybrids and fluid exchanges across group boundaries."[26] Worlds may be coming together, but languages are often starting to fade. By the third generation, there may be interest in, but little understanding of or access to, the language. With hybrids, there is always the question of how much the component parts they depend on are acknowledged or replenished. Without its sources, the city of hybrids too will fade.

How can *this* Babel—the one we live in, not the muddled myth—actually work?

The threats above demand their own targeted responses, but one thing we can do proactively is build a linguistic infrastructure, a real right to language that ensures information, interpretation, and education in every mother tongue. This requires an unprecedented push beginning in courts, hospitals, and schools, and it's ultimately about the interaction of language and power at every level, reaching deep into our mouths and our minds.

Language policy, far from perfect but in many ways much more advanced in countries like Canada, Switzerland, and India, remains almost nonexistent in the US. More than just official regulations, it's also about "unofficial, covert, de facto, and implicit mechanisms, connected to language beliefs and practices," the kinds of things that dominant-language speakers hardly even notice.[27] Almost any right or service becomes impossible to claim without communication and mutual understanding. Language justice, a new framework only just being developed, recognizes that no other form of justice can be served—racial, social, economic, environmental, or otherwise—unless support for languages is built in, as with phone tree or touch screen options that start by asking your language, or similar provisions for the blind or deaf.

For now there is little hope at the international, national, or even state levels, but in cities like New York there are glimmers of what a linguistic infrastructure could look and sound like.[28] Bilingual/dual-language education, which emerged in part from the struggles of Puerto Rican parents for Spanish in the 1960s and '70s, is on the upswing.[29] Driven by both the extraordinary linguistic diversity of the city's million-plus public school students and a new consensus about the benefits of mother-tongue education and multilingualism, the city has recently opened or expanded hundreds of new bilingual programs in thirteen languages. Multilingual pre-K and 3-K programs, funded by the city but run at the community level, could also have an enormous impact if sustained, though it may take a generation to see how well these programs are working.

Meanwhile, local laws passed since 2003 go beyond the patchwork solutions of the past and mandate support for those with limited English proficiency who need vital services.[30] Implementation is a serious problem, but at least officially there is a commitment to supporting the current ten "citywide" languages, all of which have upward of one hundred thousand speakers just in the five boroughs. This is why you now see public health messages in Russian, licensing information in Chinese, and subway notices in Haitian Creole. The task is enormously complicated, though not necessarily prohibitively expensive—especially if local community experts like those at the Indigenous Interpreters Collective can be involved, rather than outsourcing to exploitative private companies.[31]

All this may be more than any other city has ever tried to do, but it remains very little given the scale of the challenge and the opportunity. An increasing number of other forward-thinking cities are following suit. After all, diversity is a competitive advantage. Many urbanites now want "the world next door," or at least a "global cultural supermarket"[32] where as outsider-consumers they can enjoy the afternoon at a Korean spa, grab Ethiopian food for dinner, and catch the new film from Norway. Bloggers eat foods from every nation without ever leaving the city, finding Finnish food fairs and savoring Senegalese specialties. YouTube polyglots discover that cities are the ultimate accessible language learning playgrounds.[33]

This is all well and good, but the real world-in-the-city cannot just be a spectacle where diversity is an asset or an amenity.[34] It has to be less about restaurants and "glocal" tourism and more about the day-to-day needs and desires of neighbors who speak hundreds of languages. Many, like the six speakers in this book, are already powerfully resisting the constant and profoundly unnecessary erosion of language, culture, and knowledge experienced in almost all immigrant communities. They need support.

There is a version of the city in which English, Chinese, Spanish, and other widely spoken languages are useful lingua francas, not killer languages baselessly touting their own superiority. Where there is space for smaller languages to thrive in homes and community contexts. Where speakers of every language have access to the information and interpretation they need. Where multilingualism is a priority, and everyone has the options and resources to maintain and develop their ancestral and community languages, not to mention learning new ones. In this imaginary but not impossible New York, differences would be recognized, interpreted, and *enjoyed*, not wished away or weeded out.

At certain times, in certain corners of Queens, it's almost within earshot. Already the borough is "probably the greatest social experiment in history," as the city's foremost demographer Joseph Salvo has put it. The neighborhood of Jackson Heights, once open to white Protestants only, has become the most diverse square mile in the country, if not the world.[35] An unassuming apartment building in Corona can be home to Uzbeks, Afghans, Indians, Pakistanis, Bangladeshis, Koreans, Filipinos, Ukrainians, Russians, Argentines, Colombians, Dominicans, Puerto Ricans, Peruvians, African Americans, and Guyanese constantly exchanging food and home remedies.[36] Flushing is a "city of gods" where Hindus, Buddhists, Sikhs, Christians, Jews, and Muslims of many denominations can all have houses of worship within minutes of each other, thanks in part to zoning regulations.[37] Ethnographers of the 7 train, the so-called International Express which cuts through the heart of the borough, describe how this distinctly unglamorous "public space in motion" keeps moving forward not in spite of but because of its "shifting cargo of passengers who represent the peoples of the world."[38]

The quintessence of twenty-first-century Queens, in all its negative capability, is getting-by and letting-live and going-about-your-business. What has been written of a building in Hong Kong applies equally to the pragmatic peace that reigns here: "People from more or less warring societies the world over come. But they do not fight with each other, as they might in their home countries—or at least if they do occasionally quarrel, the quarrels are soon enough set aside in [the] universal striving to make money."[39] Money is not everything, but the key to cosmopolitan coexistence here may likewise be thoroughly mundane.

Precisely because it's riddled with problems and nowhere close to utopia, yet still part of the most looked-to city on the planet, Queens could in some ways be a bizarro model for diversifying cities, towns, and suburbs everywhere, not to mention the thousands of sending communities from which people migrate. There is a remarkable record of tolerance precisely here, where the city (and the world) is at its most diverse. While diversification in the short term can bring challenges,[40] the example of Queens strongly suggests that more difference over time means less conflict, and that it matters how contact happens, is managed, and is mediated. Deep difference can come to seem utterly natural.

The idea that people who speak differently can't get along is just as wrong as the idea that people who speak the same will always get along. We won't all learn to speak each other's languages, but a few words can go a long way, and at a minimum we need to grow familiar and comfortable with hearing them all the time. We need ways to communicate, which is why the city has not one but a dozen lingua francas. We need people who speak four, five, or six languages, the constant connectors who are on every block in certain parts of Queens.

We need language keepers, who keep up endangered ways of speaking, knowing, and being, despite the loneliness and the pressure, reflecting everything we are.

The linguistic life of a great city is impossible to capture. In 1954, the legendary sound archivist Tony Schwartz released *New York 19*, an audio portrait of the Manhattan zip code where he lived. He apparently had plans to do something similar for a single city block. Almost by accident, ELA's archive is now a partial record of the most linguistically diverse city in history. An organization called the Interstellar Foundation wants to send some of our recordings to the moon, hoping that humans will find them there hundreds or thousands of years in the future. They were inspired by the Golden Records, launched way out into the universe on the *Voyager* spacecraft in 1977. From those recordings in a mere fifty-five languages, any extraterrestrials out there with a turntable are expected to learn something about life on Earth. The Rosetta Project goes further, etching microscopic parallel texts in a thousand languages onto nickel disks that will be blasted into space and buried deep in the earth. We have to hope that someone out there is listening, but in the meantime: we all can.

# Acknowledgments

To the six speakers: Rasmina, for your bravery and generosity; Husniya, for your perseverance in dreams; Boris, for your spirit of ceaseless invention; Ibrahima, for your storytelling and hospitality; Irwin, for your maestro's touch; and Karen, for your teachings in language and life—we miss you.

To the Endangered Language Alliance, above all puxku Daniel Kaufman (and Amalia, Dahlia, and Ammiel!), as well as Bob Holman, Juliette Blevins, Habib Borjian, Charles Häberl, Patrick White, and so many others.

To my agent Bonnie Nadell, for clear vision and constant support.

To my editor Peter Blackstock, Emily Burns, and everyone at Grove Atlantic, for believing in this book and seeing it through.

To the editors who commissioned essays and reporting: Charles Petersen (*n+1*), Sarah Leonard (*Dissent*), David Wolf (*The Guardian*), Chris Cox (*Harper's*), Moira Weigel and Ben Tarnoff (*Logic*).

To Nawang Gurung and Diki Bista, Sienna Craig, Mark Turin, Maya Daurio, and Jason Lampel—friends and colleagues in key endeavors.

To Thelma Carrillo, Marco Castillo, Jackie Alvarez, and the members of El Concejo de Los Pueblos Originarios—la lucha sigue.

To Coleman Donaldson, for timely assistance with N'ko.

To linguists George van Driem, Scott Delancey, Tom Owen-Smith, Chaofen Sun, Sun Hongkai, Peter Austin, Jim Matisoff, Randy LaPolla, Dominic Yu, and to my Linguistics colleagues at Columbia

(Meredith Landman, John McWhorter, and Bill Foley), as well as my teaching assistants (Matt Malone, Austin Dean, Rose Kim, and Emily Kohn) and inspiring students.

To those who supported the work materially and intellectually: the Endangered Languages Documentation Programme, especially Mandana Seyfeddinipur; the Gotham Center, especially Peter-Christian Aigner and Mike Wallace; New America, including Awista Ayub, Sarah Baline, and all my fellow fellows; National Geographic; the American Council of Learned Societies; the New York Foundation for the Arts; the National Endowment for the Humanities; and the Café Royal Cultural Foundation.

To MacDowell, the Yaddo Corporation, the Sitka Fellows Program, and Connie Casey and Harold Varmus for extraordinary gifts of time and space.

To the many other writers, artists, and thinkers met along the way.

To sustaining friends: Karan Mahajan, Nick Casey, Greg Wayne, Francesca Mari, Tom Wolf, Jack Chung, Alex Pasternack, Alex Dubilet, Jessie Hock, Tom Stammers, Paddy Bresnihan, Tehseen Noorani, Adam Forman, Michael Leibenluft, Jason Glick, Nick McDonell, John Kluge, Christine Mahoney, Tyson Reist, Michael Alpert, Maya Jasanoff, Sewell Chan, Angel Acosta, Michael Casper, Aaron Halegua, Zach Levine, Nick Frisch, Ben Knelman, Katherine Stirling, Adam Horowitz, Simon Shuster, Liz Skeen, Henry Rees-Sheridan, Natalie Galpern, Nicole Galpern, L. Lefkowitz, and many others.

To my parents.

To C. Hatakeyama, A. Durrell, and Café de los Fiordos.

To the essential workers.

To all language keepers.

# A Note on Sources

This book is focused on endangered, minority, and primarily oral languages about which little has been written, as used in a city about which too much has been written.

My primary debt is to the speakers of those languages and to the oral record they have transmitted. In addition to all the unrecorded moments and conversations, the thousands of video and audio recordings made by the Endangered Language Alliance since its founding in 2010 constitute a fundamental primary source that has made the writing of this book possible. There is no doing justice to the wild breadth of this ever-unfinished corpus, from two Koda men in Bangladesh talking about fishing to public health messages recorded by a Mam-speaking New Yorker. As of 2024, over seven hundred of these videos in around one hundred different languages are freely available on ELA's YouTube channel (youtube.com/@elalliance), for the most part edited and subtitled. These videos can also be found embedded within ELA's Languages of New York City map (www.languagemap.nyc). More raw materials are also gradually being made available at ELA's Internet Archive repository (https://archive.org/details/elalliance).

ELA's recordings have informed this book throughout, though I have only cited a handful here. I have been involved with the making of many of them, but Daniel Kaufman is the force behind even more, and above all they are the work of hundreds of speakers, as well as linguists, videographers, transcribers, and others. Nearly all the languages mentioned in this book are represented in one way or another. Take a spin around ELA's YouTube channel and have a listen.

In addition, there are now several extraordinary digital archives located around the world that are focused on preserving endangered-language materials and making them accessible to a variety of users through the internet. To appreciate these efforts, DELAMAN (Digital Endangered Languages and Musics Archives Network) is a good starting point. Among its members are the Endangered Language Archive (where my Trung and Seke recordings are housed), the Language Archive based at the Max Planck Institute and the Archive of the Indigenous Languages of Latin America, among others.

As for written sources, I am deeply indebted to hundreds of authors of very different kinds of texts, which are cited in the Notes where they come up. Below is a much more limited set of key sources which I have consulted repeatedly and can recommend as further, sometimes specialist, reading. They are listed alphabetically and by the chapter to which they are most connected:

## I. Thousands of Natural Experiments

Austin, Peter K. "Language Documentation 20 Years On." In *Endangered Languages and Languages in Danger: Issues of Ecology, Policy and Human Rights*, edited by Martin Pütz and Luna Filipović, 147–70. Amsterdam: John Benjamins, 2016.

Davis, J. L. "Resisting Rhetorics of Language Endangerment: Reclamation through Indigenous Language Survivance." *Language Documentation and Description* 14 (2017): 37–58.

Evans, Nicholas. *Words of Wonder: Endangered Languages and What They Tell Us*. 2nd ed. Hoboken: Wiley-Blackwell, 2021.

Evans, Nicholas, and Stephen C. Levinson. "The Myth of Language Universals: Language Diversity and Its Importance for Cognitive Science." *Behavioral and Brain Sciences* 32, no. 5 (2009): 429–48.

Hale, Ken. "Endangered Languages: On Endangered Languages and the Safeguarding of Diversity." *Language* 68, no. 1 (1992): 1–42.

Harrison, K. David. *When Languages Die: The Extinction of the World's Languages and the Erosion of Human Knowledge*. Oxford: Oxford University Press, 2008.

Heller-Roazen, Daniel. *Echolalias: On the Forgetting of Language.* Princeton: Princeton University Press, 2005.

Himmelmann, Nikolaus P. "Language Documentation: What Is It and What Is It Good for." *Essentials of Language Documentation* 178, no. 1 (2006): 1–30.

Kaufman, Daniel and Ross Perlin, "Invisibilization of Indigenous Languages in Urban Centers." In Global Language Justice, edited by Lydia H. Liu and Anupama Rao. With Charlotte A. Silverman. New York: Columbia University Press, 2023.

Kaufman, Daniel, and Ross Perlin. "Language Documentation in Diaspora Communities." In *The Oxford Handbook of Endangered Languages*, edited by Kenneth Rehg and Lyle Campbell, 399–418. Oxford: Oxford University Press, 2018.

Leonard, Wesley Y. "When Is an 'Extinct Language' Not Extinct?" In *Sustaining Linguistic Diversity: Endangered and Minority Languages and Language Varieties*, edited by Kendall A. King, Natalie Schilling-Estes, and Lyn Fogle, 23–33. Washington, DC: Georgetown University Press, 2008.

McDonnell, Bradley, Andrea L. Berez-Kroeker, and Gary Holton, eds. *Reflections on Language Documentation 20 Years after Himmelmann 1998* (Language Documentation & Conservation Special Publication 15). Honolulu: University of Hawai'i Press, 2018.

Nettle, Daniel, and Suzanne Romaine. *Vanishing Voices: The Extinction of the World's Languages*. Oxford: Oxford University Press, 2000.

Perley, Bernard C. "Zombie Linguistics: Experts, Endangered Languages and the Curse of Undead Voices." *Anthropological Forum* 22, no. 2 (2012): 133–49.

Perlin, Ross. "Radical Linguistics in an Age of Extinction." *Dissent* 61, no. 3 (2014): 70–75.

Perlin, Ross, Daniel Kaufman, Mark Turin, Maya Daurio, Sienna Craig, and Jason Lampel. "Mapping Urban Linguistic Diversity in New York City: Motives, Methods, Tools, and Outcomes." *Language Documentation and Conservation* 15 (2021): 458–90.

Treuer, Anton. *The Language Warrior's Handbook: How to Keep Our Languages Alive No Matter the Odds*. St. Paul: Minnesota Historical Society Press, 2020.

## II. Past

Andriani, Luigi, Ross Perlin, and Daniel Kaufman. "*Dialetti* in Diaspora: Loss and Retention in Italian New York." In *Italian(s) Abroad: Italian Language and Migration in the Cities of the World*, edited by Francesco Goglia and John Hajek. Berlin and Boston: De Gruyter, forthcoming.

Bayor, Ronald H., and Timothy Meagher, eds. *The New York Irish*. Baltimore: Johns Hopkins University Press, 1997.

Benson, Kathleen, and Philip M. Kayal. *A Community of Many Worlds: Arab Americans in New York City*. New York: Museum of the City of New York, 2002.

Bercovici, Konrad, *Around the World in New York*. New York: The Century Company, 1924.

Binder, Frederick, and David Reimers. *All Nations under Heaven: An Ethnic and Racial History of New York City*. New York: Columbia University Press, 1996.

Burrows, Edwin G., and Mike Wallace. *Gotham: A History of New York City to 1898*. Oxford: Oxford University Press, 1999.

Campanella, Thomas J. *Brooklyn: The Once and Future City*. Princeton: Princeton University Press, 2020.

Chen, Hsiang-Shui. *Chinatown No More: Taiwan Immigrants in Contemporary New York*. Ithaca: Cornell University Press, 1992.

England, Sarah. *Afro Central Americans in New York City*. Gainesville: University Press of Florida, 2006.

Feliciano-Santos, Sherina. "How Do You Speak Taíno? Indigenous Activism and Linguistic Practices in Puerto Rico." *Journal of Linguistic Anthropology* 27, no. 1 (2017): 4–21.

Foner, Nancy. *From Ellis Island to JFK: New York's Two Great Waves of Immigration*. New Haven and London: Yale University Press and New York: Russell Sage Foundation Press, 2000.

Foner, Nancy, ed. *New Immigrants in New York*. New York: Columbia University Press, 2001.

Foner, Nancy, ed. *One Out of Three: Immigrant New York in the Twenty-First Century*. New York: Columbia University Press, 2013.

Gabaccia, Donna. *From Sicily to Elizabeth Street: Housing and Social Change among Italian Immigrants, 1880–1930*. Albany: State University of New York Press, 1984.

García, Ofelia, and Joshua Fishman, eds. *The Multilingual Apple: Languages in New York City*. Berlin and New York: De Gruyter Mouton, 2002.

Gehring, Charles Theodor. *The Dutch Language in Colonial New York: An Investigation of a Language in Decline and Its Relationship to Social Change*. Bloomington: Indiana University, 1973.

Jackson, Kenneth T. *The Encyclopedia of New York City*. New Haven and London: Yale University Press, 1995.

Kasinitz, Philip, John Mollenkopf, and Mary Waters, eds. *Becoming New Yorkers: Ethnographies of the New Second Generation*. New York: Russell Sage Foundation, 2004.

Newman, Michael. *New York City English*. Berlin and Boston: De Gruyter, 2014.

Noordegraaf, Jan. "A Language Lost: The Case of Leeg Duits ("Low Dutch")." *Academic Journal of Modern Philology* 2 (2013): 91–108.

Saed, Zohra. "Samsa on Sheepshead Bay: Tracing Uzbek Foodprints in Southern Brooklyn." In *Eating Asian America: A Food Studies Reader*, edited by Robert Ji-Song Ku, Martin F. Manalansan, and Anita Mannur. New York: NYU Press, 2013.

Sivertsen, Karen. "Babel on the Hudson: Community Formation in Dutch Manhattan." PhD diss., Duke University, 2007.

Wallace, Mike. *Greater Gotham: A History of New York City from 1898 to 1919*. Oxford: Oxford University Press, 2017.

## III. Present

### Rasmina - सेके, སེ་སྐད་ (Seke)

Craig, Sienna. "Migration, Social Change, Health, and the Realm of the Possible: Women's Stories between Nepal and New York." *Anthropology and Humanism* 36, no. 2 (2011): 193–214.

Craig, Sienna. "Place, Work and Identity between Mustang, Nepal and New York City." *Studies in Nepali History and Society* 7, no. 2 (2002): 355–403.

Craig, Sienna. *The Ends of Kinship: Connecting Himalayan Lives Between Nepal and New York*. Seattle: University of Washington Press, 2020.

Gurung, Nawang, Ross Perlin, Daniel Kaufman, Mark Turin, and Sienna Craig. "Orality and Mobility: Documenting Himalayan Voices in New York City." *Verge: Studies in Global Asias* 4, no. 2 (2018): 64–80.

Honda, Isao. "A Sketch of Tangbe." In *Themes in Himalayan Languages and Linguistics*, edited by Mark Turin and Tej Ratna Kansakar, 49–64. Heidelberg and Kathmandu: South Asia Institute and Tribhuvan Univerisity, 2003.

Honda, Isao. "Grammaticalization of Deictic Motion Verbs in Seke." In *Himalayan Languages: Past and Present*, edited by Anju Saxena, 285–310. Berlin and New York: De Gruyter Mouton, 2011.

Honda, Isao. "Seke Phonology: A Comparative Study of Three Seke Dialects." *Linguistics of the Tibeto-Burman Area* 25, no. 1 (2002): 191–210.

Ramble, Charles. *The Navel of the Demoness: Tibetan Buddhism and Civil Religion in Highland Nepal*. Oxford: Oxford University Press, 2008.

Sherpa, P. Y. "Sustaining Sherpa Language and Culture in New York," *Book 2.0* 9, no. 1–2 (2019): 19–29.

Van Driem, George. "Trans-Himalayan." In *Trans-Himalayan Linguistics*, edited by N. Hill and T. Owen-Smith, 11–40. Berlin and Boston: De Gruyter, 2014.

## Husniya - X̌ik (Wakhi)

Bashir, Elena. 2009. "Wakhi." I*n The Iranian Languages*, edited by Gernot Windfuhr, 825–62. London and New York: Routledge, 2009.

Grjunberg, Aleksandr L., and Ivan M. Steblin-Kamenskij. *Vaxanskij jazyk.* (*Jazyki Vostočnogo Gindukusha*.) Moscow: Akademia Nauk SSSR, 1976.

Lorimer, D. L. R. *The Wakhi Language*. London: University of London, 1958.

Obrtelová, Jaroslava. "From Oral to Written: A Text-Linguistic Study of Wakhi Narratives." PhD diss., Uppsala Universitet, 2019.

Paxalina, Tatjana N. *Pamirskie Jazyki*. (*Jazyki Narodov Azii i Afriki*.) Moscow: Akademia Nauk SSSR, 1969.

Perlin, Ross, Daniel Kaufman, Habib Borjian, and Husniya Khujamyorova. "Wakhi in New York: Multilingualism and Language Contact in a Pamiri Diaspora Community." In *Iranian Heritage and Minority Languages*, edited by Anousha Sedighi, 293–326. Berlin and Boston: De Gruyter, 2023.

## Boris - ייִדיש (Yiddish)

Bleaman, I. L. "Outcomes of Minority Language Maintenance: Variations and Change in New York Yiddish." PhD diss., New York University, 2018.

Fishman, J. A. *Yiddish in America: Socio-Linguistic Description and Analysis*. The Hague: Indiana University and Mouton, 1965.

Katz, Dovid. *Words on Fire: The Unfinished Story of Yiddish*. New York: Basic Books, 2007.

Nove, C. R. "The Erasure of Hasidic Yiddish from Twentieth Century Yiddish Linguistics." *Journal of Jewish Languages* 6, no. 1 (2018): 109–41.

Perlin, Ross. "What Was the *kultur-tuer*?" *In geveb*, August 2015. www.ingeveb.org/blog/what-was-the-kultur-tuer.

Sandler, Boris. *Lamed-vovnikes fun mayn zikorn* [The Hidden Righteous Ones in My Memory]. New York: Forverts Oysgabe, 2010.

Sandler, Boris. *Mit a shlikhes keyn Moskve* [With a mission to Moscow]. New York: Yiddish Branzhe, 2022.

Schaechter-Viswanath, G.,and P. Glasser, eds. *Comprehensive English Yiddish Dictionary (Based on the Lexical Research of Mordkhe Schaechter)*. Bloomington: Indiana University Press,

Shandler, Jeffrey. *Adventures in Yiddishland: Postvernacular Language and Culture*. Berkeley: University of California Press, 2005.

## Ibrahima - ߒߞߏ (N'ko)

Diané, Baba Mamadi. *Dictionnaire Kandjamadi Franç-N'KO (Kodofolan Kanjamadi Franç.-N'ko)*. Cairo: Kanjamadi, 2014.

Donaldson, Coleman. "Clear Language: Script, Register and the N'ko Movement of Manding-Speaking West Africa." PhD diss., University of Pennsylvania, 2017.

Donaldson, Coleman. "Linguistic and Civic Refinement in the N'ko Movement of Manding-Speaking West Africa." *Signs and Society* 7, no. 2 (2019): 156–85.

Donaldson, Coleman. "Orthography, Standardization, and Register: The Case of Manding." In *Standardizing Minority Languages*, edited by Pia Lane, James Costa, and Haley De Korne, 175–99. London and New York: Routledge, 2017.

Donaldson, Coleman. "The Role of Islam, Ajami Writings, and Educational Reform in Sulemaana Kantè's N'ko." *African Studies Review* 63, no. 3 (2020): 462–86.

Kane, Ousmane Oumar. *The Homeland Is the Arena: Religion, Transnationalism, and the Integration of Senegalese Immigrants in America*. Oxford: Oxford University Press, 2011.

Oyler, Dianne W. "Re-Inventing Oral Tradition: The Modern Epic of Souleymane Kanté." *Research in African Literatures* 33, no. 1 (2002): 75–93.

Oyler, Dianne W. "The N'ko Alphabet as a Vehicle of Indigenist Historiography." *History in Africa* 24 (1997): 239–56.

Stoller, Paul. *Money Has No Smell: The Africanization of New York City*. Chicago: University of Chicago Press, 2010.

Stoller, Paul. *Yaya's Story*. Chicago: University of Chicago Press, 2021.

Vydrine, V. *Manding-English Dictionary (Maninka, Bamana)*. Vol. 1. St. Petersburg: Dimitry Bulanin Publishing House, 1999.

Wyrod, Christopher. "A Social Orthography of Identity: The N'ko Literacy Movement in West Africa." *International Journal of the Sociology of Language* 2008, no. 192 (2008): 27–44.

## Irwin - Nahuatl

Hill, Jane H., and Kenneth C. Hill. *Speaking Mexicano: Dynamics of Syncretic Language in Central Mexico*. Tucson: University of Arizona Press, 1986.

Kaufman, Daniel. "The Mixtec Language in New York: Vitality, Discrimination, and Identity." In *Multilingualism and Pluricentricity: A Tale of Many Cities*, edited by John Hajek, Catrin Norrby, Heinz L. Kretzenbacher, and Doris Schuepach. Berlin and Boston: De Gruyter, forthcoming.

Pribilsky, Jason. *La Chulla Vida: Gender, Migration and the Family in Andean Ecuador and New York City*. Syracuse: Syracuse University Press, 2007.

Remeseira, Claudio Iván, ed. *Hispanic New York: A Sourcebook*. New York: Columbia University Press, 2010.

Smith, Robert C. *Mexican New York: Transnational Lives of New Immigrants*. Berkeley: University of California Press, 2006.

### Karen - Lunaape (Lenape)

Baker, Joe, Hadrien Coumans, and Joel Whitney. *Lenapehoking: An Anthology*. New York: The Lenape Center and Brooklyn Public Library, 2023.

Goddard, Ives. *Delaware Verbal Morphology: A Descriptive and Comparative Study*. London: Taylor and Francis, 1979.

Goddard, Ives. "Linguistic Variation in a Small Speech Community: The Personal Dialects of Moraviantown Delaware." *Anthropological Linguistics* 52, No. 1 (2010): 1–48.

Goddard, Ives. "Pidgin Delaware." *Creole Language Library* 17 (1996): 43–98.

Goddard, Ives. "The Origin and Meaning of the Name Manhattan.'" *New York History* 91.4 (Fall 2010): 277–93.

Grumet, Robert. *Manhattan to Minisink: American Indian Place Names of Greater New York and Vicinity*. Norman: University of Oklahoma Press, 2013.

Grumet, Robert. *The Munsee Indians: A History*. Norman: University of Oklahoma Press, 2009.

O'Meara, John. *Delaware-English, English-Delaware Dictionary*. Toronto: University of Toronto Press, 1996.

O'Meara, John. "Intransitive Verbs with Secondary Objects in Munsee Delaware." *Algonquian Papers-Archive* 23 (1992).

Soderlund, J. R. *Lenape Country: Delaware Valley Society before William Penn*. Philadelphia: University of Pennsylvania Press, 2014.

Weslager, C. A. *The Delaware Indians: A History*. New Brunswick: Rutgers University Press, 1999.

### IV. Future

García, Ofelia. "Educating New York's Bilingual Children: Constructing a Future from the Past." *International Journal of Bilingual Education and Bilingualism* 14, no. 2 (2011): 133–53.

Jones, Reece. *White Borders: The History of Race and Immigration in the United States from Chinese Exclusion to the Border Wall.* Boston: Beacon Press, 2021.

Kaufman, Daniel, and Ross Perlin. 2019. "Surveying Indigenous Latin American Languages in NYC: A report to the NYC Department of Health." Endangered Language Alliance. www.elalliance.org.

# Notes

## Preface: The Limits of My Language

1. I use the term Dominant American English because Standard English, General English, American English, and US English all risk naturalizing the dominance of this particular variety, the origins of which are still much debated.
2. The "critical period hypothesis" remains a contested topic in language acquisition studies, with some scholars suggesting a range of ages, others pointing to a suite of factors only loosely correlated with age, and still others disputing that there is any critical period at all. A classic early articulation of the theory is Eric Lenneberg, *Biological Foundations of Language* (New York: Wiley, 1967).
3. Most students in Europe begin learning a second language by the age of nine. In China, the study of English begins around the same age, if not earlier.
4. Linguists would conventionally use angle brackets here, e.g. <r>, to represent an orthographic convention, whereas a phonetic representation of the actual sound would be in brackets, e.g. [ʁ], and between slashes if discussed as a phoneme (within the language's entire sound system), e.g. /ʁ/. Begging forgiveness from all linguists, I am going to use /. . ./ throughout for all of these simply to set apart from the surrounding text, not to comment on the orthographic, phonetic, or phonemic status of the segment under discussion.
5. See Richard Scholar, *Émigrés: French Words That Turned English* (Princeton: Princeton University Press, 2022).
6. Chinese is cited as the ultimate difficult language—a paragon of incomprehensibility—in a range of languages that includes Finnish, Hebrew, Hungarian, Tagalog, and others. In Chinese, one can say that something is as hard as 天書 tiānshū, *heavenly script*. See the delightful Arnold Rosenberg, "The Hardest Natural Languages," *Lingvisticae Investigationes* III, no. 2 (1979): 323–39.
7. Jerry Norman, *Chinese* (Cambridge, UK: Cambridge University Press, 1988), 1. "Few language names are as all-encompassing as Chinese."

   Here and elsewhere I use the traditional characters which I started on and which are still standard in Taiwan, Hong Kong, and many overseas Chinese communities, as opposed to the simplified characters adopted in mainland China, which usually have fewer strokes. In New York, both systems are in use.
8. Perry Link, *An Anatomy of Chinese* (Cambridge, MA: Harvard University Press, 2013), 245.
9. Sun Hongkai's work has spanned an extraordinary range of languages spoken within China's present-day borders, including Trung and the related language Anong. A rare work of his that has been translated, annotated, and supplemented by Fengxiang Li,

Ela Thurgood, and Graham Thurgood is G. Liu and Hongkai Sun, *A Grammar of Anong: Language Death under Intense Contact* (Boston: Brill, 2009).

In 2006–07, I studied for an MA in Language Documentation and Description at the Endangered Languages Academic Programme at SOAS, a program unique in having this focus at the time.

10. Trung is in the Nungish branch of the Tibeto-Burman family, which includes several little-known languages straddling the China-Myanmar border. See Ross Perlin, "A Grammar of Trung," *Himalayan Linguistics* 18, no. 2 (2019): 4–8.
11. Trans-Himalayan (van Driem, "Trans-Himalayan") is the most recent and neutral term for the language family, which many linguists have traditionally referred to as Sino-Tibetan (while using the term Tibeto-Burman for a subgroup of this same family). No one disputes that all Sinitic (i.e., Chinese) languages are part of this family, but there is disagreement over how to describe their place in it and, more broadly, how language families should be named, whether after well-known languages within them, or more neutrally.
12. Linguists, like anthropologists, write fieldwork memoirs, e.g., Don Kulick, *A Death in the Rainforest: How a Language and a Way of Life Came to an End in Papua New Guinea* (New York: Algonquin Books, 2019), and Daniel Everett, *Don't Sleep, There Are Snakes: Life and Language in the Amazonian Jungle* (London: Profile Books, 2009).
13. Because there is no /v/ consonant, /v/ in used for the Trung practical orthography is the neutral schwa vowel. See Perlin, "A Grammar of Trung," 66–68.

## I. Thousands of Natural Experiments

### A Room on Eighteenth Street

1. Officially the Joshua Fishman Library, it consists of the late linguist's collection of sociolinguistics books, recently donated to ELA by his family.
2. The Jehovah's Witnesses website, in over one thousand languages, is by far the most multilingual. For a study of how few languages are "ascending" in the digital realm, see András Kornai, "Digital Language Death," *PLoS ONE* 8, no. 10 (2013), e77056. Progress has been made in the last decade, but there are no signs that the internet will ever come close to fully representing real-world linguistic diversity.
3. The oft-cited figure is that one language is lost (i.e., a last native speaker passes away) every two weeks. A more recent estimate from the Catalogue of Endangered Languages (ELCat) found that the rate may be closer to one every three months. Neither number can be precise given all the complexities involved in defining both what is a language and who counts as a "last speaker", not to mention how little is concretely known about the linguistic situation in key parts of the world.
4. One source of this oft-cited statistic is probably David Crystal, *Language Death* (Cambridge, UK: Cambridge University Press, 2000), 14. Again, exact numbers will vary depending on definitions and speaker numbers, but the broad strokes here are undeniable.
5. As with spoken languages, there are fundamental challenges involved in enumerating sign languages, and even more so given how little is known about them by outsiders. As of this writing, Ethnologue (David M. Eberhard, Gary F. Simons, and Charles D. Fennig eds., *Ethnologue: Languages of the World*, 25th ed. [Dallas: SIL International,

2022], www.ethnologue.com) lists 159 sign languages while Glottolog, with different criteria, lists 215 (Harald Hammarström, Robert Forkel, Martin Haspelmath, and Sebastian Bank. Glottolog 4.7. Leipzig: Max Planck Institute for Evolutionary Anthropology, 2022, www.glottolog.org). It's unclear how many are in active use. See also James Woodward, "Endangered Sign Languages," in *The Oxford Handbook of Endangered Languages*, ed. Kenneth L. Rehg and Lyle Campbell (Oxford: Oxford University Press, 2018), 168–202.

6. Hyperdiversity (or deep diversity) here refers straightforwardly to the significant quantitative increase in the number of language varieties and registers known and used in cities today. For the more theoretical concept of superdiversity, more commonly used in Europe, see Steven Vertovec, "Super-Diversity and Its Implications," *Ethnic and Racial Studies* 30 (2007): 1024–54; Jan Blommaert and Ben Rampton, *Language and Superdiversity* (London: Routledge, 2015), 31–58.

   Superdiversity can be a useful term for indexing the different dimensions of contemporary migration, but so far (among other shortcomings) has done little to illuminate the dynamics of urban linguistic diversity and bring visibility to speakers of endangered, minority, and Indigenous languages in cities. See Nancy Foner, Jan Willem Duyvendak, and Philip Kasinitz. "Introduction: Super-Diversity in Everyday Life,". *Ethnic and Racial Studies*, 42, no. 1 (2019): 1–16. See also Daniel Kaufman and Ross Perlin, "Invisibilization of Indigenous Languages in Urban Centers," in Global Language Justice, edited by Lydia H. Liu and Anupama Rao. With Charlotte A. Silverman. New York: Columbia University Press, 2023.

7. In fact, the whole region spoke Lenape, or a spectrum of closely related dialects now grouped under that name. Here and throughout, for clarity, we follow the practice of most speakers and researchers in calling the language Lenape at the broadest level (with Lunaape the spelling in the contemporary orthography itself). As will be explained, it can be more precise to use the later term Munsee when referring specifically to the northern varieties that would have been used in the New York area and are used today in Canada. Lenni Lenape is no longer used. Delaware is a name given by European settlers, occasionally still used.
8. In their important ethnic and racial history of the city, *All Nations under Heaven*, Binder and Reimers "highlight those groups which, because of their numbers, time of arrival, and significance, illustrate clearly the major themes in our story."
9. For example, in a talk called "Greenberg's 16th Slain in the Bronx," Daniel used his fieldwork with speakers of Garifuna in the Bronx to show how a supposedly universal principle proposed by linguist Joseph Greenberg (his "16th Universal") doesn't hold up.
10. Requests of all sorts also come to ELA from courts, translation companies, artists, filmmakers, etc.
11. ELA's way of documenting the impacts was to commission, post, and create English summaries for daily ten-minute audio diaries from speakers of a dozen Indigenous Himalayan and Latin American languages. Together with later interviews including community leaders, there were ultimately hundreds of entries totaling over one hundred hours: an amchi, *Tibetan doctor*, trying to help frightened patients; an expectant mother talking about being pregnant during such a time in Loke; a Mayan deliverista doing mutual aid work, among others. See Ross Perlin, Nawang Gurung, Maya Daurio, Sienna Craig, Daniel Kaufman, and Mark Turin, "Who Will Care for the Care Worker? The COVID-19 Diaries of a Sherpa Nurse in New York City," *Issues*,

June 22, 2021; Sienna Craig, Nawang T. Gurung, Ross Perlin, Maya Daurio, Daniel Kaufman, Mark Turin, and Kunchog Tseten, "Global Pandemic, Translocal Medicine: The COVID-19 Diaries of a Tibetan Physician in New York City," *Asian Medicine* 16 (2021): 58–88.

## A Home in Queens

1. UN Missions can be important, more "official" sites for small language communities without much other infrastructure. Of course, thousands of UN employees, mission staff, and related others live all over the city. On the one hand, there are the nearby residential towers favored by diplomats and officials—like the one where the Israeli ambassador cheerfully shares the elevator with his counterparts from Iran, Iraq, Italy, and Saudi Arabia (one of whose four wives is Japanese but speaks perfect Arabic, according to the Russian doorman), while discreet US–North Korea negotiations take place in a private apartment.

   On the other hand, there is a place like Roosevelt Island, which may seem like the opposite of an "ethnic neighborhood" but is in fact a highly multilingual zone where many UN employees live. When the UN was initially based in Queens after its founding, many lived in Parkway Village, a purpose-built complex of 109 buildings still standing in Briarwood. One need it served was to provide housing for the many employees and delegates of color given the racial segregation of the broader housing market at the time.

   It's important to note too that even "geographically restricted nonimmigrants" otherwise barred from entering the US, such as Muammar Gaddafi, Saddam Hussein, and members of the Iranian diplomatic corps, receive special C-2 visas enabling access to the UN. They just have to stay within a twenty-five-mile radius of the curiously determined "mile zero" of Columbus Circle.
2. To give one example, among those who died was Jupiter Yambem, who was born in Manipur in northeast India and was working at Windows on the World on September 11, 2001. Yambem was a founder of the North American Manipur Association, an organization representing speakers of the minority language Meitei which was originally based in Brooklyn but is now in Queens.
3. The language referred to as Serbo-Croatian in the former Yugoslavia was spoken natively by Serbs, Croatians, Bosnians, and Montenegrins, as well as by most others in the country to varying extents. Since the country's breakup, it has become customary to refer to these as separate languages or, awkwardly, as Bosnian-Croatian-Serbian-Montenegrin (BCSM). There are certainly real differences between them, especially in writing where those differences may now be widening, but there is also typically a high degree of mutual intelligibility.
4. Val di Non today is part of the Italian province of Trento/Trentino, but was under Austro-Hungarian rule through the First World War. The first Nonesi came to the US in the early twentieth century and settled near the Hudson River piers on Manhattan's West Side before moving to north Brooklyn, Ridgewood, and beyond—parallel to but separate from Italian communities from which many felt distinct. Small communities of several dozen families kept the community going through church, choral groups, bocce games, and family visiting on Sundays. Other Nonesi communities formed in places like Hazelton, Pennsylvania, and Roxbury, Wyoming, very different from Italian Americans. See John W. Cole and Eric Robert Wolf, *The Hidden Frontier: Ecology and Ethnicity in an Alpine Valley* (New York: Academic Press, 1974).

5. See Martha Hutter, *Gottscheerisch: An Introduction to the Language of the Gottschee Germans* (self-pub., 1994).

   The most promising situation for the language seems to be in New York, where many have passive knowledge of the language and some use it at home. The relative absence of Standard German is probably one key factor. Some Gottscheer New Yorkers now in their fifties learned it from their parents, who spoke only Gottscheerish, according to Anja Moric, "The Maintenance of Gottscheerish, the Dialect of Gottschee Germans in Slovenia, Austria, Germany, Canada and the USA," *Razprave in Gradivo: Revija za Narodnostna Vprasanja* 61 (2010): 92–119.
6. At Morscher's Pork Store it's now often Polish on both sides of the counter but Standard German on the beautiful old sign out front: Tischlein Deck Dich! (*Table, Deck Yourself!*), a line from a famous Brothers Grimm fairy tale about a magically self-catering table.
7. The soccer field is Metropolitan Oval.
8. This is Valentino Food Market.
9. Along with Yorkville in Manhattan, Ridgewood was one of the most concentrated German neighborhoods in the country and home to various organizations sympathetic to the Nazi party, like the Efedende (*Friends of the New Germany*). In April 1934, five thousand people rallied at Ridgewood Grove Arena in support of boycotting Jewish merchants who were themselves boycotting Nazi Germany. Five years later, in his article "Pull His Whiskers!" A. J. Liebling describes an evening of staged wrestling in the same arena, with ethnic, nationalist, and racist prejudices on full display.
10. For the case of a Kosovar-Polish romance in Brooklyn, where the two lovers navigate intelligibility between Polish and Serbo-Croatian, see Stacy Sullivan, *Be Not Afraid, For You Have Sons in America: How a Brooklyn Roofer Helped Lure the US into the Kosovo War* (New York: St. Martin's Press, 2004), 85–86. The book describes how Florin Krasniqi, a Brooklyn roofer, became an important player in raising funds, running guns, and bringing New York Kosovar volunteers to the Kosovar Liberation Army in the 1990s.
11. A number of scholars have taken up this idea: "One feature of Hackney and other super-diverse areas that may be especially likely to lead to positive intergroup social relations is the absence of any one majority national origin or ethnoracial group that dominates numerically, culturally, and politically." Nancy Foner, Jan Willem Duyvendak, and Philip Kasinitz, "Introduction: Super-Diversity in Everyday Life," 8.

## A Snapshot of Babel

1. See Ross Perlin, Daniel Kaufman, Mark Turin, Maya Daurio, Sienna Craig, and Jason Lampel, "Mapping Linguistic Diversity." Unsurprisingly given the importance of language in Canadian politics, the Canadian census asks several considerably more granular questions about language. In the US Census, the preeminence of English is assumed from the get-go, and the other languages into which the census is translated are all major ones. Response rates are lowest precisely in the urban areas where linguistic diversity is highest, reflecting a basic lack of trust that may be tied to past experiences of persecution or marginalization, as well as current immigration status. In 2020, ELA worked with New York City's official census outreach efforts in an attempt to mitigate some of these problems.
2. See the Languages of New York City map at www.languagemap.nyc. Typical American Community Survey data for New York lists just over one hundred "languages,"

of which the actual component languages of nearly a fifth are unclear (e.g., "Other Specified Native American"). By my estimation, this data may be broadly accurate, though not without serious problems, for the largest sixty or so languages. Even the most comprehensive register for the metropolitan area, a special census data dive made over a decade ago, listed fewer than two hundred "languages."

Another guerrilla census worth noting was "Wordsearch—A Translinguistic Sculpture" created by the German artist Karin Sander, which listed 62,500 words from the different mother tongues of 250 New Yorkers. All were arranged in small-print columns on a Business section spread in the October 4, 2002, issue of the *New York Times*, next to and almost indistinguishable from the current mutual fund prices. Each word donated was supposed to have a special significance for the speaker and was then translated into every one of the other 249 languages. Going to embassies was one way to gather the words, I learned from Franziska Lamprecht, who worked on the project, "but a great advantage of New York embassies is that in about sixty percent of them there's someone from the Philippines sitting behind the reception desk—and in the Philippines they speak 172 different languages."

3. A community should reserve the right to remain invisible, but also to dictate the terms of its own visibility. Locations were "fuzzed" and not always directly referenced as one way of addressing privacy concerns. No group has asked to be left out of ELA's language map, and most have embraced it. For some, it can be a revelatory experience to see their language accorded any kind of public recognition. One time we met a young Senegalese-French man, new to the city, who was moved to find his heritage language, Baïnounk, in the very first place he looked, among the Senegalese languages in the Bronx. He eagerly called over his wife, who is from Congo-Brazzaville and speaks Monokutuba, a language not then on the map and of which she may be the only speaker in the city. Another time, on a street corner in the Bronx, a roughly ten-year-old kid started closely scanning the section of the map for where we were standing. "It begins with a G," he said, trying to remember the name of the language that his family, apparently, is not passing on to him. But he found it there with the force of discovery: "Garifuna!"
4. See Tarry Hum, *Making a Global Immigrant Neighborhood: Brooklyn's Sunset Park* (Philadelphia: Temple University Press, 2014).
5. For a good overview of what constitutes a "Jewish language," see Sarah Bunin Benor, "Towards a New Understanding of Jewish Language in the Twenty-First Century," *Religion Compass* 2, no. 6 (2008): 1062–80. Among those spoken along Ocean Parkway, arguably the most diversely Jewish street in the world, are Juhuri, Bukhori, Ladino, Judeo-Shirazi, and various forms of Judeo-Arabic, though most are shifting fast to English, Hebrew, Russian, or Persian and many can get by in Arabic, Azeri, Tajik, Uzbek, and other languages. Others are more common in Queens and on Long Island. Biblical Hebrew and Talmudic Aramaic are the languages of countless synagogues and yeshivas, and "Yeshivish" is the name for a new style of speaking that seamlessly mixes these liturgical languages with English and Yiddish.
6. Some academics favor the term "minoritized" over "minority" as a reminder that many groups are not or were not minorities in their own territories, but came to be so after they were colonized by, subsumed by, or otherwise encountered larger populations.
7. Jan Morris, *Manhattan '45* (Baltimore: Johns Hopkins University Press, 1998), 175.
8. A historian of immigration calls it "America's quintessential immigrant city, with a long history of ethnic succession and immigrant inclusion," characterized by extreme

heterogeneity. Nancy Foner, "How Exceptional Is New York? Migration and Multiculturalism in the Empire City," *Ethnic and Racial Studies* 30, no. 6 (2007): 999–1023.

9. Immigrants likely constituted a majority in earlier periods, but a recorded twentieth-century peak of just over 40 percent was reached in 1910. After bottoming out in 1970 under 20 percent, the foreign-born percentage has again climbed over 35 percent. See Arun Peter Lobo and Joseph J. Salvo, *The Newest New Yorkers: Characteristics of the City's Foreign-Born Population* (City of New York, Department of City Planning, Office of Immigrant Affairs, 2013), 10.
10. Yet "the outlook associated with New York's cosmopolitan experience has been unable to establish itself as an American standard." See Thomas Bender, "New York as a Center of Difference," in *The Unfinished City* (New York: The New Press, 2002), 185–98.
11. Suketu Mehta, *This Land Is Our Land: An Immigrant's Manifesto* (New York: Vintage, 2020).
12. There are linguists starting to look at (greater) Paris the way ELA has looked at New York, specifically the team behind Langues et Grammaires en Île-de-France (LGIDF), consisting of Rebekah Rast, Elena Soare, and Anne Zribi-Hertz, with connections to several local universities, institutes, and archives. See www.lgidf.cnrs.fr.
13. See Panikos Panayi, *Migrant City: A New History of London* (New Haven and London: Yale University Press, 2020).
14. The British Nationality Act of 1948 was one such policy. Much though not all of postcolonial literature and thought, however radical, has taken place in colonial languages—a sociolinguistic reality which has even been justified as subversive. "To conquer English may be to complete the process of making ourselves free," as Salman Rushdie put it. Those leading the charge were already the products of a profound linguistic shift, usually cut off from a linguistic past which itself had remained chronically underdeveloped.
15. Ingrid Piller, "Dubai: Language in the Ethnocratic, Corporate and Mobile City," in *Urban Sociolinguistics*, eds. Dick Smakman and Patrick Heinrich (London: Routledge, 2017), 77–94.
16. Gordon Mathews, *Ghetto at the Center of the World: Chungking Mansions, Hong Kong* (Chicago: University of Chicago Press, 2011).
17. For the work of ELA's Toronto branch, see www.elalliance.com.
18. For a richly detailed portrait of São Gabriel, see Sarah Shulist, *Transforming Indigeneity: Urbanization and Language Revitalization in the Brazilian Amazon* (Toronto: University of Toronto Press, 2018). Despite São Gabriel's substantial and very linguistically diverse Indigenous population, the prospects for Indigenous languages there are not encouraging.
19. For the Multilingual Manchester project, see mlm.humanities.manchester.ac.uk. For Graz, see multilingual.uni-graz.at.
20. See, for example, Catherine Besteman, *Making Refuge: Somali Bantu Refugees and Lewiston, Maine* (Chapel Hill: Duke University Press, 2016).
21. Panethnicity occurs "among immigrant groups who have entered host societies with regional, national origin, and language differences and, over time, have come together and developed panethnic identities." See Dina Okamoto and G. Cristina Mora, "Panethnicity," *Annual Review of Sociology* 40 (2014): 219–39.
22. United Nations Human Settlements Programme and United Nations Office of the High Commissioner for Human Rights, "Urban Indigenous Peoples and Migration:

A Review of Policies, Programmes, and Practices" (Nairobi: UN-HABITAT and OHCHR, 2010).

23. The city is an ever-changing human concentrate, wrote E. B. White, "peculiarly constructed to absorb almost anything that comes along." He meant the enormous events that happen every day, but this could just as well apply to the appearance and disappearance of languages and communities over decades. E. B. White, *Here Is New York* (1949; repr., New York: The Little Bookroom, 1999).

## A Brief Guide to Radical Linguistics

1. Nicholas Evans, *Dying Words, Endangered Languages and What They Have to Teach Us*, (New York: Wiley-Blackwell, 2009) 1–11.
2. In linguistics, as in other fields, there are "splitters" and "lumpers" who tend to see more difference and more similarity, respectively. These statistics draw on Eberhard et al., Ethnologue, still the most comprehensive database despite its issues, which lists 7,151 "known living languages" as of this writing. Glottolog, an emerging alternative even more in the "splitter" camp, lists over eight thousand "languoids," including families, languages, and dialects, without trying to provide estimates of speaker numbers.
3. The quote is usually attributed to Yiddish linguist Max Weinreich, who recounted and commented on it. See Alexander Maxwell, "When Theory Is a Joke: The Weinreich Witticism in Linguistics," Beiträge zur Geschichte der Sprachwissenschaft, 28, no. 2 (2018): 263–92.
4. See Raf Van Rooy, *Language or Dialect?: The History of a Conceptual Pair* (Oxford: Oxford University Press, 2020). Though the terminology may vary, colonial notions of "language" (official, standardized, and written) versus "dialect" (no official status, unstandardized, primarily oral) are very much alive in many of New York's immigrant communities. While possibly finding some support in the way these terms are used in American contexts, these notions seem to draw most readily on distinctions made in immigrants' societies of origin, e.g., *lengua/lenguaje* versus *dialecto* in Mexico, *lingua* versus *dialetto* in Italian contexts, 語言 *yǔyán* versus 方言 *fāngyán* (and sometimes 土話 *tǔhuà*) in China, etc. The linguistic criterion of mutual intelligibility often plays little or no role in these distinctions.
5. Roman Jakobson, "On Linguistic Aspects of Translation," in *On Translation*, ed. Reuben Brower (Cambridge, MA: Harvard University Press, 1959), 236.
6. Harold Hammarstrom, "Linguistic Diversity and Language Evolution," *Journal of Language Evolution* 1, no. 1 (2016): 19–29.
7. See Tom Güldemann, Patrick McConvell, and Richard A. Rhodes, eds., *The Language of Hunter-Gatherers* (Cambridge, UK: Cambridge University Press, 2020).
8. See Ulrike Zeshan and Connie de Vos eds., *Sign Languages in Village Communities: Anthropological and Linguistic Insights* (Berlin and Boston: De Gruyter, 2012).
9. Rebecca Green, "A Grammar of Gurr-goni (North Central Arnhem Land)" (PhD thesis, Australian National University, 1995).
10. See Douglas H. Whalen, Margaret Moss, and Daryl Baldwin, "Healing through Language: Positive Physical Health Effects of Indigenous Language Use," *F1000 Research* 5:852 (2016).
11. Linguistic claims can be considered reliable only if based on reliable evidence from a broad cross section of the world's languages. One recent survey found that current mainstream theories about sentence production draw on data from at most 0.6 percent of the world's languages, mostly Indo-European. See T. Florian Jaeger and Elisabeth

J. Norcliffe, "The Cross-Linguistic Study of Sentence Production," *Language and Linguistics Compass* 3, no. 4 (2009): 866–87.

12. For Pirahã, see Daniel Everett, "Cultural Constraints on Grammar and Cognition in Pirahã: Another Look at the Design Features of Human Language," *Current Anthropology* 46, no. 4 (2005): 621–46. For Salish, see Dale Kinkade, "Salish Evidence against the Universality of 'Noun' and 'Verb,'" *Lingua* 60, no. 1 (1983): 25–39.
13. For example, see Luisa Maffi, "Linguistic, Cultural, and Biological Diversity," *Annual Review of Anthropology* 34 (2005): 599–617.
14. Antonio De Nebrija and Magalí Armillas-Tiseyra, "On Language and Empire: The Prologue to Grammar of the Castilian Language," *PMLA* 131, no. 1 (2016 [orig. pub. 1492]): 197–208.
15. The linguist Leanne Hinton telescopes the most common scenario into a sentence: "The decline of linguistic diversity in the world is linked to the world political economy which invades and takes over the territories of indigenous peoples, threatens the ecosystems in which they live, wipes out their traditional means of livelihood, and (at best) turns them into low-caste laborers in the larger society in which they must now live on the margins." See Leanne Hinton, "Language Revitalization: An Overview," in Leanne Hinton and Ken Hale, eds. *The Green Book of Language Revitalization in Practice* (New York: Academic Press, 2001), 18.
16. For Light Warlpiri, see Carmel O'Shannessy, "Light Warlpiri: A New Language," *Australian Journal of Linguistics* 25, no. 1 (2005): 31–57. For Nicaraguan Sign Language , see Richard J. Senghas, Ann Senghas, and Jennie E. Pyers, "The Emergence of Nicaraguan Sign Language: Questions of Development, Acquisition, and Evolution," in Sue Taylor Parker, Jonas Langer, Constance Milbrath, eds., *Biology and Knowledge Revisited* (London: Taylor and Francis, 2005), 305–24. Emojis, however linguistically interesting, don't meet the bar.
17. Marianne Mithun, *The Native Languages of North America* (Cambridge, UK: Cambridge University Press, 1999), 1–12.
18. Michael Krauss, "The World's Languages in Crisis," *Language* 68, no. 1 (1992): 5: "For the whole USA and Canada together, a similar count is only a little less alarming: of 187 languages, I calculate that 149 are no longer being learned by children; that is, of the Native North American languages still spoken, 80 percent are moribund." Over thirty years later, the principal change is in the number of language revitalization efforts underway, especially in North America, but the degree to which these are producing new native or fluent speakers remains unclear.
19. A "built-up" language is sometimes referred to, using the German, as an Ausbausprache, *language by development*, as opposed to an Abstandsprache, *language by distance* (which has not gone through the development process). The history of these terms is itself intriguing, linked to a German linguist with strong Nazi associations who had a special interest in activating Germanic "linguistic islands" in the US. See H. Kloss, "'Abstand Languages' and 'Ausbau Languages,'" *Anthropological Linguistics* 9, no. 7 (1967): 29–41.
20. See Deborah Tannen, "New York Jewish Conversational Style," *International Journal of the Sociology of Language* 30 (1981): 133–49.
21. One starting point for the massive literature on the cognitive benefits of bilingualism is the work of Ellen Bialystok, *Bilingualism in Development: Language, Literacy, and Cognition* (Cambridge, UK: Cambridge University Press, 2001).
22. A state-of-the-art guide is Julien Meyer, *Whistled Languages: A Worldwide Inquiry on Human Whistled Speech* (New York: Springer, 2015).

23. Most prominent of all the missionary linguistics organizations is the Summer Institute of Linguistics, which is the publisher of the Ethnologue database and may be responsible for more language documentation work than all the world's linguistics departments combined.
24. See Krauss, "The World's Languages in Crisis" and the other widely cited manifesto of the time: Ken Hale, "Endangered Languages: On Endangered Languages and the Safeguarding of Diversity." *Language* 68 no.1 (1992): 1–42. Himmelmann, "Language Documentation," is credited as helping to define language documentation as the field's response.
25. The mobilization of linguists was plainly inspired by biologists, conservationists, policymakers, and ordinary people mobilizing against the Sixth Extinction, man-made this time, of plant and animals. Likewise, the five hundredth anniversary of 1492 was a signal moment for a global Indigenous movement already growing since the 1960s.
26. See Nicholas Evans and Stephen C. Levinson, "The Myth of Language Universals: Language Diversity and Its Importance for Cognitive Science," *Behavioral and Brain Sciences* 32, no. 5 (2009): 429–48.
27. Usually called the "Boasian triad" after the pioneer fieldworker Franz Boas, the dictionary-grammar-corpus triad has been emphasized and cited much more in the past twenty years as part of the new language documentation.
28. Key contributors to the discussion include Wesley Leonard, Jennie Davis, and Bernard Perley. See Davis, "Resisting Rhetorics," Leonard, "Extinct Language," and Perley, "Zombie Linguistics," for examples.
29. For my proposal for and genealogy of radical linguistics, see Perlin, "Radical Linguistics."
30. In *Going to Extremes*, the writer Joe McGinniss memorably imagines the appeal (and absurdity) of "modern life" from an Indigenous perspective as a "way of life that enabled people to heat their homes simply by turning a dial; that permitted them to consume that which they had not had to kill themselves; and that gave them money, apparently, for doing no more than sitting in a warm building all day, playing with pieces of paper, and talking to each other on the telephone."
31. Linguistic difference arguably takes a new if less differentiated form when Irish people speak Irish English instead of Irish.
32. See Alisdair MacIntyre, *After Virtue: A Study in Moral Theory* (London: Duckworth, 2007 [1981]), 256. "The story of my life is always embedded in the story of those communities from which I derive my identity."
33. A 2019 survey was able to find 245 revitalization efforts ongoing worldwide, with most launched since 2000—though this is surely only a slice of the total based on research limitations. See Gabriela Pérez Báez, Rachel Vogel, and Uia Patolo, "Global Survey of Revitalization Efforts: A Mixed Methods Approach to Understanding Language Revitalization Practices," *Language Documentation and Conservation* 13 (2019): 446–513.

    For a brilliant description of and guide to "language warrior" work from the inside, see Anton Treuer, *The Language Warrior's Handbook: How to Keep Our Languages Alive No Matter the Odds* (St. Paul: Minnesota Historical Society Press, 2020).
34. As Gaiutra Bahadur writes: "Those of us engaged in this daily struggle against loss know that it's possible to 'have' a language on many levels. We know that it's possible for a language to resonate emotionally even when it has been literally lost. We know that, even when slurring the surmised remains of our once-upon-a-time language or parroting it without understanding it's possible to wrap our tongues possessively

around the world it expresses and implies." See Gaiutra Bahadur, *Coolie Woman: The Odyssey of Indenture* (Oxford: Oxford University Press, 2016), 8.

35. In a signal recent exception, the Canadian government settled a lawsuit brought by 325 First Nations over "cultural genocide" for around $2 billion, of which a large amount may be earmarked for language revitalization.
36. Morpehemes are bolded here and throughout purely for ease of reading.
37. This is a very simplified account, like everything else in this section, not addressing all the vagaries of constituent order, including the possibility of a language being "NODOM," or having no dominant order. See Matthew S. Dryer, "Order of Subject, Object and Verb," in WALS Online, ed. Matthew S. Dryer and Martin Haspelmath, 2013, www.wals.info/chapter/81. As for other aspects of linguistic typology, the World Atlas of Linguistic Structures is an essential source; now likewise its successor Grambank and the assorted databases of the Glottobank consortium.
38. See Lyle Campbell, "Language Isolates and Their History, or, What's Weird, Anyway?" *Annual Meeting of the Berkeley Linguistics Society* 36, no. 1 (2010).

## II. Past

### Minority Port

1. Grumet, *Munsee Indians*, 40–42, imagines in some detail a composite settlement along the Bronx River.
2. Goddard, "Origin and Meaning."
3. See Anthony Stevens-Acevedo, Tom Weterings, and Leonor Alvarez Francés, *Juan Rodriguez and the Beginnings of New York City* (New York: CUNY Dominican Studies Institute, 2013).
4. By the time of the English conquest in 1664, as much as a quarter of the population was African, including a substantial free population. See Joyce Goodfriend, *Before the Melting Pot: Society and Culture in Colonial New York City, 1664–1730* (Princeton: Princeton University Press, 1994), 10.
5. See Bertrand Van Ruymbeke, "The Walloon and Huguenot Elements in New Netherland and Seventeenth-Century New York: Identity, History and Memory," *Revisiting New Netherland: Perspectives on Early Dutch America*, by Joyce Goodfriend (Boston: Brill) 41–54.
6. See Burrows and Wallace, *Gotham*, 31–33, for the "sparse and ambiguous" details of slavery in New Amsterdam. The system expanded and changed greatly under the English.
7. "In 1666, for instance, Domingo the Negro was called to court to translate Jan Angola's testimony into Dutch . . . Although it is not known what language they spoke in court, it was likely Kikongo or Kimbundu given Jan's Angolan heritage." Jeroen Dewulf, "'A Strong Barbaric Accent': America's Dutch-Speaking Black Community from Seventeenth-Century New Netherland to Nineteenth-Century New York and New Jersey," *American Speech* 90, no. 2 (2015): 134.
8. Richard Dickerson, "Abstracts of Early Black Manhattanites," New York Genealogical and Biographical Record 116, no. 2 (April 1985): 100–104.
9. Sivertsen, "Babel on the Hudson," 214.
10. See Pierre Swiggers, "Munsee Borrowings from Dutch: Some Phonological Remarks," *International Journal of American Linguistics* 51, no. 4 (1985): 594–97.
11. Sivertsen, "Babel on the Hudson," 214.

12. David Steven Cohen, "How Dutch Were the Dutch of New Netherland?" *New York History*, Vol. 62 (January 1981).
13. The North Frisian islands of Amrum and Föhr sent many immigrants to New York in the late nineteenth century. "The majority of Föhr Frisians who emigrated to New York before 1929 came from the western part of Föhr and spoke Fering" and perhaps had knowledge of Low German and High German as well. Over time they became increasingly integrated with other Germanic communities in New York. See Robert Kleih, "Postvernacular Identity in Two North Frisian Immigrant Communities in the USA," *11th Workshop on Immigrant Languages in the Americas* (Somerville, MA: Cascadilla Proceedings Project, 2022), 66.
14. See John Romeyn Brodhead, Berthold Fernow, and Edmund Bailey O'Callaghan, State of New York Legislature, *Documents Relative to the Colonial History of the State of New York*, vol. 14 (1883; repr., Albany: Weed, Parsons and Co., 1901), 42–44.
15. Father Isaac Jogues, "Novum Belgium," in *Narratives of New Netherland, 1609–1664*, ed. J. Franklin Jameson (New York: Barnes & Noble, Inc., 1953), 259.

    There is no list of the eighteen languages. Lenape and several African languages certainly should be included, but it's possible that this number (however calculated) included only the kinds of European varieties that Director General Willem Kieft might have recognized as languages. Given the high number, this must have extended beyond familiar national languages (e.g., Dutch, French, German, Spanish, Portuguese, Danish, Swedish, Norwegian, Finnish, Polish, Bohemian/Czech, Italian, Arabic, and possibly Turkish) and may have included regional varieties like Frisian, Flemish, Walloon, Venetian, and possibly other Germanic and eastern European varieties.
16. Only the skipper and the boatswain are Dutch, while the others include a Portuguese soldier, a Swedish student, a Spanish barber, a French merchant, a Neapolitan, a poor English nobleman, a "High-Dutch [i.e., German] Gentleman," and the apparent Polish speaker "Popolski." See A. Donck and H. C. Murphy, *Vertoogh van Nieu Nederland; and Breeden raedt aende Vereenichde Nederlandsche provintien: Two Rare Tracts, Printed in 1649–'50. Relating to the Administration of Affairs in New Netherland* (New York: Baker, Godwin & Co., printers, 1854).
17. Coming from the Polish-Lithuanian Commonwealth, Kuršius was referred to as a Lithuanian at the time, but his precise ethnolinguistic identity, like that of a number of other New Amsterdammers, is a matter of debate. See James S. Pula and Pien Versteegh, "Were There Really Poles in New Netherland?" *Polish American Studies* 73, no. 2 (2016): 35–55.
18. Charles Lodwick's 1692 letter was collected in *Collections of the New-York Historical Society*, 2nd ser., vol. II (New York: New-York Historical Society, 1849), 243–50.
19. In 1712 the Anglican chaplain wrote that "it is possible to learn Hebrew here as well as in Europe, there being a synagogue of Jews, and many ingenious men of that nation from Poland, Hungary, Germany &c." Goodfriend, *Before the Melting Pot*, 151.
20. Goodfriend, *Before the Melting Pot,* 92.
21. See Jill Lepore, *New York Burning: Liberty, Slavery, and Conspiracy in Eighteenth-Century Manhattan* (New York: Vintage, 2006).
22. Goodfriend, *Before the Melting Pot*, 104.
23. See Jan Noordegraaf, "A Language Lost: The Case of Leeg Duits ('Low Dutch')." *Academic Journal of Modern Philology* 2 (2013): 91–108. Instead of the contemporary Dutch term "Nederlands," they probably knew the language as Nederduits (Low Dutch), or even just as taal (*language*). For how Dutch changed over time, see also

Charles Gehring, *The Dutch Language in Colonial New York: An Investigation of a Language in Decline and Its Relationship to Social Change* (Bloomington: Indiana University, 1973).

24. See Gertrude Lefferts-Vanderbilt, *The Social History of Flatbush: And Manners and Customs of the Dutch Settlers in Kings County* (New York: D. Appleton, 1909).
25. On Mohawk-Hudson Dutch, see L. G. Van Loon, *Crumbs from an Old Dutch Closet: The Dutch Dialect of Old New York* (The Hague: Martinus Nijhoff, 1938); J. Dyneley Prince, "Jersey Dutch Dialect," *Dialect Notes*, vol. III, 1910, 459–84.
26. See Dewulf, "A Strong Barbaric Accent." Pinkster was a hybrid holiday with Dutch and African American elements. Tap dancing has been described as a fusion of practices brought by enslaved Africans with the jigs of Irish and English immigrants, which took off in face-offs between Black and Irish dancers in the Five Points, as described in Brian Seibert, *What the Eye Hears: A History of Tap Dancing* (New York: Macmillan, 2015).
27. Shane White, "A Question of Style: Blacks in and around New York City in the Late 18th Century," *Journal of American Folklore* 102, no. 403 (1989): 23–44.
28. In 1776 these were the words of Samuel Shaw, the mayor of Boston. Did New York's complex international entanglements make it more fit to be a Loyalist bastion during the American Revolution?
29. The first half of the nineteenth century also seems to have been the period when the city was first blanketed in text—not only newspapers and books but signs, posters, banknotes, which even down to today have been overwhelmingly in English and generally far less diverse than the city's oral speechways. See David Henkin, *City Reading: Written Words and Public Spaces in Antebellum New York* (New York: Columbia University Press, 1998).

    Henkin notes the irony of such a multilingual city presenting such a monolingual face, but hypothesizes that most New Yorkers of this period could read most "texts" that the city presented both because of spreading literacy and because most immigrants of the period were familiar with Latin-based alphabets.
30. William Labov, *The Social Stratification of English in New York City* (Cambridge, UK: Cambridge University Press, 2006), 338.
31. See Newman, *New York City English*.
32. Ira Rosenwaike, *Population History of New York City* (Syracuse: Syracuse University Press, 1972). It's interesting to note that domestic migrants to the early nineteenth-century city banded together in societies just as overseas ones did, with Massachusetts and Connecticut traders forming the New England Society of New York, for example, just as the city's Scottish mercantile elite formed the St. Andrew's Society. See Sven Beckert, *The Monied Metropolis: New York City and the Consolidation of the American Bourgeoisie, 1850–1896* (Cambridge, UK: Cambridge University Press, 2014), 46–47.
33. Kenneth Nilsen, "Irish in Nineteenth Century New York," in *The Multilingual Apple: Languages in New York City*, ed. Ofelia García and Joshua A. Fishman (Berlin and New York: De Gruyter Mouton), 53–70.
34. Most moved upstate but a few, including the famous publisher John Peter Zenger, remained in the city. In fact, not all were originally Palatine dialect speakers: there were also Hessians, Swiss, and others. See Philip L. Otterness, *Becoming German* (Ithaca: Cornell University Press, 2013).
35. Bayor and Meagher, *The New York Irish*, 46.
36. N. Sumner and A. Doyle, eds., 2020. *North American Gaels: Speech, Story, and Song in the Diaspora*, vol. 2 (Montreal: McGill Queen's Press MQUP), 8.

37. Kenneth E. Nilsen, "The Irish Language in New York, 1850–1900," in Ronald Bayor and Timothy Meagher, eds., *The New York Irish* (Baltimore: Johns Hopkins University Press, 254.
38. John Ridge, "Irish County Societies in New York, 1880-1914" in Bayor and Meagher, *The New York Irish*), 276.
39. Nilsen, "Irish in Nineteenth Century New York."
40. This building, which was not a boarding house, was at 411 West Sixteenth Street, and the number is based on the 1910 census. Many would have been servants, laborers, cooks, etc. See "Irish Speakers and the Empire City," accessed November 26, 2021, www.irish-empire-city.nmwolf.net.
41. Bayor and Meagher, *The New York Irish*, 405.
42. Stanley Nadel, *Kleindeutschland (Little Germany): New York City's Germans, 1845–1880* (Champaign: University of Illinois Press, 1990).
43. Ibid, 37.
44. Similar numbers in the same period left India and Southern China for Southeast Asia and the Pacific, while another series of migrations brought people mostly from European Russia to Central and Northeast Asia. Within the Americas, Portuguese immigrants went overwhelmingly to Brazil, just as Spaniards went to Argentina and Cuba, but the US received a majority of the total, including members of every ethnolinguistic group. A higher percentage returned than is generally acknowledged, particularly in certain groups, but this only extends and complicates the migration's impact. See Tara Zahra, *The Great Departure: Mass Migration from Eastern Europe and the Making of the Free World* (New York: W. W. Norton & Company, 2016).
45. Migrants themselves may have heard the name as kestl gartl, meaning *belted box*, an apt description, as in Sholem Aleichem's classic Yiddish novel *Motl, Peyse the Cantor's Son*: "We haven't seen America yet because we're still in 'Kestl Gartl.' That is, that's what it was once called. Now it's not called kestl gartl anymore, but 'Ellis Island.'"
46. Małgorzata Szejnert's *Ellis Island: A People's History* is a powerful recent account of the place and its mythologies, as seen largely from the other side of the ocean—though Szejnert migrated to New York, for a time, in the 1980s.
47. In 1942, YIVO held a contest for the best autobiography by a Jewish immigrant on the theme "Why I Left the Old Country and What I Have Accomplished in America." Aaron Domnitz's autobiography, quoted here (138), was chosen from over two hundred entries, translated from Yiddish, and included as one of the nine life stories in J. Cohen, *My Future Is in America: Autobiographies of Eastern European Jewish Immigrants* (New York: NYU Press, 2008).
48. Binder and Reimers, *All Nations under Heaven*, 105.
49. Thomas Kessner. 1976. *The Golden Door: Immigrant Mobility in New York City, 1880–1915*. New York: Oxford University Press, 174.
50. Burrows and Wallace, *Gotham*, 1039–58.
51. See Endangered Language Alliance, "Languages of New York."
52. For the detailed demographics of Galician migration, see, among other sources, Bieto Alonso Fernández, *Obreiros alén mar: Mariñeiros, fogoneiros e anarquistas galegos en New York (1900–1930)* (Santo Tirso, Portugal: A Nosa Terra, 2006).
53. See Nan Ickeringill, "The Bretons: A Poor Province's Gift to New York Restaurants," *New York Times*, February 22, 1967, which cites the newspaper *France-Amerique* for the number twelve thousand. Kenneth Nilsen cites "more than 20,000 Breton speakers in the greater New York area during the last decades of the 20th century" in John

T. Koch, *Celtic Culture: A Historical Encyclopedia*, vol. 1 (*A—Celti*) (Santa Barbara: ABC-Clio, 2006), 384.

Today, the Breton Association of New York (BZH-NY) still has its membership and continues to hold cultural events on a regular basis. A newer organization, Breizh Amerika, builds transnational ties between Bretons in Brittany and those in the city, who now number two to three thousand at most, according to the organization's founder, Charles Kergaravat.

54. The terminology, as so often in the history of languages, is complex. Many sources from the period use the now archaic term Ruthenian, which seems to encompass Ukrainian, Belarusian, and Rusyn. And in fact the names "Russian," "Ruthenian," and "Rusyn" do all go back to the same root, which seems to have come from speakers of an entirely unrelated Finnic language. At various times, Rusyns in America have named and identified their institutions as Russian, Ukrainian, Carpatho-Rusyn, and Lemko.
55. Warhol's parents both spoke Ruthenian, and the artist understood it enough to use it in 1980, when he met Pope John Paul II, who knew the language from his own upbringing in southern Poland. Though Warhol famously said "I come from nowhere," his family in fact came from Mikova in what is now Slovakia. See Andrew Higgins and Miroslava Germanova, "Andy Warhol Said He Came from 'Nowhere.' This Is It," *New York Times*, October 7, 2018.
56. Lemko-OOL still exists, with six branches across New York and New Jersey. For the fascinating story of how Skhimba made and sold his recordings (out of an ice cream store in Clifton, New Jersey, among other places), see Bogdan Horbal and Walter Maksimovich, *Lemko Folk Music on Wax Cylinders (1901–1913) and American Records (1928–1930)* (Lviv: self-pub., 2008).

    The city's "ethnic" (i.e., non-English-language) entertainment and recording industries produced thousands of records, including music and skits in a wide range of now-endangered genres and languages. Made by and for immigrants, but often with an influential transnational reach, these records preserve and serve as clues to a whole forgotten history of Rusyn instrumentalists, Sicilian comics, and western Armenian singers—as well as hundreds of unique examples of language mixing, particularly with English. See Richard Spottswood, *Ethnic Music on Records: A Discography of Ethnic Recordings Produced in the United States, 1893–1942, Vol. 7: Record Number Index, Matrix Number Index* (Champaign: University of Illinois Press, 1990); Eric Byron, *Crank Up the Phonograph: Who We Are and Where We Came from in Early Sound Recordings* (self-pub., 2015), retrieved from www.crankupthephonograph.com.
57. See Luigi Andriani, Ross Perlin, and Daniel Kaufman, "*Dialetti* in Diaspora: Loss and Retention in Italian New York," in *Italian(s) Abroad: Italian Language and Migration in the Cities of the World*, edited by Francesco Goglia and John Hajek. (Berlin and Boston: De Gruyter, forthcoming).
58. Gabaccia, *From Sicily*, 60–61, describes Little Italy's Elizabeth Street as "socially fragmented by village chains." She analyzes distinctive patron saint names in census listings to determine these; in other cases, parish records have been used for a similar analysis.
59. Mike Wallace, *Greater Gotham: A History of New York City from 1898 to 1919* (Oxford: Oxford University Press, 2017), 696. See also Gerald Meyer, *Vito Marcantonio: Radical Politician, 1902–1954* (Albany: SUNY Press, 1989), 114–15.
60. Mary Elizabeth Brown, *The Italians of the South Village* (New York: Greenwich Village Society for Historic Preservation, 2007), 12.

61. See www.lungblock.nyc; Stefano Morello, personal communication, September 14, 2020.
62. Simona Frasca, *Italian Birds of Passage: The Diaspora of Neapolitan Musicians in New York* (New York: Springer, 2014), 21.
63. An oft-cited example is Luigi "Papa" Fugazy, a Piedmontese who arrived in New York in 1869 and founded all manner of businesses and initiatives for his fellow immigrants, including a bank, before being honored by the Italian government and dying in a Bleecker Street townhouse in 1930.
64. Gay Talese, *Unto the Sons* (New York: Random House Trade Paperbacks, 2006), 206.
65. Peter Vellon, *A Great Conspiracy against Our Race* (New York: NYU Press, 2014), 22–24.
66. Nancy Carnevale, *A New Language, a New World: Italian Immigrants in the United States, 1890–1945* (Champaign: University of Illinois Press, 2010), 25–26.
67. See Endangered Language Alliance, "The Old Father and the Modern Son," YouTube, 2017. It was in this context that a new Sicilian poetry scene, led by Provenzano and others at Arba Sicula, took root in the city. In Queens alone at the time, there were dialetti-dominant clusters speaking Sicilian, Nones, Friulian, Campanian (Cilentano and Irpino), Molisan, Abruzzese, Southern Lazio (Ciociaro), and Istrioto/Istro-Venetan/Istro-Romanian. See Andriani et al., "*Dialetti* in Diaspora."
68. Hermann W. Haller, "Italian Speech Varieties in the United States and the Italian-American Lingua Franca," Italica 64, no. 3 (1987), 396. The census listed three hundred thousand "Italian" speakers in 1980, and as many as four hundred fifty thousand in 1930, when an even larger number would have spoken forms of Sicilian, Calabrese, etc.
69. Andriani et al., "*Dialetti* in Diaspora" includes a deep dive into one "archaic" dialect from the town of Casamassima in Puglia, as preserved in the home of a single family in Jersey City.

## Survivor City

1. This is not meant to be an exhaustive list of all survivor communities in the New York area, but one focused specifically on linguistic minorities who came to the city in large numbers during this particular period.
2. Warren Lehrer and Judith Sloan, *Crossing the BLVD: Strangers, Neighbors, Aliens in a New America* (New York: W. W. Norton and Co., 2003).
3. Ashrafuzzaman Khan moved to Pakistan, then to the United States after the war, and lived in Jamaica, Queens, where he was active in the Islamic Circle of North America. See Ellen Barry, "Bangladesh Sentences 2 Expatriates to Death for War Crimes," *New York Times*, November 3, 2013.
4. On Jakiw Palij in Queens, see Debbie Cenziper and Justine Coleman, "'Get the Nazi out of New York,'" *Washington Post*, September 1, 2018.
5. Joseph Berger, "God Said Multiply, and Did She Ever," *New York Times*, February 19, 2010.
6. This is the writer Nikos Bakos, whose blog *Jadde* took inspiration from his father's notion of ta mere mas, *our parts*, referring to the approximately thirty Dropoli villages, but Bakos has widened the angle of aperture to encompass "Bosnia to Bengal." New York is part of this, writes Bakos, "because that's where I live, that's where I'm from, because it's only from a vantage point that's both heterogeneous and external that the phenomena I'll be talking about can be apprehended in their fullness and because that's where, more than any other single place or any single time in history,

the cosmopolitan ideal that motivates me has manifested itself in one actual, throbbing, hopelessly chaotic and deeply sure of itself city." See jaddeyekabir.com.

7. By day, a whole recording industry flourished—as late as the 1960s, the ethnomusicologist Zev Feldman remembers hanging out and picking up 78s and LPs recorded and sold by the Albanian owner (born in Istanbul, later of Bucharest) of the Balkan Phonograph Company on Twenty-Ninth and Eighth.

   A range of musicians from Dave Brubeck to Leonard Bernstein were fans of the scene. Eighth Avenue also had a summer scene in the so-called Yogurt Belt of the Catskills around Tannersville, where there were Armenian-owned and -visited hotels.

   See Sylvia Angelique Alajaji, *Music and the Armenian Diaspora: Searching for Home in Exile* (Bloomington: Indiana University Press, 2015). Harold Hagopian of Traditional Crossroads Records has worked hard to preserve this music, notably in the album *Armenians on 8th Avenue*. With its annual festival running for the last four decades, the Zlate Usne (*Golden Festival*) has in some ways revived and extended the Eighth Avenue scene, making New York a site of intensely felt musical crossings involving dozens of languages from the Balkans and beyond.

8. Many moved further into Bergen County but continued to speak and create in the language, including the Fort Lee–based singer Onnik Dinkjian and writer Charles Kasbarian in Teaneck, who published the *Dikranagerdtsi Vernacular Handbook*.

9. The city's earliest known Greek community was on Madison Street on the Lower East Side, later moving north to Manhattan's Twenties and Thirties. The collapse of the Ottoman Empire, the Greek Civil War of the 1940s, and late periods of economic turmoil all fueled the Greek community's growth, but the largest number came between 1965 and 1980 and settled in Astoria.

   Most Pontic Greeks seem to have come in the same period. Today, only a few hundred speakers of the Pontic language remain in the New York area, according to Dmitri Molohidis, though those who speak Greek and maintain a Pontic identity are more numerous. Another community member, Costas Tsilfidis, believes that 90 percent of the seven hundred families in Norwalk are Pontic and that most of them still speak the language, and all have a genocide connection. Most came in the 1960s or '70s and found work in the factories emptied out by the Vietnam War.

10. As times changed, the Captive Nations Committee faded, and after 1989 Natho started courting Middle Eastern diplomats and building ties with the new autonomous republics in the Circassian homeland (within Russia). When he died in New York in 2021 at the age of ninety-three, Natho was mourned in all the languages of the global Circassian diaspora he had done much to connect.

11. See Kadir Natho, *Memoirs* (Bloomington: Xlibris Corporation, 2010), 308, 378.

12. Scott Moss, *A History of the Tolstoy Foundation 1939–1989* (Valley Cottage, NY: Tolstoy Foundation, 1989), 11–27.

13. For Kalmyk identity and perceptions of other groups, see Elsa-Bair M. Guchinova, "Kalmyks in the United States," *Anthropology and Archeology of Eurasia* 41, no. 2 (2002), 7–22. Besides Howell and Brooklyn, the other large Kalymk American community, most of whose members came from the Don River rather than the Volga, lives in north-central Philadelphia.

14. Purev Navdid, personal communication, June 29, 2017. Purev himself was born in Kyrgyzstan "during the exile," just a few years after the deportation. Like many others, Purev's family returned to their village in Kalmykia when they could, a decade later. It was there that he started picking up Kalymk before the family moved to Elista,

the capital city, and life switched completely to Russian. He noted a recent plan to offer Kalmyk language classes in the US, but scheduling proved impossible.

15. Mikhail Kizilov, "The Krymchaks: Current State of the Community," in *Euro-Asian Jewish Yearbook 5768* (*2007/2008*), ed. Mikhail Chlenov (Pallada, 2009), 271–72.
16. See Julia Krivoruchko, "Judeo-Greek," in *Handbook of Jewish Languages*, ed. Lily Kahn and Aaron Rubin (Boston: Brill, 2016), 194–225. In addition to linguistic differences, there is also a specific Romaniote rite in terms of Jewish liturgical practice and cantillation. Besides the Lower East Side, other Romaniote congregations, which also included some Ladino-speaking Sephardim from Greece, formed in Bensonhurst, Harlem, and the Bronx.
17. The distinguished writer/translator Rae Dalven, herself a Ioanniote Jew whose family came to New York, has brief remarks on the language in Rae Dalven, *The Jews of Ioannina* (Port Angeles, WA: Cadmus Press, 1990). See also Nicholas Alexiou, "Romaniote Jews in the United States," *Journal of Modern Hellenism* (2006): 169–79. Joseph M. Papo, *Sephardim in Twentieth Century America: In Search of Unity* (San Jose, CA: Pelé Yoretz Books, 1987), 311–12.
18. For ELA's work on Ladino/Judeo-Spanish, see www.elalliance.org/languages/judeo-spanish, with links to interviews piecing together the history of Ladino in New York with a dozen remaining speakers and semispeakers. Names for the language are noted in Tracy K. Harris, *Death of a Language: The History of Judeo-Spanish* (Newark, DE: University of Delaware Press, 1994). See also David Bunis, "Native Designations of Judezmo as a 'Jewish Language,'" in *Studies in Language, Literature and History Presented to Joseph Chetrit*, ed. Yosef Tobi and Dennis Kurzon (Jerusalem: Carmel, 2011), 41–81.
19. Few Haketia speakers ended up in New York as compared to France, Canada, and Spain, but one, Alicia Sisso Raz, is particularly active with her Voces de Haketia project.
20. See Devin Naar, "'Impostors': Levantine Jews and the Limits of Jewish New York," in *The Jewish Metropolis* (Boston: Academic Studies Press, 2021), 115–46; Devin Naar, "From the 'Jerusalem of the Balkans' to the Goldene Medina: Jewish Immigration from Salonika to the United States," *American Jewish History* 93, no. 4 (2007): 435–73. Ladino-speaking socialists published a songbook and several Ladino newspapers and organized with Puerto Rican workers in East Harlem. The first Ladino novella published in the US was the story of a Sephardic factory worker who develops a socialist consciousness and organizes other workers.
21. Claudio Iván Remeseira, ed., *Hispanic New York: A Sourcebook* (New York: Columbia University Press, 2010), 76; Piri Thomas, *Down These Mean Streets* (New York: Vintage Books, 1967).
22. Naar, "Impostors," 137.
23. For an intimate look into a Bronx Izmirli home, see Gloria Ascher, "Proverbs and Expressions from a Bronx Izmirlí Family: Toward a Sephardic View of the World," *Shofar: An Interdisciplinary Journal of Jewish Studies* 10, no. 1 (1991): 49–56. At the time, nearby 170th Street was full of stores owned by Greek Jews, according to a member of the community who grew up there. Ladino was the everyday language of his home, while Greek was used by his parents when they didn't want him to understand.
24. Leonard Plotnik, "The Sephardim of New Lots," *Commentary* 25 (1958): 28.
25. Carol Silverman, *Romani Routes: Cultural Politics and Balkan Music in Diaspora* (Oxford: Oxford University Press, 2012).

26. Kalderash Vlax is still one of the main Romani languages spoken in New York. For the term porrajmos, see Ian Hancock, "On the Interpretation of a Word: Porrajmos as Holocaust," The Romani Archives and Documentation Center (2006).
27. Barnet Schecter, *The Devil's Own Work: The Civil War Draft Riots and the Fight to Reconstruct America* (New York: Walker Books, 2007).
28. This led to "sister cities of the unlikeliest of pairings: Palestine, Texas, and Syracuse, New York; Norfolk, Virginia, and Roxbury in Boston; Brookhaven, Mississippi, and Bloomington, Illinois." Isabel Wilkerson, *The Warmth of Other Suns: The Epic Story of America's Great Migration* (New York: Penguin, 2020), 243.
29. The linguist was William Stewart. See Carey Winfrey, "Linguist Seeking to Legitimize Gullah Language," *New York Times*, March 29, 1977; John Holm, *Pidgins and Creoles: Vol. 2, Reference Survey* (Cambridge, UK: Cambridge University Press, 1988), 491.
30. See Irma Watkins-Owens, *Blood Relations: Caribbean Immigrants and the Harlem Community, 1900–1930* (Bloomington: Indiana University Press, 1996).
31. Wallace Thurman, "An Introduction to Contemporary Harlemese, Expurgated and Abridged," in *Classic Fiction of the Harlem Renaissance*, ed. William Andrews (Oxford: Oxford University Press, 1994).
32. Ibid, 339.
33. William Leap, *Language before Stonewall: Language, Sexuality, History* (London: Springer Nature, 2019), 351.
34. Irving Lewis Allen, *The City in Slang: New York Life and Popular Speech* (Oxford: Oxford University Press, 1995). Arguably every major city has the kind of lexical culture Allen describes so well, with each locally resonant word opening onto a different history. One extraordinary example is Buenos Aires, where the historic local argot known as Lunfardo, forged when the city was as much an immigration hub as New York, even has its own academy.
35. James Weldon Johnson, *The Book of American Negro Poetry* (New York: Harcourt, Brace and Company, 1922), xli.
36. For a description of three Brazilian mães de santo (*mothers of saints*) who are bringing Candomblé knowledge and practice to New York, see Marcelo Niel, "ÀwọnỌnà Mímọ́: Axé Women in New York City and Their Sacred Paths," *Studia Religiologica*, no. 3 (2018): 209–18.

## Indigenous Metropolis

1. See American Indian Community House, "Sacred Spaces," for several important oral histories, including those of Louis Mofsie and Gloria Miguel.
2. "Indigenous" refers here to the Americas, where the term is in widest use today, and as such is capitalized. On a per capita basis, many smaller cities in the Midwest and West, like Tulsa and Tucson, have higher percentages of Native people than New York due to the recency of European settlement and the proximity of large reservations belonging to larger tribes on or near their original territory. Another factor was the Indian Relocation Act of 1956, by which the federal government encouraged people to leave their reservations by covering moving expenses and vocational training in designated western cities. This may be interpreted as economic opportunity on the one hand, the attempted erasure of Indian country on the other, but one clear result was the growth of new urban Native communities.

3. Alaska Natives are very few in New York, so American Indian will be used here as shorthand. Starting in 1960, you could declare your own race or ethnicity on the US Census, instead of the census worker declaring it for you; starting in 2000, you could declare more than one race or ethnicity. Across the intervening decades, the Native American population grew much, much faster than the general population—mostly due to people newly identifying as Native, not new births.
4. See Matthew Malone, "Native Americans in New York City," (Endangered Language Alliance, forthcoming), www.elalliance.org.
5. Minik was among the six Inuit men and women brought to the city in 1897 by the explorer Admiral Robert Peary, then returning from one of his early trips to Greenland. Already sick after reaching Newfoundland, they contracted tuberculosis in New York. Four of the six died, including Qisun, but his seven-year-old son Minik survived and remained in the city for over a decade, mostly under the care of William Wallace, chief curator and superintendent of the Natural History Museum. At first there were just three people in the city with whom he communicated: Esther Enutsiak, an Inuk woman from Labrador who had originally come with a group to be exhibited at the 1893 world's fair in Chicago and stayed in New York afterwards; Franz Boas, the founding figure of anthropology in America, who had learned the related but quite different Inuktitut language of Baffin Island; and Matthew Henson, the extraordinary African American explorer who was born to a family of Maryland sharecroppers and played a leading role in seven of Peary's polar expeditions. Henson, who learned to speak excellent Inuktun, considered himself the first person to reach the North Pole. When he wasn't in the far north, he lived in northern Manhattan's Dunbar Apartments, a Harlem Renaissance hub that was also home to W. E. B. Du Bois, Paul Robeson, A. Philip Randolph, and Countee Cullen.

   Ultimately, the teenage Minik learned English and began to lose his own language. Discovering that his father's skeleton had been displayed at the Natural History Museum, he made anguished pleas for a proper burial, enlisting the city's newspapers in his cause. As a disaffected eighteen-year-old, he made his way back to Greenland, eventually relearning Inuktun and the Inuit way of life, but still caught between worlds. By then Minik was strongly attached to English, using it whenever he could with visiting explorers, and a few years later he returned to New York—only to die soon after in the influenza epidemic of 1918. See Kenn Harper, *Give Me My Father's Body: The Life of Minik, the New York Eskimo* (New York: Simon and Schuster, 2001).

   For other cases, see Pamela Newkirk, *Spectacle: The Astonishing Life of Ota Benga* (New York: Harper Collins, 2015); Claire Prentice, *The Lost Tribe of Coney Island: Headhunters, Luna Park, and the Man Who Pulled Off the Spectacle of the Century* (New York: New Harvest, 2014).
6. After becoming the first Native American graduate of Stanford in 1898 and then doing graduate work at Harvard, Oskison moved to New York and became a professional journalist and later novelist, writing in English but often on Native American themes. Oskison was a fixture of the city's literary scene for decades, and his autobiography is more about who met whom at luncheons than any overt reflection on what it meant to be Native or "mixed race" in the city in the early 1900s. More striking are his encounters with the city's immigrant diversity and the fact that Oskison spent a year working and living at one of the "settlement houses" on the Lower East Side, helping impoverished Jewish greenhorns. His free evenings were

spent listening to "gypsy music" and drinking Hungarian wine at cafés by the East River.

7. See Benjamin Lee Whorf, *Language, Thought, and Reality: Selected Writings of Benjamin Lee Whorf* (Cambridge, MA: MIT Press, 2012). Regarding Hopi, the influential rebuttal is Ekkehart Malotki, *Hopi Time: A Linguistic Analysis of the Temporal Concepts in the Hopi Language*, Trends in Linguistics. Studies and Monographs, vol. 20 (Berlin and New York: Mouton Publishers, 1983). More generally, see John H. McWhorter, *The Language Hoax: Why the World Looks the Same in Any Language* (Oxford: Oxford University Press, 2014).
8. See Linda Waggoner, *Starring Red Wing!: The Incredible Career of Lilian M. St. Cyr, the First Native American Film Star* (Lincoln, NE: University of Nebraska Press, 2019).
9. See American Indian Community House, "Sacred Spaces."
10. Billed as a "Native American and multicultural festival," Drums Along the Hudson is run by Lotus Music and Dance, whose executive and artistic director Kamala Cesar, herself a dancer in the Bharatanatyam tradition of South India, was born in Brooklyn to a Filipino father and a Mohawk mother—though the latter hid her identity from her daughter. It was Cesar's discovery of this later in life that led her to found the festival.
11. These were linked to the fact that Inwood Hill Park at the time was a focus for "weekend archaeologists" like Reginald Pelham Bolton, who were inspired by the island's last old-growth forest to uncover and revive the Native past.
12. According to the *New York Evening Post* (Henry Beckett's 1935 column "A Good Time on a Quarter"), the traditionally attired princess, also known as Marie Noemie Boulerease Constantine Kennedy, was Cherokee from Oklahoma by way of Louisiana and lived in her cottage from 1926 to 1936, until Parks Commissioner Robert Moses moved quickly to evict her. As Moses recalled in his memoir, *Public Works: A Dangerous Trade*: "In the middle [of the park] was a kiln where an Indian princess taught ceramics under dubious auspices. She had a son who didn't work. Both were on relief, and the relief checks were delivered to the princess at a mailbox fastened to a tree. The hullabaloo about disturbing the princess, the kiln, the old tulip tree, and other flora and fauna was terrific."

    Ironically, Moses had established an Indian village at Jones Beach just a few years earlier, with three tipis for children to use as clubhouses and artifacts on loan from the Natural History Museum. Rosebud Yellow Robe, who was Lakota Sioux from South Dakota, directed it for twenty years and became more famous than Princess Naomi thanks to radio and television.
13. "New York Indian Colony Now Has Its Own Club," *New York Times*, February 6, 1927; "Mrs. Mary Newell, Leader of Indians, Dies in Queens," *New York Times*, October 29, 1938. See also D. K. Miller, *Indians on the Move: Native American Mobility and Urbanization in the Twentieth Century* (Chapel Hill: University of North Carolina Press, 2019).
14. Waggoner, *Starring Red Wing!*, 273.
15. For a contemporary outside journalistic source, see Joseph Mitchell, "The Mohawks in High Steel," in *Up in the Old Hotel* (New York: Pantheon, 1992), 267–90. For a linguistic overview, see Marianne Mithun and Wallace Chafe, "Recapturing the Mohawk Language," in *Languages and Their Status*, ed. Timothy Shopen (Philadelphia: University of Pennsylvania Press, 1979), 3–33. See also the work of poet Maurice Kenny.

The story goes that thirty-three men from the community died on a single day in 1907 when the Quebec Bridge collapsed. The widows decided that the men should "boom out" from then on to work on projects all over to reduce the risk of such a catastrophic loss happening again, although New York became the major hub.

Less is known about the Mohawks who remained as Little Caughnawaga faded, but their presence has been continuous. From the 1950s into the 1970s, the Indian League of the Americas, many of whose 250 members were reportedly Mohawk, held regular meetings at Scandinavian sports clubs in Bay Ridge. Mohawk ironworkers not only helped build the World Trade Center but returned after 9/11 for the careful, hellish work of dismantling what remained of the towers.

16. Henry Gass, "Why the Mohawks Are No Longer Walking the High Steel," *Globe and Mail*, August 23, 2013.
17. Mofsie became a public school teacher and worked for thirty-five years on Long Island, and the Miguels became deeply involved in the city's art, theater, and dance worlds—Muriel Miguel founded Spiderwoman, a pioneering Indigenous women's theater—and Thunderbird kept growing.

    McBurney powwow after-parties took place at another quintessential New York location just across the street: an outpost of the Blarney Stone, of the vanished chain of divey Irish pubs.
18. New federal funding for urban Indians enabled the AICH to get off the ground with space and staff, but dictated a depoliticized approach focused on serving specific community needs. The AICH tackled health care, job placement, and substance abuse treatment. For years it ran houses that hundreds of Native people stayed in or passed through: Survival House on the Lower East Side and Spirit Lodge in Clinton Hill, which consisted of two connected brownstones.
19. Around the world, from the Toba barrios of greater Buenos Aires to "the Block" in the Sydney suburb of Redfern, there are urban Indigenous communities, little recognized and highly marginalized but sometimes of long standing. In both Canada and Australia, the urban Indigenous population is increasing much faster than the general urban population.
20. Ben Geboe, personal communication, October 30, 2021.
21. See William L. Leap, *American Indian English* (Salt Lake City: University of Utah Press, 2012).
22. The term Taíno was coined by none other than Constantine Samuel Rafinesque, of the Walam Olum hoax.
23. Richard Kearns, "The Return of the Taïnos/Our Own 'Lost Tribe,'" *El Hispano* (October 1997–February 1998).
24. Sherina Feliciano-Santos, "How Do You Speak Taíno? Indigenous Activism and Linguistic Practices in Puerto Rico," *Journal of Linguistic Anthropology* 27, no. 1 (2007): 14.
25. "The puertorriqueñas usually treated us very well and took us under their wing," writes the Honduran Garifuna Aida Lambert, who moved to 111th Street in Harlem in 1965. See Aida Lambert, "We Are Black Too: Experiences of a Honduran Garifuna," in *The Afro-Latin@ Reader: History and Culture in the United States*, ed. Miriam Jiménez Román and Juan Flores (Chapel Hill: Duke University Press, 2010), 431–33.
26. The *Drama of King Shotaway* was performed in Lower Manhattan by Brown's African Grove Theater, the first Black theater in the country. Unfortunately, little is known about the production or how the Caribbean-born Brown came to take up the theme of the Garifuna struggle, but its creation is suggestive on multiple levels.

27. Sarah England, *Afro Central Americans in New York City* (Gainesville: University Press of Florida, 2006), 24–25.
28. After the expulsion of the Garifuna in 1795, the British repopulated the island with enslaved Africans, who developed the English-based Vincentian Creole, also spoken in New York today.
29. Five to six hundred languages from over one hundred families are estimated for South America in Harald Hammarström, "Linguistic Diversity and Language Evolution," *Journal of Language Evolution* 1, no. 1 (2016): 19–29.
30. Mexico's Instituto Nacional de Lenguas Indígenas (INALI) is responsible for the official numbers. See also Ethnologue.
31. Blake Gentry, Marianne Richardson, Diego Piña Lopez, and Joseph Watkins, "Indigenous Language Migration along the US Southwestern Border—the View from Arizona," *CHANCE* 34, no. 3 (2021): 47–55.
32. Rachel Nolan, "A Translation Crisis at the Border," *New Yorker*, December 30, 2019.
33. Mayan communities settling in smaller towns beyond the New York area include Q'anjob'als in Indiantown, Florida, and Ixils in Centreville, Virginia, and Dover, Ohio.
34. Numerous sources mention "pioneer migrants" at least in passing. A century ago, the aptly nicknamed cobbler "Cristoforo Colombo" told tales and sent remittances that ultimately lured half his Italian village to America. (Foner, *From Ellis Island*, 23, 61). Don Miguel Yanes, who came from Concepción de Oriente to Westbury, Long Island, in the late 1970s and was later known as "the godfather," claims that a thousand of his fellow townspeople followed him. (Sarah J. Mahler, *American Dreaming: Immigrant Life on the Margins* [Princeton: Princeton University Press, 1995], 52–53.) Mario Coria, from the flower town of Tuxpan in Mexico, happened to land a gardening job in Bridgehampton in 1977, and within three decades some five hundred Tuxpeños had followed his lead and made their way to the Hamptons for similar work (Nathan Thornburgh, "Inside the Life of the Migrants Next Door," *Time* 167, no. 6 [2006], 34–45). Further afield, Dang Moua's role in bringing Hmong people to Merced, California, has the force of a full-on foundation story (Anne Fadiman, *The Spirit Catches You and You Fall Down: A Hmong Child, Her American Doctors, and the Collision of Two Cultures* [New York: Macmillan, 2012], 229–31).
35. Clemente Sajquiy Ramirez, personal communication, June 24, 2016.
36. See Pribilsky, *La Chulla Vida*, 56, 67. The collapse of the panama hat industry in the mid-twentieth century played a key role. The trade already linked many Ecuadorians to New York.
37. The New York Quechúa Initiative has been teaching the language at ELA and elsewhere to a mix of students, including many from Peru of Indigenous or mestizo descent who were not raised speaking the language.
38. Those from the region with mixed identity are also "often described, not altogether positively, as cholos (cholas)" with "linguistic features that blend Spanish with a rich set of Quichua words and phrases as well as its 'singsong' cadences." The term may come from the Kichwa chulla (shuj lla). See Pribilsky, *La Chulla Vida*, 38–39.
39. Kate Swanson, "From New York to Ecuador and Back Again: Transnational Journeys of Policies and People," *Annals of the American Association of Geographers* 108, no. 2 (2018): 390–98.
40. Pribilsky, *La Chulla Vida*, 164–66.
41. Ibid, 117–18.

## Global Microcosm

1. Examples include *The Soul of the Street: Correlated Stories of the New York Syrian Quarter* (1900) by the Scottish-Canadian journalist Norman Duncan, who several years later actually went to cover Syria, Palestine, Arabia, and Egypt for *Harper's Magazine*. All-around shyster Chuck Connors led "slumming" tours as the self-declared "Second Mayor of Chinatown" (giving deference to Tom Lee, the "Chinese mayor").

   As cringe-inducing as Connors's act sounds today, bound up in a whole history of "internal" Orientalism, it's notable that he started by capitalizing on the immense voyeuristic interest of other New Yorkers in slang-talking, working-class "Bowery Boys," of which he claimed to be an exemplar in his 1904 memoir *Bowery Life*.
2. According to Bercovici's autobiography, he grew up learning Greek, Romanian, French, and German in what was then the Austro-Hungarian Empire, in the multiethnic region where the Danube meets the Black Sea. He writes that he formed a close connection with the local Roma through his nursemaid and her family, and through his father's work as a horse trader—a connection developed in some of his later writing. After his father was killed in a pogrom in Galați when Bercovici was eleven, the family left for Paris, where he studied the organ and helped paint the puddled iron of the Eiffel Tower. From there he moved to Montreal, where he worked for a Yiddish newspaper, and then the Lower East Side, where he made artificial flowers in a sweatshop, sold clocks door to door, shoveled snow, played the organ at a nickelodeon, branched out into farming and blacksmithing, and eventually made his way in journalism. See Konrad Bercovici, *It's the Gypsy in Me: The Autobiography of Konrad Bercovici* (Read Books, 2007).
3. Bercovici, *Around the World*, 14–15. Bercovici's obituary speeds through the dozens of books he wrote on every imaginable topic, his attempt to write screenplays in Hollywood, his semisuccessful lawsuit against Charlie Chaplin over *The Great Dictator* (allegedly Bercovici's idea), and his reputation as a social gadfly at the Algonquin Round Table and elsewhere. But the most interesting section of the obit is "Neighbors Complained," describing how at one point Bercovici gave up his home on West Ninety-Second Street and moved several blocks away "because his former neighbors and landlord had complained about parties to which he had invited Negroes, Chinese, Russians, assorted Balkans, gypsies and representatives of every other nationality and race." See "Konrad Bercovici Is Dead at 80," *New York Times*, December 28, 1961.
4. Bercovici, *Around the World*, 3–4. He fever-dreams the city as "a bazaar at the gateway of a new world" with "wand-risen castles and palaces," "trains winding like illumined snakes . . . hundreds of ferry-boats like giant glow-worms," and commuters like "lava flowing down from the top of a volcano."
5. For example, Joseph Berger, *The World in a City: Traveling the Globe through the Neighborhoods of the New New York* (New York: Ballantine Books, 2009). Here Berger, a *New York Times* metro reporter, explicitly focused on post-1965 ethnic neighborhoods like Bukharian Rego Park and Afghan Flushing.
6. Bercovici, *Around the World*, 23. He transports us with images of theaters, restaurants, and musical cafés, but with little sense of what's happening in homes and schools. In Greenwich Village, he speculates that nine-tenths of the "bead-shops and toy-shops and antique shops and tea shops" have been opened by Boston transplants. Without evidence, the English are placed in New Jersey on the other side of the Hudson/English Channel.

7. See Linda K. Jacobs, *Strangers in the West: The Syrian Colony of New York City, 1880–1900* (New York: Kalimah Press, 2015).
8. Kathleen Benson and Philip M. Kayal, *A Community of Many Worlds: Arab Americans in New York City* (New York: Museum of the City of New York, 2002), 10.
9. Ibid, 29.
10. The Alien and Sedition Acts of 1798, parts of which still remain in place, marked an early but ultimately very limited effort to target outspoken immigrants.
11. For an excellent study of the nativist turn that led to the 1924 Johnson-Reed Immigration Act, see Daniel Okrent, *The Guarded Gate: Bigotry, Eugenics, and the Law That Kept Two Generations of Jews, Italians, and Other European Immigrants out of America* (New York: Scribner, 2020).
12. Jones, *White Borders*, 117.
13. Jan Morris, *The Great Port: A Passage through New York* (New York: Harcourt, Brace & World, 1969), 112.
14. Jones, *White Borders*, 76–78.
15. Ibid, 81.
16. For an account of how New York elites consciously tried to project an image of the city as quintessentially American, see A. M. Blake, *How New York Became American, 1890–1924* (Baltimore: Johns Hopkins University Press, 2006).
17. The 1952 McCarren-Walter Act, while banning various political undesirables, repealed the blanket ban on Asian immigration but with minuscule quotas.
18. For the national impact of the 1965 act, see Nancy Foner, *One Quarter of the Nation: Immigration and the Transformation of America* (Princeton: Princeton University Press, 2022).
19. Jones, *White Borders*, 90–93.
20. See Lauren Hilgers, *Patriot Number One: American Dreams in Chinatown* (New York: Crown, 2018) for an immersive study of Zhuang Liehong, a Chinese activist and immigrant from Wukan fleeing a battle over land rights, who arrives in Flushing on a tourist visa and waits for his asylum application to come through. Zhuang "pursues a number of money-making schemes, including a logistically convoluted and barely profitable personal-shopping business, which involves schlepping to an outlet mall north of the city to buy up discounted designer goods and resell them to moneyed customers back in China." At the same time, he travels across the US to protest the government crackdown in his village. On August 13, 2006, the first congress of the Democratic Party of China was convened at the Sheraton Hotel in Flushing.
21. Speakers of the Ryukyuan languages of Okinawa, at least a small number of whom are in the New York area, are an important exception. The first wave of Korean New Yorkers consisted largely of students, Protestants, and refugees from Japanese occupation, as captured in Younghill Kang's 1937 novel *East Meets West*. In the second half of the twentieth century, Koreans expanded throughout the city, with Manhattan's Koreatown a cultural and culinary showcase while most people moved into Queens or ultimately the suburbs of Bergen County, New Jersey, which is now also a major Japanese hub. A century ago, Japanese New Yorkers were concentrated on West Sixty-Fifth Street in Manhattan, thanks to the Ichiriki and Taiyo boarding houses, and later clusters appeared in the East Village and Astoria. Around 1900, the area around the Brooklyn Navy Yard had small Chinese, Japanese, and Filipino communities, including in the latter many discharged sailors who could legally become US citizens.

22. Many Southeast Asian (e.g., Malaysian, Vietnamese) New Yorkers are ethnic Chinese and speak both the national language and a Sinitic mother tongue like Hokkien, Cantonese, or Teochew. For the Cambodian refugee community in the Bronx, see Eric Tang, *Unsettled: Cambodian Refugees in the New York City Hyperghetto* (Philadelphia: Temple University Press, 2015).
23. Saed, "Samsa on Sheepshead Bay."
24. See Habib Borjian, "What Is Judeo-Median—and How Does It Differ from Judeo-Persian?" *Journal of Jewish Languages* 2, no. 2 (2014): 117–42.
25. Habib Borjian and Daniel Kaufman, "Juhuri: From the Caucasus to New York City," *International Journal of the Sociology of Language* 237 (2016): 59–74.
26. Habib Borjian and Ross Perlin, "Bukhori in New York," Cahier de Studia Iranica 57: 15–27.
27. The café where I met with Boris was subsequently raided by the FBI for its ties with Turkey's Hizmet movement, which is led by the cleric Fethullah Gülen from his Pennsylvania exile.
28. See Dina Dahbany Miraglia, "An Analysis of Ethnic Identity among Yemenite Jews in the Greater New York Area" (PhD diss., Columbia University, 1983); Joseph Sutton, *Magic Carpet: Aleppo-in-Flatbush: The Story of a Unique Ethnic Jewish Community* (New York: Thayer-Jacoby, 1979); Benjamin Hary, "Judeo-Arabic in Its Sociolinguistic Setting," *Israel Oriental Studies*, vol. 15: Language and Culture in the Near East: Diglossia, Bilingualism, Registers. R. Drory and S. Izre'el, eds., 73–99; Ella Shohat, "The Question of Judeo-Arabic," *Arab Studies Journal* 23, no. 1 (2015): 14–76.
29. Until the 1960s, the Syro-Malabar Catholic Church (which is in communion with Rome) used a distinctive Syro-Malabar Syriac as the liturgical language of their chants, but today most singing is in the vernacular language of Malayalam. Father Joseph Palackal, an ethnomusicologist and priest from the Syro-Malabar community now living in Queens, has done extensive work to document remaining knowledge of the Syriac chants.
30. See Jorunn Jacobsen Buckley, "The Ducks That Came to the Marshes," in *The Mandaeans: Ancient Texts and Modern People* (Oxford: Oxford University Press, 2002). For a description of the language largely based on data from the speaker Nasser Sobbi from Queens (faute de mieux), see Charles Häberl, *The Neo-Mandaic Dialect of Khorramshahr*, Semitica Viva vol. 45 (Wiesbaden: Otto Harrassowitz Verlag, 2009).
31. For Turoyo, see C. M. Weaver and G. A. Kiraz, "Turoyo Neo-Aramaic in Northern New Jersey," *International Journal of the Sociology of Language* 237 (2016): 19–36. ELA has recorded stories, proverbs, and memories with Ghaith Hadaya, a speaker of Surath (also called Chaldean Neo-Aramaic), the language of over one hundred thousand Chaldeans worldwide, originally spoken in the plain of Mosul and Iraqi Kurdistan.
32. International Mother Language Day is a UN-sanctioned observance held every February 21 because of events connected to the Bengali language movement, including a group of students at the University of Dhaka who were killed while protesting the imposition of Urdu in what was then East Pakistan. In Bengali, the day is known as ভাষা আন্দোলন দিবস Bhasha Andolôn Dibôs (*Language Movement Day*).
33. Eva Gerharz and Corinna Land, "Uprooted Belonging: The Formation of a 'Jumma Diaspora' in New York City," *Journal of Ethnic and Migration Studies* 44, no. 11 (2018): 1881–96.

34. See Jennifer Gonnerman, "Fighting for the Immigrants of Little Pakistan," *New Yorker*, June 19, 2017.
35. Abraham Lotha, personal communication, December 29, 2021. Speakers, who generally also know the Nagaland lingua franca Nagamese, live scattered across New Jersey, Manhattan, Brooklyn, and Long Island.
36. There is also a thriving community of Madrasis, Guyanese of Tamil origin who espouse a particular form of Hinduism. Between their forty or so mostly private, unofficial temples, usually in people's backyards, and their new forms of public worship and self-organization, they are finding Queens the ideal place to take on centuries-old stigmas and taboos. See Mathieu Claveyrolas, "Guyanese Madrasis in New York City: 'It's All about Progress!'" *DESI La Revue*. Diasporas: Études des singularités indiennes, in *Political Mobilisations of South Asian Migrants. Global Perspectives*, DESI no. 5, eds. Anne-Sophie Bentz and Lola Guyot (Pessac, France: Presses Universitaires de Bordeaux, 2021), 49–77.
37. See Nancy Foner and George M. Fredrickson, eds., *Not Just Black and White: Historical and Contemporary Perspectives on Immigration, Race, and Ethnicity in the United States* (New York: Russell Sage Foundation, 2004), 11–12.
38. Lise Winer and Lona Jack, "English Caribbean Creole in New York," in *The Multilingual Apple: Languages in New York City*, eds. Ofelia Garcia and Joshua Fishman (Berlin and New York: De Gruyter Mouton, 2002), 301–38.
39. At least in London, where Jamaicans are the largest Black population, there is more evidence of stable transmission for Patwa than for other immigrant languages. Formal recognition as a language may be beside the point, or perhaps even actively harmful. See Christian Mair, "Language, Code, and Symbol: The Changing Roles of Jamaican Creole in Diaspora Communities," *AAA: Arbeiten aus Anglistik und Amerikanistik* 28, no. 2 (2003): 231–48.
40. The total number of New Yorkers who speak French as a second or third language is probably higher, partly due to the large numbers of people who arrived from Francophone West Africa beginning in the 1990s.
41. This completely upends the picture from the census, which among other things lumps the African languages it does record into inscrutable categories like the vaguely geographic grouping of "Kru, Ibo, Yoruba." "Niger-Congo," a language family recognized by the census as having over five thousand "speakers" in New York City, is revealed by ELA's data as likely involving dozens of languages, especially Twi, Igbo, and Wolof.
42. For a closer look at African and African American ties in Harlem, including pan-Africanist currents preceding the mass migration of the seventies and eighties, see Boukary Sawadogo, *Africans in Harlem: An Untold New York Story* (New York: Fordham University Press, 2022). Sawadogo also draws a comparison, in terms of intellectual currents and influence, with Paris as a Black diaspora capital in the 1940s.
43. On hometown associations, see Agyemang Attah-Poku, "Asanteman Immigrant Ethnic Association: An Effective Tool for Immigrant Survival and Adjustment Problem Solution in New York City," *Journal of Black Studies* 27, no. 1 (1996): 56–76.
44. See Jonny Steinberg, *Little Liberia: An African Odyssey in New York City* (New York: Random House, 2011).
45. According to witnesses, they killed sixty-seven people, abducted sixteen girls, and raped ninety-three women, if not more. All of the residents fled, most to camps in the region. For Nasseruddin's telling, see Endangered Language Alliance, "Zaghawa Tawila," 2010, www.archive.org/details/ZaghawaTawila.

## III. Present

### Rasmina - सेके, སེ་སྐད་ (Seke)

1. Of course, the city has seen many other kinds of vertical villages as well, with the extreme concentration of different kinds of communities often leading to extraordinarily specific settlement patterns. One particularly well-documented example, thanks to the forty thousand pictures and four hundred hours of music recorded by the photographer Eugene Smith, was the famous "Jazz Loft" at 821 Sixth Avenue, a dilapidated five-story building in the Flower District where hundreds of the greatest jazz musicians of the era lived, hung out, and jammed between 1957 and 1965. A more banal example once mentioned in passing to the author: a network of University of Georgia graduates occupying and passing through a single Williamsburg building over the course of two decades.
2. Anthropologists, economists, and others have studied dhikuti and similar systems around the world. For a description of the very similar dikur system used by Thakali people, who are near neighbors of Seke speakers in Mustang and speak a closely related language, see Michael Vinding, *The Thakali: A Himalayan Ethnography* (Chicago: Serindia Publications, Inc., 1998), 127–33. See also F. A. J. Bouman, "ROSCA: On the Origin of the Species," *Savings and Development* XIX, no. 2 (1995): 129; Alaine Low, *A Bibliographical Survey of Rotating Savings and Credit Associations* (London: Oxfam, 1995).
3. Tontine is a French word based on the name of the Neapolitan banker Lorenzo de Tonti, who in 1653 first proposed a quickly rejected scheme that sounds like *Survivor* for finance geeks: everyone pays in to get an annuity, which grows for the survivors as the other subscribers die. Both word and concept morphed while crossing Francophone Africa, Southeast Asia (Cambodia, Malaysia, Singapore), and eventually Latin America (where tontine became tanda). On May 17, 1792, it was likewise a tontine that launched under the buttonwood tree where people used to do business in Lower Manhattan. A tontine funded by the sale of 203 shares at £200 each led to the establishment of the Tontine Coffee House as a proper hub for all kinds of trading at the corner of Wall and Water Streets. That lasted until 1817, when the traders reformed, reorganized, and rented a dedicated space up the block, known from 1863 as the New York Stock Exchange. The tontine itself wrapped up seven years later, having given birth to the most powerful financial institution in history. There were seven surviving beneficiaries, who had just been kids at the time the tontine was established.
4. Clifford Geertz, "The Rotating Credit Association: A Middle Rung in Development," *Economic Development and Cultural Change* 10, no. 3 (1962): 241–63.
5. Founded in 1982 as a corner store in Woodside, H Mart at the time of writing had over eighty stores worldwide, doing over a billion dollars annually in revenue.
6. Ava Chin, *Mott Street: A Chinese American Family's Story Of Exclusion And Homecoming*. Penguin: New York, 2023.
7. Michel S. Laguerre, *American Odyssey: Haitians in New York City* (Ithaca: Cornell University Press, 1984), 52, 96.
8. Craig, *The Ends of Kinship*, is a masterful experimental ethnography of the deep and evolving ties between Mustang and New York.
9. Himalayan is increasingly a preferred English term, perceived as politically neutral, to refer broadly to people from the whole high-altitude region including Tibet, northern Nepal, northern India, Bhutan, etc. "Himalaya" itself is a Sanksrit word usually

translated as *abode of snow*, and in general few languages inside the region had a single toponym to refer to the region and/or the mountain range as a whole.

10. See Glenn Hendricks, *The Dominican Diaspora: From the Dominican Republic to New York City—Villagers in Transition* (New York: Teachers College Press, 1974).
11. Zohra Saed and Sahar Muradi, *One Story, Thirty Stories: An Anthology of Contemporary Afghan American Literature* (Fayetteville: University of Arkansas Press, 2010).
12. Of course, there is creative placemaking by English speakers too, e.g., the memorable toponymy of the Five Percenters: Manhattan/Harlem ("Mecca") and Brooklyn ("Medina"), The Bronx ("Pelan"), Queens ("the Desert"), and Staten Island as "Shaolin" or "Savior's Island."
13. Aaron Reiss and Jenny Ye, "A Road by Any Other Name," 2017, in *This American Life*, podcast.
14. These names "should not be seen as mere mispronunciations, but rather as cleverly (if not always consciously) construed strategies whereby immigrants could bring their worldview to bear on their accommodation to New York." Hannah Kliger and Rakhmiel Peltz, "Yiddish in New York: Communicating a Culture of Place," in García and Fishman, *Multilingual Apple*, 93–116.
15. There has been an attempt to get Dawson Street, which leads to the park, officially renamed Joseph Chatoyer Way.
16. Scott Hanson, *City of Gods: Religious Freedom, Immigration, and Pluralism in Flushing, Queens* (New York: Fordham University Press, 2016).
17. The informal enclitic pronoun te, given a usage that extends to strangers, may suggest a more complex interpretation, such as *bowing to the divine in you.*
18. There is some variation in how the villages are referred to. In Loke/Tibetan, the villages are known as Tshug, Tsele, Gyaga, Te, and Taye; in Nepali, they are Chhusang, Chele, Gyakar, Tetang, and Tangbe. Nepali /ch/ is equivalent to Tibetan /ts/, and Seke speakers will now sometimes slip back and forth between the two, such that the village may be called Chuksang.
19. The "1.5 generation" refers to those born abroad who largely grow up after emigrating. See Philip Kasinitz, John Mollenkopf, and Mary Waters, eds., *Becoming New Yorkers: Ethnographies of the New Second Generation* (New York: Russell Sage Foundation, 2004), 270.
20. See Honda, "Seke Phonology," Honda, "A Sketch of Tangbe," and Honda, "Grammaticalization in Seke." Years later in Nepal I met the remarkable Phurpha Tsering, a speaker who has been singlehandedly collecting materials, thus far unpublished, on his own Tangbe dialect.
21. See Paul Kay, Brent Berlin, Luisa Maffi, and William Merrifield, "Color Naming across Languages," *Color Categories in Thought and Language* 21, no. 2 (1997).
22. As always, the use of a more general term doesn't mean that speakers can't specify what part of an *arm-hand* or *leg-foot* they mean—whether by using terms like *lower* or *upper* or with terms like *elbow* or *finger* that do exist.
23. Fieldworks Language Explorer, also known as FLEx, is an essential language documentation tool used at ELA and elsewhere, produced by the Summer Institute of Linguistics.
24. André-Georges Haudricourt, "Two-Way and Three-Way Splitting of Tonal Systems in Some Far Eastern Languages," *Tai Phonetics and Phonology* (1972): 58–86.
25. It's a question of what's called "orthographic depth," where "shallow" writing systems are easy to pronounce right off the bat while "deep" ones are harder, reflecting historical developments. English and Tibetan would be examples of deep orthographies, Spanish of a relatively shallow (or "phonetic" and consistent) one.

26. Alexandra Y. Aikhenvald, *Evidentiality* (New York: Oxford University Press, 2004).
27. In Tibetan, a sentence like *There is a mouse over there* can serve as a simplified example of how evidentiality works. If you see the mouse with your eyes, the sentence should end with the evidential marker **dug**, whereas if you infer the mouse's presence (for example, you saw footprints but not the mouse itself), it should end with **yod sa red**. If you know from hearsay, general knowledge, or inference from general facts (for example, the mouse is there every day), you end with **yod kyi red**. You end with **yod red** if you want to be noncommittal or secretive, or if you simply don't know how you know the mouse is over there, it's just a guess or a hunch.
28. A year later the Karmapa's Tibetan opera about the life of the saintly historical figure Milarepa premiered in Queens. Besides being the longest and most virtuosic performance of lip-syncing I have ever seen, the performance was notable for drawing a large audience of his Chinese followers.
29. See Ramble, *Navel of the Demoness*.
30. See Charles Ramble and Christian Seeber, "Dead and living settlements in the Shod-yul of Mustang." Ancient Nepal 138, 107–30 (1995) and Charles Ramble, "Se: Preliminary Notes on the Distribution of an Ethnonym in Tibet and Nepal," in *Les Habitants du Tait du Morule: Etudes recueillies en hommage à Alexander W. Macdonald*, ed. Sarnten Kannay and Philippe Sugant (*Nanterre: Societe d'Ethnologie*, 1997), 485–513; David P. Jackson, "Notes on the History of Se-rib, and Nearby Places in the Upper Kali Gandaki Valley" (1978).

    In "Seke Phonology," Honda reports that one of his Tshugsang informants had visited Khingar and Phalyak about fifty years previous and found several old people speaking Seke.
31. Linguistic evidence for this, but also from Zhangzhung in general, is sparse. See Isao Honda, "Some Notes on 'Gold' and 'Road' in Zhangzhung and Tamangic," *Senri Ethnological Studies* 75 (2009): 99–117.
32. Examples include the Maoist insurgency in Nepal, the Naxalite rebellion in India, Hmong resistance, and the world's longest civil war in Myanmar. See James C. Scott, *The Art of Not Being Governed: An Anarchist History of Upland Southeast Asia* (Singapore: NUS Press, 2010).
33. Nicolas Tournadre, "The Tibetic Languages and Their Classification," *Trans-Himalayan Linguistics: Historical and Descriptive Linguistics of the Himalayan Area* 266, no. 1 (2014): 105–29.
34. Key works on Tamangic languages are the following: Chantyal (Michael Noonan with Ram Prasad Bhulanja, Jag Man Chhantyal, and William Pagliuca, *Chantyal Dictionary and Texts* [Berlin and New York: De Gruyter Mouton, 1999]), Nar-Phu and other languages of Manang (Kristine Hildebrandt, "Nar and Phu Lexical and Discourse Material" [SOAS, Endangered Languages Archive, collection MPI121152, 2011], accessed September 1, 2019), Thakali (Stefan Georg, *Marphatan-Thakali: Untersuchungen zur Sprache des Dorfes Marpha im Oberen Kali-Gandaki-Tal/Nepal*, LINCOM Studies in Asian Linguistics 2 [Munich: LINCOM, 1996]), Tamang (Martine Mazaudon, "Tamang," in *The Sino-Tibetan Languages*, ed. Graham Thurgood and Randy LaPolla [London: Routledge, 2003], 291–314), and Gurung (W. W. Glover, *Sememic and Grammatical Structures in Gurung (Nepal)* [Dallas: Summer Institute of Linguistics, 1974]).
35. Seke speakers talk of Loke speakers making fewer caste distinctions and being in this sense "not as educated," as one puts it. Yet in a gully below the Upper Mustang capital

of Lo Monthang sits the lower-caste zone of Trokpo—from here, too, many have left for New York, where one's status is not immediately forgotten.

36. See Endangered Language Alliance, "After Us, No One Will Speak," YouTube, 2018.
37. The amount of time required for transcription can vary greatly depending on the quality of recording, one's familiarity with the language, the nature of the material, and other factors.
38. For more on ergativity, see, for example, Robert M.W. Dixon, *Ergativity* (Cambridge, UK: Cambridge University Press, 1994)
39. Galen Murton, "Nobody Stops and Stays Anymore: Motor Roads, Uneven Mobilities, and Conceptualizing Borderland Modernity in Highland Nepal," in *Routledge Handbook of Asian Borderlands* (London: Routledge, 2018), 315–24.
40. Himalayan nightlife in Queens didn't start with Thamel, however. Previously, at least some of this crowd would probably have been at the Monastery or the Nunnery, two nearby Irish bars in this once Irish neighborhood that were given those nicknames by their many Tibetan Buddhist patrons, based on how their color schemes suggested those Buddhist institutions in the Himalaya. Some of the dozens of Himalayan-owned restaurants that have opened nearby in the last decade also discreetly have music, dancing, or parties in their basements or upstairs rooms.
41. Nicolas Tournadre, "The Dynamics of Tibetan-Chinese Bilingualism: The Current Situation and Future Prospects," *China Perspectives* (2003): 45.
42. Susan Hangen and Luna Ranjit, *Snapshots of the Nepali-Speaking Community in New York City: Demographics and Challenges* (New York: Adhikaar, 2010).
43. There is a further layer of "Tibetan": a spectrum of what linguists call registers based not on geography but on tradition and social context, including shesa, *polite speech*; kä kyüma, *ordinary speech*; chökä, *Dharma language* (for religion and philosophy); and yikkä, *literary Tibetan*; not to mention "slang" and "secret languages" associated with particular professions. See Nicolas Tournadre, *Manual of Standard Tibetan* (Ithaca: Snow Lion, 2003), 25–29.
44. Estimates range from twenty thousand to fifty thousand.
45. Gurung et al., "Orality and Mobility."
46. Endangered Language Alliance, 2021, "Songs and Singers of the Himalaya," YouTube, 2021.
47. Corey Kilgannon, "Night and Day," *New York Times*, December 13, 2009.
48. See Nicole Hong, "N.Y.P.D. Officer Is Accused of Spying on Tibetans for China," *New York Times*, September 21, 2020. Charges were later dropped.
49. Several hundred people attended the 2016 Himalayan Town Hall organized by city agencies, Himalayan organizations, and the city council member Daniel Dromm (who represented Jackson Heights).
50. See Pasang Yangjee Sherpa, "Sustaining Sherpa Language and Culture in New York," *Book 2.0* 9, no. 1–2 (2019): 19–29.
51. With "Lhapso Land," named for the Sherpa New Year, the kyidug is inadvertently following in the footsteps of many other groups that have sought new possibilities of community maintenance through inexpensive but expansive space upstate. Founded in 1952, Soyuzivka, a nearby Ukrainian cultural center/hotel/spa/camp focusing on arts and sports, stretches over two hundred acres and includes twenty buildings named for Ukrainian cities and built in the traditional Carpathian resort style. Elsewhere in the Catskills there are Latvian-, Lemko-, and Yiddish-speaking summer colonies, to name just some of the Eastern European groups.

## Husniya - X̌ik (Wakhi)

1. As used by linguists, Pamiri is a geographic grouping, not a genealogical linguistic one in the sense of having a shared innovation that neatly separates them from other Iranian languages. Yet most Pamiri languages are quite closely related and may be converging further.
2. Husniya says her eight-year-old nieces in Dushanbe, currently going to Tajik school and planning to switch to Russian, are now speaking Persian with each other thanks to this channel, which wasn't available before.
3. For more information on the Pamiri Stories series published by ELA, see www.elalliance.org/our-work/revitalization/storybooks.
4. Certain well-traveled words, names, and phrases stretch farther and last longer than empires. Another example across this same zone are tales of the trickster antihero Molla Nasreddin and the nearly just as mythical Alexander the Great (a.k.a. Iskender, Sikandar).
5. Endangered Language Alliance, "A Wakhi Grandmother from Pakistan to Brooklyn," YouTube, 2018.
6. The phenomenon is particularly advanced in western areas of the Alps, but there are similar phenomena in mountainous areas worldwide—e.g., around Kilimanjaro, the High Atlas, the West Caucasus, and the Sapporo Mountains.
7. The Pamir Knot was the original bam-e dunya, *roof of the world*, a Persian term only later calqued into English and shifted east to the central Himalaya, thanks to British colonial activities and the nineteenth-century discovery that Chomolungma was the world's highest peak.
8. Shibboleth crimes have not always been easy to substantiate—as in the so-called parsley massacre of 1937, when Dominican soldiers were said to have forced Haitians to pronounce perejil, the Spanish word for *parsley*. If they could pronounce it the Spanish way the soldiers considered them Dominican and let them live, but if they pronounced it the French or Creole way they considered them Haitian and executed them.
9. See Vlad Ilkevich, "Dushan-Bangers: Female Voices of 1980s Tajik Pop," EastEast, undated, www.easteast.world/en/posts/291.
10. Dastarkhan, a Turkic word, is used across Central and South Asia and sometimes beyond to refer to both the tablecloth itself and the whole space and setting for the meal.
11. G. R. van den Berg, "Literary Afterlives: Mediaeval Persian Poets and Strategies of Legitimisation in the Oral Poetry of the Ismāʿīlī's of Tajik Badakhshan," *Jerusalem Studies in Arabic and Islam* 45 (2019): 355–80.
12. See Richard K. Wolf, "The Musical Poetry of Endangered Languages," *Oral Tradition* 35 (2021): 103–66.
13. Richard Wolf's film *Two Poets and a River* contains rare and wonderful footage juxtaposing Qurbonsho, a singer from Vrang in Tajikistan who started in the 1990s and inspired new compositions in Wakhi, and Daulatsho in Afghanistan, who began writing in Wakhi around 2006, inspired both by other Afghan Wakhis and by Pakistani Wakhis—"a new way of using our language," he calls it.

## Boris - ייִדיש (Yiddish)

1. Though the words in this expression are of Germanic origin, the reference is apparently to the Hebrew Bible, specifically Psalms 90:4: "For a thousand years in Thy sight are but as yesterday when it is past" (in the King James translation).

Here and elsewhere I use the YIVO transliteration system for rendering Yiddish in Latin letters.

2. Revernacularization is the preferred term. For a period, there was a vision of a single bilingual Hebrew-Yiddish literature, with many writing in both languages. See Naomi Brenner, *Lingering Bilingualism: Modern Hebrew and Yiddish Literatures in Contact* (Syracuse: Syracuse University Press, 2016). For how Yiddish underlies much of Hebrew (a.k.a. "Israeli"), see Ghil'ad Zuckermann, "A New Vision for Israeli Hebrew: Theoretical and Practical Implications of Analyzing Israel's Main Language as a Semi-Engineered Semito-European Hybrid Language," *Journal of Modern Jewish Studies* 5, no. 1 (2006): 57–71.
3. Besides the ghosts and the resurrected corpses, Singer lists as reasons the fact that Yiddish itself might somehow resurrect, as Hebrew did, and finally that "Yiddish may be a dying language but it is the only language I know well. Yiddish is my mother language and a mother is never really dead."
4. Vivien Schweitzer, "Evgeny Kissin Will Indulge His Love of Yiddish Poetry at Carnegie Hall," *New York Times*, December 13, 2015. The other writer is Emil Kalin, who came from Romania to Israel at the age of four and grew up speaking Hebrew but started teaching himself Yiddish while in the Israeli army. "Where does he come by all of this?" marvels Boris, citing the mature style of Kalin's recent *Bukareshter shriftn* (*Bucharest Writings*).
5. Perlin, "What Was the *kultur-tuer*?"
6. Of course, even dominant cultures fall out of conversation with themselves, so that many poets today don't feel they need to have heard of Auden.
7. Max Weinreich, *History of the Yiddish Language*, vol. 1, ed. Paul Glasser, trans. Shlomo Noble, with the assistance of Joshua A. Fishman (New Haven and London: Yale University Press, 2008).
8. The example is my own, but a fortuitously similar one appears on the website of the Jewish Languages Project with which ELA is affiliated.
9. See Michael Weisser, *A Brotherhood of Memory: Jewish Landsmanshaftn in the New World* (New York: Basic Books, 1985). Most lasted for the lifetime of just one "generation," approximately 1900–1970. Though sometimes seen as "conservative," "backward-looking," and "fusty," they also played a key role in aid efforts during the world wars and after the Holocaust, though the New Deal reduced the need for their mutual-aid component.
10. The complex story of Yiddish in Israel is taken up in Yael Chaver, *What Must Be Forgotten: The Survival of Yiddish in Zionist Palestine* (Syracuse: Syracuse University Press, 2004), and Rachel Rojanski, *Yiddish in Israel: A History* (Bloomington: Indiana University Press, 2020).
11. Yiddish has left at least a trace in what linguist Anna Verschik calls Jewish Russian, "a cluster of post-Yiddish varieties of Russian used as a special in-group register by Ashkenazic Jews in Russia." Jewish Russian is sometimes equated with or compared to the particular Yiddish-influenced variety of Russian long spoken in Odessa in today's Ukraine. Though Jewish Russian has been little studied outside the former USSR, for the past half century Brooklyn's "Little Odessa" (Brighton Beach and the surrounding neighborhoods) has represented a major concentration of Russian-speaking Jews and appears to be a site for use of the ethnolect.
12. An alternate translation of the title, *Hidden Saints I Recall*, is no closer to the mark. As yet, there is no English translation of the book itself.
13. For the English translation, see Boris Sandler, *Red Shoes for Rachel: Three Novellas* (Syracuse: Syracuse University Press, 2017).

14. A similar community developed on a smaller scale in eastern Queens, as memorably described by the novelist Sergei Dovaltov in *A Foreign Woman*. From that nucleus of Jewish refuseniks has grown a much larger and more diverse Russian-speaking zone in eastern Queens, encompassing parts of Forest Hills and Kew Gardens and including Bukharian Jews, non-Jewish Russians, and Central Asian Muslims.
15. An unforgettable portrayal of the whole post-Soviet milieu is the Georgian movie *Brighton 4th*, in which a retired Georgian wrestler comes to Brighton Beach to bring home his son, who is living there with a Georgian opera-singer-turned-doorman and an Uzbek portrait artist.
16. Belz in Moldova is not to be confused with Belz in Poland or with Belz in Ukraine, where the Belzer Hasidim are from. The Belzers now form one of the largest Hasidic communities in Borough Park as well as elsewhere in New York and New Jersey.
17. From the point of view of Yiddish dialectology, Bessarabian Yiddish falls under Southeastern (a.k.a. Ukrainian) Yiddish. The irony of the secular klal "standard" being based on the now highly endangered Northeastern (a.k.a. Lithuanian) variety is increasingly recognized, and the Southern (a.k.a. Polish/Hungarian) Yiddish used in Hasidic communities is now by dint of demographics the de facto standard.
18. Boris's mother's "shtetl" was actually an agricultural colony, where Jews farmed land originally granted by the Romanian king. Mărculești (as it is now known in Moldovan) is the subject of Matthew Mishory's 2015 documentary *Absent*, about the massacre of its entire Jewish population in 1941 by the Romanian army. His father's family was from Rîbnița on the Ukrainian border.
19. Numbers vary. See Wolf Moskovich, "Bessarabia," *YIVO Encyclopedia of Jews in Eastern Europe* (2010).
20. Mikhail Krutikov, "Introduction," in *Stones Don't Bear Witness: A Historical Novel of the Kishinev Pogrom,* ed. B. Sandler and B. Zumoff (New York: KTAV Publishing House, 2011). The Yiddish title is completely different.
21. Boris Sandler *Lamed-vovnikes fun mayn zikorn* [The Hidden Righteous Ones in My Memory]. (New York: Forverts Oysgabe), 8–9.
22. In Yiddish, the Night of the Murdered Poets is known as Harugey Malkus, in reference to ten martyred rabbis in Roman times. Likewise emphasizing echoes and continuities, the usual Yiddish term for the Holocaust is Khurbn, *Destruction*, linking it to the similarly named destruction of the First and Second Temples in Jerusalem.
23. Mensch in Yiddish means both *person* and *ethical upstanding person*—the latter is the source of the (Jewish) English word. In this passage, the Yiddish original behind both *person* and *mensch* is mensch.
24. Steven J. Zipperstein, *Pogrom: Kishinev and the Tilt of History* (New York: Liveright Publishing, 2018).
25. Russian translations of certain Yiddish authors, notably Sholem Aleichem, were available, as well as a few ideologically correct newspapers in Yiddish: *Der Birobidzhaner Shtern* and the Israeli communist newspaper *Der Veg*. Boris bought Yiddish books, which were hard to find, privately from other Jews.
26. See Christa Whitney's 2019 oral history with Boris Sandler for the Yiddish Book Center: Boris Sandler Oral History Interview, interviewed by Christa Whitney, Yiddish Book Center's Wexler Oral History Project, Brooklyn, New York, May 6, 2019.
27. Yiddish traditionally has a dual orthographic system, where words of Germanic and Slavic origin are typically spelled "phonetically" while Hebrew and Aramaic words are spelled as they would be in those languages. The Soviet Yiddish orthography, in Boris's view, was a well-intentioned effort to broaden literacy as part of the Soviet

Yiddish school system of the 1920s and '30s. The issue became hopelessly political, and the Soviet orthography has fallen completely out of use. See Gennady Estraikh, *Yiddish in the Cold War* (London: Routledge, 2017).

28. Boris believes there are now at most a few thousand Jews still living in the country, principally in Kishinev, Belz, and Bender. He was last there for the hundredth anniversary of Shraybman's birth (in 2014). Shraybman remained in Moldova until his death.
29. In the film, Boris points out that there are no common Jewish surnames based on the demonyms for New York, Paris, or Amsterdam, even though those cities have large Jewish populations. In a jaunty patterned cap and leather jacket and somehow calling to mind Werner Herzog, he interviews Shraybman and provides Yiddish commentaries (a first in the Soviet Union) as classic interwar Yiddish pop music from New York plays. It ends with him crossing names out of the phone book. Boris also produced a film called *Don't Give Up Yiddish* during this same period.
30. Reasons for choosing Bainbridge Avenue included the fast transit connections to Manhattan and the availability of green space. Roosevelt, New Jersey, was also considered. See Janina Wurbs, *Generationenübergreifender Jiddischismus: Skizzen kultureller Biographien der Familie Beyle Schaechter-Gottesman*, vol. 11 (Postdam: Universitätsverlag Potsdam, 2018).
31. A. Mac Póilin, "Belfast's Neo-Gaeltacht," in *Bringing Our Languages Home*, ed. L. Hinton, (Berkeley: Heyday, 2013), 141–63; F. Mac Ionnrachtaigh, *Language, Resistance and Revival: Republican Prisoners and the Irish Language in the North of Ireland* (London: Pluto Press, 2013).
32. See the critique in Dovid Katz, "The Yiddish Conundrum: A Cautionary Tale for Language Revivalism," in *The Palgrave Handbook of Minority Languages and Communities*, ed. Gabrielle Hogan-Brun and Bernadette O'Rourke (London: Palgrave Macmillan, 2019), 553–87.
33. Wurbs, *Generationenübergreifender Jiddischismus*, 97–114.
34. For the secular Yiddish school system in the US (including supplementary, afternoon, and Sunday schools), see Naomi Prawer Kadar, *Raising Secular Jews: Yiddish Schools and Their Periodicals for American Children, 1917–1950* (Waltham: Brandeis University Press, 2016).
35. The *svive* was called Enge-Benge, after a counting rhyme made popular by Sholem Aleichem: "Enge benge / stupe stenge / artse bartse / gele shvartse / eygele feygele khik." See Rachael Kafrissen, "Enge Benge Revisited," *Jewish Currents*, December 1, 2007.
36. Schaechter first found his calling as a zamler, a collector of songs and tales and tidbits, in a Displaced Persons camp outside Vienna. As in Moldova, the DP camps, where a million "nonrepatriable" Holocaust survivors were stuck before eventually managing to scatter to the US, Canada, Australia, and Israel, were a place where non-Hasidic Jewish children often spoke Yiddish, for a few years anyway.

    Two other major linguist-heroes in New York at the time, though not part of Bainbridge, played a key role in establishing Yiddish in the academy: historian Max Weinreich and his son Uriel Weinreich at Columbia University, who pioneered the study of language contact in linguistics.
37. "A Bronkser Suriname," in the words of Itsik Gottesman, Shaechter's son and a prominent contemporary Yiddish klal-tuer himself, referring to the territorialist project of carving out a Yiddish-speaking territory in Suriname.
38. Fortunately, the prefixes to many Yiddish words begin with aleph. The great unabridged dictionary can be said to have begun as the modest idea of Nahum Stutshkov, the

Yiddish lexicographer, playwright, and radio personality in New York who assembled the monumental *Oytser fun der yidisher shprakh* (*Treasury of the Yiddish Language*), a Yiddish thesaurus. Its chief impresario was Yudl Mark, who published the four volumes beginning with aleph between 1961 and 1980. Containing nearly fifty thousand entries and thirty-three thousand subentries, the *Comprehensive English-Yiddish Dictionary* published in 2016 is the closest thing to a result. *The Great Dictionary of the Yiddish Language* is a new opera in progress by Alex Weiser and Ben Kaplan about this effort.

39. See Alec Eliezer Burko, "Saving Yiddish: Yiddish Studies and the Language Sciences in America, 1940–1970" (PhD diss., The Jewish Theological Seminary of America, 2019). Yet the New York Yiddishists ignored Hasidic Yiddish and its regrowth: see C. R. Nove, "The Erasure of Hasidic Yiddish from Twentieth Century Yiddish Linguistics," *Journal of Jewish Languages* 6, no. 1 (2018): 109–41.
40. Just obtaining a quality wire recorder—he took a job at a local dealership to get one—and shlepping it on the subway from Sunnyside every day was no small matter. I first learned of the Stonehill recordings when I joined the Jewish People's Philharmonic Chorus, directed by Mordkhe Schaechter's son Binyumen and singing a kind of Yiddish choral music I didn't know existed in a once-grand room at the Marseilles, which is now senior housing. Miriam Isaacs has been working to make the Stonehill archive available.
41. Aaron Lansky, *Outwitting History: The Amazing Adventures of a Man Who Rescued a Million Yiddish Books* (New York: Algonquin Books, 2004).
42. See Wurbs, *Generationenübergreifender Jiddischismus*.
43. Put succinctly: "The prime desire of the immigrant generations of East European-born Jews in the United States (or Canada, Britain, Australia, South Africa, as well as France, Argentina, and various others), whether they came before the war, or as Holocaust survivors, was to build a good and tranquil life where their children and grandchildren could thrive on a level playing field with anyone else and rise to the highest positions of personal success and achievement. Anecdotally, and sometimes not only anecdotally, that could mean, say, sweatshop toiler immigrants worried that their children might have some slight trace of a foreign accent or mannerisms in places like America that would hinder them becoming a doctor or lawyer or 'at least an accountant.'" Katz, "The Yiddish Conundrum," 565.
44. For more on young Yiddishism during this period, especially in New York, see Joshua Friedman. "Yiddish Returns: Language, Intergenerational Gifts, and Jewish Devotion" (PhD diss., University of Michigan, 2015).
45. See Jeffrey Shandler, *Adventures in Yiddishland: Postvernacular Language and Culture* (Berkeley: University of California Press, 2005).
46. One midrash states that the Jewish people survived enslavement in Egypt in part because they (supposedly) did not change their language—a point about language maintenance not in any way meant to suggest that Moses (Moishele!) was a Yiddish speaker.
47. On the practical side of how the community established and maintained itself in Williamsburg, see Nathaniel Deutsch and Michael Casper, *A Fortress in Brooklyn: Race, Real Estate, and the Making of Hasidic Williamsburg* (New Haven and London: Yale University Press, 2021).
48. In terms of today's map, the Unterland is more or less "the northwestern corner of Romania, in East Slovakia, and in Carpathian Ruthenia. In a wider sense, it also comprises the rest of Transylvania and the mountainous parts of East Slovakia and

Carpathian Ruthenia." See Steffen Krogh, "How Yiddish Is Haredi Satmar Yiddish?" *Journal of Jewish Languages* 6, no. 1 (2018): 5–42.

49. Interestingly, there have been steps to combat this in the Hasidic community. See Ayala Fader, "Literacy, Bilingualism, and Gender in a Hasidic Community," *Linguistics and Education* 12, no. 3 (2001): 261–83; Ayala Fader, "Reclaiming Sacred Sparks: Linguistic Syncretism and Gendered Language Shift among Hasidic Jews in New York," *Journal of Linguistic Anthropology* 17, no. 1 (2007): 1–22.
50. Katz, "The Yiddish Conundrum," explores this "conundrum" with verve.
51. Is this one reason among many why secular urban people abandon their languages—discomfort not only with their traditional and often religious associations but also with the vexed questions of belief, adherence, or traditionalism more broadly?
52. OTD = off the derech, or *path* of Hasidism. As many of the recent OTD memoirs have touched on, lack of English skills is one of the things that can make it difficult to leave the community.
53. Rose Waldman, "Lost Yiddish Words," *Tablet*, December 11, 2020.
54. The great feminist writer Ellen Willis captured what was happening early on, relating the story of her bal-tshuve brother Mike. Traditional Judaism, wrote Willis, offered an aimless seeker "absolute values to which [he] could dedicate his life; a new and exciting subject to study; a close-knit religious community; a stable, secure social structure." Willis was initially shocked—"In my universe, intelligent, sensible people who had grown up in secular homes in the second half of the twentieth century did not embrace biblical fundamentalism"—until she went to see for herself. See Ellen Willis, "Next Year in Jerusalem," *Rolling Stone*, April 21, 1977.
55. Eliza Shapiro and Brian M. Rosenthal, "In Hasidic Enclaves, Failing Private Schools Flush with Public Money," *New York Times*, September 11, 2022. Remarkably, the story was published with a Yiddish translation, clearly done by a translator from within the Hasidic community—apparently a first not only for the *Times* but perhaps for any non-Yiddish newspaper.
56. Samuel Norich, the longtime publisher of both the English and Yiddish editions of the *Forward* who still serves in multiple roles with the larger organization, told me that the commitment to socialism remained in the bylaws until 1967 (when it was replaced by a commitment to social justice), but that "socialism probably had ceased to be an animating idea several decades earlier" and that "the last year the *Forverts* endorsed the Socialist Party candidate for President was 1932."
57. In 1917, there were eight Yiddish dailies in the US with a combined circulation over six hundred thousand. The *Forward* was also one of the first truly national newspapers in any language, with editions not only in eastern cities like Philadelphia and Boston, but later in Chicago, Detroit, Cleveland, Milwaukee, St. Louis, and Los Angeles, with a national advertising network. See Brian Dolber, "'Digging in the Dark': The *Forward*'s Advertising Strategy in the 1920s," *Media and Culture in the US Jewish Labor Movement* (London: Palgrave Macmillan, 2017), 13–49.
58. Isaac Metzker, *A Bintel Brief: Sixty Years of Letters from the Lower East Side to the Jewish Daily Forward* (New York: Schocken, 2011).
59. However, of the four Nepali newspapers in New York City (*Vishwa Sandesh*, *Everest Times*, *Khasokhas*, and *Nepalaya*)—all struggled during the COVID-19 pandemic and were turning entirely to digital.
60. For instance, Brazilians in New York in the 1990s would regularly record or videotape sixty- to ninety-minute messages to send to family and friends back home. See Maxine L. Margolis, *Little Brazil: An Ethnography of Brazilian Immigrants in New York*

*City* (Princeton: Princeton University Press, 1993). Voices of New York was a website that highlighted and translated into English the best work of many of the city's "ethnic media" outlets.

61. "A minority were younger people who had studied Yiddish in university and achieved sufficient literacy to be able to read often sophisticated texts. Most readers usually read all of an issue of the paper." Samuel Norich, personal communication, March 3, 2023.
62. This unbelievably prolific Yiddish Fernando Pessoa—who also wrote the six-volume *Oysgebrente likht* (*Extinguished Lights*) on his experiences during the Holocaust—had already done the same for decades at other Yiddish newspapers in Paris and New York before he came to the *Forward* in 1987 (while continuing to edit *Der Yidisher Kempfer*!).
63. *Vorwärts* was the name of the German Social Democrats' New York newspaper. Here and elsewhere German New Yorkers, especially socialists, were a help and inspiration to Yiddish-speaking socialists, with German-Yiddish intelligibility clearly a bridge. *Foroys* was also the name of an actual Yiddish newspaper in Mexico City.
64. The Russian *Forward* lasted around a decade. Conceived by newly arrived New Yorker Vladimir (Velvl) Yedidovitch, a former high-ranking Soviet naval officer who was born in Vilna and steeped in Yiddish, it was "a beautiful and intellectual newspaper," according to Boris. After Yedidovitch, it was edited by Leonid Shkolnik, who learned Yiddish as an adolescent and became editor of the *Birobidzhaner Shtern*. The paper "was sold for a pittance to its enemies—a nasty dirty thing," says Boris.
65. "Guilty pleasure" is Samuel Norich's phrase, and he notes that articles on Haredi/Hasidic topics get more than double the readership of others, closer to fifty thousand unique visitors per month—with these readers exclusively using mobile devices.
66. In 2019, soon after Boris's retirement, the Forward Association stopped printing both the English and Yiddish editions, and the latter has palpably faded to what Boris calls a "bulletin" of several pieces of online content per week, mostly translated or drawn from elsewhere. Norich notes that there are still two full-time staff members as well as a few regular freelancers, and that two to three videos are posted each week, including "Yiddish Word of the Day."
67. Trep is a *flight of stairs*. Other translations for trepverter could be *staircase wit*, or *words that come too late*, and there is a clear parallel in the French l'esprit du escalier and German Treppenwitz, with calquing from the former likely. As Saul Bellow writes in *Herzog*, "At first there was no pattern to the notes he made. They were fragments—nonsense syllables, exclamations, twisted proverbs and quotations or, in the Yiddish of his long-dead mother, *Trepverter*—retorts that came too late, when you were already on your way down the stairs."

## Ibrahima - ߒߞߏ (N'ko)

1. Mahmoud Sangaré, ߦߌ ߞߏ ߛߎߟߋߡߊ߯ߣߊ ߞߊ߲ߕߍ ߡߍ߲߫؟ [Who Is Sulemaana Kantè?] (Bamako, Mali, 2011). In Donaldson, "Orthography, Standardization, and Register," 89.
2. The publication was Maruwa's *Nahnou fi Afriqya* (*We in Africa*). Maruwa later became a prominent founder of Arabic, English, and French newspapers in Beirut, and in the 1950s helped innovate Arabic typography for the then-popular Linotype machine.
3. Donaldson, "The Role of Islam," 464–65.
4. Oyler, "Re-Inventing Oral Tradition," 79–82.

5. Wyrod, "Social Orthography," 32–33.
6. Djibril Tamsir Niane, "An Epic of Old Mali" (New York: Longman, 1965), 87. As told to Niane by the jeli Mamadou Kouyaté, this has become the "classic" version of the West African Sundiata epic.
7. Wyrod, "Social Orthography," 33.
8. K. Konadu-Agyemang, B.K. Takyi, and J.A. Arthur, *The New African Diaspora in North America: Trends, Community Building, and Adaptation* (Lanham, MD: Lexington Books), 97–102.
9. Cheikh Anta Babou, "Brotherhood Solidarity, Education and Migration: The Role of the Dahiras among the Murid Muslim Community of New York," *African Affairs* 101, no. 403 (2002): 151–70.
10. Stoller, *Money Has No Smell*, 17.
11. The market was closed by the Giuliani administration and later moved to 116th Street, where it operates today as the Malcolm Shabazz African Market. Stoller, *Money Has No Smell*, 13.
12. Stoller, *Yaya's Story*.
13. Stoller, *Money Has No Smell*.
14. S. Kántɛ, ߒߞߏ ߞߊ߲ߜߍ ߞߎ߲ߓߊߓߊ (*N'ko' Kangbè Kùnbabá'*) [The Big Book of N'ko Grammar], ed. M. Jàrà (Bamako: Bakoroba, 2008). In Donaldson, "Orthography, Standardization, and Register," 83–84, 92.
15. Ibid, 30.
16. Donaldson, "Clear Language," 137–67.
17. Ibid, 209.
18. Donaldson, "Linguistic and Civic Refinement," 12–18.
19. Ibid, 159. There seems to be slight variation in the terminology of the English translation, with Development and Justice sometimes substituted for each other.
20. Oyler, "The N'ko Alphabet," 249.
21. Coleman Donaldson, "The Role of Islam, Ajami Writings, and Educational Reform in Sulemaana Kantè's N'ko," *African Studies Review* 63, no. 3 (2020): 462–86.
22. Oyler, "The N'ko Alphabet," 248.
23. Wyrod, "Social Orthography," 41. There is some hope of reaching non-Manding communities with N'ko as well, but it's not clear whether this can be accomplished.
24. See V. Vydrin, "New Electronic Resources for Texts in Manding Languages," in *Searching for Sharing: Heritage and Multimedia in Africa*, vol. 7, ed. D. Merolla and M. Turin (Cambridge, UK: Open Book Publishers, 2017), 109–22.
25. Johanna Drucker, *Inventing the Alphabet: The Origins of Letters from Antiquity to the Present* (Chicago: University of Chicago Press, 2022).
26. There is a debate between those who see a divide, e.g., Jack Goody, ed., *Literacy in Traditional Societies* (Cambridge, UK: Cambridge University Press, 1968), and those who see orality and literacy as practices embedded in particular social contexts, e.g., Brian Street, *Literacy in Theory and Practice* (Cambridge, UK: Cambridge University Press, 1984).
27. William Smalley, Chia Koua Vang, and Gnia Yee Yang, *Mother of Writing: The Origin and Development of a Hmong Messianic Script* (Chicago: University of Chicago Press, 1990).
28. For the rapid progression of Pahawh Hmong from handwriting to wood block to heroic attempts under wartime conditions to make a Pahawh typewriter by hand with traditional Hmong silversmith and blacksmith technology, see Smalley et al., *Mother of Writing*, 104–7. Nearly twenty years later, there was finally progress towards word

processing on computers, thanks to work with IBM funded by supporters. Though Pahawh Hmong can be typed and used in various applications today, leaders of the movement in the US have found it hard to keep up classes and stimulate the interest of the younger generation.

29. "Though isolated from one another, these cases exhibit conspicuous similarities: speakers of a minority language experience violent conflict resulting in a community crisis, a prophet emerges with a new cultural and spiritual program presented in terms of both a return to traditional ways of life and the building of a modern nation, and a supernatural entity reveals an authentic indigenous script to the prophet who teaches it to his followers. The prophet maintains that the new script will bring a corrective influence on a suffering society, the perceived degeneration of which is viewed [as] a driving cause of political marginalization and ill fortune." See Piers Kelly, *The Last Language on Earth: Linguistic Utopianism in the Philippines* (Oxford: Oxford University Press, 2021), 244.
30. See Piers Kelly, "The Invention, Transmission and Evolution of Writing: Insights from the New Scripts of West Africa," in *Paths into Script Formation in the Ancient Mediterranean*, ed. Silvia Ferrara and Miguel Valério (Rome: Studi Micenei ed Egeo Anatolici, 2018), 189–209. Kelly points out that weavers, tailors, and carpenters were involved in their development. Exhibited at MOMA in 2022, the artist Frédéric Bruly Bouabré's Bété syllabary, developed around the same time as N'ko, makes the artistry of orthography explicit.
31. Thousands of Vai men were in the Grassfields of Cameroon right at the time of the invention of the Bamum script. The men were working for the Germans as carriers and soldiers to "pacify" the peoples of the interior. Staten Island's Cape Mount Association uses Vai characters on the program at their annual celebration. Konrad Tuchscherer, personal communication, October 22, 2021.
32. Konrad Tuchscherer and Paul Hair, "Cherokee and West Africa: Examining the Origins of the Vai Script," *History in Africa* 29 (2002): 427–86. George Guess, known as Sequoya, lived from 1770 to 1843 in Tennessee. He was nonliterate but observed those around him, and his refined 1821 system was approved by the Cherokee Nation and spread widely for decades among thousands, including in books and newspapers. The earliest known example of Vai writing was found on the house of Austin Curtis, a Cherokee trader who had settled in Vai country just a few years earlier. It's not clear whether Curtis knew the Cherokee syllabary, or how he might have been connected to Bukele, but missionaries were soon creating Cherokee-inspired syllabaries for languages as disparate as Bassa (also in Liberia) and Cree (in Canada).
33. Oyler, "Re-Inventing Oral Tradition," 87.
34. The phrase is given in Charles Bird, "Poetry in the Mande: Its Form and Meaning," *Poetics* 5, no. 2 (1976): 89–100, but for consistency it is rendered here in N'ko and interpreted into a Latin-based (Maninka) form, with thanks to Coleman Donaldson.
35. For a fascinating broader discussion, see Susie J. Tanenbaum, *Underground Harmonies: Music and Politics in the Subways of New York* (Ithaca: Cornell University Press, 1995).
36. David C. Conrad, "From the Banan Tree of Kouroussa: Mapping the Landscape in Mande Traditional History," *Canadian Journal of African Studies/Revue canadienne des études africaines* 42, no. 2–3 (2008): 384–408.
37. Lisa Feder, *Jeliya at the Crossroads: Learning African Wisdom through an Embodied Practice* (London: Springer Nature, 2021), 122.
38. David Racanelli, "Diasporic Jeliya as a Collaborative Trade in New York City," *African Music: Journal of the International Library of African Music* 9, no. 1 (2011): 136–53.

39. Beginning in 1997, New York's Center for Traditional Music and Dance ran a program called Badenya, producing concerts of jeliw music. The resulting recording from the project is *Badenya: Manden Jaliya in New York City*, Smithsonian Folkways, SFW 40494, 2002.
40. The scene is described in Feder, *Jeliya at the Crossroads*, 146.
41. Donaldson, "Clear Language," 10.
42. At least initially, the 2022 release of Google Translate for Bambara, the first Manding (and West African) language to be supported, does use the official Latin system.
43. Microsoft, "Can an Alphabet Save a Culture?" undated, news.microsoft.com/stories/people/adlam.html.

## Irwin - Nahuatl

1. Rebecca Ann Dufendach, "Nahua and Spanish Concepts of Health and Disease in Colonial Mexico, 1519–1615" (PhD diss., University of California, Los Angeles, 2017), 60–61.
2. Some of Irwin's poetry, translated in collaboration with Daniel Kaufman, is being published by ELA.
3. The pre-Hispanic settlement is today a site called Tlilostoc.
4. The number of languages is from Ethnologue; the number of speakers is from INEGI (Instituto Nacional de Estadística y Geografía). 2020. Censo de Población y Vivienda 2020. Mexico, D.F.: INEGI. www.inegi.org.mx.
5. Hill and Hill, *Speaking Mexicano*, 90–91.
6. Ibid, 90–91.
7. Ibid, 22.
8. Ibid, 156–177. Also heavily used from Spanish are "function words and particles, including discourse and conversational eleemnts, logical connectives, conjunctions, prepositions, exclamations, and hesitation forms," especially de and que.
9. Ibid, 251.
10. James Richard Andrews, *Introduction to Classical Nahuatl*, vol. 1 (Norman: University of Oklahoma Press, 2003), 18.
11. For more on desindianización and the ongoing force of Indigenous lifeways in the "México profundo" (*deep Mexico*) from which so many Mexican New Yorkers come, see Guillermo Bonfil Batalla and Philip A. Dennis, *México Profundo: Reclaiming a Civilization* (Austin: University of Texas Press, 1996).
12. Hill and Hill, *Speaking Mexicano*, 404.
13. "According to village residents, about fifty years ago, Mexicano could be heard everywhere in the village. In the past, as you walked down the dirt roads, you would pass a person and they would greet you in Mexicano; children playing games would tease and joke in Mexicano, and young children would talk to older people in Mexicano, a sign of respect . . . [Now] Spanish was the dominant language. The younger people spoke Spanish; if elders were not present, then Mexicano was not used." See Rosalva Mojica Lagunas, "Nahuatl in Coatepec: Ideologies, Practices and Management for Linguistic and Cultural Continuance," *International Review of Education* 65, no. 1 (2019), 67–86.
14. Even today, says Irwin, there are only five people from the town in New York and another five in Minnesota—tiny numbers compared to the thousands from Atlixco, Tulcingo, etc.
15. Smith, *Mexican New York*, 19.

16. Alison Mountz and Richard A. Wright, "Daily Life in the Transnational Migrant Community of San Agustin, Oaxaca, and Poughkeepsie, New York." *Diaspora: A Journal of Transnational Studies* 5.3 (1996): 403–28.
17. Many Mixtec speakers have also migrated internally to or near northern cities like Culiacán and Tijuana—way stations, sometimes, en route to the US, where some, however, remain.
18. Kaufman, "The Mixtec Language." In the name of unity, some speakers may prefer to refer to Mixtec in terms of different varieties of one language.
19. See the story of Marta in Leslie A. Martino-Vélez, *Indigenous Mexicans in New York City: Immigrant Integration, Language Use, and Identity Formation* (PhD diss., City University of New York, 2022). Born in the Mixtec-speaking town of Telotepec in Guerrero, she has never been to Mexico City or anywhere else in the country beyond the city of Tlapa. At the age of twenty-nine, she made her way to the border, crossed on foot, and came by bus to East Harlem to join a partner already in the city. She was unusual, but by no means unique, in knowing only basic Spanish—a language she is trying to learn in New York. She never attended school, though others from a similar background might have on average around five years of formal education. Now she lives in a rented room in someone's else apartment with her two small children, one of whom is enrolled in a local Head Start program with twenty other local children from Mixtec- and Nahuatl-speaking backgrounds (of 142 total). There are few known cases, here or elsewhere, of parents fully transmitting an Indigenous language to their children after emigrating. As a result, some Indigenous children end up "between languages," with no real mother tongue. Over half of those at the Head Start program were in speech therapy or likely to start soon.
20. See Stephanie Wood, ed., *Online Nahuatl Dictionary* (Eugene, OR: Wired Humanities Projects, College of Education, University of Oregon), "ayecotli", nahuatl.uoregon.edu.
21. A new coinage, like Italian "pomodoro" (literally *golden apple*), doesn't really change the equation.
22. Restaurant workers come from every conceivable background—with glaring back-of-house versus front-of-house inequities often tied to perceived or actual language skills—but it's telling that nearly one in ten of the city's three-hundred-thousand-plus restaurant workers lives in Irwin's neighborhood, the nexus of Jackson Heights, Elmhurst, and Corona. One out of every twelve private-sector jobs in the city is in the restaurant industry, which doesn't even encompass all the cafeteria, catering, import-export, and other food businesses. Most of those jobs are in a bewilderingly diverse range of tiny establishments reflecting the cuisines of at least 150 different countries. See Office of the New York State Comptroller, "The Restaurant Industry in New York City: Tracking the Recovery," (Albany, NY: Office of the State Deputy Comptroller for the City of New York, 2020).
23. Smith, *Mexican New York*, 27.
24. Immigrants' place at the bottom is confirmed by the fact that the vast majority of the thousands of canners redeeming the five-cent deposit on beverage containers, and thus contributing significantly to the city's recycling, are Latin American (often Indigenous) and Chinese (often not native Mandarin speakers). Sure We Can, a Brooklyn-based organization run by a "street nun" originally from Spain's Basque country, helps organize and speak for the lateros (*canners*) and huíshōurén (*recycle people*) as they are called in Spanish and Chinese, respectively.

25. One such cart, which started out with hot dogs in 1990 on the southeast corner of Fifty-Third Street and Sixth Avenue before switching to gyros, pita, and rice for its mostly Muslim taxi-driver customers, is now a global phenomenon with hundreds of locations. Thanks to The Halal Guys and their canny franchise development strategy, "halal," no longer just a designator of adherence to Islamic dietary law but a New York–born fusion of Middle Eastern and Mediterranean flavors, is now more or less the city's official street food, seemingly going global like hot dogs, pizza, and bagels before it. Golden Krust, the Jamaican chain which started with a susu in the Bronx, may be doing something similar for Caribbean food and Jamaican-style patties, with over one hundred locations nationwide.
26. Past occupational niches can now seem incredibly specific, like the Czech immigrants known for manufacturing pearl buttons, the Balkan New Yorkers involved in freight handling, the Sicilian-speaking asphalt men from Castrofilippo who settled mostly in Astoria, or the "ice men," many originally from in and around Bari in Puglia, who delivered door to door the huge chunks of ice cut from lakes upstate and sometimes hauled hundreds of pounds of it up tenement stairs.
27. First referring to just the flour, the word cemita made its way from Aramaic into Andalusian Arabic into Old Spanish and finally to Mexico, with both Italian semolina and the Turkish simit being distant cousins.
28. Molli is a generic word meaning *sauce* or *something ground* in Nahuatl, but Irwin hears a resonance with the word olini, which is *to move* or *stir*.
29. Lagunas, "Nahuatl in Coatepec," 228.
30. Hill and Hill, *Speaking Mexicano*, 121–22, 343.
31. The nineteenth-century author is Ignacio Manuel Altamirano, who came from a Nahuatl-speaking community in Guerrero and uses a lot of Nahuatl phrasing in his Spanish-language works, according to Irwin.
32. James Lockhart and Bernardino de Sahagún, *We People Here: Nahuatl Accounts of the Conquest of Mexico*, vol. 1 (Berkeley: University of California Press, 1993), 4.
33. See Kevin Terraciano, "Reading between the Lines of Book 12," *The Florentine Codex* (Austin: University of Texas Press, 2021), 45–62.
34. Lockhart and de Sahagún, *We People Here*, 50.
35. Horacio Carochi, *Grammar of the Mexican Language: With an Explanation of Its Adverbs (1645)* (Stanford: Stanford University Press, 2002), 247–48.
36. The title "Ome Poali Uan Yei", (*Forty-Three*) is literally (2 x 20) + 3, because Nahuatl has a vigesimal, or base-20, system, and each score is divided into fives, such that chicuacempohualli (*twenty-six*) breaks down as (5+1) + (1 x 20). Mayan and Inuit languages share a similar pattern (vigesimal with a quinary sub-base, in number-speak), but all nondecimal number systems today can be considered endangered.
37. This pioneering organization is called CIELO (Comunidades Indígenas en Liderazgo).
38. Daniel Kaufman and Ross Perlin, "Surveying Indigenous Latin American Languages in NYC: A Report to the NYC Department of Health" (New York: Endangered Language Alliance, 2019).
39. Translation is the term usually used for written materials, while interpretation is primarily oral and may be simultaneous.
40. For translocal, see, e.g., Katherine Brickell and Ayona Datta, eds., *Translocal Geographies* (Farnham, UK: Ashgate Publishing, Ltd., 2011). For transnationalism, a much more widely discussed term, see, e.g., Nina Glick Schiller, Linda Basch, and Cristina

Blanc-Szanton, "Towards a Definition of Transnationalism," *Annals of the New York Academy of Sciences* 645, no. 1 (1992): ix–xiv. Randolph Bourne's 1916 "Trans-National America" argued (against the melting pot model) that cosmopolitanism and multiculturalism should define the country much as they had already come to define the New York Bourne loved.

41. ELA has recorded an account of the movement in Me'phaa (Tlapanec) by Juan Solano. A journalistic account is Josh Dzieza, "Revolt of the Delivery Workers," *Verge*, September 13, 2021.

## Karen - Lunaape (Lenape)

1. There have been many convenings, panels, and exhibits in just the last few years, and land acknowledgments, sometimes with a few words in Lenape, are an increasingly common ritual at liberal institutions across the city. See in particular the work of the Lenape Center, created by Native artists and activists including members of the Oklahoma tribe, as described in Joe Baker, Hadrien Coumans, and Joel Whitney, *Lenapehoking: An Anthology* (New York: The Lenape Center and Brooklyn Public Library, 2023).
2. Grumet, *Manhattan to Minisink*, 1, 191. More surprising still are the nearly two hundred place-names listed by Grumet that, thought to be Native, are "imports, inventions, invocations, or impostors." It's telling of how, at a certain later point, white settlers actively embraced Native names as romantic and authentically American, without really being able to access or coin actual Lenape names.
3. Many have likely encountered "Mannahatta" thanks to Eric Sanderson's *Mannahatta: A Natural History of New York City*, which uses part of Whitman's poem as an epigraph, and is otherwise a marvelous reconstruction of the present-day city's precolonial environment.
4. Goddard, "Origin and Meaning."
5. APA Institute, "Oral Histories: Jim Rementer," YouTube, February 23, 2017.
6. As remembered by Jim Rementer in Baker et al., *Lenapehoking*, 135–50.
7. See Grumet, *Munsee Indians*. For the broader phenomenon of "playing Indian," see Philip Joseph Deloria, *Playing Indian* (New Haven and London: Yale University Press, 1988).
8. Ives Goddard, review of *First Manhattans: A Brief History of the Munsee Indians*, by Robert S. Grumet, *New York History* 92, no. 4 (2011): 290–302.
9. Theodore Roosevelt, *The Winning of the West: The War in the Northwest*, vol. 7. (New York: G. P. Putnam's Sons, 1902), 9.
10. APA Institute, "Oral Histories: Jim Rementer," YouTube, 2017.
11. There may be more evidence for this further south. See Goddard, "Pidgin Delaware," and Soderlund, *Lenape Country*, which is focused on the lower Delaware Valley.
12. See www.talk-lenape.org, which includes recordings of Nora Thompson Dean. Revitalization efforts in Oklahoma are ongoing.
13. Goddard, "Linguistic Variation."
14. Karen has also taught at Ramapough and in Kingston. Heather passed away in 2019. Classes became virtual with the onset of the COVID-19 pandemic in March 2020.
15. APA Institute, "Oral Histories: Chief Vincent Mann," YouTube, 2017.
16. See American Indian Community House, "Sacred Spaces: Honoring Our Elders and Our Stories of Living Culture with Chief Reggie," YouTube. 2020.

17. Sewanhacky is one Native name, recorded by the Dutch in land deeds of the 1630s, that has been understood to mean Long Island and is thought to mean *place of shells*. At the time, Long Island was a center for the production of wampum, the shell "money" that fueled Native-settler exchanges. The word may actually reflect language mixing more than any "pure" Indigenous original, with -hacky a variation on -hoking, and sewan the "jargon" word for *wampum*, based on a very different Lenape word. See Paul Otto, "'This is that which . . . they call Wampum': Europeans Coming to Terms with Native Shell Beads," *Early American Studies* 15, no. 1 (2017): 1–36.
18. See Allison McGovern, "Disrupting the Narrative: Labor and Survivance for the Montauketts of Eastern Long Island" (PhD diss., City University of New York, 2015).
19. At some point, Jefferson also seems to have collected eighty words of Munsee, but this and many of his other unpublished papers were thrown overboard and badly damaged by a river gang when he was shipping them home to Virginia at the end of his presidency.
20. See Julian Granberry, *Modern Mohegan: The Dialect of Jits Bodunaxa* (Munich: LINCOM, 2003).
21. Roger Williams, *A Key into the Language of America* (1643, repr., Carlisle, MA: Applewood Books, 1997).
22. The Wôpanâak Language Reclamation Project was founded by Jessie "Little Doe" Baird in 1993 and represents a collaboration between four Wampanoag communities. The Bible is John Eliot, *Mamusse Wunneetupanatamwe Up-Biblum God* (1663, Cambridge, MA: Samuel Green).
23. Andrew Newman, "The Walam Olum: An Indigenous Apocrypha and Its Readers," *American Literary History* 22, no. 1 (2010): 26–56.
24. T. Konishi, "The Semantics of Grammatical Gender: A Cross-Cultural Study," *Journal of Psycholinguistic Research* 22 (1993): 519–34.
25. Goddard, *Delaware Verbal Morphology*.
26. O'Meara, *Delaware-English*.
27. On October 16, 1679, the Frisian traveler Jasper Danckaerts, seeking a site to settle his sect, met an old Lenape man named Tantaqué from what is now Hackensack. As Danckaerts writes in his journal:

    > We asked him, where he believed he came from? He answered from his father. "And where did your father come from?" we said, "and your grandfather and great-grandfather, and so on to the first of the race?" He was silent for a little while, either as if unable to climb up at once so high with his thoughts, or to express them without help, and then took a piece of coal out of the fire where he sat, and began to write upon the floor. He first drew a circle, a little oval, to which he made four paws or feet, a head and a tail. "This," said he, "is a tortoise, lying in the water around it," and he moved his hand round the figure, continuing, "This was or is all water, and so at first was the world or the earth, when the tortoise gradually raised its round back up high, and the water ran off of it, and thus the earth became dry." He then took a little straw and placed it on end in the middle of the figure, and proceeded, "The earth was now dry, and there grew a tree in the middle of the earth, and the root of this tree sent forth a sprout beside it and there grew upon it a man, who was the first male. This man was then alone, and would have remained alone; but the tree bent over until its top touched the earth, and there shot therein another root, from which

came forth another sprout, and there grew upon it the woman, and from these two are all men produced."

This is the first recorded mention of Turtle Island. Danckaerts later confirmed it with another Lenape speaker, living in what is now Bayonne. Other tribes of the Northeast were ultimately found to tell a similar story. The idea of a "World Turtle" appeared in ancient India and China, too, leading to that famous maxim about infinite regress, in defiance of every story of origins: "It's turtles all the way down."

As for Tantaqué, local settlers said he had saved their lives some years back, quietly leaving them fish during a famine. According to Danckaerts, who met him only a few more times, he was a jolly drunk, generous to a fault, the essence of a holy fool. See Jasper Danckaerts, *Journal of Jasper Danckaerts* (1913), www.gutenberg.org, accessed July 30, 2022.

28. Jennifer Adese and Robert Alexander Innes, *Indigenous Celebrity: Entanglements with Fame* (Winnipeg: University of Manitoba Press, 2021).
29. Nicholas Evans, "The Last Speaker Is Dead: Long Live the Last Speaker!" in *Linguistic Fieldwork*, ed. P. Newman and M. Ratliff (Cambridge, UK: Cambridge University Press, 2001), 250–81.
30. William W. Elmendorf, "Last Speakers and Language Change: Two Californian Cases," *Anthropological Linguistics* 23, no. 1 (1981): 36–49.
31. Cornish, of Cornwall, was thought gone with Dolly Pentreath in 1777, but six speakers were found a century later, and there are said to be a thousand revivalists today. As of the early 2000s, Laghu on Santa Isabel Island in the Solomons was "considered to have become extinct but five speakers were subsequently identified." See Osahito Miyaoka, Osamu Sakiyama, and Michael Krauss, *The Vanishing Languages of the Pacific Rim* (Oxford: Oxford University Press, 2007), 277.

## IV. Future

1. Just as urban areas were seen only as places for languages to vanish, they have also long been considered epicenters of ecological disaster, doing nothing but devastating the areas of high biodiversity where humans usually plant them. Indeed, rampant urbanization worldwide is continuing to threaten many native species and environments today, but there is also a growing recognition, against all expectations, that "urban arks" can shelter nonnative species with nowhere else to go.

Partly it's the "law of escape," whereby species thrive once away from their pests, parasites, or predators. Many are also adapting or evolving at remarkable speed, proving that genetic diversity and trait differences can actually be enhanced in urban environments. In addition, urban humans, inadvertently or not, are creating all sorts of new opportunities for species with different niches, not only domesticates and commensals (all the breeds of dogs, races of rats, varieties of virus, etc.).

The result, as an ecologist puts it very technically, is that surviving native species, together with introduced or colonizing nonnative species, are forming "unique no-analogue ecological communities: species assemblages that have never existed elsewhere in space or time." So it is that Central Park, an inviting and well-situated patch of green along the Atlantic Flyway, hosts over two hundred species of annually migrating birds. Greater Miami is a global hot spot for reptile and amphibian diversity, with a reported 117 species. The red-crowned amazon, a parrot endangered at home in northeastern Mexico, is thriving in Los Angeles. It also matters that cities are places subject to intensive scrutiny, where diversity and difference are not only concentrated, but sought, sorted, and appraised.

See Max R. Lambert and Colin M. Donihue, "Urban Biodiversity Management Using Evolutionary Tools," *Nature Ecology and Evolution* 4, no. 7 (2020): 903–10; H. B. Shaffer, "Urban Biodiversity Arks," *Nature Sustainability* 1 (2018): 725–27. Thanks to Cecil Howell for raising some of these questions.

2. Sarah Pierce and Jessica Bolter, "Dismantling and Reconstructing the US Immigration System," in *A Catalog of Changes under the Trump Presidency* (Washington, DC: Migration Policy Institute, 2020).
3. Jason Schachter, Pete Borsella, and Anthony Kapp, "New Population Estimates Show Covid-19 Pandemic Significantly Disrupted Migration Across Borders" (US Census Bureau, December 21, 2021).
4. Muzaffar Chishti and Julia Gelatt, "Mounting Backlogs Undermine US Immigration System and Impede Biden Policy Changes" (Migration Policy Institute, February 23, 2022).
5. Steven Camarota and Karen Zeigler, "Estimating the Illegal Immigrant Population Using the Current Population Survey" (Center for Immigration Studies, March 29, 2022).
6. There are several differences in terms of the process and legal status, but one is that asylees claim asylum when setting foot on US soil while refugees typically must seek refugee status from outside the country.
7. A variety of factors may be at work, from the views and practices of particular judges to the types of asylum seekers and the available support sytems for them in different locations.

   The federal Goverment Accountability Office reported on geographic disparities in similar cases from 2007 to 2014: Government Accountability Office, "Asylum: Variation Exists in Outcomes of Applications Across Immigration Courts and Judges," November 14, 2016.

   More recent data from the Transactional Records Access Clearinghouse at Syracuse University shows a similar pattern, though rates may be changing. See Paul Moses and Tim Healy, "Here's Why the Rejection Rate for Asylum Seekers Has Expanded in America's Largest Immigration Court in NYC," *The Daily Beast*, December 2, 2019.
8. "The Touray Tower Fire in the Bronx," *Gambia Times*, January 18, 2022.
9. As Suketu Mehta puts it, with Mumbai by comparison a city of people from villages. LaGuerre, *American Odyssey*, 38–39, gives a sense of how this worked in the Haitian case: "A peasant who decides to migrate to New York will go first to Port-au-Prince to become accustomed to city ways, to learn some English, to start transactions with a travel agent, to develop a network of contacts, and finally to apply for an exit visa from the Haitian government and an American visa from the US Consulate."

The explosion of hundreds of community gardens across New York in recent decades has tapped into the agricultural memories, skills, and desires of immigrant gardeners now growing foods from home in New York soil. Not to mention private yards: the Seke speaker planting buckwheat from Mustang, the Polish landlady bringing the seeds of certain flowers from Wrocław to Ridgewood, or the Iraqi Jewish engineer who carries on the grape-growing and wine-making traditions of his native Basra in an Upper East Side garden. See Robin Shulman, *Eat the City: A Tale of the Fishers, Foragers, Butchers, Farmers, Poultry Minders,*

*Sugar Refiners, Cane Cutters, Beekeepers, Winemakers, and Brewers Who Built New York* (New York: Crown, 2012), 258–65.

10. Ofelia García and Li Wei, "Language, Bilingualism and Education," in *Translanguaging: Language, Bilingualism and Education*. (New York: Palgrave Macmillan, 2014).
11. Ofelia García, José Luis Morín, and Klaudia Rivera, "How Threatened Is the Spanish of New York Puerto Ricans?" in *Can Threatened Languages Be Saved?* ed. Joshua Fishman (Bristol: Multilingual Matters, 2001), 57–58.

    "They left *buscando algo mejor* [looking for something better]. They gave up on the neighborhood and decided to relocate. Our restaurants used to be Spanish. The *bodegas* [stores] sold out. *Los puertorriqueños se metieron a ser maestros* [Puerto Ricans went into teaching], *en* Auto Repair Shops, Liquor Stores. But the majority went independent. *Compran ropa y venden* house to house *por la calle* [They buy clothes and sell house to house in the street] . . ."

    A related but different kind of hybrid is New York City Spanish, produced partly by what linguists call "leveling," where similar varieties from all over the world converge further (lexically, morphologically, syntactically) through contact. Much of this, at least until recently, was in the direction of Caribbean Spanish, which dominated in the city even if it was low prestige everywhere else: Mexican New Yorkers saying pique (instead of chile) for *hot sauce*, Ecuadorians saying chavos for *money*, everyone saying guagua for *bus* and dropping -s from the end of syllables—to name just a few examples.
12. J. Nortier and M. Dorleijn, "Multi-Ethnolects: Kebabnorsk, Perkerdansk, Verlan, Kanakensprache, Straattaal, etc.," in *Contact Languages: A Comprehensive Guide*, ed. P. Bakker and Y. Matras, Language Contact and Bilingualism, no. 6 (Berlin and Boston: De Gruyter, 2013), 229–71. See also John McWhorter, "What Multiethnolects Reveal about Creole Genesis," *Language Dynamics and Change* 9, no. 2 (2019): 220–37; Kara Becker and Elizabeth L. Coggshall, "The Sociolinguistics of Ethnicity in New York City," *Language and Linguistics Compass* 3, no. 3 (2009): 751–66.
13. Walt Wolfram, *Sociolinguistic Aspects of Assimilation: Puerto Rican English in New York City* (Arlington, VA: Center for Applied Linguistics, 1974).
14. In a notorious incident in 2018, lawyer Aaron Schlossberg was at a Midtown lunch spot when he started yelling at an employee and a customer to speak English. He threatened to call Immigration and Customs Enforcement in a video that quickly went viral.
15. The Yemeni Muslim owners of David's House of Brisket in Bed-Stuy, who close for Jummah on Fridays, maintain a Jewish deli complete with pastrami, pickles, and cream soda, for a mostly African American clientele. An African American baker is famed for his Jewish rugelach. An Egyptian man and his Filipina Muslim (Iranun-speaking) wife bought a Bronx ice cream company from its Jewish owner, retooling it to corner the halal ice cream market. In Los Angeles, a Thai restaurant became legendary among Mexicans and Central Americans because its poh tak, a sour and spicy seafood soup, happens to taste similar to caldo de siete mares. Greek-owned diners evolved ecumenical, ethnically inflected menus with spanakopita, matzah ball soup, chicken parm, huevos rancheros, milkshakes, and a thousand other items. Traditional New York bakeries may sell semolina rolls, soda bread, and bagels side by side.
16. An infinitely detailed map of the city would also show the microcultures of DJs, Burners, crypto bros, etc., as well as the innumerable family and friend groups

clustering in particular neighborhoods and overlapping in various ways with larger formations. Even smaller subcultures may only have the critical mass to fill a bar or a room periodically, or just enough for an ambient awareness that like-minded others are around.

17. On the valorization of (certain types of) diversity in the current mode of capitalism: "But it is a form of capitalism whose flexibility enables it to take advantage of a much wider range of things than in the past, whose diversity is not only preserved but valorized, to exploit the differences it establishes between the status of varying commodities. At the same time, it integrates these into a single forcefield, with which financial flows—that, being strictly commensurable, are indifferent to the specificities of the objects that feed them—create a form of interdependence, even a kind of solidarity. However, against this backdrop of tacit solidarity, there exist conflicts over the appropriation of profits, which depend on the way differences between things are exploited in the various forms we have highlighted. These struggles relate back to the question of who has control over the determination of these differences and their valorization: in other words, to the question of power—which, in the context of capitalism, is measured by the ability of agents to valorize certain differences, and thereby devalue differences from which their rivals hope to profit." Luc Boltanski and Arnaud Esquerre, "Enrichment, Profit, Critique: A Rejoinder to Nancy Fraser," *New Left Review* 106 (2017): 76.
18. László Krasznahorkai and Ornan Rotem, *The Manhattan Project*, trans. John Batki (London: Sylph Editions, 2017).
19. Jean Paul Sartre, "Manhattan: The Great American Desert," in *The Empire City*, ed. Alexander Klein (New York: Rinehart, 1955), 451–57.
20. For "the ethos of mixing" that defines Hackney, an area of London that bears comparison with Brooklyn or Queens, see Susanne Wessendorf, "Commonplace Diversity and the 'Ethos of Mixing': Perceptions of Difference in a London Neighbourhood," *Identities* 20 (2013): 407–22.
21. For some reason, corner stores seem to be the urban equivalent of butterflies, for which famously every language and even dialect seems to have a completely different word. As for people who call them delis, originally short for delicatessen, they are calling on an old French word for *delicacy* that got a German plural -n and then spread widely in America through Yiddish, while largely disappearing or remaining far more niche (and unabbreviated) in Europe.
22. Estimate from the Yemeni-American Merchants Association, according to Christina Goldbaum, "Behind the Counter, a New Political Force Takes on the *New York Post* and Trump," *New York Times*, April 29, 2019.
23. If anything, though, it's the ocks of New York who have become fluent in the cultures and sometimes even the languages of their customers. "He'll joke with an older Grenadian woman that he went to school with Maurice Bishop's son," writes Moustafa Bayoumi of a Palestinian New Yorker working at his family's bodega. "He curses the Haitians in Jamaican patois and the Jamaicans in Haitian Creole, to everyone's surprise and amusement. He's a curious mix that isn't so strange in Brooklyn, equally at home with Arabs, African Americans, and West Indians." Moustafa Bayoumi, *How Does It Feel to Be a Problem?: Being Young and Arab in America* (New York: Penguin, 2009), 120.

    With astonishing specificity, the ocks of New York have also learned the tastes of working-class New Yorkers. Red Hook bodega owner General Ock (real name Rahim Mohamed) is justly famous on TikTok for making things "the Ocky Way," which means anything in the store you want (packaged or otherwise) mixed on the griddle into an insane kitchen-sink chopped cheese on steroids.

24. See Kasinitz et al., *Becoming New Yorkers*.
25. Foner, "How Exceptional Is New York?," 1010.
26. Kasinitz et al., *Becoming New Yorkers*, 16. There is understandable scholarly disagreement about these complex processes of acculturation, with some referring to "a mosaic of little worlds which touch but do not interpenetrate" (Robert E. Park, "The City: Suggestions for the Investigation of Human Behavior in the City Environment," *American Journal of Sociology* 20, no. 5 [1915]: 577–612), or "intimate strangers" from "communities overlapping but not touching." (Michael Jones-Correa, *Between Two Nations: The Political Predicament of Latinos in New York City* [Ithaca: Cornell University Press, 1998], 32.)
27. David Cassels Johnson, *Language Policy* (New York: Palgrave Macmillan, 2013).
28. Politicians say the right things, but mostly it's a handful of driven civil servants at city agencies like the Department of Health, the Department of Education, and the Mayor's Office of Immigrant Affairs who are contacting ELA and smaller language communities to try to make projects happen.
29. The passage of the federal Bilingual Education Act, Title VII of the Elementary and Secondary Education Act of 1968, was important at a federal level, but implementation has fallen entirely to a small number of cities. Bilingual, dual language, and other terms have different implications. See Ofelia García, "Educating New York's Bilingual Children: Constructing a Future from the Past," *International Journal of Bilingual Education and Bilingualism* 14, no. 2 (2011): 133–53.
30. Local Law 73, passed in 2003, was the first real language access law in the city. In 2008, Executive Order 120 went further, designating "citywide languages" for which the city government has some legal obligation and requiring all agencies to make a language access plan. In 2017, Local Law 30 added teeth and numbers to what had come before.
31. Problematic private companies are usually contracted to do a lot of the heavy lifting by phone, especially for nondesignated languages. They often have to contact ELA to find interpreters, because they still cover only a fraction of the city's over seven hundred languages.
32. For this term, see Gordon Mathews, *Global Culture/Individual Identity: Searching for Home in the Cultural Supermarket* (London: Routledge: 2000).
33. One example is Frankie Light, a child of Deaf parents who grew up in Brooklyn signing American Sign Language while hearing Haitian Creole and Jamaican Patwa, set out to learn Mandarin by working at a hair salon in Flushing, and has since moved on to twenty other languages. Blogs include *Eating in Translation*, *Eat the World NYC*, and *The United Nations of Food*.
34. For a close look at two public spaces in Astoria where the rhetoric of diversity can obscure ongoing inequalities, see Sofya Aptekar, "Super-Diversity as a Methodological Lens: Re-Centering Power and Inequality," *Ethnic and Racial Studies* 42, no. 1 (2019): 53–70.
35. Before the Great Depression, this "restrictive residential community" developed by the Queensboro Corporation under Edward Archibald MacDougall had convenants specifically barring Blacks, Jews, and immigrants. See, for example, I. M. Miyares, "From Exclusionary Covenant to Ethnic Hyperdiversity in Jackson Heights, Queens," *Geographical Review* 94, no. 4 (2004): 462–83.

36. Suketa Mehta, "The Meltingest Pot," *New York Times Magazine*, October 5, 2003. This is also the source of Joe Salvo's quote earlier.
37. Hanson, *City of Gods*.
38. "Subway cosmopolitanism," with its "rider competencies" and "contextualization skills," is a survival skill that has developed in reaction to the underfunded and decrepit system's legendary crowding, danger, and filth. The "process of knowing-yet-ignoring whereby riders become 'blasé' New Yorkers" is an art of benign neglect. See Stéphane Tonnelat and William Kornblum, *International Express: New Yorkers on the 7 Train* (New York: Columbia University Press: 2017), 8, 44.
39. Mathews, *Ghetto*, 101.
40. For the argument that diversity can have a negative impact on trust, community, and civic participation, see Robert Putnam, "E pluribus unum: Diversity and Community in the Twenty-First Century: The 2006 Johan Skytte Prize Lecture," *Scandinavian Political Studies* 30, no. 2 (2007): 137–74.

    For an in-depth look at the thorny politics of ethnic succession in a neighborhood (Elmhurst, Queens) that has since become linguistically hyperdiverse, see Roger Sanjek, *The Future of Us All: Race and Neighborhood Politics in New York City* (Ithaca: Cornell University Press, 2000).

    For a global tour of tolerant diverse places, with a chapter on Queens, see Karl E. Meyer and Shareen Blair Brysac, *Pax Ethnica: Where and How Diversity Succeeds* (New York: Public Affairs, 2012).